FINAL AUTHORITY

A Christian's Guide to the
King James Bible

FINAL AUTHORITY

A Christian's Guide to the
King James Bible

William P. Grady

GRADY
PUBLICATIONS

ISBN 0-9628809-1-4
Library of Congress Catalog 92-085282

First Printing, March, 1993
Second Printing, July, 1993
Third Printing, October, 1993
Fourth Printing, January, 1994
Fifth Printing, June, 1994
Sixth Printing, January, 1995

For information, address:

Grady Publications, Inc.
P.O. Box 506
Schererville, Indiana 46375

This volume is affectionately dedicated to my faithful *helpmeet*, Linda Shannon, for being that special angel of providence from whose hands I received my first King James Bible.

"A woman that feareth the Lord,
she shall be praised."
(Proverbs 31:30b)

Acknowledgements

The author is indebted to the following team of co-laborers *"whose hearts God had touched,"* for their tireless effort in defense of our precious King James Bible:

Mrs. Linda Stubblefield for her expertise in the overall format of this book and her countless hours of diligent typesetting.

Mrs. Angie Zachary and Mrs. Linda Grady for their conscientious proofreading.

Mr. Tommy Ray and his wife Lori for the creativity and professionalism reflected in their impressive cover design.

Dr. Jack Hyles, my pastor, employer and friend, for his courageous example and costly stand for the King James Bible.

Dr. Carl Laurent and Mr. Lewis Shelton for their concentrated season of prayer specifically for this book.

Mr. Chris Stansell, Mr. Bob Hooker, Pastor Dan Woodward, Dr. Tim Young and especially Dr. Dallas Dobson for their invaluable counsel at several crucial junctures.

A special thanks to Miss Mary Purdum, Mrs. Kelly Hawkins, Mr. Paul Kruse, Mr. Phil Pins and Mr. Ray Highfill for their providential assistance during the formative stages of this work.

The deepest of love and appreciation to my wife Linda and my three precious children, Danny, Sara and Paul, for their encouragement, input, and patience during a most disrupted family schedule.

Finally, a sacred word of gratitude to Dr. Jack Patterson, *my Jonathan,* for having expounded unto me the way of God more perfectly and for convincing me to write this book.

Table of Contents

Foreword

*"Thy word is true from the beginning: and every
one of thy righteous judgments endureth for ever."*
(Psalm 119:160)

While reading the manuscript of *Final Authority*, I thought,
here is a book that tells the truth about the **Truth.**

One has only to look at our present society to see what the
absence of **Truth** has accomplished. Today many nationally
known pastors, evangelists, Christian psychologists and other
prominent Christians are endorsing, promoting and sometimes
selling a book they call the "Bible." Many of these translations,
or transliterations, leave out passages or change words that result
in robbing Christ of His Deity. They leave the impression that
Jesus was just another good man with a new philosophy. In some
passages, the new Bibles are in direct contradiction of the 1611
King James Bible.

It is impossible for both to be right. Only one can be the
Truth. *Final Authority* gives you the truth about the **Truth.** Not
many folks know where and why these other translations came
into existence, and people know even less about the men who
wrote them. There are some good books on the market today that
defend the 1611 King James Bible and point out the errors in
other translations. *Final Authority* is the only book I know that
gives you the detailed background, historic references and the
reason for the departure from the **true Word of God.**

As a close friend of the author for many years, I know of no
other person as intellectually qualified and capable of researching,
organizing and writing a book defending the **true Word of God.**

Final Authority is written in a scholarly manner, fully
documented with over 1,000 endnotes, a complete bibliography,
a detailed index, and dual glossaries of terms and proper names;
yet, it is written in an interesting way that holds one's attention.

Every student of the Bible will find *Final Authority* an
excellent reference book. It should be in every Bible-believing

pastor's library.

After reading this book, one is fully convinced that the 1611 King James Bible is the **true Word of God.**

Final Authority gives you the truth about the **Truth.**

> *"God forbid: yea, let God be true, but every man a liar; as it is written . . ."* (Romans 3:4)

— Dr. Dallas Dobson

A Personal Word

When I was a young preacher, the battle was over **how** to interpret the Bible. Now, almost half a century later, the battle is over the Bible **itself**. Then, the battle was over what the Bible **TAUGHT**. Today the battle is over what the Bible **IS**. Then, it was a battle over interpretation. Now, it is a battle over inspiration and preservation. Then, it was a battle over difference of doctrine. Now, it is a battle over where we get our doctrine. Then, it was a battle over the flow. Now, it is a battle over the source. Then, it was a battle over what Truth says. Now the battle is over what truth is. I have given the few years that I have left to the defense and propagation of the King James Bible.

Years ago I had a secretary who took dictation from me. When the first letters were given me to sign, I noticed that they were not exactly the same words that I dictated. I called her to my office to ask why. She informed me that she had changed my words a little so they could be more easily understood. I informed her that she was "fired." Every church in America should do the same to every pastor who changes the words so they will be more easily understood and to every theologian who does the same.

Think what could have happened if all of the hours that have been spent **changing** the Bible had been spent **preaching** the Bible and **spreading** its message.

Bill Grady is right in his defense of the Bible. He has worked tirelessly and, he and his family have sacrificed financially to expose the versions for exactly what they are—versions, and to show us that the King James is not **A** version, but **THE** Bible. May God bless him for it, and use it to "fire" the secretaries (theologians and preachers) who change the "dictation."

— Dr. Jack Hyles

Preface

With the attention of today's Christian already diverted by an unprecedented age of materialism, the devil's accompanying barrage of modern English "Bibles" has wrought significant confusion over the identity of the true Word of God. Such a cause for alarm is a timely application to the Psalmist's cry, *"If the foundations be destroyed, what can the righteous do?"* (Psalm 11:3)

Final Authority has been written to help dispel this confusion by presenting a logical, documented argument for the King James Bible as being *the* true Word of God for English-speaking people.

However, because of the multi-faceted nature of the issue, certain portions of this book may appear a bit technical at times. It is the prayer of this author that the reader will be faithful to the challenge, for difficult problems require diligent study. Questions about the Bible are of eternal consequence and should never be considered in a casual manner. *"Study to shew thyself approved unto God, a workman that needeth not to be ashamed, rightly dividing the word of truth."* (II Timothy 2:15)

— William P. Grady

Introduction

When the Anglican committee for revision published its Revised New Testament in 1881, it was immediately opposed by Dean John William Burgon (1813-1888), the outstanding conservative scholar within the Church of England. After witnessing his beloved nation abandon her 1611 Authorized Version for the unfounded textual theories of Drs. Brooke Foss Westcott (1825-1901) and Fenton John Anthony Hort (1828-1892), Burgon remained certain of a future return to the traditional text. Herman Hoskier, a faithful associate of the Dean, relates a touching scene from the closing years of Burgon's labor:

> Three and a half years ago (this was written in 1890) I was in Dean Burgon's study at Chichester. It was midnight, dark and cold without; he had just extinguished the lights, and it was dark, and getting cold within. We mounted the stairs to retire to rest, and his last words of the night have often rung in my ears since: 'As surely as it is dark now, and as certainly as the sun will rise tomorrow morning, so surely will the traditional text be vindicated and the views I have striven to express be accepted. I may not live to see it. Most likely I shall not. But it will come.'[1]

After nearly a century of English revision based on corrupt Alexandrian manuscripts (codices *Vaticanus* and *Sinaiticus*), a mild resurgence of pro-*Textus Receptus*, pro-Authorized Version thinking has indeed occurred. In 1979, the editors of the liberal Nestles-Aland Greek text reversed an eighty-year preference for Westcott and Hort with a token insertion of 467 *Receptus* readings into their 27th edition.

However, of far greater significance is the present consolidation among many independent fundamental Baptists toward a conviction of "King James exclusivity." This stand has been necessitated by an ever-increasing barrage of modern English revisions. Predictably, such a position is rejected by the self-styled "Christian scholar" as being intellectually unacceptable. The following reaction is typical of such end-day apostates:

Overreaction to translations by cults seeking to prop up their heresies with an aura of authority, along with the translations prepared by liberals which leap at every opportunity to play down the deity of Jesus Christ, plus numerous paraphrases masquerading as translations, caused some **untrained fundamentalists**, mostly among the laity, to claim verbal inspiration for the King James Version, while some of the more scholarly ones were satisfied to insist that only the "textus receptus" was a reliable Greek text.[2]

This volume has been designed to equip the sincere Christian ("untrained fundamentalist") with a systematic work of doctrine, history and manuscript evidences to enhance his "new look at the old Book."

Having slighted the Bible-believer for his equating of final authority with an exclusive source of reference, the critic will then declare that a "King James-only" position lacks the endorsement of historic fundamentalism. The argument goes:

We have no objection if some refuse to use or honor any translation but the King James Version. We wish them Godspeed and count them our friends. We, too, love it and seek to defend it from its critics. But we think any who make exclusive use of that translation a test of fellowship are wrong, especially when they infer a recommendation of another version—which has been translated by competent evangelical scholars—is a departure from the faith. *That is not the historic fundamentalist position!*[3]

Thus one perceives that the battle lines are drawn between those who embrace the 1611 Authorized Version as their final authority and those who would appeal to the dictates of human tradition. (Colossians 2:8)

To begin with, it must be understood that in the majority of cases, the so-called "historic fundamentalist position" (which relegates the King James Bible to an inferior status behind the nonexistent, original manuscripts) was erected by *non-soul-winning theologians*. Frankly speaking, the Greek scholar J. Gresham Machen never warranted the police protection afforded the uneducated, controversial Billy Sunday.

With few exceptions, the history of evangelism confirms that the size of a soul-winner's harvest was commensurate with his belief in the Book he was preaching. In his letter to the Thessalonians, Paul stated:

*". . . when ye received the word of God which ye heard of us, ye received it not as the word of men, but as it is in truth, the word of God, **which effectually worketh also in you that believe.**"* (I Thessalonians 2:13b)

Preachers like Gypsy Smith, who crisscrossed the Atlantic Ocean *forty-five* times in his quest for souls, were too busy winning the lost to spend time critiquing their Bibles. The roving evangelist, summarizing his antipathy for the world of intellectualism, remarked:

> I didn't go through your colleges and seminaries. They wouldn't have me . . . but I have been to the feet of Jesus where the only true scholarship is learned.[4]

Lester Roloff was equally unimpressed with dry academicism, preferring to reclaim sinners with the spiritual realities of "Dr. Law and Dr. Grace" rather than the textual fantasies of Drs. Westcott and Hort. His "exegetical" classics "Pawing in the Valley," "And the Mule Walked On," etc., constitute a homiletical style of their own.

There was, of course, the occasional exception of a dedicated soul winner succumbing to the spirit of his age. Dr. R.A. Torrey is an excellent case in point. Opponents of the King James Bible derive great security from Torrey's preference for the Revised Version. Those of us familiar with Dr. Torrey's well-intentioned, but disastrous period of study with the German school of higher criticism are not the least bit intimidated. Dr. Ed Reese writes:

> Not satisfied with the training he received in the States, he studied at the German universities of Leipzig and Erlangen in 1882-83. As a brilliant student he made great progress in school. Early in his studies he was a pronounced higher critic, but ere he had completed them, he was convinced of the falsity of his views and swung gradually back to old conservative doctrines, reversing the usual trend because of Europe's emphasis on higher criticism.[5]

Another biographer notes:

> Slowly but surely he moved away from the critical approach to the Scriptures, and accepted the "old truth" in the "old garb."[6]

Furthermore, for all his authoritative warblings about historic positions, the typical Christian scholar doesn't know half as much as you think. Although he is quick to define the limitations of inspiration (i.e., to the original manuscripts), he cannot begin to explain the doctrine itself. A survey of such intellectual "mumbo jumbo" would include:

Were we asked, then, how this work of divine inspiration has been accomplished in the men of God, we should reply, that we do not know.[7] (Louis Gaussen)

The doctrine of inspiration, because it is supernatural, presents some problems to human understanding.[8] (Lewis Sperry Chafer)

Accepting the above as the best definition of inspiration, we observe that we do not know the mode of inspiration.[9] (Henry C. Thiessen)

Of course there is a mystery connected with a product that is the result of the confluence of the human and the divine.[10] (Harold Lindsell)

What is declared is that the Scriptures are a divine product without any implication of how God has operated in producing them.[11] (Philadelphia College of the Bible lecture notes)

Exponents of the "historic fundamentalist position" argument will also cite King James advocates with inconsistency for quoting Dean Burgon since he felt that the Authorized Version could possibly be revised in the future should the correct Greek text be employed. By their inability to *"discern the signs of the times,"* (Matthew 16:3) these present-day pharisees betray a first-century heritage. As previously mentioned, the King James-only position has been necessitated by the modern Bible movement. Because *today's* conservative is surrounded by literally dozens of "perversions," *unlike the time of Burgon,* he *must* hold to *one* Book and one Book *alone* for matters of final authority!

While the "historic fundamentalist position" was emerging around the heavily promoted debut of the 1901 American Standard Version (ASV), the new arrival showed no aspirations for being used in the *sanctuary,* requesting only a humble abode in the pastor's *study* alongside his other reference tools. Having duped preachers on the merits of revision *per se,* the devil subtly laid low in patient anticipation of his carefully orchestrated end-day plethora of modern English translations. Had he dumped his entire truckload of over one hundred versions on the preachers of Torrey's day, they would never have taken his bait. While Satan got his foot in the door with the ASV, he crashed it down with the Living Bible, Reader's Digest Condensed Version, New International Version, etc. The growing alignment of frustrated independent Baptists behind the King James Bible is an attempt to rehang the door on its hinges and *slam it shut!*

Such an action is far from a departure from orthodoxy, but rather is consistent with established patterns of church history. From the ancient reactions against worldliness by Montanus, Novatian and Donatus, through the free-will advocacies of Pelagius, Arminius and Wesley; the courage of Hus and Luther; the eccentricities of Whitefield and Finney; the eschatological pioneering of Darby and Larkin; down to the resurgence of an aggressive, personal soul-winning emphasis by Rice, Roberson and Hyles—God's people have stood ready to abandon *any* "historic position" when so led by the liberating Spirit of God.

"Beware lest any man spoil you through philosophy and vain deceit, after the tradition of men, after the rudiments of the world, and not after Christ."
(Colossians 2:8)

"To employ soft words and honeyed phrases in discussing questions of everlasting importance; to deal with errors that strike at the foundations of all human hope as if they were harmless and venial mistakes; to bless where God disapproves, and to make apologies where He calls us to stand up like men and assert, though it may be the aptest method of securing popular applause in a sophistical age, is cruelty to man and treachery to Heaven. Those who on such subjects attach more importance to the rules of courtesy than they do to the measures of truth do not defend the citadel, but betray it into the hands of its enemies. Love for Christ, and for the souls for whom He died, will be the exact measure of our zeal in exposing the dangers by which men's souls are ensnared."

— Thornwell

I

Final Authority

"No man can serve two masters . . ."
(Matthew 6:24a)

The story is told that when Sir Walter Scott lay dying, he asked his son-in-law to bring him "The Book." With astonishment the young man replied, "Father, your library contains thousands of volumes, including your own works. To which book are you referring?" The veteran author immediately replied, "There is only one book which we all call 'The Book.' Bring me the Bible."

Sadly, such reverence can no longer be conveyed to our present "Bible-of-the-Month-Club" generation. Following an uncontested reign of 270 years (1611-1881), "The Book" has been challenged by an ungrateful people and must now "share" final authority with over two hundred other "The Books." Scott's noble words have become pearls before swine.

Consequently, as the children of Issachar were commended for their *"understanding of the times"* (I Chronicles 12:32), God's people of today need a similar discernment to recognize Satan's final assault on the King James Bible via an unprecedented cannonade of modern English versions. The purpose of this chapter is to provide such an insight.

It is significant that this escalating demand for bogus Bibles continues to stem from professing Christians. For example, one highly respected and nationally known Baptist pastor has recently endorsed the Living Bible as follows:

The Living Bible has ministered to me personally every morning for many years. There is no way I can measure the spiritual contribution the Living Bible has made to my ministry.

Could this influential brother have been totally awake when "ministered to" by the updated version of Elijah's run-in with the prophets of Baal?

Perhaps he is talking to someone or else is out sitting on the **toilet**. (Living Bible, I Kings 18:27)

Was his understanding and appreciation for the second coming of Christ warmly enhanced by the modern rendition?

And if someone asks them, what are these scars on your chest and your back, you will say, I got into a **brawl** at the home of a friend. (Living Bible, Zechariah 13:6)

Obviously, the modern "Bible movement" is one facet of a tremendous apostasy within twentieth-century Christendom. To discern the singular cause for such a widespread and unnatural resistance to the Holy Spirit, consider the following passage:

"No man can serve two masters: for either he will hate the one, and love the other; or else he will hold to the one, and despise the other. Ye cannot serve God and mammon." (Matthew 6:24)

Here our Saviour declares categorically that no human can submit to God and money simultaneously. All men, saved or lost, must choose between the two. Therefore, the central observation to make is that our unparalleled variety of "Bibles" just happens to coincide with an unparalleled age of materialism. To put it another way, America's Bible selection increases with her standard of living. Appreciating the reason for this will explain the growing animosity toward the King James Bible.

Because no man can serve two masters, the Christian who chooses to sell out for materialism becomes incapable of submission to God. He who willfully succumbs to the cares of this world and the deceitfulness of riches could not submit to God if he wanted! *"No man can serve two masters"!*

Once the apostate "goes for the gold," his singular, face-saving profile becomes unmistakable:

"Having a form of godliness but denying the power thereof."
(II Timothy 3:5)

(Is there any doubt that the Bible is the power of godliness?)

Because the rich young rulers of our day have become spiritually incapacitated, they will not embrace a Bible that lays exclusive claim to the English-speaking world. Instead, they will take cover behind the assurances of Christian scholarship that one conscientious translation is as good as the next. They'll embrace *anything* but a dreaded submission to *one* book.

When this concept of materialistic paralysis is comprehended, several other theological maladies are found to be related. For instance, consider the doctrine of the local church. Because of his aspiration to build bigger barns, the end-day materialist will inevitably seek membership in the non-obligatory "invisible church." When he decides to "visit around," he will be sure to avoid any church where the pastor is in charge, gravitating instead toward an elder-board structure.

Although his first-century ancestor could submit to *his* pastor's authoritative, *"Wherefore my sentence is . . ."* (Acts 15:19), today's temporal-minded religionist can only complain about "legalism." And, of course, the host of miscellaneous, non-denominational Agapé Chapels, Family Centers, etc., will always be preferred to the restrictive and reproachful tag of independent Baptist.

With an outward demeanor projecting a mere "form of godliness," *life-style evangelism* and *lordship salvation* are right around the corner. After all, "if He's not Lord of all, then He's not Lord at all," etc.

Then we have an application to the weekly sermon. Armed with an intimidating financial clout, today's parishioners have reduced their churches' *pulpit* ministries to *puppet* ministries. In dramatic fulfillment of Paul's departing admonition, *preachers* proclaiming sound doctrine have been replaced by *teachers* sharing fables such as, the blood doesn't save, etc.

In conclusion, your precious King James Bible is under attack by today's money-worshiping Christians simply because it commands the same unconditional surrender that Jesus did.

*"For he taught them as one having **authority**, and not as the scribes."* (Matthew 7:29)

The problem with the King James Bible is a problem with **final authority**.

II

The Deeds of the Nicolaitanes

"But this thou hast, that thou hatest the deeds of the Nicolaitanes, which I also hate."
(Revelation 2:6)

As this book is dedicated to helping Christians gain a better understanding of the King James Bible, we will begin by examining the Lord's basic reason for giving us His Word. The Bible, as God's supreme revelation of Himself, was bestowed upon estranged man for the sole purpose of enticing his return to a relationship of intimate fellowship. The Apostle John put it this way: *"We love him, because he first loved us."* (I John 4:19)

Whether initiating justification for the lost or imparting sanctification for the saved, the Bible remains man's heavenly lifeline for survival throughout his "pilgrim's progress." John Wesley wrote:

> I build on no authority, ancient or modern, but the Scripture. I want to know one thing—the way to Heaven: how to land on that happy shore. God Himself hath condescended to teach the way. He hath written it down in a book. O give me that book! At any price, give me that book of God.[1]

Comprehending this foundational truth will more than explain Satan's relentless aggression against the Holy Bible. To eliminate, diminish, or question the Scriptures is to jeopardize man's central communication link with his God.

This is precisely how the human race fell in the first place. Having received her Creator's clear instructions, Eve chose to entertain the "serpentine suggestion." A key insight into the way Satan attacks your King James Bible can be gained from his very first words to man.

"Yea, hath God said . . . ?" (Genesis 3:1)

Because of Eve's disastrous questioning of the revealed Word of God, the entire human race was plunged into judgment— *"For as in Adam all die . . ."* (I Corinthians 15:22)

As there is nothing new under the sun, three important lessons may be gleaned from the fall of our first parents.

1. God's messages to His children are always simple, clear and unmistakable.

The famed deist, Benjamin Franklin, once remarked that it wasn't the selections of the Bible of which he was ignorant that worried him as much as it was the Scripture with which he was already familiar. God's Words have always been easy to understand for those seeking the truth.

> *"All the words of my mouth are in righteousness; there is nothing froward or perverse in them. They are all plain to him that understandeth, and right to them that find knowledge."* (Proverbs 8:8-9)

Rebuking the whining, Living Bible advocates of his day, the fourth-century giant Chrysostom (c. 347-407) retorted:

> But still you will say, "I cannot understand it! What marvel? How shouldest thou understand it, if thou will not read nor look upon it?"[2]

It is fitting that Chrysostom was the first Christian to refer to the Scriptures as **The Bible** (in the Greek, ὁ Βίβλος; literally, "The Book").

More often than not, man's real problem with the Bible is that it is *too* plain. William Seward, an aide to the powerful eighteenth-century evangelist George Whitefield, has left us this humorous account:

> Heard of a drinking club with a negro boy attending them who used to mimic people for their diversion. One day the gentlemen bid him mimic our Brother Whitefield, which he was very unwilling to do; but they insisting upon it, he stood up and

said, *'I speak the truth in Christ; I lie not; except you repent, you will all be damned!'* This unexpected speech broke up the club which has not met since.[3]

The clarity of God's Word may be readily illustrated from our Saviour's public ministry. When Isaiah gave his nation a prophetic profile of the coming Messiah, he described Him with the words, *"He hath no form nor comeliness; and when we shall see him, there is no beauty that we should desire him."* (Isaiah 53:2b) His preaching was just as plain as His person. While the educators were stuttering, *"How knoweth this man letters, having never learned,"*(John 7:15b) no greater endorsement for Divine simplicity could be found than the words, *"and the common people heard him gladly."* (Mark 12:37c)

Appropriately, the book of Acts opens with the first preachers and writers of Scripture being described as *"unlearned and ignorant men."* (Acts 4:13) The "know-it-all scholar" remains at a loss to explain why the Holy Spirit chose to "move" (II Peter 1:21) unlettered commercial fishermen to *speak* the Word of God with *flawed grammar*. And as everything reproduces after its own kind, we are not surprised to learn that many of the catacombs' burial epitaphs contained misspelled words. The ante-Nicene Father, Lactantius (d. A.D. 315), addressed this ageless antithesis of simplicity versus complexity in his work entitled *The Divine Institutes*:

> For this is especially the case why, with the wise and the learned, and the princes of this world, the sacred Scriptures are without credit, because the prophets spoke in *common* and *simple* language, as though they spoke to the people. And therefore they are despised by those who are willing to hear or read nothing except that which is polished and eloquent; nor is anything able to remain fixed in their minds, except that which charms the ears by a more soothing sound. But those things which appear humble are considered anile, foolish and common ... Therefore they do not believe the sacred writings, because they are without any pretense; but they do not even believe those who explain them, because they also are either altogether ignorant, or at any rate possessed of little learning.[4]

When we come to the King James Bible, we are blessed to discover God's message preserved as clearly as ever. If a critic of the Authorized Version complains to you about the archaic, Elizabethan English, etc., just ask him to read I John 5:12—*"He that hath the Son hath life; and he that hath not the Son of God hath not life."*

The eternal destiny of all mankind will one day be determined by these nineteen, one-syllable words. How much plainer can you get?

2. Spiritual freedom is ensured by believing God's message.

Convinced that she could no longer understand God's words without help from the devil's "lexicon and grammar," Eve's momentary doubt led to her prolonged bondage. Such tragedy could have been avoided had she only believed her God.

When Jesus wanted to stress the importance of simple faith, he surprised everyone by embracing a child and saying, *"Except ye be converted, and become as little children, ye shall not enter into the kingdom of heaven."* (Matthew 18:3) The entire Christian life is experienced through such a childlike faith as we believe a message we do not understand, love a person we have never met, and long for a home that we have never visited. With six thousand years behind us, God's law remains unalterable—*"he that doubteth is damned."* (Romans 14:23)

Applying all of this to the King James issue, Christians would do well to simply believe whatever God has already stated on the subject. For instance, in Psalm 12:6-7 we read:

> *"The words of the LORD are pure words: as silver tried in a furnace of earth, purified seven times. Thou shalt keep them, O LORD, thou shalt preserve them from this generation for ever."*

Although these verses will be elaborated upon later, suffice it to say that God expects His children to believe His simple, clear, and unmistakable promises. God plainly said that He would preserve His words forever. The issue of today is not archaic, Elizabethan English. The issue is faith; does one believe that God is able to fulfill His promises?

> *"The LORD of hosts hath sworn, saying, Surely as I have thought, so shall it come to pass; and as I have purposed, so shall it stand: For the LORD of hosts hath purposed, and who shall disannul it? and his hand is stretched out, and who shall turn it back?"* (Isaiah 14:24, 27)

As the seminary professor attempts this very resistance, his arguments are silenced by the question of a child: "Mommy, if

God didn't mean what He said, why didn't God say what He
meant?"

3. Any man or movement which encourages doubt in God's Word is satanically motivated.

Paul warned the carnal Corinthians, *"But I fear, lest by any
means, as the serpent beguiled Eve through his subtilty, so your
minds should be corrupted from the simplicity that is in Christ."*
(II Corinthians 11:3) After nineteen centuries of fidelity, the
majority of God's people are suddenly found to be departing from
Christ's simplicity at breakneck speed. With a different English
version arriving approximately every six months to update the
"archaic" Authorized Version, a recent work promoting the King
James Bible was appropriately entitled, "Which Bible?" When
men begin to ask this question, you can be sure that Satan is
close at hand, *"For God is not the author of confusion."* (I
Corinthians 14:33)

The motives behind such intentional deception may be traced
back to the ancient sect of the Nicolaitanes. Although twice
mentioned in Revelation (2:6, 15), their appearance in church
history is unfortunately negligible. What we do know is that Jesus
stated His intense hatred for their activities. The cause for this
Divine provocation can be determined by examining the root
words for "Nicolaitanes." The footnote in the Scofield Reference
Bible states, "From *nikao*, 'to conquer,' and *laos*, 'the people,' or
'laity.' "[5]

Apparently, Nicolaitane theology divided God's people into an
unscriptural, dual class structure of clergy and laity. Whenever a
doubt-spreading "cleric" could convince a mere "layman" of his
inability to comprehend Divine revelation, he would "conquer"
him by substituting his own warbly-voiced opinions for final
authority. Rather than lead his flock by example, the Nicolaitane
heretic preferred to lord over God's heritage.

With the passing of time came the inevitable deterioration. As
local assemblies ceased hating Nicolaitane *deeds* (Revelation 2:6),
they were soon found holding Nicolaitane *doctrine* (Revelation
2:15). After inspiring the intellectually oriented secret societies of
Gnosticism for two centuries, Nicolaitane philosophy found its
most destructive fulfillment in the priestly class of Roman
Catholicism.

In keeping with our chapter's central premise of simple faith
in a simple message, Rome's rise to power was made possible by
another season of doubting God's ability to preserve His Word. By

the end of the fourth century, a number of corrupted manuscripts were circulating throughout the empire. Capitalizing on this opportunity to cause greater confusion, the Catholic scholar Jerome attempted a major revision of the "Old Latin" Bible (also known as the Itala Bible), the second-century translation revered as the preserved Word of God for Latin-speaking believers.

With the celebrated arrival of the corrupt "Latin Vulgate" in 420 A.D., the question of "Which Bible?" was soon being heard in the land. As infallibility could no longer be claimed for a *book*, it was now to be promoted in a *man*. In the year 440 A.D., Leo I became history's first authentic pope by having forcefully secured universal submission to his personal authority.

For the next ten centuries, God allowed rebellious man to experience the blessings of *Satan's* millennial kingdom. With true believers and their Bibles forced underground, this period of history became known as the "Dark Ages." Throughout this era of Nicolaitane bondage, Europe's laity wallowed in filth, ignorance, famine, despair, pestilence and barbarism.

Thanks to a "timely revision" of the "archaic" Old Latin, infant mortality rates swelled to such unparalleled levels that children were not even given names until their seventh birthday. The general population was so benighted that even the most elementary principles of personal hygiene were shrouded in mystery. It was not until the Crusaders traveled to the Middle East that the benefits of daily bathing were discovered. Prior to this, the bath was almost a monthly ritual with hefty amounts of cologne being used between washings. Concerning the statement that "truth is stranger than fiction," it was not uncommon in siege warfare to observe plague-ridden corpses being catapulted over city walls.

Such deplorable conditions continued to exist in direct proportion to the clergy's suppression of Scripture. Laymen, for example, were expressly forbidden to read the Bible by the Council of Toulouse in 1229. Thus we see that the secret to Nicolaitane dominance is the sustained ignorance of the laity; it was as the prophet Hosea wrote: *"My people are destroyed for lack of knowledge."* (Hosea 4:6a)

The great need of common men to regain direct access to the Scriptures was beautifully articulated by the fourteenth-century reformer John Wycliffe:

> What sort of Antichrist is this who, to the sorrow of Christian men, is so bold as to prohibit the laity from learning this holy lesson which is so earnestly commanded by God? Every man is

bound to learn it that he may be saved, but every layman who shall be saved is a very priest of God's own making, and every man is bound to be a very priest.[6]

Wycliffe channelled this passion into the first translation of the entire Bible in the English language. Satan's wrath fell swiftly on this project and hounded all ensuing translation efforts. (See chapter nine.)

The arrival of the Authorized Version in A.D. 1611 was met with immediate resistance by Jesuit agents from Rome. With such fury intensifying unabated, we are suddenly confronted by a most unusual phenomenon when entering the twentieth century. After nineteen hundred years of opposition from Rome, we now find that the Bible is under its greatest attack by the *Christians themselves!*

In the mid-1800's, the intellectual community was startled by the discovery of two fourth-century Greek manuscripts, *Codex Sinaiticus* (א—Aleph) and *Codex Vaticanus* (B). They received immediate preeminence as a result of their being several hundred years closer to the autographs than the oldest manuscripts available to the King James translators.

This acceptance became the catalyst for a special revision committee sanctioned in 1871 by the Church of England to improve the Authorized Version where needed. The two major culprits of this project were Cambridge professors, Dr. Brooke Westcott (1825-1901) and Dr. Fenton Hort (1828-1892).

With an entire chapter of this book being devoted to their writings (chapter 14), we need only examine a timely example of their Nicolaitane resolve for confusion. When faced with conflicting manuscript readings, Westcott and Hort theory automatically chose the more difficult-sounding text on the arbitrary conjecture that a well-meaning scribe had clarified the other. Wilbur Pickering comments on this unscholarly caprice:

> Another canon used against the "Byzantine" text is *proclive lectioni praestat ardua*—the harder reading is to be preferred. The basis for this is an alleged propensity of scribes or copyists to simplify or change the text when they found a supposed difficulty or something they didn't understand.[7]

Following a decade of activity behind closed doors (more cause for doubt), the Revised Version was released with much fanfare upon an unsuspecting public. Although the final number of unnecessary changes was never foreseen by the sincere but misguided Anglican hierarchy, the damage had nevertheless been done. Twenty years later, the Revised Version entered the United States market as the American Standard Version (1901). These counterfeit "Bibles" would set the pace for a century of confusion wrought by apostate Christians addicted to revision.

The greatest display of Nicolaitane intimidation can now be seen in the prestigious centers of higher Christian education. Here we find that Luther's "priesthood of the believers" doctrine has been subtly replaced by an esoteric priesthood of Hebrew and Greek professors who would have you believe that you cannot understand God's Word without their humble assistance. With great astuteness did the German reformer once note that Satan's first appearance in Scripture was under the *tree of knowledge.* Consider the following quote from a present-day leader of Nicolaitane thought:

> As much as Fundamentalists have loved and defended a great translation like the King James Version, they must remember that the court of last resort in doctrinal matters is not any translation, but the wording of the original Greek and Hebrew texts . . . The present-day believer should read his Bible with the faith that it is God's Word, but with the humility of recognizing that he may not be able to solve every textual problem that may exist in our Bibles. The believer may safely leave such problems to the discussions of theological and textual "experts." He should not try to become a botanist, but simply feed on the fruit of the Word. He can let the scholars chew over dry bones.[8]

This author can personally testify on behalf of many that it was only after attending a neo-evangelical college that he began to doubt the Book that had delivered him from over two decades of Catholicism. No sooner had he found shelter from the traditions of church fathers than he was introduced to the theories of textual critics. In ignorance were the opinions of Augustine and Aquinas exchanged for those of Westcott and Hort. Fortunately, the words of Galatians 4:9 came alive with liberating application:

> *"But now, after that ye have known God, or rather are known of God, how turn ye again to the weak and beggarly elements, whereunto ye desire again to be in bondage?"*

Upon examining our modern Nicolaitanes, we note a pronounced departure from the methodology of their suppressive forerunners. Whereas traditional Nicolaitanes undermined the

Scripture to bring a confused laity under *their* authority, today's Bible critics consign their victims to the most exacting taskmaster of all. Because no man can serve two masters, the modern cleric simply releases his unsubmissive, materialistic brother to his *own* recognizance.

No longer enjoined to kiss the pontifical toe, today's liberated (conquered) believer is encouraged to kiss his own toe. With everyone doing that which is right in his own eyes, Satan's ultimate goal for mankind is realized. Contrary to popular belief, the god of this world does not covet the personal loyalties of his subjects but would rather their testimony be, *"we have turned everyone to his own way."* (Isaiah 53:6)

This leads us to the all-important job description for the twentieth-century "scholar." In an age committed to escalating materialism, a Nicolaitane priest (whether Catholic, Evangelical, charismatic, or pseudo-Fundamentalist) is retained by his congregation for basically two functions—to rescue his shell-shocked parishioners from their dreaded submission to "the Book" (as opposed to any number of "reliable" translations, etc.) and to help them "cope" (salve their conscience) with their new-found "freedom in Christ" (doing their own thing, etc.).

As a lost Catholic, this author had the personal experience of observing his parish priest "minister" throughout a most bizarre slate of weekend activities. The same "father" who called out the Bingo numbers on Friday while holding a cigarette in one hand and a can of beer in the other, would secure his members' forgiveness in the confession booth on Saturday so they could appreciate his sacrificing of Christ in the Mass on Sunday. The bottom line was always the same—a wild time on Friday mandated a light penance on Saturday which insured a heavy collection on Sunday.

Similarly today, Nicolaitane preachers of the Evangelical or pseudo-Fundamentalist "order" may be recognized by the incessant charges of legalism which they level against authoritative pastors. In the name of "liberty" they would emancipate the oppressed brethren from such enslaving themes as, *"Love not the world,"* to a caring and sharing message of, "If it feels good, do it."

The world is always alert to such compromise on the part of God's people. A recent article in the *USA Weekend* had this to say concerning the "New Time" religion of Bill Hybels, pastor of Willow Creek Community Church.

To attract churchgoers today, you've got to please the

consumers. That means high-tech entertainment. Day care. Self-help groups. No pleas for money. No Bible-thumping. Happy customers from California to Maryland are eating up "fast-food religion" this Easter. Pastor Bill Hybels' answer for getting 30- and 40-year-olds into the tent: **Marketing. Ask consumers what they want, then let them (as they say at Burger King) have it their way.**[9]

This description of his Nicolaitane-styled ministry included:

A slick, show-biz service where drama and soft rock are served up on a stage washed in pink and blue spotlights. A **soft-sell sermon** is delivered.[10]

In a *Moody Monthly* article entitled "Which Bible Translation Is Best For Me?" John Kohlenberger writes:

A generation ago few people asked, "Which version of the Bible is best?" The Authorized or King James Version, had been the most popular and widely read Bible for 350 years. But an explosion of English Bible translations over the past 40 years has challenged the long reign of the King James Version. And the question "Which version of the Bible is best?" is now a common concern. It is a question not easily answered. For every Bible translation there is someone who will say it is the best of all possible versions. And the search for the best version is crowded with "experts" loaded with opinion, choked with rhetoric, confused by misused terminology, and short on objective information.
In fact there is no "best" translation . . . No translation is perfect, but most are "for the greatest part true and sufficient." **So the question is not "Which Bible is best?" But which of the many good translations is best *for you*?**[11]

Another illustration of this "have it your way" religion is the book *Decide for Yourself* by Dr. Norman L. Geisler. (You will hear more about this author in chapter 5.)
After taking 114 pages to present the eight leading "positions" on God's Word (beginning with his own opinion of the Biblical view), the former Dallas Theological Seminary professor concludes his work with the militant words:

Which view then, is right about the origin and nature of the Bible? The orthodox? The liberal? The fundamentalist? The neoorthodox? The liberal evangelical? Or the neoevangelical?

Decide for yourself.[12]

It is a sad commentary that the author has the Holy Bible, New International Version, copyright, 1978 by New York International Bible Society listed as "used by permission" along with six other outside sources from which he has quoted.

Having accentuated this particular distinctive of modern Nicolaitanes, we are reminded that their perennial activity continues to involve the subtle undermining of the preserved Word of God. Consequently, with the legitimate confusion wrought by so many "Bibles" contending for final authority, a pertinent question arises: "How do the modern revisers justify their actions in the light of God's clear promise for preservation?"

> *"The words of the LORD are pure words: as silver tried in a furnace of earth, purified seven times. Thou shalt keep them, O LORD, thou shalt preserve them from this generation for ever."* (Psalms 12:6-7)

The answer is easy. You simply *change* God's promise!

> And the words of the Lord are flawless, like silver refined in a furnace of clay, purified seven times. O Lord, you will keep **us** safe and protect **us** from such people forever. (Psalms 12:6-7, NIV)

Notice how the New International Version conveniently changes "them" to "us" and "this generation" to "such people." The consistent testimony of history condemns this rendering as totally preposterous. As a fitting example of desperate, Nicolaitane scholarship, this depraved reading was released less than one generation after six million of David's descendants (the "us" of verse 7) were exterminated by Adolph Hitler. When the mob cried out to Pilate, *"His blood be on us, and on our children,"* a new period of heartache was ushered in where Jewish people would be anything *but* "safe" and "protected." In fact, from a numerical standpoint, David's people have known only holocaust and genocide for two thousand of the three thousand years since the twelfth Psalm was penned. And for the record, their added cry, *"We have no king but Caesar,"* insured that their antagonists would be "Romans," as in Roman Catholics—Hitler, Mussolini, Himmler, Goebbels, Göring, Eichmann, and so forth. Who is lying—God or the NIV translators?

As stated previously, this corruption and thousands of similar ones are descended from the liberal textual theories of Wescott and Hort. For a closing bit of trivia, we note that the sophisticated Dr. Hort once took in a D.L. Moody preaching service. Observe his uppity disdain for the Christ-like simplicity of Moody's manner:

> Think of my going with Gray yesterday afternoon to hear "Moody and Sankey" at the Hay Market. I am very glad to have been **but should not care to go again**. All was much as I expected, except that the music was inferior, and altogether Sankey did not leave a favorable impression. Moody had great sincerity, earnestness and good sense, with some American humor which he mostly keeps under restraint, but in matter is quite conventional and common place.[13]

It is humorous to see that despite Hort's highbrow description of Moody's manner as "common," his message was convicting enough to send the good doctor running—"but I should not care to go again."

Of course, it was the preaching from a 1611 Authorized Version which so unnerved professor Hort. And herein lies the central lesson of our second chapter. Whenever a doubt-spreading Nicolaitane tries to conquer you through intimidation, just stick him with the Sword he claims he doesn't believe is real. When confronted with his high priestly credentials of superior scholarship, linguistic skills, and historic positions, etc., simply quote I John 2:27a and watch him run!

"But the anointing which ye have received of him abideth in you, and ye need not that any man teach you."

III

The Doctrines of the Nicolaitanes

"So hast thou also them that hold the doctrine of the Nicolaitanes, which thing I hate."
(Revelation 2:15)

In chapter two, we observed that the modern application for Nicolaitane deeds is supplied by the typical educator's attempt to transfer final authority from the King James Bible to his own opinions and prejudices. We will now offer a critical analysis of Nicolaitane doctrine.

The present-day confusion over so many "Bibles" has been caused by the scholar's wresting of II Timothy 3:16 to his own destruction.

> *"All scripture is given by inspiration of God, and is profitable for doctrine, for reproof, for correction, for instruction in righteousness."*

Every critic of the King James Bible would agree on two points of interpretation; the word *scripture* is always a reference to the missing originals, while *inspiration* describes the singular act when God mysteriously breathed out the very words comprising these autographs.

Combining these two concepts implies that the breath of God is in some way limited to the venerable originals and, of necessity, reduces all subsequent copies and translations to an inferior status. Consider the following statement by Dr. James M. Gray, former dean of the Moody Bible Institute and contributing editor to the Scofield Reference Bible.

Let it be stated further in this definitional connection, that *the record for whose inspiration we contend is the original record*—the autographs or parchments of Moses, David, Daniel, Matthew, Paul or Peter, as the case may be, and not any particular translation or translations of them whatever.[1]

This statement is typical with its absence of any references to Divine preservation. Without infallible preservation, we are forced to conclude that God's breath evaporated with the deterioration of His originals. The NIV's perversion of Psalm 12:6-7 is a picturesque attempt on the part of the scholar to divert your confidence in a "reliable" text from Divine Providence to mere human effort. Nicolaitane priests would substitute the science of textual criticism for the tender watch care of a sovereign God.

That most modern Christian educators appear oblivious to such a notion as *infallible preservation* should not be surprising. Westcott and Hort were of the opinion that the Biblical text they sought to reconstruct was in no way different from any other ancient document. Hort, writing of his intellectual neutrality, asserted:

For ourselves, we dare not introduce considerations which could not reasonably be applied to other ancient texts, supposing them to have documentary attestation of equal amount, variety, and antiquity.[2]

Elsewhere he stated:

In the New Testament, as in almost all *prose writings* which have been much copied, corruptions by interpolations are many times more numerous than corruptions by omissions.[3]

And again he adds:

The principles of criticism explained in the foregoing section hold good for all ancient texts preserved in a plurality of documents. In dealing with the text of the New Testament no new principle whatever is needed or legitimate.[4]

However, not only does such passivity ignore a supernatural preservation, but a Satanic persecution as well. Westcott and Hort refused to believe that the sacred text could be subject to intentional heretical alterations. Hort writes:

It will not be out of place to add here a distinct expression of

our belief that even among the numerous unquestionably
spurious readings of the New Testament there are no signs of
deliberate falsification of the text for dogmatic purposes.[5]

With the foregoing introduction considered, we will now
compare the so-called "historic fundamentalist position" against
the oldest position possible as found in the original *context* of II
Timothy 3:16. When weighed in the balances, Nicolaitane
doctrines are found wanting in the following seven particulars:

1. Their testimony is dishonest.

In fulfillment of their predicted end-time propensity for a
"form of godliness," apostate fundamentalists engage in clever
double-talk. While they don't believe in a preserved Bible, they
often deceitfully employ language that gives the impression they
believe "the very book they hold in their hands is the inspired,
inerrant, infallible Word of God." For the record, not a one of
them believes it! How can they if inspiration is limited to
autographs?

During this author's twenty-two years in Catholicism, he
became acquainted with the Jesuit doctrine of "mental
reservation." A bounce or two on this intellectual trampoline will
jar one's conscience free enough to enable him to say anything he
feels a need to say, regardless of his true inner reservations. This
Catholic practice finds its most appropriate usage when assisting
Nicolaitane scholars in their effort to overthrow the Authorized
Version with corrupt Vatican manuscripts. Note how this
convenient loophole helped Hort appear as though he believed in
a literal Hell:

> Certainly in my case it proceeds from no personal dread;
> when I have been living most godlessly, I have never been able
> to frighten myself with visions of a distant future, even while I
> 'held' the doctrine.[6]

Adherents of Nicolaitane doctrine can always be recognized by
this Jesuit technique of mental reservation. They will say one
thing while believing another. For instance, Evangelist Billy
Graham is one of the most admired men in America. Dr. Graham
has certainly earned high marks for ministerial integrity in the
wake of widespread contemporary scandal. However, when it
comes to pulpit survival, transparency is not always expedient.

In August of 1949 I was so filled with doubts about

everything that when I stood to preach and make a statement, I would say to myself: I wonder if that is the truth. I wonder if I can really say that sincerely. My ministry had gone. I then took the Bible up into the high Sierra Nevada Mountains in California. I opened it and got on my knees. I pled, 'Father I cannot understand many things in **this Book**. I cannot come intellectually all the way, but I accept it by faith to be authoritative, **the inspired** Word of the living God!'[7]

Although a sincere-appearing man in many areas, Billy Graham's position on the Bible is decidedly Nicolaitane. If he really believed what he said—that the very book he took up that mountain peak was the inspired word of God, then he has since had another mountaintop experience. The March 1991 *Saturday Evening Post* quotes the famous evangelist as stating:

In **this** book I have read the age-abiding truths of the scriptures with renewed interest and inspiration. The **Living Bible** communicates the message of Christ to our generation.[8]

Note the downward shift in terminology from an inspired Bible to personal inspiration. Observe further how "the truth" is no longer *equated with* "The Book" but is now merely *in* the Book. This is the standard neoorthodox position that the Bible *contains* the Word of God. With all due respect to Billy Graham, this switch to the Living Bible is at least consistent with his previous celebrity appearance on George Burns' "80th Anniversary in Show Business" special. Could we possibly find a sadder illustration of our present-day apostasy than the renowned Baptist evangelist helping "roast" the Hell-bound star of the movie, *"Oh, God"*?[9]

Generally, it is only when you press these religious pragmatists one-on-one that they will they share their true mental reservations. Dr. Louis Talbot (1889-1976), the first president of Biola, expressed such double-mindedness as follows:

For **public** reading and worship, so do I **prefer** the King James Version. And nothing in all the English language can compare with it for beauty and majesty and dignity of style. It is still the Bible of the people. It is familiar to most Christians, and therefore desirable for public reading, **to avoid confusion.** These are the reasons why I **use** it in the church services. Moreover, it is remarkably accurate in its translation. It was the product of forty men's work; therefore, this precluded any one man's coloring the translation with his own prejudices or inclinations. **Truly God guided the translators** who, in 1611, under the supervision of King James of England, worked so diligently at their task! Yet (now here comes the mental reservation) since that date, many valuable manuscripts, versions, and archaeological discoveries have become available to scholars; and therefore, by careful scrutiny of these **devout,** scholarly men (Westcott and Hort?) have been able to improve on the accuracy of an English translation here and there—so far as rendering the literal meaning of the original Hebrew and Greek is concerned. Accordingly, the American Standard Version and the English Revised Version, which are **practically** the same in **most** respects, are **the most accurate** translations in our English language.[10]

Robert L. Sumner confessed:

I have never even preached from the NKJV, although I consider it a superior product because I have not wanted my congregations to be distracted by word changes. Perhaps I have been wrong.[11]

This is Nicolaitane doctrine at its best. Like the rank liberal who confesses privately what he conceals publicly—such as his total rejection of Bible miracles—an apostate fundamentalist will acknowledge in confidence that the only really inspired, inerrant, and infallible Bible he believes in disappeared from the face of this earth nearly two thousand years ago! This is the *only* "militant," historic, fundamentalist position available for those who would relegate inspired Scripture solely to the autographs.

Thus, the same fighting fundamentalists who will condemn the *Reader's Digest* Bible are forced to admit under rigorous cross-examination that they don't even possess as much as a condensed version themselves since their inspired autographs are lost! After criticizing Madalyn Murray O'Hair for expelling the Bible from America's *schoolrooms*, they are exposed as ministers who cannot even profess to have Bibles in their *studies!*

Furthermore, if all of this is not embarrassing enough, the scholars have apparently yet to perceive that their "Bible-in-the-originals-only" conviction is a blunderous misnomer and a figment of their egotistical imagination. As the word *Bible* literally means *the Book*, the only Bible anyone has ever been able to see, handle or read has been, of necessity, a binding of copies. *The autographs have never been so arranged.* Apparently, that trampoline jars more than one's conscience.

2. Their method is incredible.

When someone tells you that your King James Bible is inferior to the inspired autographs, he will always cite II Timothy 3:16 as his proof-text of final authority. But such an act is preposterous! After denouncing your Authorized Version as uninspired, the double-talking Nicolaitane will then quote from it to prove that some nonexistent papers were inspired before they disappeared! Such an unscrupulous practice has been rejected since antiquity. Consider the rebuke issued in 208 A.D. by an indignant Tertullian against heretics who would "use" the Christian Scriptures to defend their position:

> Thus, not being Christians, they have acquired no right to the Christian Scriptures; and it may be very fairly said to them, "Who are you? When and whence did you come? As you are none of mine, what have you to do with that which is mine?"[12]

This question bears asking today. So much for trampolines.

3. Their terminology is unscriptural.

When the scholar's technical vocabulary is examined in the light of Scripture, a significant observation appears. Not one single Bible character in either Testament has ever been discovered using the scientific rhetoric of the modern textual critic.

Of the fifty-three verses containing the word *scripture* or *scriptures,* nineteen of them record personal commentary by Jesus. Not once does the Master show a Nicolaitane preference for a verbally inspired autograph, an older manuscript, or a more accurate rendering, etc. His disciples never heard confusing references to such jargon as interpolations, glossas, eclecticity, scholia, kepholia, colophons, neumes or onomostics. Yet despite His less-than-intellectual approach, His listeners *"were astonished at his doctrine."* (Mark 1:22a)

4. Their reasoning is inconsistent.

A common argument against the King James Bible's capacity for inspiration is that the translators themselves did not specifically claim to be inspired. Dr. W.B. Riley expressed this objection with:

> To claim, therefore, inerrancy for the King James Version . . . is to claim inerrancy for men who never professed it for themselves.[13]

This complaint dissolves when applied to the autographs. Not a single one of the forty-plus authors ever professed that his writings were *uniquely* inspired either (i.e., as being superior to any number of subsequent copies). Some expressed a longing for their words to be preserved in a book (Job 19:23), while others acknowledged confusion at their own works (Daniel 12:8).

Although Paul wrote that his letter constituted the commands of the Lord (I Corinthians 14:37), he never once expressed inerrancy. The Holy Spirit also moved him to appear as though offering his own opinions to the same church (I Corinthians 7:6, 25, 40). And as far as conjecture goes, Paul missed the same rapture he went on record as anticipating (I Thessalonians 4:17). To indict the King James Bible with the argument of silence is to invalidate Genesis through Revelation in the originals.

However, despite all of this reasoning, a pertinent question remains: Who ever said that the King James translators had to be inspired? This faulty hypothesis, known as "double inspiration" is rendered unnecessary because of "infallible preservation." If God's breath rested on the very originals He intended to preserve, wouldn't common sense dictate that the final ancestor would also have to retain inspiration?

Should the critic persist in technicalities, we would point out that II Timothy 3:16 doesn't even say that the original authors were specifically inspired. The wording of the English simply uses the word *inspiration* to describe the way in which God "gives" (note the present tense) His Scripture (the designation of which to be covered under point six); *"all scripture is given by inspiration."* Furthermore, when God does mention His manner of personal involvement with His spokesman, He employs the word "moved"; *"holy men of God spake* (not wrote) *as they were moved by the Holy Ghost."* (II Peter 1:21)

To summarize, the infallible preservation of the inspired autographs produces the preserved, infallible, inspired Word of God. To the consternation of the educated sector, "It's as simple as that."

5. Their objection is unfounded.

The challenge is also maintained that a mere translation could never possess inspiration because of a necessary loss in exact word-for-word carry over. Once again, the critic's only source of authority for this position is the silence of his opponent's supposedly defective Bible; i.e., since it is nowhere stated in Scripture that a translation can be inspired, then no translation can be inspired. (The assumption is guilty until proven innocent.)

This objection is unfounded and thoroughly rejected in both testaments. After several conversations with Pharaoh in the Egyptian tongue, Moses records them in the Hebrew original of

Exodus and thus produces an inspired translation!

If translations are exempt from inspiration, then the "historic fundamentalist position" would eradicate a significant portion of your Bible. For instance, it is obvious that Matthew never attended seminary because he doesn't write twenty-three verses of his Gospel before attempting to insert a "defective" translation into the inspired autograph.

> "Behold, a virgin shall be with child, and shall bring forth a son, and they shall call his name Emmanuel." (Matthew 1:23a)

Matthew's linguistic shortcomings are also apparent when you compare his rendering with Isaiah's, and note the words "lost in the translation."

> "Behold, a virgin shall conceive, and bear a son, and shall call his name Immanuel." (Isaiah 7:14b)

Before someone gets the idea that this is a problem peculiar to the King James Bible, he need only survey the other English translations. For instance, the New American Standard Version reading has five variants, etc.

Now, do we reject this key verse connected with the virgin birth or do we concede that inspiration can indeed rest upon a translation? The latter option is the recommended one since Matthew continues to have "problems" in this area. (See Matthew 1:23; 2:6; 2:18; 3:3; 4:15; 8:17; 9:13; etc.)

Moving to the Apostle Paul, we discover that much learning apparently did make him mad as he only lasts seventeen verses into his original of Romans before violating the "historic fundamentalist position." When attempting to edify those western Gentiles with Habakkuk 2:4, "The just shall live by faith," do you suppose he misled them by omitting the word "his"? Did inspiration cease with the loss of this word?

Could it be that the Nicolaitane intelligentsia has set a higher standard for inspiration than the Holy Spirit Himself? Have they, like Martha of old who was, "cumbered about with much serving," caused God's people to become careful and troubled about many things?

6. Their interpretation is private.

Charles H. Spurgeon once lampooned a fellow English clergyman for preaching from the text, "Abraham is dead" (John 8:52) on the Sunday following President Lincoln's assassination.

To secure irrefutable evidence that the traditional interpretation of II Timothy 3:16 is hermeneutically bankrupt, one need only refer to the immediate context.

In addition to taking our turn with the "argument of silence," we may dogmatically assert that the *scripture* of verse sixteen cannot possibly be limited to the autographs because of its providential usage in the preceding verse.

> *"And that from a child thou hast known the holy scriptures, which are able to make thee wise unto salvation through faith which is in Christ Jesus."* (II Timothy 3:15)

How could any thinking person suppose that Timothy ever saw the Old Testament originals, much less that his mother possessed them? Obviously, Timothy was reared on copies of copies.

After discovering that the Holy Spirit ignores the historic, "militant," fundamentalist position by a contextual designation of copies as Scripture, we proceed to the all-important verse sixteen. The opening, three-letter adjective *all* clarifies how much Scripture is given by inspiration of God. This is precisely why Timothy's copies were described as *"holy"* Scriptures.

That this position of limiting the word *scriptures* to the originals is a private interpretation is also borne out by a 100 percent context check of the entire Bible. Not once in any of the fifty-three verses where the word *scriptures* is found is the object in question an original. (The indirect reference in II Peter 3:16 represents the only possible example). If the "Scripture" Jesus read in the Nazareth synagogue was Isaiah's original (Luke 4:16, 17, 21), we are forced to conclude that the Ethiopian eunuch must have broken in and stolen it on his way back to Egypt (Acts 8:29, 30).

7. Their defense is desperate.

As the frustrated Nicolaitane defies the context by insisting that the *all scriptures* of verse sixteen just has to refer to the originals, we politely smile in recognition of the fact that such irrationality is standard procedure for all end-day apostates.

Whether it is the hyper-Calvinist insisting that the *all* of I Timothy 2:4, 6 and the *any* of II Peter 3:9 must refer to the elect (despite the context), or just the typical, ecstatic charismatic crying, "Don't confuse me with the Scriptures; I *know* what I've experienced," we've seen it all before.

Therefore, when the ramifications of verse fifteen begin to sink in, the scholar will inevitably submerge to the Greek in search of a way of escape. As there is pleasure in sin for a season, he is granted a momentary stay of execution by pointing out that the Greek word for *scripture* in verse fifteen (*grammata*) differs from the Greek of verse sixteen (*graphe*).

This potential, quick-fix remedy appealed so strongly to the American Standard Version committee of 1901 that they twisted verse sixteen into: "Every scripture inspired of God is profitable."

As a last resort against recognizing Timothy's Scriptures as possessing the breath of God, these scholars were willing to invent a new phenomena—two classes of Scriptures—one inspired and the other not. This fantasy, described by Dean Burgon as "the most astonishing as well as calamitous literary blunder of the age," possessed two serious flaws.

First, if Timothy's Scripture was separated from the *all scripture* of verse sixteen, what of the other fifty-one references where the Scripture is also an obvious reference to copies but employs the same Greek word as verse sixteen?

Second, in their desperation to display a superior scholarship to a supposedly shallow 1611 forerunner, the Nicolaitane priests forgot to follow a basic law of Greek syntax:

> The disputed portion of the sentence is made up of a subject (*all scripture*) and two adjectives connected by the conjunction and (*God-breathed and profitable*). The verb is omitted as is often the case in Greek. The question is where to supply the understood verb. The A.V. supplies it between the two adjectives, making one a part of the subject and the other a predicate adjective. Sound grammar would demand that if one adjective is placed in the predicate, the other should be, since they agree in case, number and gender, and are connected by the simple conjunctive and.[14]

This quote was taken from a neo-evangelical publication and is indicative of the widespread repudiation heaped upon so depraved a rendering. The desperate interpretation was to be seen no more in any of the subsequent versions. The single exception and the diehards' last resort for any wresting of Scripture remains Kenneth Taylor's Living Bible rendition:

All scripture **was** given by inspiration of God.

IV

The Transmission of the Text

"And the things that thou hast heard of me among many witnesses, the same commit thou to faithful men, who shall be able to teach others also."
(II Timothy 2:2)

Dr. J. Frank Norris taught that the study of history was second only to the Bible itself for the preacher who would gain maximum influence for God. This valuable resource will now be extended to the conscientious believer in order to gain the necessary background for the King James controversy. We will begin our survey by examining the transmission of the New Testament text.

As previously stated, Westcott and Hort believed that the sacred canon should be handled no differently than any other ancient document. The absurdity of such an approach becomes apparent when one considers the vast numerical superiority held by surviving New Testament manuscripts over other extant writings of a secular nature.

For instance, over 5,000 Greek manuscripts of the New Testament exist today ranging in size from small fragments containing two or three verses to nearly entire Bibles.[1] Their ages vary from the second to the sixteenth century; the manuscript era ending with the arrival of printing. By comparison, there exists only ten quality manuscripts of Caesar's *Gallic War* composed between 58-50 B.C. Of Livy's *History of Rome* written between 59 B.C.-17 A.D., only 35 of the original 142 books survive being represented by a mere 20 copies. Only two manuscripts remain of *The History of Tacitus* completed around 100 A.D.[2]

These numbers are even more impressive when one considers

the centuries of persecution leveled against the Holy Scriptures. It was not some glorious history of Rome which Diocletian consigned to the flames but rather the convicting record of sinful mankind. (Someone has rightly concluded that after two thousand years, we name our sons Paul and our dogs Nero!)

These writings were made on two types of material—*papyrus* and *parchment*. The papyrus was a vegetable product fashioned from the inner bark of the reed-like papyrus plant found along river banks and marshes. After drying, these strips of bark were laid side by side in a row with a second layer positioned above in a crisscross manner. The two layers were then gummed together to create a primitive form of paper.

The parchment type is animal as it came from the shaved and scraped skins of sheep, goats, and other such creatures. Also known as *vellum*, it was the more durable and costly of the two with calf and antelope skin being the most expensive. An entire antelope would furnish only about two pages of a Bible manuscript.

The kind of book with which we are familiar was not invented until the second century. Known as a *codex*, it consisted of parchment pages in a standard binding. Since the codex was unknown to the New Testament writers, the normal books of this period were recorded on scraps of papyrus. This is what the Apostle John witnessed in Revelation 5:1. The average papyrus scroll was ten inches in height and about thirty feet in length. Such was the size of a copy of Luke's Gospel.

Just as our Bibles wear out through frequent study, any manuscript possessing the endorsement of the Holy Spirit was soon thumbed to pieces through similar usage. Under a natural transmission of the text, successive generations of faithfully executed copies would share a similar fate. Because of this, only a fraction of the 5,000 surviving manuscripts have been granted notoriety for their exceptional antiquity.

Like the embarrassed bench warmer who returns to his locker with an unsoiled uniform, these overrated "ancient authorities" actually owe their unnatural survival to a continuous abandonment by God's people. That such is the case can be easily proven by observing both their individual depravities as well as their collective disagreements.

As an illustration of the latter, notice the conflict between two of the oldest and most revered of the papyrus manuscripts in existence—the *Chester Beatty* and the *Bodmer* papyri. Dated from approximately 200 A.D., they have about seventy verses in common. In just this brief stretch alone, they are found to differ with one another over seventy-three times, not including simple copyists' mistakes.[3] Predictably, such demonstrable logic and evidence is ignored by the desperate Nicolaitanes.

In contrast to this high percentage of disarray within so small a number of ancient manuscripts, there exists a reassuringly high degree of conformity among the larger body of late copies. This providential phenomenon has come to be known as the *Textus Receptus* for "received text" (i.e., the text received by the people). Also referred to as the "Majority," "Traditional," "Antiochian," and "Byzantine," this tradition represents the underlying Greek text for most of the King James translation labors of 1611.

Once again, the outstanding feature of the Received Text is its high percentage of agreement among so many thousands of independent witnesses. This agreement is often placed at about 90 percent; in other words, 90 percent of all existing manuscripts agree with one another so miraculously that they are able to form their own unique text.[4] In contradistinction to such unity, the remaining 10 percent comprises a selection of manuscripts that will both agree with the majority text in many particulars while disagreeing wildly in others. Again, let it be stated that many of these variant readings are also unique to the individual manuscript containing it; where the 10 percent disagree from the majority, these departures also disagree with each other! In his book, *The Identity of the New Testament Text*, Wilbur Pickering has helped to simplify this highly technical concept by suggesting the following professional estimate of its miraculous coherence:

> A better, though more cumbersome, way to describe the situation would be something like this: 100% of the MSS. agree as to, say, 80% of the text; 99% agree as to another 10%; over 95% agree as to another 4%; over 90% agree as to another 3%; only for 3% (or less) of the Text do less than 90% of the MSS agree.[5]

If the critic of your King James Bible is correct in his rejection of the underlying *Textus Receptus*, then he is also under the greatest pressure to account for its existence. To complain of fabrication is one thing, but to account for its universal prevalence is quite another. Whenever a large body of ancient documents are seen to be in agreement, this inexplicable harmony becomes their greatest evidence for legitimacy. Simple arithmetic confirms that the nearer a particular reading is to the original, the longer the time span will be for descendants to follow. The larger the family is, the older the original source must be. Zane

Hodges explains this concept as follows:

> The manuscript tradition of an ancient book will, under any but the most exceptional conditions, multiply in a reasonably regular fashion with the result that the copies nearest the autograph will normally have the largest number of descendants. The further removed in the history of transmission a text becomes from its source the less time it has to leave behind a large family of offspring. Hence, in a large tradition where a pronounced unity is observed between, let us say, eighty per cent of the evidence, a very strong presumption is raised that this numerical preponderance is due to direct derivation from the very oldest sources. In the absence of any convincing contrary explanation, this presumption is raised to a very high level of probability indeed.[6]

Even Hort was forced to concede:

> A theoretical presumption indeed remains that a majority of extant documents is more likely to represent a majority of ancestral documents at each stage of transmission than *vice versa*.[7]

The human factors responsible for such a widespread acclaim of this text may be traced back to the earliest years of transmission. Church history confirms that the maiden copies of Scripture were blessed with an unprecedented proliferation. For instance, Clement of Rome refers to at least eight New Testament books in his epistle to the Corinthians dated about 96 A.D. Many such similar references confirm the early existence of a burden to both propagate and receive the precious words of God.

In addition to this resolve to transcribe their sacred deposit, the first Christians were also careful to proceed with a spirit of utmost vigilance. Such caution was the natural reaction to a vicious onslaught of heretical corruption. (See chapters 5 & 6.) Having copied the very prophecies of the enemy's approach, they were suddenly confronted by their ominous fulfillment.

Fortunately, the infant churches were blessed with an array of courageous leaders, fanatically intolerant of textual depravities. John's letter to the Ephesian assembly reflects such devotion:

> *"I know thy works, and thy labour, and thy patience, and how thou canst not bear them which are evil: and thou hast tried them which say they are apostles, and are not, and hast found them liars."* (Revelation 2:2)

This fervor of the Apostolic age was passed into the second century through men like Polycarp, bishop in Smyrna (A.D. 69-155). Revered as a personal disciple of John, he perpetuated his mentor's fiery denunciation for any who would distort the Divine record. "Whosoever perverts the oracles of the Lord . . . he is the first-born of Satan."[8]

An impressive insight into the expectations of such men for conscientious scribes and transcriptional accuracy can be gleaned from the admonitions they affixed to their own writings. Irenaeus concluded his work *On the Ogdoad* with the following charge:

> I adjure you who shall copy out this book, by our Lord Jesus Christ and by his glorious advent when he comes to judge the living and the dead, that you compare what you transcribe, and correct it carefully against this manuscript from which you copy; and also that you transcribe this adjuration and insert it in the copy.[9]

However, the most significant factor which accounts for the early domination of our traditional text is in its convenient recourse to the extant originals. As the patriarchal trio of Adam, Methuselah, and Noah preserved the entire pre-flood oral tradition, the church's accessibility to New Testament autographs offered a similar security for the written record. This providential arrangement provided a fail-safe deterrent against fabrications which insured a steady transmission of faithfully executed copies.

That the originals were utilized in this very manner is confirmed by the written testimony of Tertullian as late as the year 208 A.D. In his defensive work entitled *On Persecution Against Heretics*, he rebukes the skeptics of his age with the challenge:

> Come now, you who would indulge a better curiosity, if you would apply it to the business of your salvation, run over the apostolic churches, in which the very thrones of the apostles are still pre-eminent in their places, **in which their own authentic writings are read**, uttering the voice and representing the face of each of them severally. Achaia is very near you, [in which] you find Corinth. Since you are not far from Macedonia, you have Philippi; (and there too) you have the Thessalonians. Since you are able to cross to Asia, you get Ephesus. Since, moreover, you are close upon Italy, you have Rome, from which there comes even into our own hands the very authority (of apostles themselves). How happy is its church, on which apostles poured forth all their doctrine along with their blood![10]

You will note that these recommended itineraries reflect the "traveling mercies" afforded by the empire's renowned road network and stringent military protection, known as the Pax Romana (Roman Peace). Also, the close proximity of these "apostolic churches" is to be observed. These and other such providential blessings greatly facilitated the early establishment of the *Textus Receptus*.

As stated previously, this text is also referred to as the Byzantine text. At this juncture, it would be profitable to consider the reason for such a textual designation by geographic location. The great majority of New Testament autographs were situated in the Aegean locales of Greece and Asia Minor. Quite naturally, the most dependable copies would be found circulating in the immediate vicinity of these originals. When it is realized further that not one of the autographs was dispatched to Egypt, a significant flaw appears in the Westcott and Hort theory. The manuscripts which challenge the established text of the Byzantine world, and hence, the King James Bible, are *Alexandrian* in geographic origin. They are named after Egypt's capital city of Alexandria. (See chapter 7.)

This flaw becomes even more damaging when considering the implication drawn from the contrasting methods of interpretation (hermeneutics) peculiar to the two theological centers. While Alexandria pioneered the *allegorical* or figurative style, Antioch maintained the strict *literalist* mode of orthodoxy which would naturally demand a greater regard for precise word-for-word copying.

It is noteworthy that this Byzantine superiority can be traced to her clergy's "anti-Nicolaitane" prejudice for a Bible-reading laity. McClure illustrates this pastoral burden by citing the insistence of Chrysostom (c. 347-407) that:

> Every man should read by himself at home, in the mean days and time, between sermon and sermon; that when they were at home in their houses, they should apply themselves, from time to time, to the reading of the Holy Scriptures. For the Holy Spirit hath so ordered and attempered the Scriptures, that in them, as well publicans, fishers and shepherds, may find their edification, as great doctors their erudition . . . Take the books into thine hands, read the whole story, and that thou understandest, keep it well in memory; that thou understandest not, read it again and again. Here all manner of persons, men, women; young, old; learned, unlearned; rich, poor; priests, laymen; lords, ladies; officers, tenants and mean men; virgins, wives, widows; lawyers, merchants, artificers, husbandmen, and all manner of persons, of

what estate or condition soever they be, may in this *book* learn
all things, what they ought to believe, what they ought to do, and
what they should not do, as well concerning Almighty God, as
also concerning themselves and all others.[11]

Thus we can see that in every particular, the hand of Divine
blessing was firmly establishing the *Textus Receptus* as the first
and dominant tradition of the ancient world.

It is at this juncture that the alert Bible-believer will be found
pondering the dilemma of Westcott and Hort in the face of so vast
an array of logic, statistics, and historical consideration. In
response to this irrefutable barrage, the Cambridge professors
offered only concession and conjecture.

As noted previously, Westcott and Hort were painfully aware
of the implications inherent in a large surviving manuscript
tradition. In perfect illustration of Lenin's words, "Facts are
stubborn things," the desperate Nicolaitanes made an even more
embarrassing admission, Dr. Hort writing:

> The fundamental Text of *late extant Greek* MSS. generally is
> *beyond all question identical* with the dominant *Antiochian* or
> *Graeco*-Syrian text of the *second half of the fourth century*.[12]

Having been forced to admit that the underlying Greek text of
the King James Bible was flourishing as early as the fourth
century, **making it at least as old as ℵ and B**, they concocted
an incredible fantasy to cover their tracks.

Westcott and Hort theorized that such a prevailing text type
could only be accounted for on the basis of its having been
ecclesiastically sanctioned. Without a single shred of historical
evidence for this supposed empire-wide church council, these men
simply picked out a place, Antioch; a time, A.D. 250-350; a
coordinator, Lucian; and an impressive-sounding, technical
designation, *The Lucian Recension*.

As their only way of explaining the existence of a fourth-
century *Textus Receptus*, they just *guessed* that this council
officially condemned and subsequently repressed the "true"
readings (Alexandrian) while endorsing and propagating the
"false" (Antiochian).

For a nineteenth-century version of "possibility thinking" at
its wildest, consider the following example of standard Nicolaitane
scholarship while under fire. Pickering citing Hort:

> The Syrian text must in fact be the result of a "recension" in
> the proper sense of the word, a work of attempted criticism,

performed deliberately by editors and not merely by scribes.[13]

Apparently not contented with only one make-believe get-together, the madness continued:

> An authoritative Revision at Antioch . . . was itself subjected
> to a second authoritative Revision carrying out more completely
> the purposes of the first. At what date between A.D. 250 and 350
> the first process took place, it is impossible to say with
> confidence. The final process was apparently completed by A.D.
> 350 or thereabouts.[14]

The audacity of Westcott and Hort in suggesting such a ludicrous theory was the result of a false confidence on their part. The deluded professors erroneously concluded that their position was unassailable because of the convenient absence of any *Textus Receptus* manuscripts older than *Sinaiticus* and *Vaticanus*.

That for which they totally forgot to allow was that, *"He that sitteth in the heavens shall laugh: the Lord shall have them in derision."* (Psalm 2:4) We shall now witness the complete obliteration of the Lucian Recension Theory at the hands of a Divinely prepared "threefold cord" of resistance.

I. Translations

The first of these provisions called for the Scriptures to be translated into several foreign languages, the natural outcome of early missionary activity. The significance attached to these translations when defending the King James Bible cannot be overestimated.

For instance, whenever the claims of conflicting readings are evaluated in order to determine the prevailing text (all things being equal), any version will, of necessity, outweigh any competing Greek copy. Such an ancient version will always possess the higher reliability by virtue of the unique conditions required for an accurate translation.

The presumption for this is that a serious translation effort would not have been attempted from merely a single, indiscriminate copy. The natural course of events would have ensured that a diligent search be undertaken to secure the most reliable of manuscripts. Burgon comments on this enlightening, though little-known principle of manuscript evidences:

> I suppose it may be laid down that an ancient Version
> outweighs any single Codex, ancient or modern, which can be

named: the reason being, that it is scarcely credible that a
Version—the Peshitto, for example, an Egyptian, or the
Gothic—can have been executed from a single exemplar (copy).[15]

A second reason for the value of ancient versions is in their
ability to exhibit a text which antedates the oldest Greek
manuscripts. Readings which are challenged in the Authorized
Version for their nonexistence in the "two most ancient
authorities" (*Codex Sinaiticus*, or ℵ; and *Codex Vaticanus*, or B,
fourth century) **are frequently discovered in the Syrian and
Latin translations of the *second* century**. As space does not
permit an exhaustive review of these numerous versions, we will
limit our study to the most pertinent witness for the King James
text.

For the Syrian people dwelling northeast of Palestine, there
were at least four major versions: the Peshitta (A.D. 145); the Old
Syriac (A.D. 400); the Palestinian Syriac (A.D. 450); and the
Philoxenian (A.D. 508), which was revised by Thomas of Harkel
in A.D. 616 and henceforth known as the Harclean Syriac.

True to the meaning of its name (*straight* or *rule*), the
Peshitta set the standard because of its early composition and
strong agreement with the Greek text underlying the King James
Bible. Because of the obvious embarrassment caused by this
document bearing witness to a text some two centuries older than
either ℵ or B, modern Nicolaitane scholarship has conveniently
assigned the Peshitta's origin to A.D. 415.

The first translation into a purely European tongue is known
as the Gothic version. This work was prepared in 330 A.D. by the
soul-winning missionary Ulfilas, whose name means *little wolf*.
Once again, the strength of this version is found in its age and
agreement with the *Textus Receptus*. Edward Hills cites F.G.
Kenyon's 1912 edition on New Testament criticism that, "The
type of text represented in it is for the most part that which is
found in the majority of Greek manuscripts."[16]

Thus, Ulfilas had access to King James Version readings a full
two decades *before Sinaiticus* or *Vaticanus* were copied. An
excellent example of his superior manuscripts is reflected by the
Gothic inclusion of the traditional ending to "The Lord's Prayer"
of Matthew 6:13. The familiar words, *"for thine is the kingdom,
and the power, and the glory, for ever. Amen"*, are conspicuously
absent from both of the "two most ancient authorities." There
are only eight surviving manuscripts of the Gothic version. A
sample of the Lord's Prayer in this barbaric northern dialect
would resemble the following:

Atta unsar thu in himinam. Weihnai namo thein. Quimai thiudinassus theins. Wairthai wilja theins. Swe in himina jah and airthai. Hlaif unsarana thana sinteinan gif uns himmadago. Jah aflet uns thatei skulans sijaima, swaswe jah weis afletam thaim skulam unsaraim. Jah ni briggais uns in fraistubujai. Ak lausei uns af thamma ubilin, unte theina ist thiudangardi, jah maths, jah wulthus in aiwins.[17]

The Armenian Bible is referred to as "The Queen of Versions," because of its unusually high number of extant copies (1,244). This translation was made by another soul winner, Mesrob, at approximately A.D. 400; and, it matches the readings in the King James Bible.

Then we have the Georgian version for the people dwelling between the Black and Caspian Seas of southern Russia. This translation is also thought to be the work of Mesrob.

The Egyptian translations are referred to as the Coptic and are divided into two main versions based on geography and dialect. The Sahidic represents the southern region (upper Egypt) and is dated from about the beginning of the third century while the Boharic is northern (lower Egypt) and is from as late as the sixth century. Because of their proximity to Alexandria, Coptic readings are frequently opposed to the Majority Text.

A second major translation in the "Land of Ham" is the Ethiopian of A.D. 350. As expected, corruptions abound including the presence of fourteen non-canonical books.

The first Latin translation of the Bible is known as the "Old Latin" and was made no later than A.D. 157 for the young churches established throughout the Italian Alps. The fifty extant manuscripts of this version are classified by either of their eventual twofold areas of expanded circulation—Europe or Asia. Also referred to as the Itala Bible, this venerable witness was also closely allied with the *Textus Receptus*—a full century before the so-called Lucian Recension!

Because of this, we are not surprised to learn that the Roman Bishop Damascus commissioned Jerome to revive the "archaic" Old Latin Bible in A.D. 382. As mentioned in chapter two, the completed monstrosity became known as the Latin "Vulgate" (for *received*) and was used by the devil to usher in the Dark Ages.

By contrast and in the face of this romanish recension, true Latin-speaking believers continued to perpetuate their beloved Itala through the centuries. These readings were eventually preserved through a translation into sixteenth-century Italian by

the reformer Diodati becoming the official Bible of the Albigensen
and Waldensian assemblies.[18] Satan's wrath for this pure Alpine
text was *vividly* confirmed by the blood which flowed through the
otherwise peaceful valleys amidst repeated Catholic atrocities.

Concerning Dr. Hort's view that a mere church council could
have dispelled the Word of God, the triumph of the banned "Old
Latin" exposed this theory for the foolish notion that it was.

II. Fathers

The second of these additional safeguards against the "Lucian
Recension" can be found in the writings of the church fathers.
Referred to as "patristic" testimony (for *fatherly*), they constitute
the surviving correspondence and miscellaneous works of the
church's earliest bishops and theologians. The appellation of
"father" was more endearing than authoritative, being occasioned
by the homegoing of the apostles.

Although some were affected by heresies (Luther calling these
the "church babies"), their own extant manuscripts, replete with
New Testament quotations, provide a valuable witness to the
prevailing text of the day.

At this point, it would behoove us to hear from Dr. Hort again
concerning the nonexistence of *Textus Receptus* readings prior to
his Lucian Recension:

> The text found in the mass of existing MSS. does not date
> further back than the middle of the fourth century. Before that
> text was made up, other forms of text were in vogue, which may
> be termed respectively Neutral, Western and Alexandrian.[19]

Thus we see that Hort's entire security is built upon the
absence of King James readings prior to the time in which they
were "made up," approximately A.D. 250.

To illustrate the contributing value of the church fathers, the
writings of Tertullian, Irenaeus, Hippolytus, Origen and Clement
of Alexandria have supplied us with 30,147 Scripture citings
alone. When we consider that the great majority of their
quotations agree with the *Textus Receptus*,[20] their worth is even
more appreciated. However, when it is further discovered that all
five men died anywhere from 20-150 years before ℵ and B were
copied or that all but one died even before the suggested
Recension, the readings of the King James Bible are established
beyond question.

Edward Miller (Dean Burgon's editor) summarized the massive

amount of patristic testimony at his disposal:

> As far as the Fathers who died before 400 A.D. are concerned, the question may now be put and answered. Do they witness to the Traditional Text as existing from the first, or do they not? The results of the evidence, both as regards the quantity and the quality of the testimony, enable us to reply, not only that the Traditional Text was in existence, but that it was predominant, during the period under review.[21]

Furthermore, as it was demonstrated that a single version will outweigh a single Greek copy, we find that the same principle applies to patristic evidence as well. Dean Burgon comments accordingly:

> It has been pointed out elsewhere that, in and by itself, the testimony of any first-rate Father, where it can be had, must be held to outweigh the solitary testimony of any single Codex which can be named ... For instance, the origin and history of Codexes ABℵC is wholly unknown: their dates and the places of their several production are matters of conjecture only. But when we are listening to the articulate utterance of any of the ancient Fathers, we not only know with more or less of precision the actual date of the testimony before us, but we even know the very diocese of Christendom in which we are standing. To such a deponent we can assign a definite amount of credibility, whereas in the estimate of the former class of evidence we have only inferences to guide us. Individually, therefore, a Father's evidence where it can be certainly obtained—*caeterius paribus*, is considerably greater than that of any single known Codex.[22]

With the Council of Nicea (A.D. 325) acting as their chronological watershed, church historians will generally arrange the Fathers by the era in which they lived; Apostolic (A.D. 75-150); Ante-Nicene (A.D. 150-325); and Post-Nicene (A.D. 325-500). However, an even more significant designation would be by geographical area; Western, Alexandrian and Antiochian. The relevance of this regional triad to the study of manuscript evidences should be apparent by now. Therefore, the following breakdown of the most pertinent Fathers is listed according to both criterion.

For the Apostolic Age, we have: the Western—Clement of Rome (A.D. 30-100); the Antiochian—Ignatius (A.D. 35-107) and Polycarp (A.D. 69-155); and no major Alexandrian Fathers. In the Ante-Nicene Period: the Western—Irenaeus (A.D. 120-192),

Hippolytus (A.D. 170-236), Tertullian (A.D. 150-220), and Cyprian (A.D. 200-258); the Alexandrian—Justin Martyr (A.D. 100-165), Clement (A.D. 150-217), Origen (A.D. 184-254), and Didymus (A.D. 313-398); and the Antiochian—Lucian (A.D. 250-312).

The Post-Nicene Fathers are: In the West—Augustine (A.D. 354-430); in Alexandria—Athanasius (A.D. 296-373), and Cyril (A.D. 315-386); and finally, the Antiochian—Diodorus (d. 394), Chrysostom (A.D. 345-407), Theodoret (A.D. 397-457), Basil (A.D. 330-379), Gregory Nazianzen (A.D. 329-390), and Gregory of Nyssa (A.D. 330-395).

III. Lectionaries

The third bulwark for preserving the true text and dismantling the Lucian Recension Theory is the insignificant-appearing lectionary. Of the more than 5,000 extant manuscripts, 2,143,[23] are actually classified as lectionaries. The lectionary became a popular aid to the early churches as it contained selected portions of Scripture, arranged in a particular schedule for congregational reading. The ones containing a daily selection were called *Synaxarion* while those used for special days like Easter and Christmas were known as *Menologion*.[24]

In addition to its obvious value of substantiating the predominate text style in its particular era and region, the lectionary was also called upon to serve an even greater providential purpose. If the Lucian Recension had taken place as theorized, the text type of the King James Bible would have gained exclusive usage in all of the empire's official churches, while the disavowed Westcott and Hort readings would have been banished to the underground assemblies.

What actually did occur can be determined by a simple examination of the text style contained in the government-appointed lectionaries. When these witnesses are heard, Lucian is forced from the field. Edward Hills writes:

> The Lectionaries also indicate that the Traditional text could not have been imposed on the Church by ecclesiastical authority. These, as has been stated, are manuscripts containing the New Testament Scripture lessons appointed to be read at the various worship services of the ecclesiastical year. According to the researches of Colwell (1933) and his associates, the oldest of these lessons are not Traditional but "mixed" in text. This would not be the case if Westcott and Hort's theory were true that the Traditional text from its very beginning had enjoyed official

status.[25]

From an evidence standpoint, the Lucian Recension Theory
has been surveyed from three perspectives, all negative. Westcott
and Hort have offered no proof; church history is silent; and the
threefold cord of versions, fathers, and lectionaries has confirmed
the heritage of a pre-A.D. 250 *Textus Receptus*. Yet there remains
a final voice whose testimony demands a hearing.

While musing with righteous indignation at the blasphemous
inference that a mere church council could repress the Spirit's
Sword, Burgon detected a most fateful chink in Hort's armor.
Much to the chagrin of the Cambridge duo, it was Burgon's
humorous rebuttal that the very theory they were proposing was
in reality the strongest possible argument *against* them.

As in our previous example of Nicolaitane panic concerning the
twisted interpretation of II Timothy 3:16, Westcott and Hort
missed the obvious again. Put simply, *what better evidence could
have been possibly assembled than the collective judgment of the
greatest church men of the age, whose familiarity with the oldest
and widest selection of existing manuscripts would have settled
the true text once and for all?*

Despite their fifteen-century removal from the hypothetical
scene, Westcott and Hort assumed they could simply dismiss the
verdict of antiquity with a scholastical sneer. However, like the
wash lady who inadvertently backs herself into a corner, their
entire arrogant scheme has backfired horrendously. Dean Burgon
assails at will:

> We devoutly wish that Dr. Hort's hypothesis of an
> authoritative and deliberate Recension of the Text of the New
> Testament achieved at Antioch first, about A.D. 250, and next,
> about A. D. 350, were indeed an historical fact. We desire no
> firmer basis on which to rest our confidence in the Traditional
> Text of Scripture than the deliberate verdict of Antiquity,—the
> ascertained sanction of the collective Church, in the Nicene Age.
> The *Latin* 'Vulgate' [A.D. 385] is the work of a single
> man—Jerome. The *Syriac* 'Vulgate' [A.D. 616] was also the work
> of a single man—Thomas of Harkel. But this *Greek* 'Vulgate' was
> (by the hypothesis) the product of the Church Catholic, [A.D.
> 250-A.D. 350,] in her corporate capacity. Not only should we hail
> such a monument of the collective piety and learning of the
> Church in her best days with unmingled reverence and joy, were
> it introduced to our notice; but we should insist that no
> important deviation from such a *Textus Receptus* as *that* would
> deserve to be listened to.[26]

As this chapter's objective has been to acquaint the believer with the historical transmission of the New Testament text, the real argument comes down to a credibility gap between the two professors and the entire third-century church leadership. Such are the fatal ground rules determined by Westcott and Hort themselves. Dean Burgon administers the coup de grâce:

> We are invited to make our election between the Fathers of the Church, A.D. 250 and A.D. 350,—and Dr. Hort, A.D. 1881. The issue is really reduced to *that*. The general question of The Text of Scripture being the matter at stake; (not any particular passage, remember, but *the Text of Scripture as a whole*;)—and the *conflicting parties* being but *two*;—*Which* are we to believe? *the consistent voice of antiquity*,—or the solitary modern Professor? Shall we accept the august Testimony of the whole body of the Fathers? or shall we prefer to be guided by the self-evolved imaginations of one who confessedly has nothing to offer but conjecture? The question before us is reduced to that single issue. But in fact the alternative admits of being yet more concisely stated. We are invited to make our election between *FACT* and—*FICTION* . . . All this, of course, on the supposition that there is *any truth at all* in Dr. Hort's 'New Textual Theory.'[27]

Confronted by reality and guided by expediency, another doctrine of the Nicolaitanes vanishes into obscurity. Like the ASV reading of II Timothy 3:16 before it, the Lucian Recension Theory has been subsequently abandoned by all serious scholars.

The combination of human effort and Divine Providence working through an unprecedented proliferation of copies, lectionaries, versions, and patristic writings instilled in our first preachers the needed conviction that they did, in fact, possess the very words of God. The witness of Tertullian represents the prevailing third-century assessment of just such a confidence:

> I hold sure title-deeds from the original owners themselves, to whom the estate belonged. I am the heir of the apostles. Just as they carefully prepared their will and testament . . . even so do I hold it. [28]

Thus we conclude that the faithful transmission of the New Testament text enabled our spiritual forefathers to fulfill God's primary condition for an authoritative pulpit ministry: *"And he that hath my word, let him speak my word faithfully."* (Jeremiah 23:28b)

Do *you* have it?

V

Mark 16:9-20

"And they went forth, and preached every where, the Lord working with them, and confirming the word with signs following. Amen." (Mark 16:20)

In I Peter 2:2, the baby Christian is exhorted to *"desire the sincere milk of the word"* as his mainstay to proper spiritual development. Consequently, the wise soul winner will establish his convert in the Scriptures at the earliest opportunity. However, in our present age of multiplied versions, the young believer has a most precarious path before him.

It is no secret that the cults recruit a substantial percentage of their membership from the ranks of professing born-again people. This tragedy can frequently be traced to an ambiguous marginal reference within the very Bible the new convert is attempting to study. For instance, should he pursue the typical discipleship program and begin his study with the New Testament, the poor fellow won't make it through the second book before hearing that damning question, *"Yea, hath God said?"*

While enjoying the victorious resurrection account of Mark 16 in his Old Scofield Bible, he is suddenly confronted at verse nine by the following statement:

> The passage from verse 9 to the end is not found in the two most ancient manuscripts, the Sinaitic and Vatican, and others have it with partial omissions and variations. But it is quoted by Irenaeus and Hippolytus in the second or third century.[1]

Now, what could a *Sinaitic* or *Hippolytus* possibly mean to a spiritual neophyte who still thinks the book of Job will help him find employment? Slightly dazed, he determines to forge ahead, only to be confused again at John 7:53. This time it is the account of the woman taken in adultery that is suspect (John 7:53-8:11). Having escaped an evil life himself, he senses a vicarious threat in the rejection of such a reassuring account of Divine forgiveness. And while he is scratching his head in doubt, Satan reminds him of the cool reception he has felt from some of the brethren for his less-than-cultural air since crawling out of the gutter.

About this time, the ubiquitous Jehovah's Witness rings his doorbell. Following the customary hour of haggling, our fledgling brother goes down for the count with the marginal note at I John 5:7. With his confidence in the Trinity eroded, he is soon found thumbing through a New World Translation.

On the other hand, for the converts who evade the Kingdom Hall, there awaits the more subtle blast from so-called higher Christian education. The most harmful permeation of Nicolaitane influence in today's Christian colleges is felt in the foundational course of Biblical Introduction. For a quarter of a century, the classic work in this field has been *A General Introduction to the Bible* by Geisler and Nix (Moody Press, ©1968). We will now examine this evangelical standard-bearer's particular treatment of Mark 16:9-20 against the established tenants of manuscript evidences.

The Nicolaitane propensity for confusion is apparent in their introductory statement: "This is one of the most *perplexing* of all textual problems."[2]

That a cloud of suspicion has engulfed this passage is not to be denied. While most translation committees have expressed their disdain for these verses by confining them to reproachful brackets, the more audacious have dislodged them altogether. However, it is this author's contention that the blame for such "perplexity" must be placed upon unreasonable Christian scholars for their refusal to acknowledge the truth.

Their opening dogmatic pronouncement illustrates their irrationality: "These verses are lacking in **many** of the oldest and **best** Greek manuscripts."[3]

By technical definition, the "oldest" Greek manuscripts would comprise the uncial (or majuscule) style, characterized by inch-high, block capital letters running together without breaks between words.

For our first example of Nicolaitane indifference to reality (not to mention blatant dishonesty), we submit the following statistics.

With uncials prevailing for about ten centuries, we learn that five of their number have obtained particular notoriety due to age. They are, in addition to ℵ and B; *Codex Ephraemi* (C), fourth-fifth century; *Codex Alexandrinus* (A), fifth century; and *Codex Bezae* (D), sixth-seventh century. As all five include the sixteenth chapter of Mark, we soon discover that when Geisler and Nix stated that the last twelve verses were lacking in "many" of the oldest Greek manuscripts, what they really meant was only **2 out of 5**—*Sinaiticus* and *Vaticanus*.

They are soon in trouble with another "scholarly" disclosure: "The familiar long ending (AV) of the Received Text is found in a **vast number** of uncial manuscripts (*C, D, L, W, Θ*) . . ."[4]

Having subpoenaed the remaining uncial witnesses to Mark 16, we discover that the "vast number" of corroborating majuscules is in reality **15 out of 15!**

Our next example of intellectual dementia involves the choice of vocabulary words when describing the quality of the two uncials in question, *Sinaiticus* and *Vaticanus*. Apparently for Geisler and Nix, the word *best* was the "best" they could do when portraying a pair of manuscripts which disagree with each other in over 3,000 places in the Gospels alone![5] (See chapter 8.)

Moving right along, we discover another incredible statement: "The familiar long ending (AV) of the Received Text is found in . . . **most** minuscules."[6] The uncials were gradually replaced by the cursive or minuscule-style manuscript (introduced by the scribes of Charlemagne, approximately 800 A.D.), employing lower case letters in a running-hand style with the normal break occuring between words. When Geisler and Nix said "most" minuscules contained the familiar ending, what they *really* meant to say was **600 out of 600!**[7] (And these are the kind of people who would condemn the Jehovah's Witnesses for wresting the Word of God?)

Dean Burgon epitomizes the ageless exasperation of God's people when confronted by such an unscrupulous disregard of Holy Scripture:

> **With the exception of the two Uncial manuscripts which have just been named, there is not one codex in existence, uncial or cursive, (and we are acquainted with, at least, eighteen other uncials, and about six hundred cursive copies of this Gospel), which leaves out the last twelve verses of St. Mark.**
>
> The inference which an unscientific observer would draw from this fact is no doubt, in this instance, the correct one. He

demands to be shown the Alexandrine (A), and the Parisian
Codex (C), neither of them probably removed by much more than
fifty years from the date of the Codex Sinaiticus, and both
unquestionably *derived from different originals*; and he ascertains
that no countenance is lent by either of those venerable
monuments to the proposed omission of this part of the sacred
text. He discovers that the Codex Bezae (D), the only remaining
very ancient manuscript authority—not withstanding that it is
observed on most occasions to exhibit an extraordinary sympathy
with the Vatican (B)—here sides with A and C against B and ℵ.
He inquires after all the other uncials and all the cursive
manuscripts in existence, (some of them dating from the tenth
century,) and requests to have it explained to him why it is to be
supposed that all these many witnesses, belonging to so many
different patriarchates, provinces, ages of the church, have
entered into a grand conspiracy to bear false witness on a point
of this magnitude and importance? But he obtains no intelligible
answer to this question.[8]

The credibility gap widens still further with their comments
on ancient versions. When Geisler and Nix stated that the
traditional ending is found in, "**some** Syriac manuscripts,"[9] what
they *really* meant was **all but one**—the *Sinaitic Syriac*.[10] When
they assured us that the disputed verses were in, "**most** old Latin
manuscripts . . .", we know that what they *intended* to say was
all but one—the *Codex Bobiensis* (K).[11]

Finally, there is an unusual assertion given concerning the
silence of the church fathers. "Many of the ancient Fathers show
no knowledge of it (e.g., Clement, Origen, Eusebius, *et al.*)."[12] By
now, the alert student can discern the Nicolaitanes' frequent
recourse to desperation when confronted by **facts**. Besides
containing a glaring inaccuracy concerning Eusebius, this last
remark smacks of futility in at least two other areas. Not only is
their charge of patristic ignorance ridiculously false (as we shall
presently demonstrate) but were this not the case, it would still
represent but a mere argument of silence. How weak can you get?

Although a number of the fathers labored under varying
degrees of theological deficiency, the trio recommended by Geisler
and Nix is almost as credible as their "many," "best," and
"most" manuscripts. Clement (of Alexandria) believed that
Plato's writings were inspired because they *contained* the truth,[13]
while his celebrated pupil, Origen, denied both a physical
resurrection and a literal Hell.[14] (Concerning Origen's departures
from orthodoxy, scholars are uncertain whether his mental
faculties were affected by his self-mutilation in obedience to

Matthew 19:12 or vice versa.[15]) His favorite student Eusebius prophesied that Constantine and Christ would reign together throughout eternity.[16]

As for Eusebius' unfamiliarity with the so-called "long ending," he not only knew of it, but expressed his willingness to accept *either* ending. Dean Burgon cites Eusebius' epistle to a certain Marinus as follows:

> But another ... will say that here are two readings (as is so often the case elsewhere;) and *both* are to be received,—inasmuch as by the faithful and pious, *this* reading is not held to be genuine rather than *that* nor *that* than *this*.[17]

Geisler and Nix then appeal to Jerome's testimony that "almost all Greek copies do not have this concluding portion."[18] Dr. Frederick H.A. Scrivener (leader of conservative forces within the Revision committee of 1871-1881) counters with an accent on Jerome's duplicity:

> Jerome's recklessness in statement has been already noticed (Volume II, p. 269); besides that, he is a witness on the other side, both in his quotations of the passage and in the Vulgate, for how could he have inserted the verses there, if he had judged them to be spurious.[19]

That Geisler and Nix are in desperate straits is apparent by their listing of the Latin Vulgate as one of the havens for our verses in question. In any case, these authors imply that the fathers' primary input is negative. **Nothing could be further from the truth**! There was enough positive evidence in circulation over a century ago for Dean Burgon to publish a massive 350-page volume in defense of the disputed passage entitled *The Last Twelve Verses of the Gospel According to St. Mark*. In a stinging letter to Bishop Ellicott, chairman of the Revision Committee, Burgon summarized his research as follows:

> Similarly, concerning THE LAST 12 VERSES OF S. MARK which you brand with suspicion and separate off from the rest of the Gospel, in token that, in your opinion, there is "a breach of continuity" (p. 53), (whatever *that* may mean,) between verses 8 and 9. *Your* ground for thus disallowing the last 12 verses of the second Gospel, is, that B and ℵ omit them:—that a few late MSS. exhibit a wretched alternative for them:—and that Eusebius says they were often away. Now, *my* method on the contrary is to refer all such questions to *"the consentient testimony of the most*

ancient authorities." And I invite you to note the result of such an appeal in the present instance. The verses in question I find are recognized,

In the IInd century,—By the Old Latin, and—Syriac Verss.—by Papias;— Justin M.;—Irenaeus;—Tertullian.

In the IIIrd century,—By the Coptic—and Sahidic versions:— by Hippolytus;—by Vincentius at the seventh Council of Carthage;—by the "Acta Pilati;"—and the "Apostolical Constitutions" in two places.

In the IVth century,—By Cureton's Syr. and the Gothic Verss.:—besides the Syriac Table of Canons;—Eusebius;— Macarius Magnes;—Aphraates;—Didymus;—the Syriac "Acts of the Ap.;"—Epiphanius;—Leontius;—ps.—Ephraem;—Ambrose;— Chrysostom;— Jerome;—Augustine.

In the Vth century, Besides the Armenian Vers.,—by codices A and C;—by Leo;—Nestorius;—Cyril of Alexandria;—Victor of Antioch;—Patricius;—Marius Mercator.

In the VIth and VIIth centuries,—Besides cod. D,—the Georgian and Ethiopic Verss.:—by Hesychius;—Gregentius;— Prosper;—John, abp. of Thessalonica;—and Modestus, bishop of Jerusalem.[20]

Obviously, the extant testimony of the church fathers is overwhelming. And for the reassuring benefit of a tangible illustration, note the presence of Mark 16:19 as found in its natural context within the second century work, *Irenaeus Against Heresies* (A.D. 177).

Plainly does the commencement of the Gospel quote the words of the holy prophets, and point out Him at once, whom they confessed as God and Lord; Him, the Father of our Lord Jesus Christ, who had also made promise to Him that He would send His messenger before His face, who was John, crying in the wilderness, in "the spirit and power of Elias, Prepare ye the way of the Lord, make straight paths before our God." For the prophets did not announce one and another God, but one and the same; under various aspects, however, and many titles. For varied and rich in attribute is the Father, as I have already shown in the book preceding this; and I shall show [the same truth] from the prophets themselves in the further course of this work. Also, towards the conclusion of his Gospel, Mark says: "*So then, after the Lord Jesus had spoken to them, He was received up into heaven, and sitteth on the right hand of God;*" confirming what had been spoken by the prophet: "*The LORD said to my Lord, Sit thou on my right hand, until I make thy foes thy footstool.*" Thus God and the Father are truly one

and the same; He who was announced by the prophets, and
handed down by the true Gospel; whom we Christians worship
and love with the whole heart, as the Maker of heaven and earth,
and of all things therein.[21]

Irenaeus is only one of approximately *thirty* patristic
endorsements recorded by Burgon over a century ago. Why
couldn't Geisler and Nix find them? Or if they knew of their
witness, why did they suppress this important evidence? But how
could they be ignorant when they refer to Burgon's work? The
Authorized Version A.D. 1611 is not suspect for containing Mark
16:9-20. *The Alexandrian codices are suspect for excising them!*

The final witness of our threefold cord is the unassuming
lectionary. Burgon wrote:

> But the significance of a single feature of the Lectionary, of
> which up to this point nothing has been said, is alone sufficient
> to determine the controversy. We refer to the fact that *in every
> part of Eastern Christendom* these same twelve verses—neither
> more nor less—have been from the earliest recorded period, and
> still are, *a proper lesson both for the Easter season and for
> Ascension Day.*[22]

It is noteworthy that Dean Burgon's defense of Mark's ending
has yet to be refuted. Facts are stubborn things. And yet, with
Burgon's four other scholarly works on manuscript evidences
bringing his total page count to nearly 2,000, his great potential
for good was frustrated by the solitary, patronizing remark of
Geisler and Nix that, "Defence of the Received Text (vv. 9-20) has
been made by John W. Burgon."[23]

Having dismissed Burgon's labor of a lifetime, they concluded
their "scholarly" review with the ultimate illustration of
Nicolaitane hypocrisy and obstinacy.

> It is admittedly difficult to arrive at the conclusion that any
> of these readings is the original. **But on the basis of the
> known manuscript evidence** it seems more likely that either
> Mark ended at verse 8, or the real ending is not extant. Of these
> two views the former one is more compatible with the concept of
> a complete canon.[24]

Vacillating in the spirit of Eusebius, Geisler and Nix go on
record as at least entertaining the possibility of a failure in Divine
preservation. But if the "true" ending somehow got severed from

א and B, *how can we possibly account for its accidental omission from 618 out of 618 other surviving copies?*

Heretofore, we have been examining the documented statements of these men as found in their own textbook. The remainder of this chapter will present the relevant material which was conveniently sidestepped for the sake of *self-preservation.*

Although the "scholars" have concurred in denouncing Mark 16:9-20, they have remained in hopeless disarray when attempting to explain such an incongruous ending. With every single book of the New Testament concluding on a positive note (twenty-four of them with the word "Amen"), what are we to think of such a negative ending as:

> *"And they went out quickly, and fled from the sepulchre; for they trembled and were amazed: neither said they any thing to any man;* **for they were afraid.***"*

The problem becomes even more acute when realizing that the four Gospels initially circulated as a distinct unit, but in the temporary arrangement of Matthew, John, Luke, and *Mark.*[25] (The lectionary displayed yet a third configuration but with the same ending—John, Matthew, Luke, *Mark.*)[26] We are therefore prevailed upon to believe that the earliest propagation of the "good news" of Christ's all-sufficient grace concluded with a scene of *fear* and *trembling.*

When refuted by such passages as II Timothy 1:7a which says, *"For God hath not given us the spirit of fear,"* some liberals have dug an even deeper hole for themselves with any number of desperate attempts at reconciliation. Of the several lame theories exposed by Edward Hills, one of the more fantastic ones suggested that Mark suddenly *died* at verse eight, despite the extant testimony of several fathers that he outlived the completion of his Gospel.[27]

However, of the pertinent material suppressed by Geisler and Nix, the most illuminating of all involves the actual manuscript evidence contained in א and B which tells its own story about the omission of Mark 16:9-20. Nicolaitane scholarship would have you believe that *Vaticanus* and *Sinaiticus* represent two ideal and trustworthy descendants of Mark's autograph. As such, you would expect their text to exhibit a *legitimate* omission of the "suspect" passage (being evidenced by a natural and inconspicuous flow of text from Mark 16:8 to Luke 1:1). The facts prove the opposite to be true.

If you had the *Codex Vaticanus* before you, each page
(measuring 10" x 10½") would be seen to contain three columns
of 42 lines each. Whenever the respective scribe concluded the
individual books within his codex, he would do so according to an
established pattern. After penning his final lines, he would
accentuate the book's completion by purposely leaving the
column's remaining space blank. The next book would begin at
the top of the adjacent column.

When arriving at Mark 16:9-20 however, we observe a
pronounced departure from this otherwise consistent procedure.
With Mark 16:8 terminating on line 31, we note that the
remaining eleven blank lines are followed not by a fresh column
with Luke 1, but rather by an additional 42 *blank* lines! This
space of a whole column is striking as it constitutes **the only
such occurrence in the entire 759-page manuscript**.

The reason you don't find this "gap theory" discussed in *A
General Introduction to the Bible* should be obvious. As these
fifty-three lines could have accommodated the missing twelve
verses, our "ancient authority" is suddenly seen to be a "dubious
document" at best.

Dean Burgon was wonderfully led of the Spirit to see the
deeper influence of this significant lacuna.

> *The older* manuscript from which Cod. B was copied must
> have infallibly contained the twelve verses in dispute. The copyist
> was instructed to leave them out, and he obeyed; but he
> prudently left a blank space in memoriam rei. Never was blank
> more intelligible! Never was silence more eloquent! By this
> simple expedient, strange to relate, the Vatican Codex is made to
> recite itself even while it seems to be bearing testimony against
> the concluding verses of St. Mark's Gospel, by withholding them:
> for it forbids the inference which, under ordinary circumstances,
> must have been drawn from that omission. It does more. *By
> leaving room* for the verses it omits, it brings into prominent
> notice at the end of fifteen centuries and a half *a more ancient
> witness than itself*. The venerable author of the original codex
> from which Codex B was copied, is thereby besought to view. And
> thus, our supposed adversary (Codex B) proves our most useful
> ally; for it procures us the testimony of an hitherto unsuspected
> witness. The earlier scribe unmistakably comes forward at this
> stage of the inquiry, to explain that he at least is prepared to
> answer for the genuineness of these twelve concluding verses
> with which the later scribe, his copyist, from his omission of
> them, might unhappily be thought to have been unacquainted.[28]

When examining *Codex Sinaiticus*, we discover that the shenanigans are stranger yet. Each of the slightly larger pages (leafs) of this uncial manuscript (13½" x 14") contains four, 2½"-wide columns of 48 lines respectively.

However, when viewing the conclusion of Mark's Gospel in this codex, even the novice will find his attention arrested by two pronounced signs of textual intrusion. The first of these concerns the presence of six pages unlike the other 364½ leaves in several particulars. This initial cause for suspicion is intensified further by the twofold discovery that one leaf contains Mark 16:2-Luke 1:56 while the handwriting style for all six pages matches that of the Vatican Codex B.[29]

It is noteworthy that this opinion regarding the interpolation of B's scribe enjoys a rare concurrence between both sides of the debate. And furthermore, before we discover the content of these spurious leaves, let it be recognized that the real significance of this partisan theory is that the number of Greek codices hostile to Mark 16:9-20 has been reduced by half! Dr. Scrivener brings this important observation to light:

> I have ventured but slowly to vouch for Tischendorf's notion, that six leaves of Cod. ℵ, *that containing* Mark xvi.2-Luke i.56 *being one of them*, were written by the Scribe of Cod. B. On mere identity of handwriting and the peculiar shape of certain letters who shall insist? Yet there are parts of the case which I know not how to answer, and which have persuaded even Dr. Hort. Having now arrived at this conclusion our inference is simple and direct, that at least in these leaves, Codd. ℵB make but one witness, not two.[30]

Should this codex be opened before you, the page containing Mark's ending would constitute the *recto* of leaf 29 (or the front side of page 29 laid open to your *right*), containing the four columns of Mark 16:2-Luke 1:18. On your *left* would be the *verso* (or the back of leaf 28) displaying the four columns of Mark 15:16-16:1.

When these eight columns are viewed in their adjacent setting, the second tell-tale evidence of scribal tampering becomes readily apparent. As if to illustrate the adage, "If at first you don't succeed, try, try again," B's scribe made a determined effort to cover his tracks by his subsequent elimination of Mark 16:9-20 via the excision of several whole pages. This time, instead of leaving an *entire* column blank, he ventured on a solution that is not unfamiliar to the average student of today. With Mark 16:8

concluding on line four of column six, and Luke 1:1 situated atop column seven, our deceiver appeared to be home free. However, just as the hefty sisters of Cinderella were unable to make the slipper fit, *his* sin would find him out as well. Dean Burgon explains:

> But the writing of these six columns of St. Mark is so spread out that they contain less matter than they ought; whereas the columns of St. Luke that follow contain the normal amount. It follows, therefore, that the change introduced by the *diorthota* (B's scribe) must have been an extensive excision from St. Mark:−in other words, that these pages as originally written must have contained a portion of St. Mark of considerable length which has been omitted from the pages as they now stand. If these six columns of St. Mark were written as closely as the columns of St. Luke which follow, there would be room in them for the omitted twelve verses.[31]

The total letter count for each of the four columns of leaf 29 (moving left to right) appears to be as follows: 560, 37, 678, and 668. With forty-eight lines per column, this averages out to 11.6 characters per line in column one with 14.1 and 13.9 for columns three and four respectively for a disparity factor of 2.4 characters per line.

So there you have it. And to whatever degree the critic may recoil in righteous indignation, let him be reminded that such blatant deceitfulness is but child's play when compared to the demoniacal twentieth-century cover-up by Geisler and Nix. For the final example of Nicolaitane semantics, we discover that their phrase, *"lacking* in the oldest and best Greek manuscripts" *really* means−*kept* out of *Vaticanus* and *kicked* out of *Sinaiticus!*

Our study would be incomplete without suggesting several possible causes for this exaggerated textual controversy. As previously noted (and apparently unbeknown to Geisler and Nix), Eusebius confirmed the existence of both endings in his day. A second excerpt from his epistle to Marinus reads, "The entire passage was not met with in all the copies."[32] He goes on to explain that certain scholars, himself included, were having difficulty reconciling Matthew's words of, *"In the end of the Sabbath,"* (Matthew 28:1) with Mark's timetable, *"early the first day of the week."* (Mark 16:9)

Although frequently used to oppose the traditional reading, this quote actually presents yet another blow to Westcott and

Hort. If the so-called "long ending" existed in Eusebius' day, how can it be argued that it was inserted *after* ℵ and B but *before* the time of Erasmus?

To proceed, it is taken for granted that the initial deletion of verses 9-20 would have been occasioned by either simple irresponsibility or calculated deception. Dean Burgon surmised that the former may have resulted from an accidental lectionary interference. You will recall that lectionaries consisted of selected portions of Scriptures prescribed for the public services according to either a daily or liturgical reading schedule. However, the mishandling of these books by inattentive scribes represents one of the lesser-known (and therefore more dangerous) causes of accidental textual corruption.

For instance, because the lectionary proper was not viewed as a Bible, much editorial liberty was taken when introducing the varied passages. On the few occasions when a lectionary was afforded the reciprocal opportunity to assist in the construction of a fresh New Testament manuscript, numbers of these non-inspired, precursory remarks were unfortunately absorbed into the Scripture text.

By way of illustration, *Codex Bezae* (D) (as well as a few copies of the Old Latin and Vulgate) begins John 14:1 with the interpolation, "And Jesus said unto his disciples." These very words formed the liturgical preface for John, chapter 14 in every lectionary of the ancient church.[33] Scratch one mystery.

Through no fault of their own, the lectionaries gave rise to an even greater encroachment than this. As an illustration of "the tail wagging the dog," the lectionaries' popularity influenced some to mark their inspired copies of Scriptures at the respective starting and stopping points of the corresponding lection. This was done by inserting the word, 'Αρχή (beginning) in the margin, while Τέλος (end) was frequently placed *in* the text itself. A precautionary red ink was normally used to disassociate these words from the Scriptures they were delineating.

Notwithstanding Paul's charge to in I Timothy 4:13, *"give attendance to reading,"* the fact remains that numbers of these rubrical directives found their way into the sacred canon. Dean Burgon supplies an excellent illustration of such corruption:

> Due memorable example of this practice is supplied by the Codex Bezae (D) where in S. Mark 14:41, instead of a ἀπεχει ἦλθεν ἡ ὥρα, we meet with the unintelligible απεχει Το τελος και η ωρα. Now, nothing else has here happened but that a marginal note, designed originally to indicate the end (το

τελος) of the lesson for the third day of the second week of the carnival, has lost its way from the end of verse 42 and got thrust into the text of verse 41 to the manifest destruction of the sense.[34]

Now the significance of all this becomes marvelously apparent when one discovers that a lectionary break *just happens to occur at Mark 16:8.* Dean Burgon presents scholarly documentation for at least eight different examples of lectionary types and/or ethnic church traditions that claim reading endings at verse eight. (He also lists four others that comprise Mark 16:9-20.)[35]

Thus, we recognize the possibility that such a disconcerting message as το τελος (the end) could have suddenly appeared in the text, after verse eight. (And as this accommodating of manuscripts to lectionaries was not regimented until the ninth-twelfth centuries, an incompetent scribe would have been even more confused in the earlier years when such procedures were little known.) Not only are we aware of a number of extant manuscripts that exhibit this very lectionary entry at verse eight (codices 22, 24, 36, etc.), but we have the testimony of Eusebius to that effect. After stating that the traditional ending "is not met with in all the copies," he also confirms with respect to verse eight, "For at those words, in almost **all** copies of the Gospel according to Mark, comes **the end**."[36]

Dean Burgon draws the obvious conclusion:

What if, at a very remote period, this same isolated liturgical note (το τελος) occurring at S. Mark 16:8 (which is "the end" of the Church-lesson for the second Sunday after Easter,) should have unhappily suggested to some copyist the notion that the entire "Gospel according to S. Mark," came to an end at verse 8? I see no more probable account of the matter, than this: That the mutilation of the last chapter of S. Mark has resulted from the fact, that some very ancient scribe misapprehended the import of the solitary liturgical note τέλος (or το τέλος) which he found at the close of verse 8.[37]

Such profound conjecture as this would surely satisfy the honest seeker of truth. However, there is yet a final gem of probability to consider. The Dean summarizes:

I allude to the fact that anciently, in copies of the fourfold Gospel, *the Gospel according to S. Mark frequently stood last* . . . Of course it will have sometimes happened that S. Mark 16:8 came to be written at the bottom of the left hand page of a MS. And we have but to suppose that in the case of one such Codex the next leaf, which would have been the last, was missing, (the very thing which has happened in respect of one of the Codices at Moscow) and what else could result when a copyist reached the words,

ΕΦ ΟΒΟΥΝΤΟ ΓΑΡ. ΤΟ ΤΕΛΟΣ

but the very phenomenon which has exercised critics so sorely and which gives rise to the whole of the present discussion? The copyist will have brought S. Mark's Gospel to an end there, of course. *What else could he possibly do?*[38]

Now if consideration is given to the prospect of intentional deception, a plausible motive must first be secured. When a doctrinal comparison is made between Mark 16:9-20 and the emerging Catholicism of third century Alexandria, an intriguing scenario presents itself.

Among other perversions, the roots of Roman Catholicism can be traced to an unscriptural extension of the Mosaic order beyond the prescribed borders of Calvary. With the avante-garde of Catholic theologians proclaiming a Divine disenfranchisement for the chosen people, Rome was only too humble to accept the fallen mantle. Thus, the Great Whore of Nicolaitanism has always been replete with Judaistic elements; robe-wearing priests, altars, sacrifices, candles, chants and holy days, etc. The deluded Augustine (354-430) went so far as to announce (through his book, *The City of God*) that Rome had been privileged to usher in the millennial kingdom (otherwise known as the "Dark Ages").

In their efforts to supplant Old Testament Judaism, early Catholics developed an understandable preference for the writings of Peter—chief apostle to the lost sheep of *Israel*—as opposed to those of Paul—apostle to the *Gentiles*, born out of due season.

Because of this, we are not surprised at Rome's convenient (though unsubstantiated) claim to Peter as her first Pope. The perpetuated imagery of this ancient rivalry can be seen in the contrasting cathedrals of St. Peter's in Rome and St. Paul's in London. For Catholics "in the know," however, "Pope" Peter represents quite a paradox: he was so pontifical that he refused to have his toe kissed (Acts 10:26), was so infallible that Jesus called him Satan (Matthew 16:23), was so autocratic that Paul rebuked him to his face (Galatians 2:11), and was so celibate that he had a mother-in-law (Matthew 8:14).

With the "chair of Peter" established firmly in Rome, a second prestigious tradition was circulated for the unlearned fisherman

from Galilee. Clement of Alexandria (A.D. 150-217) promoted the
idea that Mark was not the second Gospel's real author, but
merely Peter's amanuensis.[39]

In classic Nicolaitane style, the hard evidence for this
purported team effort in Rome is Clement's allegorized wresting
of I Peter 5:13, (as preserved in Kenneth Taylor's Living Bible),
cited by Eusebius as follows:

> But Peter makes mention of Mark in the first epistle, which
> he is also *said to have composed* at the same city of Rome, and
> that he shows this fact, by calling the city by an unusual trope,
> *Babylon*; thus, *"The church at Babylon, elected together with you,*
> *saluteth you, as also my son Marcus."* (I Peter 5:13)[40]

You will search in vain for any such mystical designation
throughout the sixteen chapters of Romans penned by Paul "of
Antioch" (Acts 13:1). However, with his country slighted for
autographs, Clement tried to further bridge the credibility gap by
declaring that Mark brought Peter's Gospel down to Alexandria.
Eusebius continues:

> The same Mark, *they also say*, being the first that was sent
> to Egypt, proclaimed the gospel there which he had written, and
> first established churches at the city of Alexandria.[41]

However, the overall reliability of this Clementine tradition
has been called into question by a subsequent archeological find.
In 1958, while investigating the library of the ancient Judean
monastery of Mar Saba, Professor Morton Smith from the
Department of History in Columbia University, discovered an
extant letter written by Clement.

According to Clement, Mark withheld the meatier portion of
Peter's Gospel from the general public of Alexandria. As if to cast
him as the patriarch of the "deeper life" movement, Clement
would have us believe that Mark reserved his second Gospel for
the "spiritually elite" of his parish. In his correspondence to
Theodore of the Carpocratians, note his "recorded, but not
reported" syndrome:

> Mark, then, during Peter's stay in Rome, *recorded* the acts of
> the Lord, not however *reporting* them all, for he did not indicate
> the mystical ones, but selected those which he thought most
> useful for the increase of the faith of those undergoing
> instruction.
> When Peter had borne his witness (i.e. suffered martyrdom),
> Mark arrived in Alexandria, taking his own and Peter's memoirs.
> From these he copied into his first book the things appropriate

for those who were making progress in knowledge but compiled a *more spiritual Gospel* for the use of those who were attaining perfection.[42]

With so much riding on a future acceptability of the Egyptian manuscripts, Jerome conferred upon Mark the additional posthumous honor of having been Alexandria's first bishop.[43] With this expedient reaffirming of Petrine authority (as preserved through Mark), Ham's capital city slithered into a second-place prominence, behind Rome, as one of the leading centers of Christendom.

It is noteworthy that even the Evangelical scholar, F. F. Bruce, has cast his vote against this repugnant promotional ploy:

> At any rate the story of Mark's founding the church of Alexandria is of most questionable authenticity . . . The picture of Mark as the founder of Alexandrian Christianity represents an attempt to provide the church of that city with an orthodox pedigree, one moreover which linked it closely with the Roman church, the pillar and ground of orthodoxy, and incidentally gave it quasi-apostolic status. For if Mark's association with Peter gave apostolic authority to the gospel which he penned, it equally gave apostolic lineage to the church which he founded.[44]

However, when Clement's "department of propaganda" got around to an actual reading of their celebrated claim to fame, they suddenly grew pale with but four verses remaining. With all of their treacherous manipulation of Jewish ordinances (to be perfected in the popish doctrine of *apostolic* succession), these Nicolaitane heretics found themselves confronted by a passage which threatened to expose their satanic masquerade. Like the ancient Ephraimites who were betrayed by their inability to pronounce the password *Shibboleth* (Judges 12:6), Clement's disciples experienced a similar consternation upon discovering the telltale *signs* of an *authentic* apostolic ministry!

> *"And these signs shall follow them that believe; In my name shall they cast out devils; they shall speak with new tongues; They shall take up serpents; and if they drink any deadly thing, it shall not hurt them; they shall lay hands on the sick, and they shall recover."* (Mark 16:17-18)

Since the Gospel was *"to the Jew first"* (Romans 2:9-10), and because *"Jews require a sign"* (I Corinthians 1:22), the apostles were endowed with a unique array of supernatural signs. Having anticipated a Satanic resistance through the archetypes of Jannes and Jambres (II Timothy 3:8), the Lord sustained his own, *"working with them, and confirming the word with signs following."* (Mark 16:20)

As if all of this was not intimidating enough for Clement, the context confirmed that the sign-working "believers" of verse seventeen must be the projected "believers" of verse sixteen. In other words, not only could the apostles produce these signs, but their personal converts could as well.

Just how many of these Bible-corrupting Egyptians do you suppose could have confirmed their "apostolic authority" by producing even *one* of these five signs? While Paul could affirm to the Corinthians, *"Truly the **signs of an apostle** were wrought among you in all patience, in **signs**, and **wonders**, and **mighty deeds"** (II Corinthians 12:12), the only **wonder** produced by Clement's henchmen was a **wonderment at their dilemma**.

Of the countless popes who would succumb to these same verses throughout the ensuing centuries, *Alexander VI* is a classic example. (Note the uncanny similarity of the names.) Elected at age sixty-one, despite his four illegitimate children, this contemporary of Columbus and Savanarola embarked upon an eleven-year reign of aggrandizement, adultery, and assassination. Predictably, "His Holiness" batted 0 for 5 in the "signs" department.

As Alexander preferred to "lay hands" on the naked courtesans which entertained his dinner guests,[45] he was in no position to heal the seventeen members of his own family and court who were ravaged with *syphilis*.[46] The only "speaking in tongues" he displayed was an intermittent retreat to his native Spanish which proved a growing cause of suspicion to his Italian subjects.[47]

With his plot to poison a wealthy cardinal backfiring in classic "switch-a-roo" style (Alexander and his son being poisoned by mistake),[48] the infected pope was suddenly afforded the command performance opportunity of his ministry. However, after whiling away untold hours of his thirteen-day illness in card playing,[49] the Pontiff's bluff was finally called by Mark 16:18. His black, fetid, and bloated corpse (evidence of poison) could hardly be forced into the prepared coffin.

Concerning Alexander's apostolic sign of exorcism, the only suggested case comes down to us from the Holy Father's sardonic "mourners." Will Durant informs us that, "Gossip added that a **little devil** had been seen, at the moment of death, carrying Alexander's soul to hell."[50]

As for the fifth and final sign, we don't know if Alexander was ever bitten by a serpent. We *are* aware of how the pious hypocrite was eulogized, the Florentine patriot Guicciardini stating:

> The whole city of Rome ran together with incredible alacrity, and crowded about the corpse in St. Peter's Church, and were not able to satisfy their eyes with the sight of a **dead serpent**, who, with his immoderate ambition and detestable treachery, with manifold instances of horrid cruelty and monstrous lust, and exposing to sale all things without distinction, both sacred and profane, had intoxicated the whole world.[51]

In the face of their dilemma, the Alexandrian fathers were limited to three simple alternatives. The troublesome passage could be ignored at the potential cost of repeated challenge and embarrassment. With the "collection plate" at stake, this would be least popular.

Their second option would have appeared as the most expedient. With "out of sight being out of mind," the easiest way to stifle the unreasonable demands being made on "Alexandria's first primate" would be to simply *cut them out of the Bible*. And if the break were made at verse *nine*, a convenient diversion could be found in the previously mentioned difficulties that some pious Gospel harmonizers were having with Mark's apparent contradiction of Matthew's chronology. One slash of Jehudi's penknife would solve everything!

The third solution displayed heretical ingenuity by offering such an optional replacement ending as exhibited in the Old Latin K and other scattered manuscripts. Having examined the premise of a "Catholicized Judaism," note with added significance the pre-eminence afforded to the Jewish Peter in this apocryphal conclusion:

> And all things whatsoever that had been commanded they explained briefly to those who were with *Peter*; after these things also Jesus Himself appeared and from the east unto the west sent out through them the holy and uncorrupted preaching of eternal salvation.[52]

Thus far, we have seen good cause for an ancient hostility to Mark 16:9-20 by the developing Catholic system. However, there remains for consideration a twentieth-century application to this controversy. Edward Hills made the astute observation that this passage contains the only reference to speaking in tongues made by our Saviour.

It is no coincidence that today's charismatic movement has been greatly used by the Vatican to accelerate the ecumenical process. The presence of tongues speaking on the campus of Notre

Dame University is a pretty clear signpost that all roads *do* lead to Rome.

When you read what Jesus gave as the purpose for *legitimate* spiritual gifts, you will better understand the renewed animosity to these verses. Although the throne of grace has been accessible to God's people in every age, the present charismatic emphasis on Divine healing is an unscriptural abuse of this privilege. That the authentic tongues speaking of Paul's day had an appointed end is confirmed in the clearest manner: *"whether there be tongues, they shall cease . . . . "* (I Corinthians 13:8)

Now it just so happens that the Scripture which most indicts the charismatic farce is found within the maligned passage in question. Hills cites Mark 16:20 as the key to a proper exegesis of this text.

> *"And they went forth, and preached everywhere, the Lord working with them, and **confirming the word** with signs following. Amen."*

Not only did these sign gifts fill a particular need for sign-requiring Jews, but they also provided a general authoritative endorsement on the apostles' preaching in the absence of a completed New Testament. Hills goes on to explain:

> Here we see that the purpose of the miracles promised by our Lord was to confirm the preaching of the Divine Word by the Apostles. These miracles were signs which vouched for the purity of their doctrine. Of course, then, these signs ceased after the death of the Apostles. Today we have no need of these signs, since we have in our possession the holy Scriptures.[53]

Thus we have viewed a Satanic resistance directed against these twelve verses through Catholic, Evangelical, and charismatic instrumentality. This opposition has been anything but a slipshod effort. Although confusion is the devil's persistent goal, it has never been his mode of operation. (Ephesians 6:12)

For a final illustration as to the coherence of his pernicious strategy, consider the following two-pronged attack. You will recall that the first counterfeit "Bible" under national sanction, the American Standard Version (ASV), arrived in the year 1901. Would you like to guess when the tongues speakers showed up? According to the *Dictionary of Christianity in America*, the first recorded occurrence of glossolalia (speaking in tongues) was by Agnes Ozman at Charles F. Parham's Bible School in Topeka, Kansas. The date was New Year's Day, *1901*.[54]

VI

Causes for Corruption

"For we are not as many, which corrupt the word of God."
(II Corinthians 2:17a)

It should be clear by now that the modern Bible movement is based upon the erroneous premise that a manuscript's reliability will be commensurate with its antiquity; i.e., "oldest is best." This argument has a logical appeal to the uninformed because the oldest extant copies are chronologically closer to the originals than those used by the King James translators. However, in his conservative treatise on manuscript evidences, *The Traditional Text of the Holy Gospels*, Dean Burgon observed that antiquity or primitiveness was only *one* of "Seven Notes of Truth" to be employed, the others being: consent of witnesses, or number; variety of evidence, or catholicity; respectability of witness, or weight; continuity, or unbroken tradition; evidence of the entire passage, or context; and internal consideration, or reasonableness.[1]

The "oldest is best" advocate will often resort to the analogy of a flowing stream. This line of reasoning assumes rather confidently that the closer one gets to the stream's source, the purer the water *must* be. So far, so good; however, Pickering throws in the proverbial monkey wrench:

> This is normally true, no doubt, but what if a sewer pipe empties into the stream a few yards below the spring? Then, the process is reversed—as the polluted water is exposed to the purifying action of the sun and ground, *the farther it runs the purer it becomes* (unless it passes more pipes). That is what

happened to the stream of the New Testament transmission. Very near to the source, by 100 A.D. at least, *the pollution started gushing into the pure stream.*[2]

The available manuscript evidence supports this conclusion by exhibiting both an excessive corruption in the earliest manuscripts and an exceptional coherence in the latter. While Colwell affirms, "The overwhelming majority of readings were created before the year 200,"[3] Scrivener summarizes his research as follows:

> It is no less true to fact than paradoxical in sound, that the worst corruptions to which the New Testament has ever been subjected, originated within a hundred years after it was composed; that Irenaeus and the African Fathers and the whole Western, with a portion of the Syrian Church, used far inferior manuscripts to those employed by Stunica, or Erasmus, or Stephen thirteen centuries later, when moulding the *Textus Receptus*.[4]

Even Dr. Hort conceded to this postulate of a primitive corruption. In a letter to Westcott, he acknowledged:

> . . . inaccuracy may in certain men or at certain periods run into a laxity **which is careless about words** though supposing itself faithful to sense, and which draws no sharp line between transcribing and editing, *i.e.* mending or completing. **This last characteristic naturally belongs to the early period.**[5]

While some of these perturbations were of an unintentional nature (human error or scribal carelessness, etc.), many others resulted from deliberate interference. Sometimes the tampering was heretical; at other times it was pious but misguided. The four basic types of corruptions are recognized as omissions, additions (interpolations), changes (substitutions), and transpositions (reversing word order). Omissions constitute the largest number, while additions are the smallest.

In chapter four we observed an excellent example of this ancient disorder with the *Chester Beatty* and *Bodmer* papyri. You will recall that in only seventy extant verses they disagreed with each other in seventy-three places, apart from mistakes.

When it comes to the earliest of the nearly 100 extant papyrus fragments,[6] diligent research has confirmed that corruption is the rule and not the exception. One of the oldest papyrus manuscripts in existence is P[66] (Bodmer Collection), dated at about 200 A.D.

P^{66} contains 104 leaves of John 1:1–6:11; 6:35b–14:15, and fragments of forty other pages from John 14–21. Wilbur Pickering has cited E. C. Colwell's collation of P^{66} along with P^{45} (ca. 250) and P^{75} (ca. 225) as follows:

> The nearly 200 nonsense readings and 400 itacistic (vowel interchange) spellings in P^{66} are evidence of something less than disciplined attention to the basic task. To this evidence of carelessness must be added those singular readings whose origin baffles speculation, readings that can be given no more exact label than carelessness leading to assorted variant readings. A hurried count shows P^{45} with 20, P^{75} with 57, and P^{66} with 216 purely careless readings.[7]

Pickering's personal commentary continues:

> Colwell's study took into account only singular readings— readings which no other MS. support. He found P^{66} to have 400 itacisms plus 482 other singular readings, 40 percent of which are nonsensical. "P^{66} editorializes as he does everything else—in a sloppy fashion." In short, P^{66} is a very poor copy—and yet it is one of the earliest!
>
> P^{75} is placed close to P^{66} in date. Though not as bad as P^{66}, it is scarcely a good copy. Colwell found P^{75} to have about 145 itacisms plus 257 other singular readings, 25 percent of which are nonsensical. Although Colwell gives the scribe of P^{75} credit for having tried to produce a good copy, P^{75} looks good only by comparison with P^{66}. (If you were asked to write out the Gospel of John by hand, would you make over 400 mistakes? Try it and see!)[8]

Although closer to the spring, these "ancient" papyrus manuscripts were obviously fished out of polluted waters. But the degradation continues. Dated at about A.D. 250, P^{46} is one of three manuscripts in the famed *Chester Beatty* collection. Consisting of 86 mutilated leaves, this fragment comprises eight of the Pauline epistles. Gunther Zuntz comments predictably:

> In spite of its neat appearance (it was written by a professional scribe and corrected—but very imperfectly—by an expert), P^{46} is by no means a good manuscript. The scribe committed very many blunders ... My impression is that he was liable to fits of exhaustion.[9]

Later on in his work, Zuntz castigates the scribe of P^{46} for failing to *correct* his mistakes:

The scribe who wrote the papyrus did his work very badly. Of his innumerable faults, only a fraction (less than one in ten) have been corrected and even that fraction—as often happens in manuscripts—grows smaller and smaller towards the end of the book. Whole pages have been left without any correction, however greatly they were in need of it.[10]

Arriving at the era of the ancient uncials, we discover that the waters are still murky at best. Dean Burgon comments on the confusion within Luke's account of the Lord's Prayer:

'The five Old uncials' (ℵABCD) falsify the Lord's Prayer as given by St. Luke in no less than forty-five words. But so little do they agree among themselves, that they throw themselves into six different combinations in their departures from the Traditional Text; and yet they are never able to agree among themselves as to one single various reading: while only once are more than two of them observed to stand together, and their grand point of union is no less than an omission of the article. Such is their eccentric tendency, that in respect of thirty-two out of the whole forty-five words they bear in turn solitary evidence.[11]

Burgon gives another excellent illustration of this lack of agreement among the ancient codices with his comments on Mark 2:1-12:

In the course of those 12 verses . . . there will be found to be 60 variations of reading . . . Now, in the present instance, the "five old uncials" *cannot be* the depositories of a tradition,— whether Western or Eastern,—because they render inconsistent testimony *in every verse.* It must further be admitted, (for this is really not a question of opinion, but a plain matter of fact,) that it is unreasonable to place confidence in such documents. What would be thought in a Court of Law of five witnesses, called up 47 times for examination, who should be observed to bear contradictory testimony *every time?*[12]

That both the papyrus manuscripts and the 5 ancient uncials are far worse than described can be surmised by the negative review they receive from their own promoters. Concerning P^{47}, Kurt Aland says candidly:

We need not mention the fact that the oldest manuscript does not necessarily have the best text. P^{47} is, for example, by far the oldest of the manuscripts containing the full or almost full text of the Apocalypse, but it is certainly not the best.[13]

Running out of purification tablets, Hort concedes to the hopeless disarray of the ancient uncials when trying to agree with the four Gospels' cockcrowing narrative:

> The confusion of attestation introduced by these several cross currents of change is so great that of the seven principal MSS Aleph A B C D L Δ no two have the same text in all four places.[14]

Thus far, the implication for these errors has been one of accidental or unintentional harm. When we proceed to the larger percentage of deliberate textual alterations, we are surprised to discover that a number of these corruptions were occasioned by misguided representatives of the orthodox.

For one thing, Burgon pointed out that the very format of a fourfold Gospel invited harmonizing difficulties from well-meaning neophytes (such was the complaint of Eusebius when attempting to reconcile Mark's resurrection timetable with that of Matthew). The Dean acquaints us with the nature of this "friendly fire":

> The fourfold structure of the Gospel has lent itself to a certain kind of licentious handling—of which in other ancient writings we have no experience. One critical owner of a Codex considered himself at liberty to assimilate the narratives: another to correct them in order to bring them into (what seemed to himself) greater harmony. Brevity is found to have been a paramount object with some, and Transposition to have amounted to a passion with others. Conjectural Criticism was evidently practised largely . . . and before the members of the Church had gained a familiar acquaintance with the words of the New Testament, blunders continually crept into the text of more or less heinous importance.[15]

Another type of ill-advised corruption involved a doctrinal paranoia when confronted by the challenges of heretics, especially against Christ's deity. Such was Luther's hermeneutical frustration with James that he called the inspired book "an epistle of straw."

Similarly, many a rookie soul winner (this author's experience included) has had the disconcerting encounter with some Jehovah's Witness who accentuated the passages displaying our Lord's humanity. When confronted by more exacting exegetical demands, numbers of the ancients found it easier to simply alter the text according to their theological fancy. Two examples will suffice to illustrate Burgon's adage, "To correct is to corrupt."

In Luke 2:40a, we find the words, *"And the child grew, and* **waxed strong** *in the spirit, filled with wisdom."* Because the enemies of Christianity insisted that Luke's expression *"waxed strong"* invalidated any claims to Christ's Divinity, certain of the ill-informed simply cut them out of the text. ℵ B D and L are the four survivors of such slothful expediency.[16]

Concerning Jesus' weeping over Jerusalem in Luke 19:41, the Father Epiphanius informs us that a similar fate attended this verse as well for the same precautionary motive.[17]

However, the greatest degree of abuse to which the New Testament text was subjected transpired at the hands of the Christ-denying heretics themselves. As a fitting introduction to the following survey of historical attestation, we reiterate the obstinate bias of Dr. Hort:

> It will not be out of place to add here a distinct expression of our belief that even among the numerous unquestionably spurious readings of the New Testament there are no signs of deliberate falsification of the text for dogmatic purposes.[18]

In view of the historical record, Hort's prejudicial theory engendered little support, even among his liberal contemporaries, Tischendorf attesting:

> I have no doubt that in the very earliest ages after our Holy Scriptures were written, and before the authority of the Church protected them, wilful alterations, and especially additions, were made in them.[19]

While the average soul winner of today may encounter as many as a dozen cults when witnessing, our first- and second-century forefathers were surrounded by far more than that. In his polemical work, *The Panarion,* Epiphanius mentions over 80 heretical sects warring for supremacy.[20]

Eusebius cites the indignation of one Dionysius, bishop of Corinth, (c. 170 A.D.) for the heretics' tampering with his personal correspondence as well as with the Scriptures:

> As the brethren desired me to write epistles, I wrote them, and these the apostles of the devil have filled with tares, exchanging some things, and adding others, for whom there is a wo reserved. It is not, therefore, matter of wonder, if some have

also attempted to adulterate the sacred writings of the Lord,
since they have attempted the same in other works that are not
to be compared with these.[21]

Perhaps the outstanding antagonist of this era was the
Alexandrian gnostic known as Marcion, "the Heretic." Tertullian
denounces him clearly:

> Marcion expressly and openly used the knife, not the pen,
> since he made such an excision of the Scriptures as suited his
> own subject-matter.[22]

The aforementioned intolerance of our spiritual ancestors can
be seen in the heated interchange between Marcion and Polycarp
as preserved by Eusebius:

> And the same Polycarp, once coming and meeting Marcion,
> who said "acknowledge us," he replied, "I acknowledge the
> firstborn of Satan."[23]

Polycarp's   disciple   Irenaeus   expands   on   Tertullian's
description:

> He (Marcion) mutilates the Gospel which is according to
> Luke, removing all that is written respecting the generation of
> the Lord, and setting aside a great deal of the teaching of the
> Lord, in which the Lord is recorded as most clearly confessing
> that the Maker of this universe is His Father ... In like manner,
> too, he dismembered the Epistles of Paul, removing all that is
> said by the apostle respecting that God who made the world, to
> the effect that He is the Father of our Lord Jesus Christ, and
> also those passages from the prophetical writings which the
> apostle quotes, in order to teach us that they announced
> beforehand the coming of the Lord.[24]

The exceptional number of heretics can be highlighted by the
marked   disagreement   among   their   numerous   mutilations.
Eusebius cites the second-century Father, Gaius, as follows:

> "The sacred Scriptures," says he, "have been boldly
> perverted by them ... For this purpose they fearlessly lay their
> hands upon the holy Scriptures, saying that they have corrected
> them. And that I do not say against them without foundation,
> whoever wishes may learn; for should any one collect and
> compare their copies one with another, he would find them
> greatly at variance among themselves. For the copies of
> Asclepiodotus will be found to differ from those of Theodotus.
> Copies of many you may find in abundance, altered, by the

eagerness of their disciples to insert each one his own corrections, as they call them, i.e. their corruptions. Again, the copies of Hermophilus do not agree with these, for those of Appollinius are not consistent with themselves. For one may compare those which were prepared before by them, with those which they afterwards perverted for their own objects, and you will find them widely differing . . . For neither can they deny that they have been guilty of the daring act, when the copies were written with their own hand, nor did they receive such Scriptures from those by whom they were instructed in the elements of the faith; nor can they show copies from which they were transcribed. But some of them did not even deign, or think it worth while, to mutilate the Scriptures, but directly denying the law and the prophets by their lawless and impious doctrine, under the pretext of grace, they sunk down to the lowest depths of perdition."[25]

Although the eminent Dr. Hort feigned ignorance at the implications of such testimony, Dean Burgon was only too happy to oblige:

Here is an orthodox Father *of the IInd century* inviting attention to four well-known families of falsified manuscripts of the Sacred Writings;—complaining of the hopeless divergences which they exhibit (being not only inconsistent with one another, but *with themselves*);—and insisting that such *corrected*, are nothing else but shamefully *corrupted* copies. He speaks of the phenomenon as being in his day notorious: and appeals to Recensions, the very names of whose authors—Theodotus, Asclepiades, Hermophilus, Appollonides—have (all but the first) long since died out of the Church's memory. You will allow therefore, (will you not?), that by this time the claim of the *oldest existing copies* of Scripture to be the purest, has been effectually disposed of. For since there once prevailed such a multitude of corrupted copies, we have no security whatever that the oldest of our extant MSS. are not derived—remotely if not directly—from some of *them*.[26]

The basic cause for Westcott's and Hort's inability (or refusal) to envision such an inaugural onslaught against the emerging New Testament can be traced to their dogmatic liberalism (see chapter 14). Being willfully blinded to the person of the *living* Word, they were equally incapable of perceiving the spiritual parallels to the *written* Word.

As John begins and ends his writing with the designation of Jesus as "The Word of God" (John 1:1; Revelation 19:13), we recognize the presence of a Divine similitude. Not only did *both* "Words" (living and written) minister to the common man and

with great pungency, but *both* experienced their strongest
opposition in the first and last years of their earthly existence,
per se.

With Herod's precursory slaughter of the innocents, we are not
surprised that the Scripture was also assaulted at its inception.
Similarly, the pressure brought against the Authorized Version in
these last days was foreshadowed by such encounters as, *"If thou
be the son of God, command that these stones be made bread,"*
(Matthew 4:3b), and especially, *"If thou be the Son of God, come
down from the cross."* (Matthew 27:40b)

Having surveyed an *excessive corruption* in the *earliest*
manuscripts, we will now make several observations concerning
the *exceptional coherence* in the *latter*.

The basic manuscript evidence for this tradition (known as the
Majority Text) was outlined in chapter four. Not only were
Westcott and Hort unable to explain this phenomenon, but their
consternation drove them to an *unscholarly* prejudice. Hort writes
at age twenty-three:

> I had no idea till the last few weeks of the importance of
> texts, **having read so little Greek Testament**, and dragged on
> with the **villainous** *Textus Receptus* . . . think of that **vile**
> *Textus Receptus* leaning entirely on late MSS.; it is a blessing
> there are such early ones.[27]

Note how the pious word "blessing" relates back to Jesus'
prediction that, *"They shall put you out of the synagogues: yea,
the time cometh, that whosoever killeth you will* ***think*** *that he
doeth God service."* (John 16:2)

With their relegation of the New Testament to ordinary
literature, our deluded Cambridge professors were not only
oblivious to a Satanic persecution, but to a supernatural
preservation as well. The Saviour's warning of approaching
opposition was quickly followed by this reassuring promise:
*"Howbeit when he, the Spirit of truth, is come, he will guide you
into all truth."* (John 16:13a) The exceptional coherence of the
Majority Text is nothing more than the historical fulfillment of
this upper room commitment.

The Spirit's first assignment was occasioned by the arrival of
numerous spurious writings referred to as *pseudepigrapha*.
Alluded to by Luke (cf. Luke 1:1-2), these non-inspired books
constituted the earliest irritations to the infant local assemblies.
Eusebius refers to them accordingly:

Among the spurious must be numbered, both the books called "The Acts of Paul," and that called "Pastor," and "The Revelation of Peter." Beside these, the books called "The Epistle of Barnabas," and what are called "The Institutions of the Apostles."[28]

A ninth-century catalogue by Photius listed over 280 others such as the Gospels of Thomas, Peter, Nicodemus, Barnabas, Andrew, Philip, Matthias, and Joseph; The Acts of Peter, John, Andrew, Philip, Thomas and Thaddeus; numerous "missing" epistles; and the apocalypses of Peter, Paul, Thomas and Stephen.[29]

Containing everything from the suggested childhood miracles of Jesus in Egypt to the purported bodily assumption of Mary, these writings were systematically exposed by the guiding Spirit of God. Known as the canonization of Scripture (from the Greek *kanon* for *measuring rod*), this Spirit-led sifting set apart our present 66 books from the cheap competitions of Satan. Throughout this process, the Spirit of Truth *guided* the fathers according to a fivefold check system: Did the book speak with authority, tell the truth and possess power? And was it written by a man of God and received by the people of God?

Having steered the churches from these non-inspired writings, the Holy Spirit began His lengthier mission of leading believers away from contaminated manuscripts. Dean Burgon summarizes these Divine activities:

> Before our Lord ascended up to Heaven, He told His disciples that He would send them the Holy Ghost, who should supply His place and abide with His Church forever. He added a promise that it should be the office of that inspiring Spirit not only "to bring to their remembrance all things whatsoever He had told them," but also to "guide" His Church "into all the truth," or, "the whole Truth." (John 16:13) Accordingly, the earliest great achievement of those days was accomplished on giving to the Church the Scriptures of the New Testament, in which authorized teaching was enshrined in written form . . . There exists no reason for supposing that the Divine Agent, who in the first instance thus gave to mankind the Scriptures of Truth, straightway abdicated His office; took no further care of His work; abandoned those precious writings to their fate. That a perpetual miracle was wrought for their preservation—that copyists were protected against the risk of error, or evil men prevented from adulterating shamefully copies of the Deposit— no one, it is presumed, is so weak as to suppose. But it is quite a different thing to claim that all down the ages the sacred

writings must needs have been God's peculiar care; that the
Church under Him has watched over them with intelligence and
skill; has recognized which copies exhibit a fabricated, which an
honestly transcribed text; has generally sanctioned the one, and
generally disallowed the other.[30]

This second application of Holy Spirit leadership is significant
as it reveals the true inconsistency of Nicolaitane scholarship. The
same "Christian educators" who endorse a preserved canon
stumble at the Spirit's ability to "purge the stream." For
instance, to embrace their foolish Antiochian (or Lucian)
Recension Theory, one would have to believe that the very fathers
who were spiritual enough to settle the canon *censured the pure
manuscripts by mistake*. Fuller cites Hills along this line:

> No sooner had the New Testament books been given to the
> Church through the inspiration of the Holy Spirit than the spirit
> of darkness began his endeavors to corrupt their texts and render
> them useless, but in these efforts also the evil one failed to attain
> his objective. In regard to the New Testament text as well as in
> regard to the New Testament canon God bestowed upon His
> Church sufficient grace to enable her to overcome all the wiles of
> the devil. **Just as God guided the Church to reject, after a
> period of doubt and conflict, all non-canonical New
> Testament books, so God guided the Church during this
> same period of doubt and conflict, to reject false readings
> and to receive into common usage the true New
> Testament text.**
>
> For an orthodox Christian Burgon's view is the only
> reasonable one. If we believe that God gave the Church guidance
> in regard to the New Testament books, then surely it is logical to
> believe that God gave the Church similar guidance in regard to
> the text which these books contained. Surely it is very
> inconsistent to believe that God guided the Church in regard to
> the New Testament canon but gave the Church no guidance in
> regard to the New Testament text.[31]

When carried to its logical conclusion, the Westcott and Hort
theory becomes quite an albatross for its embarrassed advocates.
Like it or not, to endorse the new "Bibles" is to believe that the
Holy Spirit failed in preserving the true Word of God for nearly
fifteen centuries. And as if this were not bad enough, one must
also ascribe to the lunacy that *two Bible-denying liberals saved
the day!* Burgon remonstrates:

> I am utterly disinclined to believe, so grossly improbable does
> it seem—that at the end of 1800 years 995 copies out of every

thousand, suppose, will prove untrustworthy; and that the one, two, three, four or five which remain, whose contents were till yesterday as good as unknown, will be found to have retained the secret of what the Holy Spirit originally inspired. I am utterly unable to believe, in short, that God's promise has so entirely failed, that at the end of 1800 years, much of the text of the Gospel had in point of fact to be picked by a German critic out of a wastepaper basket in the convent of St. Catherine; and that the entire text had to be remodelled after the pattern set by a couple of copies which had remained in neglect during fifteen centuries, and had probably owed their survival to that neglect; whilst hundreds of others had been thumbed to pieces, and had bequeathed their witness to copies made from them.[32]

In the spirit of such compromising positions as theistic evolution, the Presbyterian theologian B.B. Warfield postulated that God had worked providentially *through* Tischendorf, Tregelles, Westcott and Hort to preserve the New Testament text. Dr. Hills' objection is sustained:

But this suggestion leads to conclusions which are extremely bizarre and inconsistent. It would have us believe that during the manuscript period orthodox Christians corrupted the New Testament text, that the text used by the Protestant Reformers was the worst of all, and that the True Text was not restored until the nineteenth century, when Tregelles brought it forth out of the Pope's library, when Tischendorf rescued it from a waste basket on Mt. Sinai, and when Westcott and Hort were providentially guided to construct a theory of it which ignores God's special providence and treats the text of the New Testament like the text of any other ancient book. But if the True New Testament Text was lost for 1500 years, how can we be sure that it has ever been found again?[33]

Thus we have seen that the extant manuscript evidence supports the hypothesis of an early contamination followed by a purifying process of several centuries. As previously stated, the crystal clear water of the Majority Text cannot be explained away. For the ultimate conclusion to our premise that "the farther it runs, the purer it becomes," consider the eye-opening illustration of born-again former Supreme Court Justice Philip Mauro, as cited by David Otis Fuller:

Let us take an illustration of what we are here seeking to establish, namely, that the concurrent testimony of the manuscripts which support the Received Text conclusively establish its authenticity in parts where it differs from the new

Greek text of Westcott and Hort. For this purpose let us suppose
that a hundred copies of a certain original document in a central
business office were made by different copyists and sent to as
many different branch-offices in various parts of the world; and
suppose that, since the document contained directions for the
carrying on of the business for many generations, it had to be
copied again and again as the individual MSS. were worn out
through usage.

Suppose further that, after centuries of time, one of the
earliest copies should turn up which, upon examination, was
found to lack a word or sentence found in later copies in actual
service, and that it were deemed important to settle the question
of the authenticity of that word or sentence.

Suppose further that, for the purpose in view, a dozen of the
manuscripts then in actual use in various and far distant parts
of the world, each one being a late copy of previously used and
worn-out copies, were examined, and that the disputed word or
sentence were found in each of those late copies, is it not clear
that the authenticity thereof would be established beyond all
reasonable dispute?

Such must be the conclusion, because the absence thereof in
the ancient copy could easily be accounted for, whereas its
presence in a number of later copies, each of which came from a
distant source, could not be accounted for except on the
assumption of its genuineness.

But let us suppose that, in addition to the various copies in
use in various places, there existed certain translations (versions
in foreign languages) which translations were earlier than the
very earliest of the existing manuscripts in the original tongue;
and also that many quotations of the disputed passage were
found in the writings of persons who lived in or near the days
when the document itself was written; and suppose that the
disputed word or sentence were found in every translation and
every quotation, would not its genuineness be established beyond
the faintest shadow of a doubt?

This suppositious case will give a good idea of the strength of
the evidence in favor of the Text of the A.V. For in the settling
of that text, due weight was given to the concurrent testimony of
the numerous MSS. *in actual use in different churches, widely
separated from one another;* and also to the corroborating
testimony of the most ancient Versions and of the patristic
writings; whereas, in the settling of the Text of the R.V. the
evidence of highest grade was uniformly rejected in favor of that
of the lowest grade.[34]

Have a problem with the *Textus Receptus*? **Tell it to the
judge!**

VII

The Synagogue of Satan

> *"And I know the blasphemy of them which say they are Jews, and are not, but are the synagogue of Satan."* (Revelation 2:9b)

Having reevaluated the analogy of a flowing stream from an historical perspective, we will now investigate the source of the textual toxicants themselves.

The average Christian is unaware that the manuscripts from which the modern "Bibles" have been translated are Egyptian in origin; more specifically, Alexandrian. This lack of understanding is exacerbated by little or no knowledge of Egypt's heretical climate at that time. When these factors are appreciated, the weakness and hypocrisy behind the modern revision movement becomes more readily apparent.

For instance, in our study of the Antiochian Recension Theory in chapter four, it was observed that the Holy Spirit refused to dispatch a single autograph to Egypt. The resultant desperation for credibility was noted in chapter five with the Clementine tradition promoting the unsubstantiated claim that Mark brought his original to Alexandria.

Another area of pronounced Nicolaitane deception concerns the Alexandrian fathers. By an equating of spirituality with religious intellectualism, the typical Bible college faculty will venerate a host of Egyptian heretics from Clement to Origen.

Because these matters form such an essential part of the King James controversy, this chapter will present an indepth study of Alexandria proper, biographical sketches of Clement and Origen and the all-important Alexandrian connection to codices *Vaticanus* (B) and *Sinaiticus* (ℵ).

In the second chapter of Revelation we find John acknowledging the blasphemies of certain apostate Jews at Smyrna. These agitators were described as being of *"the synagogue of Satan."*

> *"I know thy works, and tribulation, and poverty, (but thou art rich) and I know the blasphemy of them which say they are Jews, and are not, but are the* **synagogue of Satan.***"* (Revelation 2:9)

When a search of this period is conducted for a concentration of blasphemous Jews a most enlightening discovery is made. A second-century census of Alexandria, Egypt, reveals that over 40 percent of the city's 800,000 residents were Jewish.[1] Occupying 2/5 of that city was the largest assemblage of Jews in the world at that time.[2]

However, Revelation 2:9 specifically calls for *apostate* Jews—*"which say they are Jews, and are not."* The historical fulfillment here is striking. With their initial settlement occasioned by a rebellious flight from Divine chastisement (Deuteronomy 28:68; Jeremiah 42, 43), the later and larger waves of immigrants were enticed by the materialistic overtures (cucumbers, melons, leeks, onions and garlics) of the epileptic demoniac, Alexander the Great himself.

Predictably, the strong intellectual temptation of Greek philosophy began its subtle encroachment with the apex of Judaic defection realized under the Jewish scholar, Philo (B.C. 20-A.D. 50). With a ministry that spanned both Testaments, this "renegade son of Abraham" established a theological school to promote the merger of Old Testament Judaism with Greek philosophy. Albert Newman writes:

> He was of the opinion that the Greeks had derived from the Jewish Scriptures all that was wise, true, and lofty in their thinking. It was his task, as it had been the task of others of his type, to show the complete harmony of the Divine revelation of the Old Testament with all that is best in Greek philosophy . . . The fact is that his modes of thought and views of life were fundamentally those of the Greek philosophy (a composite of Pythagoreanism, Platonism, Aristotelianism, and Stoicism), and he undertook to show by applying the allegorical system of interpretation to the Scriptures that these were not as they seemed to be, simple, unsophisticated narratives of the dealings of God with His people, but that underneath the anthropomorphic and anthropopathic representations of God and the uncouth representations of the sins and follies of the heroes and

worthies of Hebrew history, everything that was wise and exalted in Greek philosophy lay concealed.[3]

Edershiem expands upon the reckless nature of Philo's allegorical methods:

> Everything became symbolical in his hands, if it suited his purpose: numbers (in a very arbitrary manner), beasts, birds, fowls, creeping things, plants, stones, elements, substances, conditions, even sex—and so a term or an expression might even have several and contradictory meanings, from which the interpreter was at liberty to choose.[4]

As a member of one of Alexandria's most prestigious families, (his brother was a major political leader of the city[5]), Philo's expedient mastery of Greek so eclipsed that of his reproachful native tongue that his admirers said, "Plato writes like Philo."[6]

It is no coincidence that this descendant of Aaron[7] and contemporary of Jesus Christ just happened to be the chief spokesman of his city's "Great Synagogue," a colonnaded basilica so immense that a system of relay signals was used to ensure a synchronized responsive reading.[8]

When surveying the third century for an extension of Philo's blasphemy, we discover that the leaven of "Satan's synagogue" was still active. Concerning textual corruption, scholars agree that *Egyptian* manuscripts are invariably the most depraved as evidenced by the extant papyri fragments.

Such negativism from the land of Pharaoh is consistent with Bible typology. The book of Hebrews presents Egypt as a type of the world: Joseph's bones were not permitted to remain there (Exodus 13:19); God called both His nation (Exodus 15) and His Son (Matthew 2:15) from there; and He would not even accept the horses that were brought from there (Deuteronomy 17:16). The book of Acts records no missionary activity to Egypt (which accounts for their similar dearth of autographs). As if to project the entire scope of man's downward experience (contrary to the positive theories of evolution), the Bible's first book begins with God (Genesis 1:1), but ends with *"a coffin in Egypt."* (Genesis 50:26b). Were it not for the next book of Exodus (deliverance), the human race would have forever remained "six feet under." Egypt is a type of this terminus—a land of coffins.

The imagery of Egypt's capital is even sharper. While the first Alexandrians to appear in Scripture assist in the stoning of

Stephen (Acts 6:9), her sole representative of the ministry, Apollos, arrives in *ignorance* (Acts 18:25) and departs in *arrogance* (I Corinthians 6:12). The only other references to Alexandrians are in Acts 27:6, 11 and these designate the city of ownership for the two ships employed in transporting Paul to his martyrdom—and one of these *sunk!*

Furthermore, the evidence of history nominates Alexandria as one of the best examples on record of Satan's world system. To the adventurer, she promised nothing but satisfaction. As if to typify the thrills that lay ahead, Alexandria's magnificent 500-foot lighthouse (the world's first) greeted awestruck mariners some thirty miles offshore. Regarded as one of the seven wonders of the ancient world, this engineering feat in B.C. 281 by the Greek architect Sostratus, utilized a fire burning in front of a gigantic mirror to guide approaching ships into Alexandria's harbor consisting of nine miles of wharves.[9] Constructed of beautiful white marble, the lighthouse's structural configuration was threefold—a square bottom, an eight-sided middle, and a circular top. It was so renowned as an Egyptian showpiece that the word *pharos* came to mean *lighthouse.*

Pliny recorded that the city's wall measured some fifteen miles in length.[10] Within these confines, a remarkably modern city displayed paved and lighted streets, running water and sewers. These unparalleled conveniences resulted from Alexandria's booming economy led by her annual grain exports of twenty million bushels.[11] (Two-tenths of Egypt's corn production would feed Rome for four months.[12])

Durant depicts the city's character:

> Of Egypt's 8,500,000 population its capital had now some 800,000, second only to Rome; in industry and commerce it was first. "Everyone in Alexandria is busy" says a letter, questionably Hadrian's; "everyone has a trade; even the lame and the blind find work to do." Here, among a thousand other articles, glass, paper, and linen were produced on a large scale. Alexandria was the clothing and fashion center of the age, setting styles and making the goods ... It was also a tourist center, equipped with hotels, guides, and interpreters for visitors coming to see the Pyramids and the majestic temples of Thebes. The main avenue, sixty-seven feet wide, was lined for three miles with colonnades, arcades, and alluring shops displaying the fanciest products of ancient crafts.[13]

With local product availability described by the proverb, "everything could be gotten except snow,"[14] the realistic assessment of Emperor Hadrian sliced curtly through Durant's humanistic platitudes that, *"Money* was the people's god."[15]

Egypt's capital was also the educational, medical and scientific center of the ancient world. Alexandria's major shrine for intellectual idolatry was her famed library of over 700,000 papyrus rolls. With a determination to translate (into Greek) and catalogue as many literary classics as possible, her mammoth collection would be surpassed only by the libraries of Baghdad and Spain a millennium later. The librarian's office was highly coveted as it included the prestigious responsibility of tutoring the crown prince.[16]

A special section of university buildings, internationally known as "The Museum" or "Home of the Muses," offered a variety of fascinating displays for the young and impressionable.[17] After worshiping at these monuments to the mind, one could visit the nearby zoo and observe such exhibits as a bona fide Indian lion, etc.

And, of course, culture was a high priority for the aesthetically inclined of Alexandria's Hell-bound citizenry, Durant commenting, "Books had to meet the tastes of a learned and critical audience, sophisticated by science and history."[18] The humanist H.G. Wells had this to say about the dysfunctional eggheads of Alexandria's scholastic community:

> Wisdom passed away from Alexandria and left pedantry behind. For the use of books was substituted the worship of books. **Very speedily the learned became a specialized queer class with unpleasant characteristics of its own.** The Museum had not existed for half a dozen generations before Alexandria was familiar with a new type of human being; shy, eccentric, unpractical, incapable of essentials, strangely fierce upon trivialities of literary detail, as bitterly jealous of the colleague within as of the unlearned without–the Scholarly Man. He was as intolerant as a priest, though he had no altar; as obscurantist as a magician, though he had no cave. For him no method of copying was sufficiently tedious and no rare book sufficiently inaccesible. He was a sort of by-product of the intellectual process of mankind. For many precious generations the new-lit fires of the human intelligence were to be seriously banked down by this by-product.[19]

The conquering Moslem, Amr, would declare in A.D. 641:

> It is impossible to enumerate the riches of this great city, or to describe its beauty; I shall content myself with observing that it contains 4000 palaces, 400 baths, 400 theaters.[20]

However, of the many intriguing sites, none was more inspiring or subliminally suggestive as the "Soma," the venerated mausoleum of the city's founder. With Alexander's claim to deity shattered by an untimely alcohol-related death, a face-saving gesture was taken by preserving the royal remains in honey and displaying the pickled king in a glass coffin.[21] As prosperity tends to delusions of grandeur (Luke 12:18), his projected invincibility appealed to the worldly Egyptians. If Alexander could endure, Alexandrians could, too!

Overall, Alexandria was a model city, except for one point. Leaving God out of any society will inevitably lead to sin and misery. As no culture can exceed the virtue of its women, one may gauge Alexandria accordingly, Herodas reporting:

> Alexandria is the house of Aphrodite, and everything is to be found there—wealth, playgrounds, a large army, a serene sky, public displays, philosophers, precious metals, fine young men, a good royal house, an academy of science, exquisite wines, and *beautiful women.*[22]

Durant adds:

> **The city was notorious for the generosity of its women and the number of its step-daughters of joy**; Polybius complained that the finest private homes in Alexandria belonged to courtesans. Women of all classes moved freely through the streets, shopped in the stores, and mingled with the men.[23]

Such lewdness was epitomized by Cleopatra, the most famous of Alexandrian charmers.

Commenting on the decadence of Alexandria's cosmopolitan populace, Durant concedes:

> They made a volatile and inflammable mixture, quarrelsome and disorderly, intellectually clever and irreverently witty, shameless in speech, skeptical and superstitious, loose in morals and gay in mood, fanatically fond of the theater, music, and public games. Dio Chrysostom describes life there as "a continuous revel . . . of dancers, whistlers, and murderers." The canals were alive with merrymakers in gondolas at night on their five-mile sail to the amusement suburb at Canopus. There were musical contests that rivaled the horse races in raising excitement.[24]

Having promised a satisfied life, Alexandria fulfilled her role as a type of the world by producing only sorrow instead. The presenting of Pompey's severed head to Julius Caesar in Alexandria's harbor[25] and the double suicide of Cleopatra and Mark Anthony are graphic illustrations of this truth. Durant summarizes accurately:

> Egypt should have been the happiest of lands, for not only was the earth freely nourished by the Nile, but the country was the most self-sufficient in the whole Mediterranean basin—rich in cereals and fruits, cutting three crops a year, unexcelled in industries, exporting to a hundred nations, and seldom disturbed by foreign or civil war. And yet—perhaps for these reasons—**"The Egyptians,"** Josephus notes, **"appear never in all their history to have enjoyed one day of freedom."** Their wealth tempted, their semitropical lassitude suffered, one despot or conqueror after another through fifty centuries.[26]

Surely, *"the way of transgressors is hard."* (Proverbs 13:15)

> The common laborer in the factories received one obol (nine cents) a day, the skilled worker two or three. Every tenth day was a day of rest. Complaints multiplied, and strikes grew more frequent: strikes among the miners, the quarrymen, the boatmen, the peasants, the artisans, the tradesmen, even the overseers and the police; strikes seldom for better pay, since the toilers had ceased to hope for this, but of simple exhaustion and despair. "We are worn out," says a papyrus record of one strike; "we will run away"—i.e., seek sanctuary in a temple.[27]

Notwithstanding Alexandria's reign as the perfume capital of the world,[28] the lifestyle of her citizens reeked! To simply cross the street was traumatic as the poet, Theocritus, relates:

> O Heavens, what a mob! I can't imagine
> How we're to squeeze through, or how long it'll take;
> An ant-heap is nothing to this hurly-burly . . .
> O Gorgon, darling, look!—what shall we do?
> The royal cavalry! Don't ride us down!
> Eunoa, get out of the way![29]

Understandably, crime was high with legionaries patrolling in groups of four. An extant papyrus fragment gives an intriguing police report: "We are working hard because we are suppressing the uproar and anarchy in the city."[30]

Many of the realm's "professing" Christians (mostly Catholics by then) fared no better at lawfulness. In A.D. 415, the female philosopher Hypatia had a "contract" put out on her by Cyril, Alexandria's illustrious archbishop. One day, a mob of fanatical monks (led by one of Cyril's staff members) dragged the unfortunate woman from her carriage into a church. She was subsequently stripped naked and flayed alive with clam shells.[31] Her corpse was then torn to pieces and burned in a barbaric orgy. Socrates (a Christian historian not to be confused with his Greek namesake) lamented the act as "so inhuman [that it] could not fail to bring the greatest opprobrium not only upon Cyril, but also upon the whole Alexandrian church."[32] Nicolaitanes always foster religious intolerance.

Obviously, all was not as bright as the giant lighthouse implied; and eventually, this sinkhole of corruption began feeling the tremors of Divine retribution. In A.D. 215, one-half of Alexandria's military-age males were ordered massacred on suspicion of national disloyalty by the paranoid emperor, Caracalla.[33] Forty-five years later, over 50 percent of the entire population was slain by Queen Zenobia's conquering army from Palmyra.[34]

However, the most humiliating defeat was still to come. After a 23-month siege by Moslem Arabs, the city capitulated in A.D. 641. Having written to the Caliph, Omar, for instructions concerning the library, the invasion commander, Amr, made public the royal reply, "Burn the libraries, for they are contained in one book" (the Koran).[35] In perfect fulfillment of First Corinthians 1:20b—". . . *hath not God made foolish the wisdom of this world?*"—Amr distributed the contents of the "Great Library" among Alexandria's public baths, where 4,000 furnaces were fueled for six months by the papyrus and parchment scrolls.[36] The lighthouse was decimated by an earthquake in A.D. 1324.

Now according to Westcott and Hort theory, it was in this same city of Alexandria that God raised up a faculty of "Christian" scholars to preserve the New Testament text. The Oxford Dictionary of the Christian Church defines this catechetical school accordingly:

> From the later second century a theological school existed at Alexandria, which addressed itself to the propagation of the Christian faith among the **cultured** classes. It rose to its greatest prominence under Clement (c. 190-c. 202) and Origen (c. 202-31). It attracted Christians from different parts.[37]

The alert reader will notice that this definition says nothing about the school's *origin*. The concern is indeed a relative one when considering that the city's intellectual-theological character had been steeped in Greek philosophy for almost five centuries! The more we conjecture as to how Philo's paganistic foundation suddenly sported an orthodox superstructure, the more hilarious the theories become. Dr. A. Cleveland Coxe gives a typical Nicolaitane smoke screen:

> The Alexandria of Apollos and of St. Mark has become the earliest seat of Christian learning. There, already, have the catechetical schools gathered the finest intellectual trophies of the Cross; and under the aliment of its library **springs up something like a Christian university.**[38]

We acknowledge this school as the *"World's Most Unusual University"* of that day for its miraculous and mysterious metamorphosis from paganism to Christianity. Newman elaborates:

> The Alexandrian theologians with whom the scientific spirit had its birth were *Platonists* . . . Not that they had been simply brought up Platonists (as were Justin and Athenagorus, who yet, after they adopted Christianity, rejected Platonism as the work of demons); **but they remained Platonists,** and sought to explain Christianity according to the Platonic categories, in somewhat the same way in which Philo had, two centuries earlier, attempted to explain Judaism. In fact these Christian Platonists were greatly indebted to Philo.[39]

Fisher's estimation concurs:

> It was at Alexandria, the seat of all science, that philosophical theology first acquired a firm footing. The union of philosophy and theology, of which we see the beginnings in the Apologists, was there consummated. Catechetical instruction, when cultivated and inquisitive heathen converts were to be taught, necessarily assumed a new form. The school for catechumens developed itself into a school for the training of the clergy. **The Alexandrian teachers met the educated heathen on their own ground.** Instead of pouring out invectives, after the manner of Tertullian, against the Greek philosophers, **they recognized in the teachings of the Greek sages materials which Christian teachers might accept and assimilate.**[40]

Rather than accept, *"Who can bring a clean thing out of an*

unclean? not one" (Job 14:4), the Nicolaitane scholars continue
to praise the Platonists. Dr. Coxe describing the first "Christian"
headmaster of the school:

> Pantaenus, "the Sicilian bee" from the flowery fields of Enna,
> comes to frame it by his industry, and store it with the sweets of
> his eloquence and wisdom. Clement, who had followed Tatian to
> the East, tracks Pantaenus to Egypt, and comes with his Attic
> scholarship to be his pupil in the school of Christ.[41]

Had Coxe carefully read the Clementine writings, he would
have discovered that his subject did not even recognize Pantaenus
as a Christian. To the contrary, Clement depicted his mentor as
"the deepest Gnostic," possessing a perfect insight into the
significance of Christianity.[42] (Clement himself claimed the
honored title of *gnostic* often.)[43]

In harmony with the analogy of Coxe that, "Alexandria
becomes the brain of Christendom; (while) its heart was yet
beating at Antioch . . . ", Clement continued the Alexandrian
propensity for compromise. Dr. Fisher commenting:

> Clement, the first of the Alexandrian teachers whose writings
> have come down to us, is full of the thought that the mission of
> the Christian theologian is **to build a bridge between the
> Gospel and Gentile wisdom**, to point out the relations of
> Christianity to universal knowledge, to give to the religion of
> Christ a scientific form, to show how the believer may rise to the
> position of the true "Gnostic."[44]

Apparently, Clement missed I Corinthians 1:19: *"For it is
written, I will destroy the wisdom of the wise, and will bring to
nothing the understanding of the prudent."*

Philip Schaff, chairman of the ASV committee (1901), gives us
yet another ambiguous attempt at confirming Alexandrian
orthodoxy:

> From this catechetical school proceeded a **peculiar
> theology**, the most learned and genial representatives of which
> were Clement and Origen. This theology is, on the one hand, **a
> regenerated Christian form of the Alexandrian Jewish
> religious philosophy of Philo**; (What in the world does that
> mean?) on the other, a catholic counterpart, and a positive
> refutation of the heretical Gnosis, which reached its height also
> in Alexandria, but half a century earlier. The Alexandrian
> theology aims at a reconciliation of Christianity with philosophy,

or, subjectively speaking, of *pistis* with *gnosis*; but it seeks this
union upon the basis of the Bible, and the doctrine of the
church.[45]

As the natural man can be painfully perceptive of the
hypocrisy within professing Christendom, consider the following
analysis by the secular New Standard Encyclopedia:

> Alexandrian school, a name given to various groups of
> persons engaged in artistic and intellectual activities in
> Alexandria, Egypt, during the Hellenistic and Roman eras . . .
> The blending of western and eastern knowledge and thought was
> the distinguishing feature of the schools . . . **Literature of the
> Alexandrian school was based on scholarship rather than
> on originality.** The writers working in the Museum and Library
> catalogued, analyzed and edited more than they wrote.
> As the Christian Era began, the Alexandrian Jew, Philo,
> combining Jewish religious ideas with Greek philosophy,
> emphasized the mystical quality of man's relationship to God.
> Philo influenced two late second-century Greek fathers of the
> church, Clement of Alexandria and his pupil, Origen. These two
> in turn headed Alexandria's catechetical (Christian religious)
> school, where both Christian and pagan (Greek) writings were
> studied and where the philosophy later known as Neoplatonism
> evolved . . . although Neoplatonism was a pagan philosophy and
> Origen, after his death, was disowned by the church as a heretic,
> **much of the mysticism of the Alexandrian school of
> theology was absorbed into Christian thinking.**[46]

Lest these numerous citings appear redundant to the casual
observer, remember that it was an *Alexandrian text type* which
was responsible for discrediting the *Textus Receptus* and hence
our Authorized Version! For the elementary student, it should be
stated that the basic evidence which associates the ancient uncials
with Alexandria is twofold; the many times their readings are
cited by an Alexandrian father and their close similarity with the
extant Coptic (Egyptian) translations.[47] Take for consideration the
ancient uncial that was actually named after the Egyptian
capitol — *Codex Alexandrinus* (A). Our old friends Geisler and Nix
tell us:

> This well-preserved manuscript from the fifth century **ranks
> second only to B and Aleph as representative of the New
> Testament text.** Though some have dated this manuscript in
> the late fourth century, it is probably the result of fifth century
> scribes of Alexandria, Egypt.[48]

These Alexandrian scribes were so "Spirit-led" that they included within A's 773 leaves, *as inspired*, the four books of Maccabees, Baruch, letter of Jeremiah, Tobit, Judith, I and II Esdras, Song of Songs, Wisdom, Sirach, I and II Clement, the 151st Psalm, and The Psalms of Solomon.[49] Although A is less corrupt than B, Scrivener states that, "The Codex Alexandrinus has been judged to be carelessly written,"[50] and in another place pointed out its ". . . several lamentable defects."[51]

When the writings of these Alexandrian fathers are studied, a number of serious problems arise. Running the gamut from Clement's preaching against *sneezing* to Origen's denial of Hell (cited later in this chapter), they conspire to seriously reduce their own authors' credibility as trustworthy guardians of Scripture. What are we to think when even their avid supporters depict them with loony phraseology? While F. F. Bruce calls Clement, "a true Christian humanist"[52] (whatever that is), Philip Schaff confuses things further:

> Clement came from the Hellenic philosophy to the Christian faith; Origen, conversely, was *led by faith to speculation* . . . Both were Christian philosophers (square–circle) and churchly gnostics (apple–orange).[53]

Of the two "Christian philosophers," Clement was less disturbing. Born Titus Flavius Clemens about A.D. 150, probably in Athens, he grew up in abject paganism. He was drawn to some semblance of Christianity by the previously mentioned "Sicilian Bee" (Pantaenus). Having become presbyter in the church of Alexandria, he succeeded his mentor as head of the catechetical school in A.D. 190 and continued in this post until driven away by the fierce persecution of Septimus Severus in A.D. 202. With only brief glimpses of activity in Antioch and Jerusalem, there is no record of his return to Alexandria prior to his death in A.D. 220. He was succeeded at the school by the precocious eighteen-year-old known as *Adamantius* (Origen).

Apart from Clement's *three* inspired authorities and *seven* plans of salvation, he was a fairly conservative guy. Not only did he quote liberally from the standard Apocrypha, specifically calling it "the Scripture" (i.e., citing Tobit 12:8, "Fasting with prayer is a good thing" in his Stromata Book VI, Chapter XII), but also from the books that were "way out" (pseudepigrapha) and rejected by all. F.F. Bruce cites one humorous example:

From the *Gospel of the Egyptians* Clement quotes an alleged saying of Jesus, "I came to destroy the works of the female", and illustrates it with a conversation between Jesus and Salome. In reply to Salome's question, "How long will death prevail?" he said, "As long as you women give birth to children."[54]

In addition to the Apocrypha, Clement also quoted extensively from the philosophers of Greece and attributed Divine inspiration to their origin as well, Plato in particular.

> We do not, if you have no objection, wholly disown Plato. How, then, is God to be searched out, O Plato? "For both to find the Father and Maker of this universe is a work of difficulty; and having found Him, to declare Him fully, is impossible" (Plato's words from his Timaeus) . . . Well done, Plato! **Thou has touched on the truth.**[55]

In no uncertain terms, Clement crossed the line:

> And let it not be this one man alone—Plato; but, O philosophy, hasten to produce many others also, who declare the only true God to be God, **through his inspiration**, if in any measure they have grasped the truth.[56]

And in another place he comments on the writings of several philosophers with the words, "For the knowledge of God, these utterances, written by those we have mentioned through the **inspiration of God.**"[57]

Was this some of the "nectar" he received from Pantaenus? With Paul condemning philosophy in the clearest of language, Clement would have us believe that the Greeks received their perversions from God:

> Speaking generally we shall not be far wrong if we say that all things necessary and profitable for life come from God, and that philosophy was given to the Greeks as a covenant peculiarly their own, a foundation of the philosophy which is according to Christ.[58]

And as a fourth-century adherent of the universalist "fatherhood of God and brotherhood of man" dogma, he adds:

> The one and only God was known by the Greeks in a Gentile fashion, by the Jews in a Jewish fashion, by us (Christians) in a new and spiritual way. It is the same God who gave both the covenants, who vouchsafed philosophy to the Greeks, whereby

the Almighty is glorified among the Greeks. So then from Greek
training, as from that of the Law, those who accept faith are
being gathered together into **the one race of the saved people**
. . . As God willed to save the Jews by giving them prophets, so
also among the Greeks He raised up their best men to be their
prophets in their own tongue.[59]

Most fathers rejected this claptrap, Tertullian writing, "What
has Athens to do with Jerusalem?"[60] As for Clement's affinity for
Plato, should we conclude that he was ignorant or just tolerant
of the philosopher's perversions? How could any Spirit-led Gospel
preacher promote the rantings of a Hell-bound, homosexual
visionary who prescribed among other things, *socialism*,[61] *selective
breeding*,[62] *contraception* and *infanticide*,[63] and *the kidnapping of
children from their parents for a 20-year period of state-controlled
values clarification*.[64] (Sound familiar?) Throw in *capital punishment*
for dissenters and you have the basics of Plato's *Republic*. But
after all, what could you have expected from a pervert who
reclined at wine parties with naked boys serving him?[65] (Plato
"cashed in his chips" at age 80 while making merry at a
wedding.) So much for Clement's hero who had "touched on the
truth."

With Greek philosophy and the Apocrypha accepted as
Divinely authoritative, Clement was bound to have problems with
his soteriology (doctrine of salvation). From Clement's writings,
we understand that sinners can attain personal salvation through
any of a number of plans: baptism,[66] philosophy,[67] overcoming
sensuality,[68] repentance,[69] church membership,[70] faith and
works,[71] faith alone through the blood,[72] and all requiring a
gradual process.[73] One reference will suffice:

> Cleanse the temple; and pleasures and amusements abandon
> to the winds and the fire, as a fading flower; but wisely cultivate
> the fruits of self-command, and present thyself to God as an
> offering of first-fruits, that there may be not the **work alone**,
> but also the **grace** of God; and **both** are requisite, that the
> friend of Christ may be rendered **worthy** of the kingdom, and be
> counted **worthy** of the kingdom.[74]

Do you suppose Clement missed Romans 11:6?

With the Bible and salvation thrown to the wind, the sky
became the limit *literally*. Speaking of the Gentiles, Clement
boldly affirmed:

> God gave them for **worship** the **sun** and the **stars**, (wait till

you see what Origen believed about stars) which God made for the nations, saith the Law (Deuteronomy iv:19), that they might not be wholly godless, and so wholly perish.[75]

What ever happened to Acts 7:42 and Romans 1:25?
Apparently, these are the theological absurdities referred to by ASV chairman Schaff who said of Clement:

> His theology, however, is not a unit, but a confused, eclectic mixture of true Christian elements with many Stoic, Platonic, and Philonic ingredients.[76]

And, of course, with the authority of Scripture undermined, the replacement authority of CULTure was sure to take charge. (According to *Webster's Ninth New Collegiate Dictionary,* both *cult* and *culture* are from the same Latin word!) Under the chapter heading entitled "The Benefit of Culture," Clement wrote:

> For nutriment, and the training which is maintained gentle, make noble natures; and noble natures, when they have received such training, become still better than before both in other respects, but especially in productiveness, as is the case with the other creatures . . . But that some are naturally predisposed to virtue above others, certain pursuits of those, who are so naturally predisposed above others, show. But that perfection in virtue is not the exclusive property of those, whose natures are better, is proved, since also those who by nature are ill-disposed towards virtue, in obtaining suitable training, for the most part attain to excellence; and, on the other hand, those whose natural dispositions are apt, become evil through neglect.[77]

With this snobby accent on the aesthetic side of man, Clement kicks into high gear by proclaiming:

> The Lord was absolutely without emotion; (How about "Jesus wept"?) in Him no impulse of the feelings ever entered, either pleasure or grief . . . The disciple strives to become like his Master and to attain this freedom from emotion.[78]

(Now you know why Nicolaitanes warble when they talk, especially when they try to pronounce the word *God.*)
Consequently, in his work entitled *The Instructor* we find Clement taking a bold, militant stand against laughter,[79] sneezing,[80] hiccups,[81] yawning,[82] sleeping on downy feathers,[83]

extravagant pajamas,[84] pierced ears,[85] dying gray hairs,[86] mirrors,[87] baths for pleasure,[88] lady wrestlers,[89] and hanging out in barber shops.[90]

Without a single chapter devoted to *soul winning* in over 450 pages of nonsense, Clement wastes his time by writing:

> If any one is attacked with sneezing, just as in the case of hiccup, **he must not startle those near with the explosion,** and so give proof of his bad breeding; but the hiccup is to be quietly transmitted with the expiration of the breath, the mouth being composed becomingly, and not gaping and yawning like the tragic masks.[91]

If Clement were alive today, he would be more concerned about *breeding* than *bus ministries*. And this crackpot is supposed to be one of the two major defenders of God's Word? Who could possibly be enamored with such frothings? Well, maybe one:

> And when it is frankly admitted that his style is generally deficient in terseness and elegance; that his method is desultory; that his learning is undigested: we can still thankfully admire his richness of information, his breadth of reading, his largeness of sympathy, his lofty aspirations, his noble conception of the office and capacities of the Faith.[92]

(This comes from Dr. Brooke Foss Westcott—who else?)

When arriving at the life and ministry of Clement's successor, Origen Adamantius, we understand our subject to be the most influential father of the Alexandrian tradition. Recognized as the patriarch of textual criticism, his voluminous usage of Scripture (17,976 extant citings of the New Testament alone) has entrenched his authority as a force with which to be reckoned. Dean Burgon comments:

> Origen was the most prominent personage by far in the Alexandrian School. His fame and influence in this province extended with the reputation of his other writings long after his death. When a writer speaks of the "accurate copies," what he actually means is the text of Scripture which was employed or approved by Origen.[93]

The high percentage of similarity between the extant text of Origen's writings with that of ℵ and B is indicative of the sway he possessed. Because of this, he is the undisputed prima donna of modern Nicolaitane scholarship. As previously mentioned, the fruition of Philip Schaff's veneration for Adamantius was evidenced by his chairing of the ASV committee, (1901):

> Origen was the greatest scholar of his age, and the most gifted, most industrious, and most cultivated of all the ante-Nicene fathers. Even heathens and heretics admired or feared his brilliant talent and vast learning. His knowledge embraced all departments of the philology, philosophy, and theology of his day. With this he united profound and fertile thought, keen penetration, and glowing imagination. As a true Divine, he consecrated all his studies by prayer, and turned them, according to his best convictions, to the service of truth and piety.[94]

The more recent Eerdmans' *Handbook to the History of Christianity* exclaims:

> Origen was the greatest scholar and most prolific author of the early church. He was not only a profound thinker but also deeply spiritual and a loyal churchman.[95]

Born of Christian parents at Alexandria in the year A.D. 185, he soon became the ultimate example of precocity. Following the arrest of his father Leonides in the Severus persecution in A.D. 202, tradition relates that Origen attempted to join him but was hindered by an uncooperative mother who hid his clothing. The aura of his legendary youth builds upon the moving account of his correspondence with Leonides exhorting him to steadfastness. (Those clothes must have been awfully hard to find.)

Having inherited responsibility for a mother and six siblings upon his father's death, Origen felt a sudden "call" to the ministry and ascended to the presidency of Alexandria's catechetical school.

With the misguided desire of providing his students with a superior education, the newly installed teenage headmaster embarked on a course of personal study under the most celebrated pagans in the land. In the face of such Scriptures as *"Learn not the way of the heathen"* (Jeremiah 10:2), Origen:

> . . . felt it necessary to make himself more extensively acquainted with the doctrines of the Grecian schools, that he might meet his opponents upon their own ground, and for this purpose he attended the prelections of Ammonius Saccas, at that time in high repute at Alexandria as an expounder of the neo-Platonic philosophy, of which school he has generally been

considered the founder. The influence which the study of philosophical speculations exerted upon the mind of Origen may be traced in the whole course of his afterdevelopment, and proved the fruitful source of many of those errors which were afterwards laid to his charge, and the controversies arising out of which disturbed the peace of the Church during the two following centuries.[96]

Many were the errors that aroused his ecclesiastical superiors but one incident proved to be especially baneful. Stemming from a perverted interpretation of Matthew 19:12, the overzealous president *castrated* himself as a means of avoiding future temptation. He could have saved himself a lot of pain by reading Deuteronomy 23:1. Concerning Origen's preference for allegorical interpretation, it was the humorous observation of Edward Gibbons that, "It seems unfortunate that, in this instance only, he should have adopted the literal sense."[97]

Following his subsequent excommunication in A.D. 231 from the church in Alexandria, Origen migrated to Caesarea where he established a second catechetical school. His personal works were in excess of 6,000 volumes, inspiring Jerome to ask, "Which of us can read all that he has written?"[98]

Arrested and tortured during the Decian persecution of A.D. 249, Origen survived his confinement but succumbed to the ordeal's aftereffects in A.D. 254, thus ensuring himself a hero's profile in Church history.

It has often been asked, "What's in a name?" Origen's given name, *Origenes,* was strangely derived from the Egyptian divinity Or, or Horus.[99] As if to make up for this youthful stigma, he received the honorable surname of *Adamantius* as a tribute to his supposed piety and industry.

Hindsight has indeed highlighted the ADAM from Adamantius as reflective of Origen's fall (along with his descendants) in the garden of textual criticism. With regard to the original sin of departing from the *Textus Receptus,* the origin is with Origen!

Adamantius himself supplied the perfect illustration of his own humanistic character by his erroneous association of the number six (6) with *perfection.* Commenting on John 2:6, he wrote:

> And six water-vessels are reasonably (appropriate) to those who are purified in the world, which was made in **six** days—**the perfect number.**[100]

This ignorance of basic Bible numerology is in sharp contrast to the painstaking defense of Irenaeus for the traditional rendering of 666 in Revelation 13:8 against the heretical inroads of 616.[101] Errors far more serious than this have made it difficult for Origen's admirers to defend him. Note the strained attempt by Dr. Coxe:

> The great biblical scholar and critic of the first half of the third century deserves a more cordial recognition and appreciation than have always been accorded to him. **While it is true that in various matters he has strange, even wild, fancies, and gives utterance to expressions which can hardly, if at all, be justified;** while it is also true that he indulges beyond all reason (as it appears to us of the present age) in utterly useless speculations, and carries to excess his great love of allegorizing,—yet these are rather of the nature of possible guesses and surmises on numerous topics, of more or less interest, than deliberate, systematic teaching as matters of faith. He frequently speaks of them in this wise, and does not claim for these guesses and speculations any more credit than they may appear to his readers to be worth. In the great fundamentals of the Christian creed Origen is unquestionably sound and true.[102]

Would Dr. Coxe consider the *eternality of the Holy Spirit* a "great fundamental"? Origen writes:

> For even although something else existed before the Holy Spirit, it was not by progressive advancement that He came to be the Holy Spirit.[103]

Origen plainly taught that the blessed Holy Spirit was a *created being*:

> We therefore, as the more pious and the truer course, admit that all things were made by the Logos, and that the Holy Spirit is the most excellent and the first in order of all that was **made** by the Father through Christ.[104]

Would the good Dr. Coxe classify *salvation by grace* as a "great fundamental"? Of this doctrine, Origen writes:

> After these points, also, the apostolic teaching is that the soul, having a substance and life of its own, shall, after its departure from the world, be **rewarded** according to its deserts, being destined to obtain either an inheritance of eternal life and blessedness, if its actions shall have procured this for it, or to be delivered up to eternal fire and punishments, if the guilt of its crimes shall have brought it down to this.[105]

In another place, he writes:

> For as we see it not to be the case with rational natures, that some of them have lived in a condition of degradation owing to their **sins,** while others have been called to a state of happiness on account of their **merits.**[105]

But if it sounds like Origen believed in an eternal Hell, don't you buy it! The man Westcott and Hort credit with preserving the true text of Scripture believed in purgatory and a final restoration of all spirits, *including the devil!*

> But in the meantime, both in those temporal worlds which are seen, as well as in those eternal worlds which are invisible, all those beings are arranged, according to a regular plan, in the order and degree of their **merits**; so that some of them in the first, others in the second, some even in the last times, after having undergone heavier and more severe punishments, endured for a lengthened period, and for many ages, so to speak, improved by this stern method of training, and restored at first by the instruction of the angels, and subsequently by the powers of a higher grade, and thus advancing through each stage to a better condition, reach even to that which is invisible and eternal, having travelled through, by a kind of training, every single office of the heavenly powers.[107]

Confused? Do you recall the telltale sign of Nicolaitanism? Origen expands on his doctrine of purgatory:

> Heaven, in which heaven and earth, the end and perfection of all things, may be safely and most confidently placed,—where, viz., these, after their apprehension and their chastisement for the offences which they have undergone **by way of purgation,** may, after having fulfilled and discharged every obligation, **deserve a habitation in that land.**[108]

Concerning his doctrine of universal salvation, he wrote, "But those who have been removed from their primal state of blessedness have not been removed **irrevocably.**"[109]
And again:

> The end of the world, then, and the final consummation, will take place when **every one** shall be **subjected** to punishment for his sins; a time which God alone knows, when He will bestow on each one **what he deserves.** We **think**, indeed, that the goodness of God, through His Christ, **may** recall **all** His

creatures to one end, even His enemies being conquered and subdued.[110]

"Origen's orthodoxy" also promoted a belief in the preexistence of the human soul (i.e., John the Baptist was previously an angel),[111] baptismal regeneration (beginning with sprinkling infants) and transubstantiation,[112] that Christ's death was paid as a ransom to Satan[113] to allow the new birth to be entered by a "mystical kiss,"[114] while denying both the coming "bodily" resurrection[115] and millennial kingdom.[116]

Because Origen's pride relegated the Holy Spirit to a created being, he was bound to be lacking in sound hermeneutics. Concerning his popularizing of the allegorical mode of interpretation (as pioneered by Philo and opposed by the *literalist* school of Antioch) his error was not in the occasional and ancillary use of this enriching Scriptural method (Galatians 4:24), but rather in his abusive exclusion of the literal. To see beautiful typology in Genesis is one thing; to deny the historicity of the book is quite another.

> **Who is so foolish as to suppose that God, after the manner of a husbandman, planted a paradise in Eden,** towards the east, and placed in it a tree of life, visible and palpable, so that one tasting of the fruit by the bodily teeth obtained life? . . . And if God is said to walk in the paradise in the evening, and Adam to hide himself under a tree, I do not suppose that any one doubts that these things figuratively indicate certain mysteries, the history having taken place in appearance, **and not literally.**[117]

His propensity for the allegorical dismissed the literality of countless other passages such as the Passover,[118] the construction details of Solomon's Temple,[119] Jesus' wilderness temptation,[120] and the purging of Herod's temple.[121] Interestingly enough, not only did Origen endorse the Apocrypha (once writing a defense of *Susana*, the non-canonical addendum to Daniel[122]) but he credited the *Shepherd of Hermas* with inspiring his allegorical format.

> For as a man consists of body, and soul, and spirit, so in the same way does Scripture, which has been arranged to be given by God for the salvation of men. And therefore we deduce this also from a book which is despised by some—***The Shepherd***.[123]

For a man who was supposed to be God's human agent for preservation, Origen continued to voice problems with the

Scriptures. Commenting on the Greek Old Testament, he wrote:

> And in many other of the sacred books I found sometimes more in our copies than in the Hebrew, sometimes less . . . Again, through the whole of Job there are many passages in the Hebrew which are wanting in our copies, generally four or five verses, but sometimes, however, even fourteen, and nineteen, and sixteen . . . Again, in Genesis, the words, *"God saw that it was good,"* when the firmament was made, are not found in the Hebrew.[124]

And in another place, he whined:

> I do not condemn them (authors of Scripture) if they even sometimes dealt freely with things **which to the eye of history happened differently**, and changed them so as to subserve the mystical aims they had in view; so as to speak of a thing which happened in a certain place, as if it happened in another, or of what took place at a certain time, as if it had taken place at another time, and to introduce into what was spoken in a certain way some changes of their own. **They proposed to speak the truth where it was possible** both materially and spiritually, and where this was not possible it was their intention to prefer the spiritual to the material. **The spiritual truth was often preserved, as one might say, in the material falsehood.**[125]

With such little confidence in the Word of God, Origen's personal fantasies reigned supreme. Whereas Clement thought the stars were for *worship*, Origen believed they were *backslidden*! Talk about wild speculation—listen to this idiot:

> We ought first to inquire after this point, whether it is allowable to suppose that they (stars) are **living** and **rational beings**; then, in the next place, whether their souls came into existence at the same time with their bodies, or seem to be anterior to them; and also whether, after the end of the world, we are to understand that **they are to be released from their bodies**; and whether, as we cease to live, so they also will cease from illuminating the world . . . **We think then that they may be designated as living beings,** for this reason, that they are said to receive commandments from God, which is ordinarily the case only with rational beings. "I have given a commandment to all the stars." (Isaiah XLV:12) . . . And seeing that the stars move with such order and regularity, that their movements never appear to be at any time subject to derangement, would it not be the height of folly to say that so orderly an observance of method and plan could be carried out or accomplished by irrational

beings? In the writings of Jeremiah, indeed the moon is called the queen of heaven. Yet if the stars are living and rational beings, there will undoubtedly appear among them both an advance and a falling back . . . Job appears to assert that not only may the stars be **subject to sin**, but even that they are actually not clean from the contagion of it. *"The stars also are not clean in thy sight."* (Job 25:5)[126]

Notwithstanding these many absurdities, the anti-Receptus readings contained in Origen's writings (and reproduced in ℵ and B) continue to be embraced by twentieth-century Nicolaitane scholarship. Coxe stated:

He is the first great textual critic of the church . . . his commentaries contain complete texts of the portions of Scripture commented on, as well as copious quotations from other parts of Scripture . . . In the New Testament, also, **his text is also very different from that which afterwards prevailed in the church.**[127]

Whereas Hebrews 2:9b reads in the King James Bible, *"that he by the grace of God should taste death for every man,"* the graceless Origen preferred a different rendering: "For without God he tasted death for everyone. In some copies of the Epistle to the Hebrews the words are 'by the grace of God'."[128]
The star-struck commentator continues his ramblings:

He died not for men only but for all other intellectual beings too . . . It would surely be absurd to say that he tasted death for human sins and not for any other being besides man which had fallen into sin, as for example **for the stars.**[129]

One of the most horrendous of Origen's hatchet jobs concerns John 1:18. Here he calls into question the eternality of Christ:

Accordingly John came to bear witness of the light, and in his witness-bearing he cried, saying . . . "No one hath seen God at any time; **the only-begotten God**, who is in the bosom of the Father, He hath declared Him."[130]

Having written, "μονογενης Θεος," the only begotten GOD, Origen embraced the Arian position that Jesus was *created* by the Father, and therefore not total Deity.
This heresy that Jesus Christ is a "god" (not Son) begotten somewhere in eternity is found in *Sinaiticus* and *Vaticanus*, and

therefore in such modern perversions as the New American Standard Bible.

> "No man has seen God at any time, **the only begotten God,** who is in the bosom of the Father, He has explained Him." (John 1:18 NASB)

And because "birds of a feather flock together," this reading is found to represent the official theology of the Jehovah's Witnesses as given in their New World Translation:

> No man has seen God at any time, **the only-begotten god** who is in the bosom of the father is the one who has explained him. (John 1:18 NWT)

This also matches their version of John 1:1 where Jesus was presented as "a god."

As we draw our chapter to a close, the reader's attention is directed to an eerie prophecy by Dr. A.E. Brooke, an Anglican biographer of Origen. Commenting on the prospect of future "intellectual triumphs" such as those manifested by the catechetical school of Alexandria, he writes:

> And the victory over the world of thought, which was won at Alexandria in earlier times, **will be repeated,** if the struggle is carried on with the same thoroughness and boldness, in the same spirit of self-devotion, and in the same conviction that all things are ours, since we are Christ's, and Christ is God's.[131]

One need only visit the local "Bible" book store to confirm that the spirit of Origen is alive and well. May the true Bible-believer be faithful in his stand for the A.D. 1611 Authorized Version. Although it is an unpopular position at present, some day the tables will be turned!

> *"Behold, I will make them of the synagogue of Satan, which say they are Jews, and are not, but do lie; behold, I will make them to come and worship before thy feet, and to know that I have loved thee."* (Revelation 3:9)

VIII

Two False Witnesses

---

*"At the last came two false witnesses . . . But neither
so did their witness agree together."*
(Matthew 26:60b; Mark 14:59)

Having surveyed Alexandria proper and her leading Ante-
Nicene fathers, Clement and Origen, we will now examine the
most notorious survivors of this era of bedevilment, *Codex
Vaticanus* (B) and *Codex Sinaiticus* (ℵ). In conformity to the
previously discussed parallels of the *living* word with that of the
written, we note that the two false witnesses pitted against our
Saviour prefigured that of ℵ and B against the *Textus Receptus*.

By now it should be elementary that these codices owe their
notoriety to an exceptional antiquity and post-1611 discovery.
With the subsequent manifestation of this Alexandrian text in the
Revised Version of 1881 (and essentially all modern translations),
Hoskier affirms, "The text of Westcott and Hort is practically the
text of ℵB."[1] Unfortunately, this unscholarly veneration has
continued to our present day, David Beale writing:

> Since the publication of the King James Version in 1611,
> numerous manuscript discoveries have contributed to a vastly
> increased knowledge of the original Scripture languages— Hebrew
> and Greek. Although many findings, such as the famous *Codex
> Ephraemi*, or even the Dead Sea Scrolls deserve attention, the
> three most significant extant contributions toward the
> advancement of textual learning are *Codex Alexandrinus, Codex
> Vaticanus,* and *Codex Sinaiticus* . . . Highly esteemed by **all**
> biblical scholars for their **worth** and antiquity, these manuscripts
> remain among the **chief treasures** of the ancient world.[2]

However, as the two false witnesses at Jesus' trial gave conflicting testimony, ℵ and B have also perjured themselves. In his highly acclaimed 924-page collation entitled *Codex B and Its Allies*, Herman Hoskier publicized what the Nicolaitane scholar continues to suppress. Beale's "chief treasures" are so reliable that they are found **to disagree with *each other* in over *3,000* places in the Gospels alone!** Hoskier states:

> I have tabulated the major part of these differences between ℵ and B in the Gospels and given the supporting authorities on each side. They amount to Matthew−656+, Mark−567+, Luke−791+, John−1022+ for a total of **3,036**.[3]

To gain a better appreciation of this statistic, consider that the four Gospels as situated in an Old Scofield Bible consist of 153 pages; this statistic would average out to more than **19 disagreements per page!**

Now, before expanding upon the nature of these many corruptions, we will review the historical particulars of their discovery.

Because the famed *Codex Sinaiticus* was eventually abandoned as hopeless (due to its numerous textual depravities), literally being discovered in a monastery **trash can**, a significant amount of fanciful embellishment has provided the typical Nicolaitane smoke screen. Geisler and Nix begin:

> This fourth century Greek manuscript is generally considered to be the most important witness to the text because of its antiquity, accuracy, and lack of omissions. The story of the discovery of Aleph is one of the most **fascinating and romantic in textual history**.[4]

As the sinfulness of Cleopatra's affair was sugar-coated with romantic platitudes (Shakespeare's Anthony addressing Cleopatra with, "I am dying, Egypt, dying, only I here importune death awhile until of many 1,000 kisses the poor last I lay upon thy lips," blah, blah, blah.) the evil character of Aleph required a similar diversionary promotion. Concerning the "accuracy" of *Sinaiticus*, Geisler and Nix forgot to tell you that the codex contains **1,460 peculiar readings not found in any manuscript on earth, affecting 2,640 words (as compared to B's 589 readings affecting 858 words)**.[5] As to their appreciation of ℵ's "lack of omissions," the evidence would betray *Sinaiticus* as another shameful Egyptian adulteress, Burgon stating:

But indeed, Mutilation has been practised throughout. By codex B (collated with the traditional Text), no less than 2,877 words have been excised from the four gospels alone: **by codex ℵ,−3,455 words.**[6]

Returning to the illusion, May of 1844 found the German textual scholar Constantin von Tischendorf (1815-1875) snooping around in St. Catherine's Monastery, located at the base of Mt. Sinai. Beale informs us that the Count was, "searching in dusty libraries for ancient manuscripts that had survived the passing centuries."[7] As his visit was concluding, Tischendorf noticed a receptacle of discarded parchments sitting in the center of the great hall. The librarian informed him that the scraps were used to light the monastery's ovens (in the same manner in which the volumes of Alexandria's library were "checked out" permanently by the Arabs).

Upon a closer examination, Tischendorf identified 129 leaves of the Old Testament in Greek (recognized by some as the *Septuagint*). Although his excitement aroused the monk's suspicion, he was permitted to leave with 43 of the pages (portions of I Chronicles, Jeremiah, Nehemiah and Esther).

After depositing these fragments in the University library at Leipzig and publishing their contents as *Codex Frederico-Augustanus* (after his patron Frederick Augustus, King of Saxony), Tischendorf returned to St. Catherine's in 1853 to secure additional leaves. Because the prelates were still spooked, his requests were all denied.

Returning three years later (1859) under the patronage of the Russian Czar himself, Alexander II, Tischendorf was shown a nearly complete manuscript wrapped in red cloth. Beale's "dramatic" narration tells us:

> Tischendorf, concealing his excitement, casually asked permission to take it to his room that evening. "I knew that I held in my hand the most precious Biblical treasure in existence," Tischendorf later testified, "a document whose age and importance exceeded that of all the manuscripts which I had ever examined during twenty years' study of the subject." This was the most exciting moment in Tischendorf's entire life; he stayed up all night, fathoming his newly-found treasure. In his diary, the scholar writes, "Quippe dormire nefas videbatur" ("It really seemed a sacrilege to sleep.")[8]

Eventually, Tischendorf was able to convince his monkish hosts to present the codex to Czar Alexander, as he was the official protector of the Greek Orthodox churches.

Named after the site of its discovery, *Codex Sinaiticus* was placed in the Imperial Library of St. Petersburg where it remained until purchased by the British government in 1933 for 100,000£ (approximately $500,000 at that time). Residing in the British Museum's Department of Manuscripts, the codex was later published in a volume entitled, *Scribes and Correctors of Codex Sinaiticus* (London, 1938). Within two years of England's national acceptance of this depraved **Catholic** manuscript, the city of London was in smoldering ruins. *"The wicked shall be turned into hell, and all the **nations** that forget God."* (Psalm 9:17)

Whereas *Sinaiticus* was clothed in romanticism, *Vaticanus* has been shrouded in mystery. Burgon writes:

> Codex B was early enthroned on something like speculation, and has been maintained upon the throne by what has strangely amounted to a positive superstition . . . The same spirit, biased by sentiment not ruled by reason, has remained since more has been disclosed of the real nature of this codex.[9]

This manuscript was unknown to the world of textual criticism until the year 1475 when it was officially catalogued in the Vatican library. With the designation "Vaticanus" also derived from its origin, the acclaim by professing Christians of a manuscript named after the veritable headquarters of Roman Catholicism speaks volumes for our present-day apostasy.

Following its delivery to the Vatican by a certain Cardinal Bessarion, the celebrated codex was confined to several centuries of possessive seclusion, broken only by the pillaging armies of Napoleon in 1809. After a brief Parisian interlude, Codex B was returned in 1815 to an even more protective atmosphere than before.

In 1845 the English scholar, Samuel Prideaux Tregelles (1813-1875), visited Rome with the hope of inspecting the confined codex. Although he was able to see *Vaticanus*, he was not permitted to transcribe any of its readings, lamenting:

> They would not let me open it without searching my pocket, and depriving me of pen, ink and paper . . . If I looked at a passage too long the two *prelati* (prelates) would snatch the book out from my hand.[10]

In addition to some notes Tregelles claims to have smuggled

out on his cuffs and fingernails,[11] a gullible Christian public has been assured by Geisler and Nix that, "Tregelles *secretly* memorized much of it."[12]

In 1866, Tischendorf got into the act with his own Vatican pilgrimage. Though also denied permission to make an outright copy of the manuscript, he was allowed to consult and take notes on any number of particularly difficult passages. Having begun his study on February 24th, the temptation to rewrite the entire codex proved too strong to resist. After copying twenty pages in the first eight days, his breach of contract was discovered by a Prussian Jesuit spy who promptly removed the prized copy.

As if to portray himself as the eternal optimist, the exposed Tischendorf assured his fans that, "I succeeded in preparing the whole New Testament for a new and reliable edition, so as to obtain **every desired result**."[13] Dr. Fuller cites the sardonic reaction of Dr. George Bishop to Tischendorf's euphoric guarantees:

> In all Tischendorf had the manuscript before him forty-two hours and only three hours at any one time, and all but a few of those hours were spent on the Gospels; . . . **Every desired result** in forty-two hours—all but two or three of them spent on the Gospels alone! **Every desired result** in three hours' hurried glancing through 146 pages of old and stained and mutilated manuscript written on very thin vellum, in faded ink, with its letters throughout large portions touched and retouched, bearing marks of a very peculiar treatment of the Epistles of St. Paul, and confessed to have received some corrections from the first and the filling up of certain blank spaces from the beginning![14]

In 1889-1890, a photographic set of the entire codex was released to the public by Vatican authorities. Strange as it sounds, the most heralded manuscript evidence for rejecting the King James Bible **has yet to be *handled* by serious Bible-believing scholars**! People like Beale, and Geisler and Nix have chosen a "slide presentation" put together by the most treacherous international gangsters in history over the blood-washed text of the Protestant Reformation!

Perhaps the best indication of ℵ and B's ability to mesmerize their scholastic devotees is the case of Count Tischendorf and his infamous *Novum Testamentum Graece* (Greek New Testament, 1869-1872). This work was the eighth and last edition of his career. David Beale eulogizing the scholar:

Constantin von Tischendorf (1815-1875)—German Protestant, Leipzig University professor, earnest textual scholar, polished theologian, and Christian philologist—devoted his life to the discovery of the oldest surviving biblical manuscripts. His love for the sacred text was the motivating force of his life; he published more editions of the New Testament text than any other scholar. Most valuable of all of these editions is his famous *Novum Testamentum Graece* (Greek New Testament, 1869-1872). This two-volume *editio octava critica maior* remains an enormous tool for the serious student of the New Testament; the work stands as the compilation of a lifetime of sacrificial work by a master-mind and spiritual giant.[15]

Nothing could be further from the truth! With his earlier editions (his third in particular) having shied away from the "reproachful" cursives, his later investigations led him to a seasoned appreciation for the unassailable logic of the *Textus Receptus*. This apex of thought attained fruition in his seventh edition of 1859. But then that fateful **trash can** entered his life, causing the Count to take, as Dean Burgon would say, "an excursion into cloud land." Beale's "master-mind and spiritual giant" had a carnal nature, subject to pride like anyone else. Burgon relates how *Codex Sinaiticus* changed Tischendorf's career from "distinguished" to *"extinguished."*

It was perhaps to be expected that human infirmity should have influenced Tischendorf in his treatment of the treasure-trove by him: though his character for judgment could not but be seriously injured by the fact that in his eighth edition he altered the mature conclusions of his seventh **in no less than 3,572 instances**, chiefly on account of the readings in his beloved Sinaitic guide.[16]

In attributing these 3,000-plus changes to Tischendorf's "grave discredit for discernment and consistency," Scrivener adds:

The evidence of Cod. א, supported or even unsupported by one or two authorities of **any** description, proved with him sufficient to outweigh all other witnesses, whether manuscripts, versions or ecclesiastical writers.[17]

The hypnotic grip of א and B becomes nothing short of incredible when these venerated documents are subjected to even a cursory inspection. Concerning the corrupt character of *Sinaiticus*, Fuller cites Mauro that:

What we now refer to is the fact that, since this document was first inscribed, it has been made the subject of no less than ten different attempts of revision and correction. The number of these attempts is witnessed by the different chirographies of the revisers, and the centuries in which they were respectively made can be approximated by the character of the different hand-writings by which the several sets of corrections were carried out.[18]

Mauro then cites Dr. Scrivener's firsthand observations of ℵ as contained in his work, *A Full Collation of the Codex Sinaiticus*:

The Codex is covered with such alterations—i.e., alterations of an obviously correctional character—brought in by at least ten different revisers, some of them systematically spread over every page, others occasional, or limited to separate portions of the Ms., many of these being contemporaneous with the first writer, but for the greater part belonging to the sixth or seventh century.[19]

Mauro then renders the all-important inference:

Here is a document which the Revisers have esteemed (and that solely because of its antiquity) to be so pure that it should be taken as a standard whereby all other copies of the Scriptures are to be tested and corrected. Such is the estimate of certain scholars of the 19th century. But it bears upon its face the proof that those in whose possession it had been, from the very first, and for some hundreds of years thereafter, esteemed it to be so impure as to require correction in every part ... Considering the great value to its owner of such a manuscript (it is on vellum of the finest quality) and that he would be most reluctant to consent to alterations in it except the need was clearly apparent, it is plain that this much admired Codex bears upon its face the most incontestible proof of its corrupt and defective character. But more than that, Dr. Scrivener tells us that the evident purpose of the thorough-going revision which he places in the 6th or 7th century was to make the Ms. conform to manuscripts in vogue at that time which were "far nearer to our modern *Textus Receptus*."[20]

Dr. Scrivener concludes his denunciation with:

It must be confessed indeed that the *Codex Sinaiticus* abounds with similar errors of the eye and pen, to an extent not unparalleled, but happily rather unusual in documents of first rate importance; so that Tregelles has freely pronounced that "the state of the text, as proceeding from the first scribe, may be regarded as very rough."[21]

Dean Burgon gives us his impression of ℵ:

> On many occasions 10, 20, 30, 40 words are dropped through
> very carelessness. Letters and words, even whole sentences, are
> frequently written twice over, or begun and immediately
> cancelled; while that gross blunder, whereby a clause is omitted
> because it happens to end in the same words as the clause
> preceding, occurs no less than 115 times in the New Testament.[22]

Not only is the scribe of *Sinaiticus* to be indicted for his
careless and frequent transcriptional errors, but how is he to be
excused for his failure to catch and correct the same? Is it any
wonder that such *trash* wound up in a *trash can*?

For a more intricate picture of ℵ's independent character,
consider Dr. Scrivener's collation of *Codex Sinaiticus* with ABC
and D over the following passages: Matthew 27:64-28:20; Mark
1:1-35; Luke 24:24-53 and John 21:1-25.

> The relation in which Cod. ℵ stands to the other four chief
> manuscripts of the Gospels, may be roughly estimated from
> analyzing the transcript of four pages first published by
> Tischendorf, as well as in any other way. Of the *312 variations
> from the common text therein noted,* ℵ stands alone in forty-five,
> in eight agrees with ABCD united (much of C, however, is lost in
> these passages), with ABC together thirty-one times, with ABD
> fourteen, with AB thirteen, with D alone ten, with B alone but
> once (Mark 1:27), with C alone once: with several authorities
> against AB thirty-nine times, with A against B fifty-two, with B
> against A ninety-eight.[23]

Finally, to add insult to injury, *Codex Sinaiticus* was also
found to include all of the Old Testament Apocrypha as well as
the *Epistle of Barnabas* and the *Shepherd of Hermas.* Such was
the fourth-century scholarship described by Geisler and Nix as
"the most important witness to the text beginning of its
antiquity, accuracy, and **lack of omissions.**"

When we turn our attention to the *Codex Vaticanus,* we find
the modern Nicolaitane promotion as syrupy as ever, Beale
stating:

> No one knows how or when the document arrived at the
> Vatican where the apostate Church of Rome suppressed it for so

long; nevertheless, **God has graciously opened a door that no man can shut.** God has made it possible for thousands of copies of this **"gem"** to be disseminated among Bible-believing scholars.[24]

To begin with, Beale's "gem" was copied by a scribe who believed that the Roman Catholic Apocrypha books were inspired, including them all with the exception of I and II Maccabees and the Prayer of Manasses.

As to the quality of transcription, Scrivener reports that B fared no better than ℵ:

> That no small proportion of these are mere oversights of the scribe seems evident from the circumstance that this same scribe has repeatedly written words and clauses *twice over*.[25]

For the record, Dean Burgon has supplied four simple examples of this telltale sign of incompetency:

> Matthew 21:4, five words written twice over; Matthew 26:56-57, six words; Luke 1:37, three words or one line; John 17:18, six words. These however, are but a few of many.[26]

Concerning the more serious error of omissions, Burgon comments:

> The impurity of the text exhibited by these codices is not a question of opinion but of fact . . . In the Gospels . . . Codex B (Vatican) leaves out words or clauses . . . It bears traces of careless transcription **on every page.**[27]

Citing Dr. Dobbin, Scrivener expands on the omissions of *Vaticanus*:

> One marked feature, characteristic of this copy, is the great number of its omissions, which has induced Dr. Dobbin to speak of it as presenting 'an abbreviated text of the New Testament:' and certainly the facts he states on this point are startling enough. He calculates that Codex B leaves out words or whole clauses no less than 330 times in Matthew, 365 in Mark, 439 in Luke, 357 in John, 384 in the Acts, 681 in the surviving Epistles; or 2,556 times in all.[28]

This subject of omissions in a manuscript is of far more serious consequence than what is initially appreciated. The problem is exacerbated as the omitted words or phrases pop up in unison elsewhere. Remarking on the excisions of B that are mysteriously discovered in the *Textus Receptus*, Burgon asks:

> By what possible hypothesis will such a correspondence of the copies be accounted for if these words, clauses, and sentences are indeed, as is pretended, nothing else but spurious accretions to the text?[29]

We are not surprised that questions like these are entirely ignored by the scholarship of Geisler and Nix. Even Bishop Lightfoot, a known ally of א, was forced to concede that the manuscript exhibits an "impatience of apparently superfluous words."[30]

Abandoned by his associates, a desperate Dr. Hort just makes matters worse being cited by Dr. Scrivener as saying:

> That such facts 'have no bearing on either the merits or the demerits of the scribe of B, except as regards the absolutely singular readings of B,' whereas multitudes of these omissions are found in other good documents.[31]

The varied textual problems of א and B are naturally responsible for a reckless departure from the Majority Text. Burgon stating the cold facts:

> Between the first two (B and א) there subsists an amount of sinister resemblance, which proves that they must have been derived at no very remote period from the same corrupt original. Tischendorf insists that they were partly written by the same scribe. Yet do they stand asunder in every page; as well as differ widely from the commonly received Text, with which they have been carefully collated. On being referred to this standard, in the Gospels alone, B is found to omit at least 2877 words: to add, 536: to substitute, 935: to transpose, 2098: to modify, 1132 (in all 7578):—the corresponding figures for א being severally 3455, 839, 1114, 2299, 1265 (in all 8972). And be it remembered that the omissions, additions, substitutions, transpositions, and modifications, *are by no means the same in both.* It is in fact *easier to find two consecutive verses in which these two MSS. differ the one from the other, than two consecutive verses in which they entirely agree.*[32]

As the "theory" of evolution is consistently rejected by *true* science (2nd Law of Thermodynamics, etc.) the caprice of Westcott and Hort is an insult to legitimate scholarship and consistent manuscript evidences. For instance, having begun his

924-page collation with the words, "It is high time that the bubble of Codex B should be pricked,"[33] Herman Hoskier gives ample illustration of the unscholarly prejudice afforded to *Vaticanus*:

Leaving aside the claims made in the Introduction of W-H, the principles upon which the text was founded as it left Hort's hands are fixed for ever, and graven in stereotype for us; and those principles are reduced to one rule, viz., to follow B whenever that MS. has any support, be it only the adhesion of *one* other MS.[34]

Hoskier then goes on to list a few examples of such instances when B is seen to stand alone:

Matthew vii:18 ενεγκειν . . . ποιειν is read absolutely alone by B . . . and in Luke iii:33 του αμιναδαβ, omitted only by B, finds no place in Hort's text; observe also Luke v. 2 πλοια δυο order of B alone among Greeks; v. 3 εκ του πλοιου εδιδασκεν B alone.[35]

The most infamous abuse of B's "power of influence" was seen when the Revision Committee of 1871-1881 viciously attacked the Deity of Christ in I Timothy 3:16. In response to their altering of the traditional, *"God was manifest in the flesh,"* to the corrupt, *"he who* was manifest in the flesh," Burgon dispatched the following remonstrance to the committee's chairman, Bishop Ellicott:

Behold then the provision which the Author of Scripture has made for the effectual conservation in its integrity of this portion of His written word! Upwards of 1800 years have run their course since the Holy Ghost, by His servant Paul, rehearsed 'the Mystery of Godliness,' declaring this to be the great foundation fact, namely, that 'God was manifest in the flesh.' *And lo! out of 254 copies of St. Paul's Epistles, no less than 252 are discovered to have preserved that expression.* The copies whereof we speak were procured in every part of Christendom, being derived in every instance from copies older than themselves; which again were transcripts of copies older still. They have since found their way, without design or contrivance, into the libraries of every country in Europe, where they are jealously guarded . . . We submit, as a proper and just conclusion from these facts, that men who, in view of the evidence before them, would cast out of the Scripture at this vital point, the word "God", and replace it by "he who," have thereby demonstrated their unfitness for the work of revising the Greek text of the N.T.[36]

But without a doubt, the most glaring evidence of Westcott and Hort's unscholarly approach to their revered ancient codices can be seen in the *higher* percentage of the anti-Receptus readings which *they refused to use*. In fact, this inconsistency applies to all of the uncial manuscripts. Pickering, citing Burgon's comments concerning Codex D:

> An excellent illustration of the need for this criterion is furnished by Codex D in the last three chapters of Luke . . . After discussing sixteen cases of omission (where W-H deleted material from the TR) in these chapters, Burgon continues: "The *sole* authority for just half of the places above enumerated [Luke 22:19-20; 24:3, 6, 9, 12, 36, 40, 52] is *a single Greek codex* – and that, the most depraved of all – viz. 12. Beza's D. It should further be stated that the only allies discoverable for D are a few copies of the old Latin . . . When we reach down codex D from the shelf, we are reminded that, within the space of the three chapters of S. Luke's Gospel now under consideration, there are in all no less than 354 words omitted: *of which 250 are omitted by D alone.* **May we have it explained to us why, of those 354 words, only 25 are singled out by Drs. Westcott and Hort for permanent excision from the sacred Text?**[37]

Pickering objects in frustration:

> The focus here is upon Westcott and Hort. According to *their own judgment*, codex D has omitted 329 words from the genuine text of the last three chapters of Luke plus adding 173, substituting 146 and transposing 243. By their own admission the text of D here is in a fantastically chaotic state, yet in eight places they omitted material from the text on the *sole authority* of D! With the scribe on a wild omitting spree, to say nothing of his other iniquities, how can *any* value be given to the testimony of D in these chapters, much less prefer it above the united voice of every other witness?!?![38]

The question remains to be answered: Why didn't Westcott and Hort omit the other **329** words? This is Nicolaitane intellectualism at its best.

Having acquainted ourselves with the inconsistencies of these two false witnesses, we will now secure the illuminating "Alexandrian Connection." That ℵ and B owe their depraved idiosyncrasies to the land of Origen is a point that is readily conceded by "modern scholarship"; Geisler and Nix label *Vaticanus* as, "an excellent example of the Alexandrian type text,"[39] and *Sinaiticus* as, "Alexandrian in general."[40] Such a conclusion is arrived at by a corroboration of history with the manuscript evidence exhibited in the extant translations from Egypt and patristic writings of Origen.

In our previous chapter, we traced the excommunicated Adamantius to his retirement haven in Caesarea. Having founded a "Palestinian Extension" of his infamous catechetical school in Alexandria, the deceased chancellor bequeathed both his writings and the institution's leadership to his favorite pupil, Pamphilus (c. 240-309).

The new president is credited with the establishment of a massive library (the foundation deposit being Origen's vast writings), and the personal discipleship of his own eventual successor, the celebrated church historian and bishop of Caesarea, Eusebius (c. 260-c. 340). This "Pamphilian link" between Origen and Eusebius cannot be overestimated, as will be seen directly.

It would be the fate of Pamphilus to suffer martyrdom in the first of two successive waves of persecution, the initial strike being an imperial ban against the "written" word (orchestrated by Emperors Diocletian, Galerius and Maximus, A.D. 303-311) followed by the more subtle theological assault upon the "living" word—known as Arianism (named after the Alexandrian Arius, latently sanctioned by the emperor Constantine and tacitly endorsed by the compromising Eusebius). Eusebius describes the opening salvo:

> Suddenly edicts were published everywhere to raze the churches to the ground, and to destroy the sacred Scriptures ... All this has been fulfilled in our day when we saw with our own eyes, our houses of worship thrown down from their elevation, the sacred Scriptures of inspiration committed to the flames.[41]

Over the ensuing decade a serious depletion of reliable Sriptures was facilitated by the cooperation of nefarious deserters, known as *traditores*. The dearth of Bibles became even more acute as the church began receiving vast numbers of "converts" within her ranks following the ascension of Constantine the Great, the empire's first ever "Christian" *Pontifex Maximus*. (The pagan title meant *supreme pontiff* or *chief priest at Rome*;[42] this honor was retained by Constantine until his death and perpetuated in our day by the "venerable" guardian of Codex B, the "Holy Father" himself.)

To meet this need, Constantine requisitioned his good friend, the bishop of Caesarea, to supply his realm at Constantinople with fifty new Bibles.[43] Therefore, Eusebius (now nicknamed "Eusebius Pamphili" in honor of his departed mentor) repaired to the latter's memorial library, where he led a team of copyists to fulfill the Emperor's order. Enter our two false witnesses, Burgon surmising:

> Constantine applied to Eusebius for fifty handsome copies, amongst which it is not improbable that the manuscripts . . . B and ℵ were to be actually found.[44]

And that such an opinion is not restricted to Majority Text advocates is evidenced by Tischendorf's euphoric speculation that:

> Is it possible that this Bible (ℵ) could be one of the 50 copies which Emperor Constantine ordered Eusebius to place in Constantinople, his new capital?[45]

At this point, it should be emphasized for the novice that an association of ℵ and B with Egypt's capital is significant for several reasons. Not only was fourth-century Alexandria noted for her unscriptural rapprochement of philosophy with Christianity, her multitudinous and extravagant attempts at textual criticism, and the nutty theological excesses of her most celebrated fathers, but she was also the hotbed of the blasphemous, Christ-denying heresy of Arianism (the teaching that Christ was a created being). In referring to this error, Burgon writes:

> It is a circumstance that cannot fail to give rise to suspicion that the Vatican and Sinaitic MSS. had their origin under a predominant influence of such evil fame. At the very least, careful investigation is necessary to see whether these copies were in fact free from that influence which has met with universal condemnation.[46]

Thus we see that an Alexandrian connection becomes *the* blot that explains ℵ and B's numerous disfigurements, both typographically and doctrinally, as epitomized by their 3,000+ disagreements with one another in only four books. And when it is realized that Constantine and Eusebius leaned toward Arianism, the potential for treachery increases. (It is noteworthy that the emperor's *orthodox* son, Constans, sent a similar request for Bibles but to the anti-Arian Athanasius.[47])

Now as concerns the evidence for an Alexandrian influence,

one should simply look for "leeks and onions" in the readings of
ℵ and B. If it *walks* like a duck and *looks* like a duck, it probably
is a duck! Dean Burgon summarizes:

> Yet I venture also to think that it was in a great measure at
> Alexandria that the *text* in question was fabricated. My chief
> reasons for thinking so are the following: (1) There is a marked
> resemblance between the peculiar readings of Bℵ and the two
> Egyptian versions,—the Bohairic or Version of Lower Egypt
> especially. (2) No one can fail to have been struck by the evident
> sympathy between *Origen*,—who at all events had passed more
> than half his life at Alexandria,—and the text in question. (3) I
> notice that Nonnus also, who lived in the Thebaid, exhibits
> considerable sympathy with the text which I deem so corrupt. (4)
> I cannot overlook the fact the Cod. ℵ was discovered in a
> monastery under the sway of the patriarch of Alexandria, though
> how it got there no evidence remains to point out. (5) The
> licentious handling so characteristic of the Septuagint Version of
> the O.T.,—the work of Alexandrian Jews,—points in the same
> direction, and leads me to suspect that Alexandria was the final
> source of the text of B-ℵ. (6) I further observe that the sacred
> Text . . . in Cyril's Homiles on St. John is often similar to B-ℵ;
> and this, I take for granted, was the effect of the school of
> Alexandria,—not of the patriarch himself. (7) Dionysius of
> Alexandria complains bitterly of the corrupt Codexes of his day:
> and certainly (8) Clemens habitually employed copies of a similar
> kind. He too was of Alexandria.[48]

However, there is also the more indirect yet intriguing link of
ℵ and B to Origen through the traceable similarities with
Jerome's Latin Vulgate, the decisive factor being Jerome's choice
of Pamphilus' library as his primary source of translation labors.
You will recall that this library was the chief depository of
Origen's writings including his famed *Hexapla* (a manuscript of
the Old Testament with six translations in Hebrew and Greek
arranged in parallel columns for comparative study).
Dr. Frederick Nolan states:

> The striking coincidence of the Greek of the Vatican
> manuscript with the Latin of the Vulgate leads to the
> establishment of the same conclusion. This version received the
> corrections of St. Jerome during his abode in Palestine; it is thus
> only probable that the Greek copies, after which he modelled it,
> were those, which from being current in Palestine, were used in
> the monastery, into which he had retired: but these he assures
> us were of the edition of Eusebius. For this edition he had

imbibed an early partiality, through Gregory of Nazianzum, who
first put the Scriptures into his hands, who had been educated at
Caesarea in Palestine.[49]

Not only does Jerome mention his familiarity with the
manuscripts of Pamphilus and Origen, particularly that of the
latter's *Hexapla* autograph,[50] but testifies of having relied upon
them as his undisputed model. Burgon indicts the modern
revisers for having banished the words *"that ye should not obey
the truth"* in Galatians 3:1 on the sole strength of seven
manuscripts (A, B, ℵ, D, F, G, and 17). Jerome is seen as having
set the pace:

> But when he comes to the place in Galatians, he is observed,
> first to admit that the clause 'is found in some copies,' and
> straightway to add that *'inasmuch as it is not found in the copies
> of Adamantius, he omits it.'* The clue to his omission is supplied
> by his own statement that in writing on the Galatians he had
> made Origen his guide.[51]

At this juncture, it would behoove us to address the
Nicolaitane fallacy that the King James translators were deprived
of the ℵ and B readings. Beale writes:

> **Since** the publication of the King James Version in 1611,
> numerous manuscript discoveries have contributed to a vastly
> increased knowledge of the original Scripture.[52]

Robert Sumner would indict Erasmus with a similar
ignorance, pronouncing:

> Erasmus himself had no knowledge of the Alexandrian
> manuscripts. The Sinaiticus was not discovered at the monastery
> of St. Catharine on Mount Sinai until the mid-19th century and
> the Vaticanus, while in the Vatican Library at Rome since about
> the mid-15th century, was not available for use by outsiders until
> near the dawn of the 20th century . . . To say those "who used
> the 'Received Text' down through the centuries had access" to
> them, "but rejected them as corrupt," is a long, *long* way from
> the facts.[53]

The hypocrisy of these statements is unbelievable when one
realizes that these same readings of *Sinaiticus* and *Vaticanus*
were very much before the scholars of the 1611 Authorized
Version as represented *in the Latin Vulgate*.

Concerning Sumner's asinine statement about Erasmus, the

tabloid-style editor is the one who is a "long *long* way from the facts." Scrivener (citing Tregelles) relates how the Catholic Sepulveda corresponded with Erasmus in 1533, promoting the "merits" of Codex B:

> Tischendorf says truly enough that something like a history might be written of the futile attempts to collate Cod. B, and a very unprofitable history it would be. The manuscript is first distinctly heard of (for it does not appear to have been used for the Complutensian Polyglott) through Sepulveda, to whose correspondence with Erasmus has been seasonably recalled by Tregelles . . . after noticing as a weighty proof of excellence its agreement with the Latin version . . . against the common Greek Text . . . , he furnishes Erasmus with 365 readings as a convincing argument in support of his statements . . . It seems, however, that he had obtained some account of this manuscript from the Papal Librarian Paul Bombasius as early as 1521 (see Wetstein's Proleg. N.T., vol. i. p. 23).[54]

With four editions of his Greek New Testament behind him, the 67-year-old accomplished scholar was not impressed. Two years later, Erasmus published his fifth and final edition (a year before his death), yet Geisler and Nix have the audacity to say, "It was still based on the Byzantine text type," and "contained readings *from very late manuscripts.*"[55]

However, returning to our initial purpose, we have found that the easiest way to trace ℵ and B to the pen of Origen is to simply observe not only a parallel of *style* but of the *readings* themselves. Being familiar with Origen's writings, Dr. Hoskier gives us a preview of that father's telltale mode of editing:

> The points in which we are specially entitled to look for innovations are: (1) curious and ingenious readings, such, for instance, as those which we have noticed in St. Mark and St. Luke; (2) the removal of words, clauses, or entire sentences which a man of fastidious taste might regard as superfluities or repetitious; (3) a fearless and highly speculative mode of dealing with portions of the New Testament which might contain statements opposed to his prepossessions or present difficulties which even his ingenuity might be unable to solve.[56]

Bishop Marsh adds:

> Whenever therefore grammatical interpretation produced a sense which in Origen's opinion was irrational or impossible, in other words irrational or impossible according to the philosophy

which Origen had learnt at Alexandria, he then *departed* from
the literal sense.[57]

We are not surprised that such are the very peculiarities
exhibited throughout the defaced leaves of codices *Sinaiticus* and
Vaticanus. Dean Burgon states:

> Origen, and mainly BℵD, are not to be regarded as wholly
> independent authorities, but constitute a class. The proof of this
> position is to be found in various passages where the influence of
> Origen may be traced, such as in the omission of Yἱοῦ τοῦ Θεοῦ
> 'The Son of God'—in Mark 1:1; and of ἐν ᾿Εφέσῳ- 'at Ephesus'-
> in Ephesians 1:1; in the substitution of Bethabara (St. John 1:28)
> for Bethany; in the omission of the second part of the last
> petition of the Lord's prayer in St. Luke, of ἔμπροσθέν μου
> γέγονεν in John 1:27.
>
> He is also the cause why the important qualification εἰκῆ
> ('without a cause') is omitted by Bℵ from St. Matthew v.22; and
> hence, in opposition to the whole host of Copies, Versions,
> Fathers, has been banished from the sacred Text by Lachmann,
> Tischendorf, W.-Hort and the Revisers.[58]

A final illustration of Origen's self-willed eclecticism will
suffice, Burgon stating:

> It is plain, from the consent of (so to speak) all the copies,
> that our Saviour rejected the Temptation which stands second in
> St. Luke's Gospel with the words,—'Get thee behind me, Satan.'
> But Origen officiously points out that this (quoting the words) is
> precisely what our Lord did not say. He adds a reason—'He said
> to Peter, "Get thee behind Me, Satan."; but to the devil, "Get
> thee hence," without the addition "behind Me"; for to be behind
> Jesus is a good thing.'[59]

We will now conclude our chapter on the two false witnesses
with the most substantive evidence of all by referring to the
discovery of a *colophon* on ℵ. A colophon is a scribal note placed
at the end of a manuscript giving pertinent information regarding
the transcription. Dean Burgon relates:

> But in connecting B and ℵ with the Library at Caesarea we
> are not left only to conjecture or inference. In a well-known
> colophon affixed to the end of the book of Esther in ℵ by the
> third corrector, it is stated that from the beginning of the book
> of Kings to the end of Esther the MS. was compared with a copy
> 'corrected by the hand of the holy martyr Pamphilus,' which

itself was written and corrected after the Hexapla of Origen. And a similar colophon may be found attached to the book of Ezra. It is added that the Codex Sinaiticus . . . and the Codex Pamphili . . . manifested great agreement with one another. The probability that ℵ was at least in part copied from a manuscript executed by Pamphilus is established by the facts that a certain 'Codex Marchalianus' is often mentioned which was due to Pamphilus and Eusebius; and that Origen's recension of the Old Testament, although he published no edition of the Text of the New, possessed a great reputation. On the books of Chronicles, St. Jerome mentions manuscripts executed by Origen with great care, which were published by Pamphilus and Eusebius. And in Codex H of St. Paul it is stated that that MS. was compared with a MS. in the library of Caesarea 'which was written by the hand of the holy Pamphilus.' These notices added to the frequent reference by St. Jerome and others to the critical MSS., by which we are to understand those which were distinguished by the approval of Origen or were in consonance with the spirit of Origen, shew evidently the position in criticism which the Library at Caesarea and its illustrious founder had won in those days. And it is quite in keeping with that position that ℵ should have been sent forth from that 'school of criticism.'[60]

What more can be added to such a documented presentation of evidence than a parting comment from the world of Nicolaitane scholarship?

> But we have not been able to recognize as Alexandrian **any** readings of B in **any** book of the New Testament which it contains.[61]
>
> – Dr. Hort, Synagogue of Satan

IX

Bathed in Blood

"And I saw the woman drunken with the blood of the saints, and with the blood of the martyrs of Jesus."   (Revelation 17:6a)

The history of the English Bible is a history which has literally been "bathed in blood." On the morning of February 8, 1555, Reverend John Hooper, Bishop of Gloucester (known as the "Father of Puritanism") was led to the stake in his own cathedral city to burn in the presence of his grieving parishioners. Noted by Foxe for his "fervent desire to the love and knowledge of *Scripture*,"[1] the selfless pastor attempted to assuage their grief with the words, "True it is that death is bitter, and life is sweet; but alas! consider that the death to come is more bitter, and the life to come is more sweet."[2] Foxe's contemporary account continues:

> Command was now given that the fire should be kindled. But because there were not more green fagots than two horses could carry, it kindled not speedily, and was a pretty while also before it took the reeds upon the fagots. At length it burned about him, but the wind having full strength at that place, and being a lowering cold morning, it blew the flame from him, so that he was in a manner little more than touched by the fire.
> Within a space after, a few dry fagots were brought, and a new fire kindled with fagots, (for there were no more reeds) and those burned at the nether parts, but had small power above, because of the wind, saving that it burnt his hair and scorched his skin a little. In the time of which fire, even as at the first

flame, he prayed, saying mildly, and not very loud, but as one without pain, "O Jesus, Son of David, have mercy upon me, and receive my soul!" After the second fire was spent, he wiped both his eyes with his hands, and beholding the people, he said with an indifferent, loud voice, "For God's love, good people, let me have more fire!" and all this while his nether parts did burn; but the fagots were so few that the flame only singed his upper parts.

The third fire was kindled within a while after, which was more extreme than the other two. In this fire he prayed with a loud voice, "Lord Jesus, have mercy upon me! Lord Jesus receive my spirit!" And these were the last words he was heard to utter. But when he was black in the mouth, and his tongue so swollen that he could not speak, yet his lips went until they were shrunk to the gums: **and he knocked his breast with his hands until one of his arms fell off**, and then knocked still with the other, while the fat, water, and blood dropped out at his fingers' ends, until by renewing the fire, his strength was gone, and his hand clave fast in knocking to the iron upon his breast. Then immediately bowing forwards, he yielded up his spirit. Thus was he three quarters of an hour or more in the fire.[3]

Such were the horrific conditions which forged the pioneer translations of the King James Bible, the likes of which were as far removed from the profit-oriented Hortian school as their variant readings remain to date. A familiarity with *Fox's Book of Martyrs* will illuminate the integral ratio of a resurgence in translation activity commensurate with a weakening of Catholic totalitarianism.

Historians will generally point to the attendance of three British bishops (those of London, York and Lincoln) at the Council of Arles in A.D. 314[4] as the earliest recorded presence of Christianity in England. The British monk Pelagius (c. 360-c. 420) is also recognized as the earliest proponent of man's free will (as opposed to the systems of his contemporary, Augustine and Reformation-era Calvin). However, in his *Ecclesiastical History of the English Nation*, the Venerable Bede acknowledges a distinct (though distorted) evidence of British Christianity as early as A.D. 156.[5]

Scholars agree that the English congregations radiated a more primitive brand of Christianity than that practiced on the Continent. The factor most responsible for this dual standard was the obvious geographical contribution made by the English Channel. This natural barrier of Providence (a persistent hindrance to as recent a victim as Adolph Hitler) enhanced Britain's spiritual climate. While Europe was succumbing to the leavening effects of Roman Catholicism, the insulated British Isles were experiencing revival under such spiritual giants as Piranus (325-430), Servanus (450-543), Drostan (470-540), Finbar (490-578), Patrick (389-461), Columba (521-597) and Columbanus (543-615).

Patrick personally testified of having immersed thousands of adult men[6] from the over 300 local assemblies which he started. (This is why Ireland means "Island of the Saints.") Numbers of these preachers became fruitful missionaries. Especially noteworthy was the Gospel station of Iona (off the west coast of Scotland) founded by the soul-winning Columba. Although the Celtic Christianity of Britain and Ireland fell short of the New Testament standard, it was light-years ahead of the Continent's "Papal Mafia."

Prior to their eventual "miraculous conversion" under Pope Gregory's invading "missionaries" (armed with literal "swords of the spirit"), these humble believers differed with Rome in several outstanding particulars: they denied the doctrines of transubstantiation, Mariolatry, infant sprinkling, and prayers for the dead; they refused the vow of celibacy; and they rejected the ecclesiastical monstrosity of apostolic succession.

This satanic subjugation of Britain was facilitated by the marriage of King Ethelbert to a Roman Catholic woman from Paris named Bertha. Ethelbert learned quickly who was going to wear the pants in the family when "Big Bertha" imported her own Catholic Bishop for the ceremony.[7]

Thus when the Benedictine Abbot, Augustine, arrived to do a little "witnessing" for Gregory, he found Ethelbert's fields *"white unto harvest."* Ten thousand Englishmen were *sprinkled* during the Christmas season of A.D. 597.[8] Of course, the official Bible of "Christianized" England would now become Jerome's Latin Vulgate.

However, many others refused to submit to the Pope's authority. Back-to-back conferences between Augustine (supported by the Frankish armies of Clovis) and the recalcitrant British bishops accomplished nothing. Augustine even resorted to a fake healing of a blind Saxon but to no avail.[9] The exasperated abbot finally expired with the Venerable Bede relating the epitaph on his tombstone:

> Here rests the Lord Augustine, first archbishop of Canterbury, who, being formerly sent hither by the blessed Gregory, bishop of the city of Rome, and by God's assistance supported with miracles, reduced King Ethelbert and his nation from the

worship of idols to the faith of Christ, and having ended the days of his office in peace, died the 26th day of May, in the reign of the same king.[10]

The ensuing centuries witnessed an ebb-and-flow relationship between the two religious factions with the light of true Christianity nearly extinguished by the 14th century.

By this time, the English language was in its second major stage of development known as Middle English (the Old English period ushered in by the 5th century Germanic invasions of the Angles, Saxons and Jutes promptly concluded with the conquest in 1066 by the Danish/French-speaking Normans).

Throughout these many centuries, very little Scripture was translated into the tongue of the common man. The earliest effort of any kind was a selection of Bible stories communicated by poetry. Referring to one Caedmon as the "unlettered poet of Whitby," Bede says that he:

Sang the creation of the world, the origin of man, and all the history of Genesis, and made many verses on the departure of the children of Israel out of Egypt, and their entering into the promised land, with many other histories from Holy Writ; the Incarnation, Passion, and Resurrection of our Lord, and His ascending into heaven; the coming of the Holy Ghost, and the preaching of the apostles; also the terror of judgment to come, the horror of the pains of hell, and the joys of heaven."[11]

This token effort was followed by several partial translations such as: the Psalms by Aldhelm (A.D. 640-709); the Gospels by Egbert (d. 766); the Ten Commandments and portions of Exodus and Acts by Alfred the Great, King of England (A.D. 849-901); and various Old Testament selections by Aelfric "The Grammarian" (c. 955-c. 1020).[12] It is interesting that Aelfric's translation selections were limited by King Ethelred II to the Bible's warlike books (including some Apocryphal books) to invigorate his English subjects with a fighting spirit in the wake of Danish invasions (978-991).[13]

Although partially deceived by Augustine's promises, Bede displayed a high regard for God's Word. Describing the monk's race against death to complete his final chapter, McClure cites the moving account by Bede's biographer, Cuthbert, as follows:

Toward evening of the day of his death, one of his disciples said, "Beloved teacher, one sentence remains to be written." "Write it quickly, then," said the dying saint; and summoning all his strength for this last flash of the expiring lamp, he dictated the holy words. When told that the work was finished, he answered, "Thou sayest well. It is finished!" He then requested to be taken up, and placed in that part of his cell where he was wont to kneel at his private devotions; so that, as he said, he might while sitting there call upon his Father. He then sang the doxology,—"Glory be to the Father, and to the Son, and to the Holy Ghost!" and as he sang the last syllable, he drew his last breath.[14]

Among the several Middle English versions would be included Ormin's poetical paraphrase of the Gospels and the book of Acts (c. 1200) as well as the literal translation of the Psalter by one William of Shoreham (c. 1320) also known as the "Hermit of Hampole."[15]

This brings us to the age of John Wycliff (1330-1384). For having broken up the fallow ground over a century before the great body of English reformers, Wycliff (also spelled Wycliffe, Wiclyff, Wyclif, Wiclif, Wicklif, etc.) was heralded as the "Morning Star of the Reformation." These initial strains of light emanated from Wycliff's monumental life's work—*the first translation of the entire Bible into English.*

John Wycliff was born into an age ripe for reform. The zenith of Rome's power had been evidenced by her ability to marshall the crusading armies of Europe. However, her overall prestige, enhanced by the victorious first campaign in 1095, was steadily diminished throughout the seven ignominious defeats which followed (1147-1291). Thirty thousand boys and girls from France and Germany perished in the infamous Childrens' Crusade of 1212.

Basically, the Crusades were initiated by the "burden" of "Holy Mother Church" for her Palestinian *coffers.* With several generations of young men enticed to their deaths by offers of plenary indulgences (free trips to Heaven), the sobered survivors gradually began to see the light. The escalating resentment against the clergy was intoned through verse:

> When men are hot with drinking wine
> And idly by the fire recline,
> They take the cross with eager boast
> To make a great crusading host.
> But with first glow of morning light
> The whole Crusade dissolves in flight.[16]

While the fruition of this disgust would be realized with Luther's 95 Theses in 1517, England would begin rattling the cage as early as the mid-14th century. The catalyst for this precursory English challenge stemmed indirectly from a second major papal embarrassment. Historians have metaphorically classed the period of 1309-1378 as *The Babylonian Captivity* because of France's successful political maneuvering of the papacy's headquarters from Rome to Avignon. There was no love lost, therefore, between England and the "new" Roman/French Catholicism throughout her subsequent *100 Years' War* with France (1337-1453).

The breach became even greater when negotiations to resolve the conflict disintegrated into another period known as *The Great Schism* (1378-1417). This era offered the world *two* "His Holinesses," one in Avignon and one in Rome. In the year 1409, Alexander V became Pope number *three*, making his official claim to "Peter's chair." (He joined Gregory XII [1406-1415] in Rome and Benedict XIII [1394-1409] at Avignon who were already fulminating anathemas at one another, "in Christian love" of course.) Schaff comments on the resulting shift in power to England's monarchy:

> The struggles of previous centuries against the encroachment of Rome upon the temporalities of the English Church was maintained in this period. The complaint made by Matthew Paris that the English Church was kept between two millstones, the king and the pope, remained true, with this difference, however, the king's influence came to preponderate. Acts of parliament emphasized his right to dictate or veto ecclesiastical appointments and recognized his sovereign prerogative to tax Church property. The evident support which the pope gave to France in her wars with England and the scandals of the Avignon residence were favorable to the crown's assertion of authority in these respects.[17]

Born of Saxon blood near the village of Wycliff in Yorkshire, John Wycliff became the chief spokesman for patriotic Englishmen through this period of emancipation. His rise to a place of scholastic eminence was swift. Excelling at Oxford, he was named king's chaplain in 1366 while receiving his doctorate in 1374. However, he soon turned his intellectual guns on Rome, Schaff relating:

> In sermons, tracts and larger writings, Wyclif brought Scripture and common sense to bear. His pen was as keen as a

Damascus blade. Irony and invective, of which he was the master, he did not hesitate to use. The directness and pertinency of his appeals brought them easily within the comprehension of the popular mind.[18]

In his condemnation of doctrinal abuse, Wycliff anticipated the later reformers' attitude toward immoral prelates, excessive territorial holdings, religious extortion, heresies such as purgatory, transubstantiation, the priesthood and auricular confession. Wycliff despised these false teachings as leaving the masses in spiritual ignorance and thus holden to Rome.

Few were spared the "Damascus blade." He blasted the pope as "the anti-Christ, the proud worldly priest of Rome, and the most cursed of clippers and cut-purses."[19] As the monks of his day were known for their taste for "good food and bad women,"[20] Wycliff depreciated their monasteries as "dens of thieves, nests of serpents, houses of living devils."[21]

In language that rivaled Luther's, he wrote that the priests:

> Take poor men's livelihood, but they do not oppose oppression; they set more price by the rotten penny than by the precious blood of Christ; they pray only for show, and collect fees for every religious service that they perform; they live in luxury, riding fat horses with harness of silver and gold; they are robbers . . . malicious foxes . . . ravishing wolves . . . gluttons . . . devils . . . apes.[22]

As no country can rise higher than the morals of its women, a contemporary account gave low marks to this all-important barometer of feminine purity (as was the case of Alexandria).

> In those days arose a great rumor and clamor among the people, that wherever there was a tournament there came a great concourse of ladies of the most costly and beautiful, but not of the best, in the kingdom, sometimes forty or fifty in number, as if they were a part of the tournament, in diverse and wonderful male apparel, in party-colored tunics, with short caps and bands wound cord-wise round their head, and girdles bound with gold and silver, and daggers in pouches across their body, and then they proceeded on chosen coursers to the place of tourney, and so expended and wasted their goods and vexed their bodies with scurrilous wantonness that the rumor of the people sounded everywhere; and thus they neither feared God nor blushed at the chaste voice of the people.[23]

Understandably, this moral declension insured England a dismal horizon at best. Dr. Green summarizes:

It was a time of shame and suffering such as England had never known. Her conquests were lost, her shores insulted, her fleets annihilated, her commerce swept from the sea; while within she was exhausted by the long and costly war, as well as by the ravages of pestilence.[24]

Although Wycliff's humbled nation was primed for repentance, his stiff-necked, religious detractors presented formidable opposition. As his fiery denunciations intensified, so did the threat of physical violence. To counter this danger, the Lord raised up a powerful protector in John of Gaunt, the Duke of Lancaster (favorite son of Edward and younger brother to the better-known, though temporal-minded Black Prince).

The longer Wycliff labored, the more certain he became that his beloved England needed something other than his sermons and tracts. They needed the Bible! In his writing entitled *The Wicket*, he exclaims with emotion:

> If God's Word is the life of the world, and every word of God is the life of the human soul, how may any Antichrist, for dread of God, take it away from us that be Christian men, and thus to suffer the people to die for hunger in heresy and blasphemy of men's laws, that corrupteth and slayeth the soul.[25]

In consequence of this need, Wycliff gave the rest of his life to complete the first translation of the entire Bible into the English language. With little knowledge of Greek or Hebrew, he based his work primarily on Latin manuscripts. Although modern scholarship stresses Wycliff's reliance upon the Vulgate's readings, a later revision of the work by John Purvey which brought the translation back in tune with Jerome makes it evident that Wycliff had access to some old Latin manuscripts. Purvey's later defection to Rome sheds added light on the issue.[26]

Regardless of the Latin consistency, the new Bible represented the first ever for the English-speaking people. Because printing had yet to be discovered, the manuscript had to be copied by hand necessitating an exorbitant price tag. (It required about 10 months of steady work by an experienced copyist.) The *rental* fee for only an hour with so costly a treasure was an entire load of hay,[27] while McClure tells us that a *purchase* price neared "four marks and forty pence," the equivalent of a clergyman's entire year's salary.[28]

The arrival of printing prompted the eerie prophecy, "Let us hope that the low *pricing* of the Bible may never occasion the low *prizing* of the Bible."[29] (Believers in our present day are sadly acquainted with the fulfillment of this concern.)

Despite the cost and circumvention of original languages, Wycliff's contribution to the work of Christ was received by and speedily propagated among a hungry people. (This was accomplished primarily through the reformer's followers, deridingly referred to as the "Lollards" [meaning "babblers"]).

Foxe informs us:

> So scanty was the supply of Bibles at this time, that but few of those who craved its teaching could hope to possess the sacred volume. But this lack was partly made up by the earnestness of those whose interest was awakened in the Bible. If only a single copy was owned in a neighborhood, these hard-working laborers and artisans would be found together, after a weary day of toil, reading in turn, and listening to the words of life; and so sweet was the refreshment to their spirits, that sometimes the morning light surprised them with its call to a new day of labor, *before they thought of sleep.*[30]

McClure cites a contemporary poem which depicts this spirit of joyous liberation:

> But to outweigh all harm, the Sacred Book,
> In dusty sequestration wrapt too long,
> Assumes the accents of our native tongue;
> And he who guides the plow, or wields the crook,
> With understanding spirit now may look
> Upon her records, listen to her song,
> And sift her laws,—much wondering that the wrong,
> Which faith has suffered, Heaven could calmly brook,
> Transcendent boon! noblest that earthly king
> Ever bestowed to equalize and bless
> Under the weight of mortal wretchedness.[31]

A portion of Wycliff's Bible from John 17:1-3 reads:

> "These thingis Jesus spak; and whanne he hadde cast up hise eyen into thi hevene, he seide: 'Fadir, the our cometh; clarifie thi sone, that thi sone clarifie thee; as thou hast yovun to hym power on ech fleische, that al thing that thou hast yovun to hym, he yyve to hem everlastynge lilf. And this is everlastynge lilf, that thei knowe thee very God aloone and whom thou hast sent, Jesu Christ."[32]

Understandably, the Catholic reaction was sheer panic! While one priest lamented, "The jewel of the clergy has become the toy of the laity,"[33] Henry de Knyghton elaborated:

> This Master John Wiclif hath translated the gospel out of Latin into English, which Christ had intrusted with the *clergy and doctors* of the Church, that *they* might minister it to the laity and weaker sort, according to the state of the times and wants of men. So that, by this means, the gospel is made vulgar and made more open to the laity . . . than it used to be to the *most learned* of the clergy and those of the best understanding! And what was before the chief gift of the clergy and doctors of the Church, is made for ever common to the laity.[34]

As would be the case with Martin Luther, Wycliff was providentially spared the martyr's stake, succumbing to a stroke while officiating in his church at age sixty-four in the year 1384. His enemies were ecstatic, the prelate Walsingham eulogizing:

> On the feast of the passion of St. Thomas of Canterbury, John Wicklif—that organ of the devil, that enemy of the Church, that author of confusion to the common people, that idol of heretics, that image of hypocrites, that restorer of schism, that storehouse of lies, that sink of flattery—being struck by the horrible judgment of God, was struck with palsy, and continued to live in that condition until St. Sylvester's Day, on which he breathed out his malicious spirit into the abodes of darkness.[35]

However, although history has forgotten the name Walsingham, the name of Chaucer has lived on, perhaps in consequence of *his* memorial to Wycliff:

> A good man was there of religioun
> That was a pore Persone of a town;
> But rich he was of holy thought and werk;
> He was also a lerned man, a clerk,
> That Christes gospel trewly wolde preche.
>
> This noble ensample to his shepe he gaf,
> **That first he wrought and after that he taught.**
>
> A better priest I trow that nowhere non is,
> He waited after no pompe ne reverence;
> Ne maked him no spiced conscience,
> But Christes lore and his apostles twelve
> He taught, **but first he folwed it himselve.**[36]

(As an interesting aside, Wycliff's influence may have been a factor in Chaucer's later renunciation of his life's works—*The Canterbury Tales, Troilus and Criseyde,* and *The Book of the Duchess* as "worldly vanities," having expressed the burden "that I may be one of those at the day of doom that shall be saved."[37])

The wrath of the Nicolaitanes exploded in 1401 with the following decree being passed by Parliament:

> Our sovereign lord the King, . . . by the assent of the estates and other discreet men . . . assembled in Parliament, has granted, established and ordained that no one within the . . . realm or any other dominions subject to his royal Majesty shall presume to preach openly or secretly without first seeking and obtaining the license of the local diocesan, always excepting curates in their own churches, persons who have hitherto been so privileged, and others permitted by canon law; and that henceforth no one either openly or secretly shall preach, hold, teach or instruct, or produce or write any book, contrary to the Catholic faith or the determination of holy Church, nor shall any of the [Lollard] sect hold conventicles (unorganized gatherings for worship) anywhere or in any way keep or maintain schools for its wicked doctrines and opinions; and also that henceforth no one shall in any way favor anybody who thus preaches, conducts such or similar conventicles, keeps or maintains such schools, produces or writes such books, or in any such manner teaches, informs or excites the people . . .
>
> And if any person within the said kingdom and dominions is convicted by sentence before the local diocesan or his commissioners of the said wicked preachings, doctrines, opinions, schools and heretical and erroneous instruction, or any of them, and if he refuses duly to abjure the same . . . , then the sheriff of the county . . . and the mayor and sheriffs or sheriff, or the mayor and bailiffs of the city, town or borough . . . nearest the said diocesan or his said commissioners . . . , shall, after such sentences are proclaimed, receive those persons . . . **and shall cause them to be burned before the people in a prominent place**, in order that such punishment may strike fear into the minds of others, to the end that no wicked doctrines and heretical and erroneous opinions (against the Catholic faith, the Christian law, and the determination of holy Church), nor their authors and favorers, be sustained . . . or in any way tolerated.[38]

In the year 1415, the Council of Constance had Wycliff's books and bones burned and the ashes dumped in the Severn River (which flowed through his town). Thomas Fuller remarking:

Thus this brook has conveyed his ashes into Avon, Avon into Severn, Severn into the narrow seas, they into the main ocean. And thus the ashes of Wiclif are the emblem of his doctrine, which is now dispersed all the world over.[39]

Because of such edicts, many godly Lollards were not as fortunate as their spiritual father. Local prosecutors' records tell of groups meeting here and there to read "in a great book of heresy *all one night* certain chapters of the evangelists in English."[40] Foxe adding:

The Lollards were tracked to the lonely, unfrequented places where they met, often under shadow of night, to worship God. Neighbor was made to spy upon neighbor; husbands and wives, parents and children, brothers and sisters, were beguiled or forced to bear witness against each other. The Lollards' prison again echoed with the clanking of chains; the rack and the stake once more claimed their victims.[41]

Convictingly enough for today's lukewarm Christians, one of the common charges brought against these godly believers was not only their *possession* of a Wycliff Bible but their ability ". . . to repeat from it by heart."[42]

Among the many burning victims were: John Badby, a tailor, 1410; two London merchants, Richard Turming and John Claydon at Smithfield, 1415; William Taylor in 1423; William White, 1428; Richard Hoveden, 1430; Thomas Bagley, 1431; and Richard Wyche in 1440.[43]

Joan Broughton became the first woman to burn at the stake in England, perishing at Smithfield with her daughter, Lady Young, beside her![44]

The history of the *real* English Bible is a history *unlike that of the NIV and other generic counterfeits constructed with a preference for* א *and B*; it is a history that is **bathed in blood**. Foxe continues:

One Christopher Shoemaker, who was burned alive at Newbury, was accused of having gone to the house of John Say, and "read to him, out of a book, the words which Christ spake to his disciples . . . " In 1519 seven martyrs were burned in one fire at Coventry, "for having taught their children and servants the Lord's prayer and the ten commandments in English . . ." Jenkin Butler accused his own brother of reading to him a certain book of Scripture, and persuading him to hearken unto the same. John Barret, goldsmith, of London, was arrested for having recited to his wife and maid-servant the Epistle of St. James, without a book ... Thomas Phillip and Lawrence Taylor were arrested for reading the Epistle to the Romans and the first chapter of St. Luke in English.[45]

In picturesque fulfillment of Fuller's analogy, Wycliff's ashes had barely reached Bohemia (modern Czechoslovakia) before the godly Englishman was being honored posthumously as "The Fifth Evangelist."[46] A full thirteen years before the reformer's corpse was desecrated, John Hus (1372-1415) was recognized as the outstanding advocate of "heretical Wycliffism" at the University of Prague. This spreading of Wycliff's doctrine by Hus resulted in Bohemia's treasured legacy as "The Cradle of the Reformation." Schaff writing on Hus:

> It was well known that it was Wyclif's cause which he was representing and Wycliffian views that he was defending, and Wyclif's writings were wide open to the eye of members of the university faculties. He made no secret of following Wyclif, and being willing to die for the views Wyclif taught. As he wrote to Richard Wyche, he was thankful that "under the power of Jesus Christ, Bohemia had received so much good **from the blessed land of England.**"[47]

At the Roman Catholic Council of Constance where Hus was betrayed and condemned to die, the official sentence also credited an **English** spark with having ignited the flames of European reformation:

> The holy council, having God only before its eye, condemns John Huss to have been and to be a true, real and open heretic, the disciple not of Christ **but of John Wyclif.**[48]

The influence of England's first Bible translator can also be traced, indirectly, to the Florentine reformer, Girolamo Savonarola (1452-1498). Placed at the feet of Luther and at the side of Wycliff and Hus in the monument of the Reformation at Worms, the converted Dominican was reached primarily through the ministry of the **Bohemian** Brethren.[49]

Wycliff's primacy for Scripture can be seen in Savonarola's disdain for his ignorant contemporaries, writing:

> The theologians of our time have soiled everything by their unseemly disputations as with pitch. They do not know a shred of the Bible, yea, they do not even know the names of its books.[50]

The courage of Wycliff can be seen in Savonarola's sermons, described by Schaff as "flashes of lightning and reverberations of thunder."[51] Denouncing the standard abuses of Catholicism, he wrote:

> It begins in Rome where the clergy make mock of Christ and the saints; yea, are worse than Turks and worse than Moors. They traffic in the sacraments. They sell benefices to the highest bidder. Have not the priests in Rome courtesans and grooms and horses and dogs? Have they not palaces full of tapestries and silks, of perfumes and lackeys? Seemeth it, that this is the church of God?[52]

Two years before inciting a mob to bring Savonarola to the stake, the perverse Alexander VI had his bribe of a "red hat" (cardinal's position) scorned, the reformer declaring his preference for a crimson crown, *reddened with blood.*[53]

With so much influence stemming from a solitary English translator during the primitive manuscript era, the coming of Gutenberg's moveable type was destined to "blow the doors off." And with the first full-length book printed being the Gutenberg Bible in 1456 (a Latin Vulgate which took six months to typeset), the proverbial "handwriting" was seen on the wall. While Martin Luther called the art of printing "the last and best gift of Providence,"[54] the Catholic Rowland Phillips, in a sermon preached at St. Paul's Cross, London, in the year 1535, frightfully remarked, "We must root out printing or printing will root us out."[55]

Rome's paranoia with the resurgence of God's Word was also manifested against the study of Hebrew and Greek (in vogue since the fall of Constantinople in 1453 forced a westward retreat of Greek scholars and manuscripts). The University of Cologne's Conrad of Hersbach warned:

> They have found a language called Greek, at which we must be careful to be on our guard. It is the mother of all heresies. In the hands of many persons I see a book, which they call the New Testament. **It is a book full of thorns and poison.** As for Hebrew, my brethren, it is certain that those who learn it will sooner or later turn Jews.[56]

Rome's fears were justified, as her corner on the market of ignorance was about to be shattered. Durant relates about sixteenth-century Europe:

Literacy was spreading. Books were pouring forth from sixteen publishers in Basel, twenty in Augsburg, twenty-one in Cologne, twenty-four in Nuremberg; . . . The trade in books was a major line in the busy commerce of the fairs at Frankfurt, Salzburg, Nördlingen, and Ulm. "Everybody nowadays wants to read and write," said a contemporary German; and another reported: "There is no end to the new books that are written."[57]

One of the notable participants in this age of intellectual renewal was the Rotterdam scholar, Desiderius Erasmus (1469-1536). As mentioned in a previous chapter, he is credited with producing the first printed edition of the Greek New Testament (1517). Because of this epoch-making contribution to the history of the English Bible (his five pioneer editions, especially his third, would set the standard for the follow-up works of Stephen, Beza and Elzevir—all decidedly anti-‍א and B), his character, scholarship and spirituality have been continuously assailed by opponents of the King James Bible.

If Erasmus was a "deadbeat," the government heads of Europe were too busy courting his citizenship to take notice; he was offered and declined professorships at the Universities of Leipzig and Ingolstadt; Frances I invited him to his personal court in France; Pope Paul III attempted to entice him to Italy with a cardinal's hat; and King Charles of the Netherlands offered him a position as a personal counselor. The man known as the "journalist of scholarship" received the following invitation from country number *five*:

I propose therefore that you abandon all thought of settling elsewhere. Come to **England**, and assure yourself of a hearty welcome. You shall name your own terms; they shall be as liberal and honorable as you please . . . We shall regard your presence among us as the most precious possession that we have . . . We shall ask nothing of you save to make our realm your home . . . Come to me, therefore, my dear Erasmus, and let your presence be your answer to my invitation.[58] (Henry VIII, King of England)

Although grounded early in Catholicism through no fault of his own (an uncle sent him and his brother to a Catholic monastery after the plague-related deaths of their parents), Erasmus was orthodox enough to speak out against the Church's manifold abuses, reject her Vulgate readings, and manifest the most non-Catholic attitude of all—*an intense burden to put God's Word into the hands of the common man.* Erasmus, writing of the Scriptures, says:

I would have those words translated into all languages, so
that not only Scots and Irishmen, but Turks and Saracens might
read them. I long for the plowboy to sing them to himself as he
follows the plow, the weaver to hum them to the tune of his
shuttle, the traveler to beguile with them the dullness of his
journey.[59]

This holy desire was soon to be realized. In 1534, Martin
Luther (1483-1546) used Erasmus' second edition to bestow upon
his beloved Germany her first complete Bible inspiring the
Reformation adage, "Erasmus laid the egg and Luther hatched
it."[60] (Was it mere coincidence that Erasmus' first edition was
printed the very year [1517] that Luther posted his 95 theses?)

Other native translations followed quickly: the French versions
of Lefevre and Olivetan, 1534 and 1535; Biestkens' Dutch work
in 1558; the Swedish Uppsala Bible by Laurentius in 1541; a
Spanish translation by Cassiodoro de Reyna in 1569; the Danish
Christian III Bible in 1550; the Czech version of 1602 and the
Italian translation by Diodati in 1607, to name but a few.

However, as history confirms a distinctive *westbound*
movement of truth, the full force of Erasmus' labors were yet to
be felt. As all of Europe lay within the reach of threatening papal
armies, the time for "Japheth's enlargement" (Genesis 9:27) had
come. Known only to the mind of God, the ultimate manifestation
of His Word was destined for another language, *English*, and in
another land, *America*, **a safe 3,400 miles from "His
Holiness."** The era of Tyndale had arrived!

William Tyndale was born about 1483 near the village of
North Nibley. Ordained to the priesthood in 1502, he
distinguished himself at Oxford, earning his M.A. in 1515. He
later transferred to Cambridge where he became acquainted with
Erasmus and his Greek New Testament. While undergoing this
time of reflection, he experienced a spiritual enlightenment
similar to that of Luther.

The more he studied this new-found treasure, the deeper his
burden became for his fellow Englishmen to share in the same.
It was during this formative period that Tyndale's classic
exchange occurred with a certain fanatical papist. Antagonized by
his inability to refute Tyndale's Biblical reasoning, the
exasperated priest shouted, "It were better for us to be without
God's laws than the Pope's," whereupon an indignant Tyndale
rejoined:

I defy the Pope, and all his laws; and if God spare my life, ere
many years, **I will cause a boy that driveth the plough to
know more of the Scripture than *you* do!**[61]

With these daring words representing his lifelong motivation,
Tyndale set out to deliver his benighted countrymen from the
hopelessness of Romanism, declaring:

> *Which thing only moved me to translate the New Testament.*
> Because I had perceived by experience, how that it was
> impossible to establish the lay people in any truth, *except the
> Scriptures were plainly laid before their eyes in the mother
> tongue.*[62]

Tyndale's request for lodging with the renowned Cuthbert
Tonstal, Bishop of London, was met with a cool rejection. As the
Bethlehem innkeeper denied shelter to the "living" Word, the
indifferent prelate turned a similar deaf ear to Tyndale's labor
pains for the "written" Word, neither proprietor having known
the time of their visitation.

The Lord countered this snubbing by sending Tyndale a
sympathetic merchant who not only opened his London residence
to the reformer, but paid him 10£ sterling to pray for his "father
and mother, their souls, and all Christian souls."[63] However, after
six months of translating, Tyndale detected an augmented
hostility by the local officials against his project. Much of this
pressure was attributable to Henry VIII's appeasement of Rome
in anticipation of his controversial application for annulment of
his marriage to the "sonless" Queen Catherine. Tyndale sadly
concluded:

> Wherefore I perceived that not only in the bishop of London's
> palace, but in all England, there was no room for attempting a
> translation of the Scriptures.[64]

In the face of such foreboding conditions, Tyndale departed his
homeland for Germany in 1524, little knowing that he would
never again set foot on English soil. (Ironically, Foxe called
Tyndale, "The Apostle of England."[65]) With an initial lodging
secured in Hamburg, the fugitive made an immediate pilgrimage
to Wittenberg.[66] The patronage denied Tyndale by Tonstal was
more than compensated for by the audacious Dr. Luther who
would unashamedly assert, "I have been born to war and fight
with factions and devils."[67]

Dr. J. R. Green captured the contagion of Luther's spirit with his narrative of Tyndale's visit:

> We find him on his way to the little town which had suddenly become the sacred city of the Reformation. Students of all nations were flocking there with an enthusiasm which resembled that of the Crusades. "As they came in sight of the town," a contemporary tells us, "they returned thanks to God with clasped hands, for from Wittenberg as heretofore from Jerusalem the light of evangelical truth had spread to the utmost parts of the earth." It was at Luther's instance that Tyndale translated there the gospels and epistles.[68]

Tyndale would receive much courage for his future trials from the rugged German whose personal outlook on troublemakers was that, "You cannot meet a rebel with reason. Your best answer is punch him in the face until he has a bloody nose."[69]

With his heart stirred, Tyndale commenced his pioneer effort of producing an English Bible translated directly from the original languages. His was an exceptional endowment for such a momentous venture. The professor Herman Buschius described Tyndale to Spalatin as:

> A man so skilled in the seven languages, *Hebrew*, Greek, Latin, Italian, Spanish, English, and French, that which ever he spake, you would suppose it his native tongue.[70]

This erudition was confirmed by Tyndale's appearance before the Cologne printers Quental and Byrchmann before a year was expired. However, unbeknown to Tyndale, Luther's archenemy, the Catholic theologian John Cochlaeus, Dean of the Church of the Blessed Virgin at Frankfurt, was hot on his trail. By now, the Catholics in Germany were fit to be tied with Bibles coming out of their ears, Cochlaeus complaining:

> Luther's New Testament was so much multiplied and spread by printers that even tailors and shoemakers, yea, even women and ignorant persons who had accepted this new Lutheran gospel, and could read a little German, studied it with the greatest avidity as the fountain of all truth. Some committed it to memory, and carried it about in their bosom. In a few months such people deemed themselves so learned that they were not ashamed to dispute about faith and the gospel not only with Catholic laymen, but even with priests and monks and doctors of divinity.[71]

Cochlaeus was not about to allow this nightmare to spread into England. One day he accidentally overheard some printers discussing Tyndale's work. By loosening them up with some wine, he was startled to discover that an English New Testament was already in the press. After seeing only ten sheets completed, Tyndale was warned of the approaching magistrates. Aided by his amanuensis, William Roye, he was able to transfer the precious documents to Worms, leaving one frustrated "father" in the dust.

From the comparative safety of Luther's "backyard," the first 3,000 copies of Tyndale's New Testament were completed in 1525 by the Worms printer, Schoeffer, and smuggled back to England in barrels, bales of cloth and sacks of flour. Unlike Wycliff's translation from Latin manuscripts, Tyndale's work was directly from the Greek, but more than that—from the *Textus Receptus* of Erasmus' second and third editions. (Erasmus rejected the Vulgate's ℵ and B readings, paving the way for hundreds of Smithfield martyrs to perish over the Majority Text.)

Having been alerted by Cochlaeus of the pending "importation of pernicious merchandise,"[72] the English clergy were watching the ports. Many of the Bibles were intercepted and ceremoniously burned at St. Paul's Cross in London by Tonstal who called it, "a burnt offering most pleasing to Almighty God."[73] The smug bishop claimed to have found 2,000 errors in it. Sir Thomas More added, "To study to find errors in Tyndale's book were like studying to find water in the sea."[74] (More was later beheaded.)

Undaunted, Tyndale exclaimed in the spirit of his German mentor:

> In burning the book they did none other thing than I looked for; no more shall they do if they burn me also, if it be God's will that it should be so.[75]

However, despite this devilish effort, many of the reproachful volumes were dispersed throughout the land (about 50,000 by some estimates[76]). The pains taken to protect these New Testaments can be gleaned from a sober believer who wrote:

> Fierce whiskered guards that volume sought in vain,
> Enjoyed by stealth, and hid with anxious pain;
> While all around was misery and gloom,
> This shewed the boundless bliss beyond the tomb;
> Freed from the venal priest,—the feudal rod,
> It led the sufferer's weary steps to God:
> And when his painful course on earth was run,
> This, his chief wealth, descended to his son.[77]

That the liberating power of Tyndale's New Testament was cause for alarm with the Catholics is evidenced by Bishop Nikke's letter to his superior, which read in part: "It passeth my power, or that of any spiritual man, to hinder it now, and if this continue much longer it will undo us all."[78]

With the heat turned up, Tyndale removed himself to Marburg in 1528, where he was protected by Philip the Magnanimous, Landgrave of Hesse. After working on the Pentateuch for about a year, he set sail for Hamburg but suffered shipwreck and the loss of a freshly completed manuscript of Deuteronomy.

After a delayed arrival in Hamburg, he took residence with an elderly widow, Margaret Van Emmerson, where he completed his translation of Genesis through Deuteronomy. Upon his appearance in the free city of Antwerp (to arrange for the printing of these new books), he devised an ingenious plan for replenishing badly needed funds. Here it was learned that the foolish Bishop Tonstal, driven to desperation by the spreading of Tyndale's New Testaments, had attempted to save the day by removing them from the market via legitimate purchase. However, unbeknown to Tonstal, the intermediary merchant which he had approached, Augustine Pakington, was a sympathetic supporter of Tyndale. Foxe picks up this marvelous account of poetic justice:

> A few weeks later Pakington entered the humble lodging of Tyndale, whose funds he knew were at a low ebb. "Master Tyndale," said he, "I have found you a good purchaser for your books." "Who is he?" asked Tyndale. "My lord bishop of London." "But if the bishop wants the books it must be only to burn them." "Well," was the reply of the shrewd merchant, "what of that? The bishop will burn them anyhow, and it is best that you should have the money to print others instead." And so the bargain was made: "The bishop had the books, Pakington had the thanks, and Tyndale had the money." "I am the gladder," quoth Tyndale, "for these two benefits shall come of it: I shall get money to bring myself out of debt, and the whole world will cry out against the burning of God's Word. The overplus of the money that remains shall enable me to correct the said New Testament, and then newly to print the same again, and I trust the second will be much better then ever was the first that I printed." After this the newly printed Testaments came thick and fast into England. The bishop then sent for Pakington again and asked how it came that the books were still so abundant. "My lord," replied the merchant, "truly I think it were best for you to buy up the stamps too by which they are

imprinted." *That this advice was not followed it is needless to
state.*[79]

With the profit from this newest "customer," Tyndale released
his Pentateuch in 1530 through the printing house of Hans Luft,
Marsburg, with his translation of Jonah being published in
Antwerp the following year.

About this time the church's animosity towards Tyndale was
at an all-time high. In addition to the despised translations, his
various diatribes against Rome were not winning him many
friends: *The Parable of the Wicked Mammon* in 1528; *The
Obedience of a Christen Man and How Christe Rulers Ought to
Governe* in 1530; and his *Practyse of Prelates* also in 1530. One of
his marginal notes in Jonah likened England to Nineveh.

Early in 1535, a trusting Tyndale was betrayed by an
undercover Catholic agent, Henry Phillips, who had gained the
reformer's confidence. Following Phillips' last-minute borrowing
of forty shillings from his generous victim, the pair departed
Tyndale's boardinghouse for dinner. The treacherous Phillips
pretentiously insisted on his "friend" going before him. Once
outside the door, Phillips, in the spirit of Judas Iscariot, pointed
at him from behind his back, as the prearranged sign for waiting
officials. The aged saint was promptly committed to the dungeon
of the nearby fortress of Vilvorde, eighteen miles north of
Antwerp.[80]

As his Master's arraignment before Pilate, Tyndale's character
was unquestioned, impressing even the emperor's prosecutor to
regard him as, "homo, doctus, pius, et bonus," – "a learned, pious
and good man."[81]

Throughout his eighteen-month imprisonment, Tyndale
suffered accordingly. One of the saddest extant documents in all
of church history (taken from the archives of the Council of
Brabant) is a letter written in Latin and in the reformer's own
hand to the governor of Vilvorde, perhaps the Marquis of Bergon:

> I believe, right worshipful, that you are not unaware of what
> may have been determined concerning me. Wherefore I beg your
> lordship, and that by the Lord Jesus, that if I am to remain here
> through the winter, you will request the commissary to have the
> kindness to send me, from the goods of mine which he has, a
> warmer cap, for I suffer greatly from cold in the head, and am
> afflicted by a perpetual catarrh, which is much increased in this
> cell; a warmer coat also, for this which I have is very thin; a piece
> of cloth, too, to patch my leggings. My overcoat is worn out; my
> shirts also are worn out. He has a woollen shirt, if he will be

good enough to send it. I have also with him leggings of thicker cloth to put on above; he has also warmer night-caps.

And I ask to be allowed to have a lamp in the evening; it is indeed wearisome sitting alone in the dark. But **most of all** I beg and beseech your clemency to be urgent with the commissary, that he will kindly **permit me to have the Hebrew Bible, Hebrew grammar and Hebrew dictionary, that I may pass the time in that study.** In return may you obtain what you most desire, so only that it be for the salvation of your soul. But if any other decision has been taken concerning me, to be carried out before winter, I will be patient, abiding the will of God, to the glory of the grace of my Lord Jesus Christ; whose Spirit (I pray) may ever direct your heart. Amen.   W. Tindalus[82]

Indeed it was the Lord's will not only for His servant to pass through that winter but the following spring and summer as well. We are confident that he recovered his linguistic aids as he left behind the completed translation of Joshua through II Chronicles.

With the autumn leaves of 1536 signaling the sure approach of another winter, the time for Tyndale's departure had arrived. Condemned by the emperor's decree in the assembly at Augsburg, the date of execution was set for October 6. Foxe transports us to the somber scene:

Brought forth to the place of execution, he was tied to the stake, strangled by the hangman, and afterwards consumed with fire, at the town of Vilvorde, A.D. 1536; crying at the stake with a fervent zeal, and a loud voice, **"Lord! open the King of England's eyes."**[83]

As the faithful Tyndale was concluding his life's work with a last, garbled prayer for the King's illumination, he could not have known that Heaven's answer was already on the way. McClure relates the miraculous testimony that:

What is strangest of all, and is unexplained to this day, at the very time when Tyndale by the procurement of English ecclesiastics, and by the sufferance of the English king, was burned at Vilvorde, a folio-edition of his Translation was printed at *London*, with his name on the title-page, and by Thomas Berthelet, the king's own patent printer. **This was the first copy of the Scriptures ever printed on English ground.**[84]

Yet even more significant than this mysterious stroke of Providence was the official sanctioning *by Henry himself* of *two* English Bibles within a year of Tyndale's martyrdom. The first of these was the Coverdale Bible, named after Tyndale's former proofreader at Antwerp, Miles Coverdale (1488-1569).

The Coverdale Bible holds the unique honor of representing the first *complete* English Bible ever printed. Like Wycliff, Coverdale was deficient in the original languages so his work consisted of Tyndale's New Testament and Pentateuch with the remaining Old Testament books being rendered primarily from Luther's German translation, with moderate indebtedness to the Vulgate and the Swiss Zurich Bible.

Although Coverdale was forced to publish his first edition in Cologne (1535), he very prudently dedicated it to the King of England and was also careful to exclude the controversial style of marginal notes associated with the Tyndale Bible. It is not hard to understand Henry's willingness to personally license such a Bible (Coverdale Second Edition of 1537) when the cover page shows him seated and crowned, with a drawn sword and a dedicatory page crediting him as "defender of the faith."

Coverdale's diplomacy was in keeping with the King's recent break with Rome over control of the English churches. Although not a renouncing of Catholic doctrine, the Act of Supremacy approved by Parliament on November 11, 1534, was certainly a major step towards an English Reformation.

The second Bible to gain official sanction that year was another adventure in discretion. Known as the Matthew Bible, this translation was actually made by John Rogers (c. 1500-1555) who used the pseudonym Thomas Matthew because of his well-known association with Tyndale. The Matthew Bible's fundamental improvement was the valuable inclusion of Tyndale's "dungeon works" of Joshua through II Chronicles. With Tyndale's Pentateuch and New Testament basically intact, the Coverdale Bible filled in the gap as Rogers secured some assistance from the French versions of Lefevre and Olivetan. Like the Coverdale Bible, Rogers' was also licensed by the King which made it legal to buy, read, reprint or sell.

On the lighter side, the Matthew Bible is sometimes referred to as the "Wife-Beater's Bible" because of the anti-ERA note at I Peter 3 which reads,

> "If she be not obedient and healpfull unto hym [he] endeavoureth to beate the feare of God into her heade, that therby she maye be compelled to learne her dutie, and to do it."[85]

Next came the Great Bible of 1538, named after its exceptional size at 16½" by 11". This was basically a revision of the Matthew

Bible by Miles Coverdale with little change apart from the excising of Rogers' controversial marginal notes. The Great Bible had the distinction of being the first Bible to be officially authorized for public use in England's churches, being required to be literally chained to some piece of church furniture where the parishioners might "resort to the same and read it."[86] With Henry's obesity perhaps forcing thoughts of eternity upon him (having gotten so fat that the had to be hoisted upon his horse by pulleys), the King officially sanctioned the Great Bible with, "In God's name, let it go abroad among our people!"[87] No doubt Tyndale smiled and for obvious reasons. On January 28, 1547, Henry VIII himself went the way of all the earth.

The new king, Edward VI, was certainly a breath of fresh air as he was decidedly *Protestant* (the son of Jane Seymour who died twelve days after his birth). Although a sickly lad of but nine, he showed an exceptional devotion to spiritual things, McClure writing:

> This intellectual and pious child was one of those "who trembled at God's Word," which he loved and venerated; and which had "free course and was glorified" during his brief reign. At his coronation, three swords were brought, to be carried before him, in token that three realms were subject to his sway. The precocious prince said that yet another sword must be brought; and when the attending nobles asked what sword that might be, he answered,—"The Bible!" That, said he, "is the sword of the Spirit, and is to be preferred before these swords. That ought, in all right, to govern us, who use the others for the people's safety, by God's appointment." Adding some similar expressions, he commanded the Sacred Volume to be brought, and to be borne reverently before him in the grand procession.[88]

Before succumbing to consumption at age sixteen (1553), the pious Edward would authorize thirty-five editions of the New Testament, and fourteen of the entire Bible.[89]

Such a saturation of Scripture was a providential stroke in preparation for the following six years of Bloody Queen Mary (daughter of Catherine). Because she was as fanatically Catholic as her half-brother was Protestant, hundreds of Englishmen fled to the Continent in anticipation of the wrath to come.

A number of these intellectual pilgrims rendezvoused in Geneva (known as the Holy City of the Alps) to form the first *committee* to attempt a translation of the Bible. Such men as Theodore Beza, John Knox, William Whittingham and Miles Coverdale labored six years to produce the celebrated Geneva

Bible in 1560. Although this Bible was the first to feature numbered verses and italics, its main achievement was the Hebrew to English rendering of Ezra through Malachi, thus representing *the first English Bible translated entirely out of the original languages.*

With the highly promoted Bishops' Bible of Queen Elizabeth's reign (1568) never getting off the ground (the only improvements being cosmetic; i.e, lots of pictures, thicker, more expensive paper, etc.), the Geneva Bible remained the people's Bible until the 1611 Authorized Version.

However, in keeping with our chapter title, "Bathed in Blood," 300 English Christians were called upon to keep the home fires burning *literally* by perishing in the flames of Smithfield.

As fate would have it, John Rogers became the "protomartyr" of Mary Tudor's reign of terror, Foxe recording:

> On the 4th of February, in the year 1555, in the morning, the prisoner was warned suddenly by the keeper's wife, to prepare himself for the fire. Being sound asleep, he could scarcely be awakened. At length being roused, and told to make haste, he said, "Is then this the day? If it be so, I need not be careful of my dressing."
>
> Now when the time had come, the prisoner was brought from Newgate to Smithfield, the place of his execution. Here Woodroofe, one of the sheriffs, asked him if he would change his religion to save his life; but Rogers answered, **"That which I have preached I will seal with my blood."** . . . It is related, that "Rogers' wife and eleven children, ten of whom were able to walk and one was at the breast, met him by the way as he went toward Smithfield (repeating the 51st Psalm). This sorrowful sight of his own flesh and blood did not move him; but he constantly and cheerfully took his death with wonderful patience in the defence of Christ's Gospel."[90]

Green adds that, "he died *bathing his hands in the flames* as if it had been in cold water."[91]

Truly did John the Beloved write, *"And I saw the woman drunken with the blood of the saints, and with the blood of the martyrs of Jesus"* (Revelation 17:6a). Beloved, these brothers and sisters laid down their lives for the readings contained in the King James Bible! **How can we forget them?**

A young boy was brought before the evil Bishop Bonner who asked him if he thought he could bear the flame, whereupon the courageous lad, without flinching, placed his hand into the flame of a nearby candle.[92]

Shall we dismiss the sweet Joan Clarke who was obliged to light the fagots that were to burn her own father, William Tilfrey, in 1506?[93] What of the crippled, sixty-eight-year-old Hugh Laverick being burned alongside the blind John Aprice on May 15, 1556? Foxe relating:

> When Hugh Laverick was secured by the chain, having no further occasion for his crutch, he threw it away saying to his fellow-martyr, while consoling him, "Be of good cheer my brother; for my lord of London is our good physician; he will heal us both shortly—thee of thy blindness, and me of my lameness." They sank down in the fire, to rise to immortality![94]

Are we to abandon *their* Bible to embrace the readings of their murderers? Can we disavow Thomas Watts' kissing of his own stake?[95] Or James Baynham's brave words, "for in this fire I feel no more pain than if I were in bed; for it is as sweet to me as a bed of roses."[96] Is one Collins to be unremembered after burning at the stake *alongside his own dog?*[97] Or how about the memories of Martin Bucer and Paulus Phagius whose dead bodies were dug up and, while still in their coffins, chained to the stake and burned?[98] In the Channel Islands, a pregnant woman was even burned at the stake. *While suffering the flames, the woman delivered her baby, only to have "the fair man-child" retrieved and cast back to the mother's side to be burned with her.*[99]

There is only one story that can adequately conclude our chapter, "Bathed in Blood." It is the moving letter of a condemned prisoner attempting to encourage a number of fellow victims. However, Richard Roth's epistle is probably unlike any that you have ever seen before. When you reach the closing, you will know why it was reproduced in its entirety:

O dear Brethren and Sisters,
How much reason have you to rejoice in God, that He hath given you such faith to overcome this bloodthirsty tyrant (Bishop Bonner) thus far! And no doubt He that hath begun that good work in you, will fulfill it unto the end. O dear hearts in Christ, what a crown of glory shall ye receive with Christ in the kingdom of God! O that it had been the good will of God that I had been ready to have gone with you; for I lie in my lord's Little-ease by day, and in the night I lie in the Coalhouse, apart from Ralph Allerton, or any other; and we look every day when we shall be condemned; for he said that I should be burned within ten days before Easter; but I lie still at the pool's brink, and every man goeth in before me; but we abide patiently the Lord's leisure,

with many bonds, in fetters and stocks, by which we have received great joy of God. And now fare you well, dear brethren and sisters, in this world, but I trust to see you in the heavens face to face.

O brother Munt, with your wife and my sister Rose, how blessed are you in the Lord, that God hath found you worthy to suffer for His sake! with all the rest of my dear brethren and sisters known and unknown. O be joyful unto death. Fear it not, saith Christ, for I have overcome death. O dear heart, seeing that Jesus Christ will be our help, O tarry you at the Lord's leisure. Be strong, let your hearts be of good comfort, and wait you still for the Lord. He is at hand. Yea, the angel of the Lord pitcheth His tent round about them that fear Him, and delivereth them which way he seeth best. For our lives are in the Lord's hands; and they can do nothing unto us before God suffer them. Therefore give thanks to God.

O dear hearts, you shall be clothed in long white garments upon the mount of Sion, with the multitude of saints and with Jesus Christ our Savior, who will never forsake us. O blessed virgins, ye have played the wise virgins' part, in that ye have taken oil in your lamps that ye may go in with the Bridegroom, when he cometh into the everlasting joy with Him. But as for the foolish, they shall be shut out, because they made not themselves ready to suffer with Christ, neither go about to take up His cross. O dear hearts, how precious shall your death be in the sight of the Lord! for dear is the death of His saints. O fare you well, and pray. The grace of our Lord Jesus Christ be with you all. Amen, Amen. Pray, pray, pray!

Written by me, **with my own blood,**
"Richard Roth"[100]

(Roth was burned September 17, 1557.)

X

Hampton Court

"Where the word of a king is,
there is power."
(Ecclesiastes 8:4a)

The dawn of November 17, 1558, found "Bloody" Mary dead. The murders of 300 Christians including Ridley, Latimer and Cranmer had left her nearly insane. It has been suggested to this author that the epithet "Bloody" was not so much in consequence of her villainous character as it was in the idea of her being *cursed* by the "blood" of Christ. The degeneracy of this application has insured Mary's anathema the infamous distinction of having become the filthiest word in an Englishman's vocabulary. Because *"he that sitteth in the heavens shall laugh"* (Psalm 2:4), her efforts to revive a British subjection to Rome backfired profoundly.

In the spirit of Tertullian's "the blood of the martyrs is the seed of the church," Newman states:

> This persecution aroused a mighty reaction that made England forever Protestant. It has well been said that "the excesses of this bloody reaction accomplished more for the Protestantization of England than all the efforts put forth under Edward's reign." [1]

With the ascendancy of the "throned vestal," Elizabeth's forty-five-year reign became a paradox of Scripture proliferation (one hundred thirty different editions of the Bible and New Testament being issued[2]) offset by a policy of religio-political expediency.

The twenty-five-year-old queen wisely inaugurated her rule

with Proverbs 25:5 in mind: *"Take away the wicked from before the king, and his throne shall be established in righteousness."* As the embers of Smithfield were still smoldering, Elizabeth outlawed all Catholic services and literature, destroyed religious images and required oaths of allegiance for all clergymen, educators, lawyers, magistrates and university graduates. The first offense of espousing papal authority over England was punishable with life imprisonment; the second, by capital punishment. By 1590, all of England's churches were Protestant.

However, with three-fourths of her subjects professing Catholicism, she made some attempt to pacify them by retaining an element of their liturgy within the Anglican services. Latourette writes:

> Yet she wished such an ordering of the Church of England as would satisfy as many of her subjects as possible. Therefore she sought to make it include both Catholic and Protestant elements.[3]

Obviously, such actions strained relations with the Puritan majority (of England's Protestants) dedicated to a "purifying" of Catholic elements. Elizabeth's ultimate attempt at distancing herself from such rabble-rousers was seen in her challenging of the Geneva Bible with the highly promoted Bishops' Bible of 1568. Notwithstanding the title page depicting the Queen in royal garb accompanied by royal arms, the Bishops' Bible gained no more than a notoriety for being "a compromise—a dignified and 'safe' version for public reading."[4]

This penchant for appeasement was characteristic of the later years of Protestantism in general. Blessed by the Reformation's initial gains of one European nation after another, an inevitable complacency settled in, followed by divisive theological controversies. While Rome was regrouping at the Council of Trent, the misguided followers of Luther and Calvin began persecuting Anabaptists for "rocking the boat" (i.e., for their willingness to abstain from *any* control—state or ecclesiastical).

Green writing:

> But at the very instant of its seeming triumph, the advance of the new religion was *suddenly* arrested. The first twenty years of Elizabeth's reign were a period of suspense. The progress of Protestantism gradually ceased. It wasted its strength in theological controversies and persecutions, above all in the bitter and venomous discussions between the Churches which followed Luther and the Churches which followed Calvin. It was degraded

and weakened by the prostitution of the Reformation to political ends, by the greed and worthlessness of the German princes who espoused its cause, by the factious lawlessness of the nobles in Poland and of the Huguenots in France. Meanwhile the Papacy succeeded in rallying the Catholic world around the Council of Trent . . . At the death of Elizabeth, therefore, the temper of every Protestant, whether in England or abroad, was that of a man who, after cherishing the hope of a crowning victory, is forced to look on at a crushing and irremediable defeat. The dream of a reformation of the universal Church was utterly at an end. The borders of Protestantism were narrowing every day, nor was there a sign that the triumph of the Papacy was arrested.[5]

However, our all-wise God was not about to be caught off guard. In contradistinction to the various European translations of the Bible, another language (English) and another land (America) were subsequently elected for the remnant *within* the remnant. The greatest revivals of the New Testament age would result from the preaching of an *English* Bible, while mankind's greatest achievement of individual liberty would be inaugurated by a *Baptist* pastor in a place called "Providence" (Roger Williams' Rhode Island settlement becoming the first government in history predicated on total religious freedom established in the year 1638, a mere 27 years after the Authorized Version was completed).[6]

The responsibility for sanctioning this new English translation would fall upon another man of "Providence," his name, by Divine commemoration, becoming synonymous with the product of his decree. With the death of the seventy-year-old, heirless Elizabeth, the Tudor dynasty was replaced by the line of Stuart in the person of James I, formerly James VI of Scotland (1567-1603).

James was the son of another infamous Mary—the Catholic "Mary, Queen of Scots" (1542-1587). Following his mother's imprisonment for sedition against her half-sister, Elizabeth, James VI was crowned King of Scotland (July 29, 1567) at but thirteen months of age. (This was only five months after his father, Henry Stuart, Lord Darnley, Mary's second husband, was killed by a bomb blast in his home.) As a young man of twenty, he would come to understand why his mother professed to fear the prayers of John Knox more than all the armies of Scotland. On the 8th of February, 1587, the Queen's wig fell off her severed head as it rolled from the axeman's block; at only forty-four years of age, *her* hoary head was a crown of "gory."[7]

Because of his watershed involvement with the 1611
Authorized Version, James was destined for unprecedented
satanic opposition. In a manner reminiscent of the unscrupulous
attention directed by the press against Franklin Delano
Roosevelt's crippled legs, historians have generally begun their
similar attempt at undermining King James by surveying *his* less-
than-handsome physical features. While Strayer simply states,
"he did not inspire confidence as a political leader,"[8] the Catholic-
trained Durant noted such observations as:

> His manners were rough, his gait ungainly, his voice loud, . . .
> weak legs, slightly swollen paunch . . . knobby nose . . . stammering
> and absolute, wagging too loosely his burry tongue.[9]

Fisher digresses to his character, adding, "He lacked common
sense, could never take a comprehensive view of a great question,
and was inflated with self-conceit."[10] France's King Henry IV
called him, "the wisest fool in Christendom."[11]

This author is a bit dismayed at Durant's opinion that the
King was, "a little *lazy*, resting on Elizabeth's oars,"[12] when this
same "slouch" was able to master Latin, Greek, and French
fluently[13] by the age of *eight*, no less[14] (in addition to being
schooled in Italian and Spanish).

Furthermore, it was no mean accomplishment for James to
have gained the combined loyalties of such traditional belligerents
as the Scotch and the English people, their first ideological
rapprochement in over a millennium.

As to the King's political detractors, it is more than
coincidental that the battle lines were soon drawn in the arena
of *final authority*. Receiving his inspiration from the autocratic
rulers of Old Testament Israel, James locked horns with
Parliament over his philosophical belief in "The Divine Right of
Kings." In a speech to Parliament in 1610, he said:

> The state of monarchy is the supremest thing upon earth, for
> kings are not only God's lieutenants upon earth and sit upon
> God's throne, but even by God himself they are called gods . . .
> I conclude then this point touching the power of kings with this
> axiom of divinity: that to dispute what God may do is blasphemy,
> . . . so it is sedition in subjects to dispute what a king may do in
> the height of his power. But just kings will ever be willing to
> declare what they will do, if they will not incur the curse of God.
> I will not be content that my power be disputed upon, but I shall
> be willing to make the reason appear of all my doings, and rule
> my actions according to my laws.[15]

His was a literal interpretation of Proverbs 16:10, *"A divine sentence is in the lips of the king: his mouth transgresseth not in judgment."*

The extent of Satan's wrath against James ranged from the spells cast by primitive Druids to the assassination attempts of sophisticated Jesuits. The King frequently wore protective padding beneath his robes to deflect the blades of would-be assailants.[16]

However, to discover the vilest attacks against his person, we must look to the 20th-century writings of *apostate Christians!* With the major encyclopedia sets such as Americana (1991), Britannica (1992), Collier's (1990), World Book (1988), New Standard (1990), Chambers (1973), Academic America (1989), and even the Catholic Encyclopedia for Home and School (1960) completely silent on the matter, an article in *Moody Monthly* categorically reports that King James was an *open homosexual!* (In over twenty pages of copy, the editors of the *Dictionary of National Biography* do not so much as allude to the rumor one time.) Writing in the July/August 1985 issue, Karen Ann Wojahn states in her report on "The Real King James":

> A French nobleman, Esme Stuart D'Aubigny arrived in Scotland. A distant cousin of James, the 38-year-old father of five traded affection for a position in the court and became James' homosexual partner . . . When one of his homosexual partners was convicted of murder and sentenced to death, James granted him a reprieve and financed his retirement to the country. The king continued to live in open homosexuality.[17]

Characteristically, "Sister" Wojahn gave zero documentation for either charge; her sole piece of evidence represents a pathetic attempt at twisting one of James' statements. Without a hint at the context (much less the source), she quotes him as saying:

> I am neither a god nor an angel, but a man like any other. Therefore I act like a man and confess to loving those dear to me more than other men.[18]

How she attributes James' admission to "acting like a man" to a confession of homosexuality constitutes a major stumbling block to thinking people. In her same tabloid-styled report, she blasted the "power-crazed," newly appointed king (of England) for being so eager to claim his throne that he "left his *pregnant wife* Anne in Edinburgh and mounted a horse for London."[19] Are we now to conclude that James was *bisexual*?

Should King James be indicted for playing political favorites
and for spending considerable time with his male advisors, then
a similar charge must be made against the likes of Ulysses S.
Grant, who was said to be vulnerable to "flattery and to the kind
attentions of his staff," known as the "jolly dogs."[20]

If the editors of *Moody Monthly* were so interested in using
twisted facts to crusade against supposed immorality, why would
they waste time speculating on the sexuality of King James when
the extant letters of Dr. Hort provide a far greater selection of
material that can be easily distorted by the dishonest scholar?
Writing to John Ellerton, Hort states:

> My dear Ellerton—you are a bad bad boy to leave me without
> a letter from July to January, and accordingly my first letter for
> the New Year shall be devoted to stirring you up.[21]

And in another letter he lamented, also to Ellerton:

> On coming up here, I find you levanted, (*"chiefly Brit*: to run
> away from a debt") and so I am left in wretched solitude, for
> there is not a single man up whom I know at all intimately; so
> pray come hither and read as you intended . . . but do not be
> guilty of the horrible treachery of leaving me any longer without
> any other company than the excessively shadowy and
> 'questionable shapes' of Pindar, Thucydides, and Juvenal
> (literary works); in short, I am vegetating, and, if you do not
> come to my aid, a vegetable I shall be all my days, without hope
> of becoming an animal, much less a 'human.'[22]

And then there is the particularly "sick" excerpt (to his wife,
no less) which reads:

> To-day's post has brought an answer at last from Westcott.
> He has had a boy very ill in his house, which has much occupied
> him. (It would be worth while being a boy ill in his house, to be
> tended by him!)[23]

The honest, simple truth is that people like Wojahn attack
King James out of an inability to submit to *final authority*! It is
the King James *Bible* that they are really out to undermine. The
deep-seated, unscholarly prejudice of this writer is evidenced by
her earlier attempt at reading the king's mind. Commenting on
his prideful anticipation of the Hampton Court meeting, she
wrote:

Here was an opportunity to debate with great scholars. *I shall be Solomon,* he thought *and the tribes will come to me for judgment.*[24]

Invariably, Nicolaitane scholarship will fail to mention two pertinent *facts*. The man responsible for this rumor was an ousted aide with an ax to grind who waited until after James was deceased to slander him. Dr. Gipp writes:

> Anthony Welden had to be excluded from the court. Weldon swore vengeance. It was not until 1650, *twenty-five years after the death of James* that Weldon saw his chance. He wrote a paper calling James a homosexual. Obviously, James, being dead, was in no condition to defend himself. The report was largely ignored since there were still enough people alive who knew it wasn't true.[25]

Furthermore, if James *were* "funny," he would have to be the first queer on record to write a serious commentary on the book of *Revelation*,[26] as well as a devotional entitled "Meditations on the Lord's Prayer."[27] In fact, Wojahn is caught talking out of both sides of her mouth by suggesting this very paradox of an "open homosexual" coming to the light so his deeds could be reproved:

> Had James applied his own **vast knowledge of the Word of God**, he might have become one of the respected heroes of the Christian faith. Indeed, he once wrote these lines for his son and heir: "If then you would enjoy a happy reign, observe the statutes of your heavenly King."[28]

On April 5, 1603, four days after Elizabeth's death, the new king departed for London. Before arriving at his destination, he was intercepted by an august delegation of Puritan ministers who presented him with a statement of grievances against the Church of England. With close to a thousand signatures attached thereto (10% of the English clergy), it came to be known as the *Millenary Petition*. The king responded by dispatching a proclamation, "touching a meeting for the hearing, and for the determining, things *pretended to be amiss in the church.*"[29]

The conference was held on the 14th, 16th, and 18th days of January, 1604, at *Hampton Court*, the largest of the royal palaces (containing 1,000 rooms), located on the north bank of the Thames River, fifteen miles southwest of central London. Considered a safe distance from the plague-ridden capital, the

imminent deaths of over 30,000 Englishmen[30] would set a most
somber mood for discussing issues of eternality.

Appointed by James himself, the Puritan delegation of four
was led by John Rainolds, president of Corpus Christi College at
Oxford, followed by Lawrence Chaderton, Thomas Sparke and
John Knewstubs. Excluded on the opening day, these men were
led into the King's privy chamber on Monday, January 16th, to
face over fifty high church officials (including the Archbishop of
Canterbury) led by Richard Bancroft, Bishop of London.

The chairman's convictions were easily detectable from his
invitation to discuss "things *pretended* to be amiss in the
church." Although James appreciated the Puritans' anti-Catholic
position, he strongly disapproved of their Presbyterian form of
government as a threat to his royal absolutism. On one occasion,
he stated that "presbytery and monarchy agreed together as well
as God and the devil."[31] The King's best-remembered words
expressing his fears of a Puritan-sponsored ouster of his
politically supportive Bishops was his cliché, "No Bishops–No
King."[32] Having been exposed to these excesses in his previous
administration, he had no intention of subjecting his newest
realm to such a confining Calvinistic theocracy, vowing to "harry
them out of the land, or else do worse."[33]

As the meeting progressed, subjects of lesser importance began
causing even more dissension. One of these bears mentioning
with regard to James' purported homosexuality. Paine writes:

> The Puritans, though not so much Rainolds, opposed wedding
> rings. James, who spoke of his queen as "our dearest bedfellow,"
> said, "I was married with a ring and think others scarcely well
> married without it." James had a good time with jokes; when
> Rainolds, unmarried, questioned the phrase in the marriage
> service "with my body I thee worship," the king said, "Many a
> man speaks of Robin Hood who never shot his bow; if you had a
> good wife yourself, you would think that **all the honor and
> worship you could do to her would be well bestowed.**"[34]

After having one request after another denied, Dr. Rainolds
finally struck the nerve that has since changed the world. Paine
relates the historic interchange:

> "May your Majesty be pleased," said Dr. John Rainolds in his
> address to the king, "to direct that the Bible be now translated,
> such versions as are extant not answering to the original."
> Rainolds was a Puritan, and the Bishop of London felt it his duty
> to disagree. "If every man's humor might be followed," snorted

His Grace, "there would be no end to translating." King James was quick to put both factions down. "I profess," he said, "I could never yet see a Bible well translated in English, but I think that of Geneva is the worst." These few dissident words started the greatest writing project the world has ever known.[35]

When it came to the topic of an English Bible, the King was only too aware that his prosperous subjects owed their "national debt" to the liberating doctrines of Holy Scripture. Having abandoned the Catholicism of his own mother, James had observed firsthand that, *"The entrance of thy words giveth light"* (Psalm 119:130). Green commenting:

> No greater moral change ever passed over a nation than passed over England during the years which parted the middle of the reign of Elizabeth from the meeting of the Long Parliament. England became the people of a book, and that book was the Bible. It was as yet the one English book which was familiar to every Englishman; it was read at churches and read at home, and everywhere its words, as they fell on ears which custom had not deadened to their force and beauty, kindled a startling enthusiasm . . . The popularity of the Bible was owing to other causes besides that of religion. The whole prose literature of England, save the forgotten tracts of Wyclif, has grown up since the translation of the Scriptures by Tyndall and Coverdale. No history, no romance, no poetry, save the little-known verse of Chaucer, existed for any practical purpose in the English tongue when the Bible was ordered to be set up in churches . . . As a mere literary monument, the English version of the Bible remains the noblest example of the English tongue. Its perpetual use made it from the instant of its appearance the standard of our language. But for the moment its literary effect was less than its social. The power of the book over the mass of Englishmen showed itself in a thousand superficial ways, and in none more conspicuously than in the influence it exerted on ordinary speech. It formed, we must repeat, the whole literature which was practically accessible to ordinary Englishmen; and when we recall the number of common phrases which we owe to great authors, the bits of Shakespeare, or Milton, or Dickens, or Thackeray, which unconsciously interweave themselves in our ordinary talk, we shall better understand the strange mosaic of Biblical words and phrases which colored English talk two hundred years ago. The mass of picturesque allusion and illustration which we borrow from a thousand books, our fathers were forced to borrow from one . . . But far greater than its effect on literature or social phrase was the effect of the Bible on the character of the people at large. Elizabeth might silence or tune the pulpits; but it was

impossible for her to silence or tune the great preachers of justice, and mercy, and truth, who spoke from the book which she had again opened for the people. The whole moral effect which is produced nowadays by the religious newspaper, the tract, the essay, the lecture, the missionary report, the sermon, was then produced by the Bible alone. And its effect in this way, however dispassionately we examine it, was simply amazing. The whole temper of the nation was changed. A new conception of life and of man superseded the old. A new moral and religious impulse spread through every class . . . the whole nation became, in fact, a Church.[36]

However, at the time of James' coronation, an unfortunate spirit of rivalry was escalating between the Geneva Bible and the Bishops' Bible. By far, the Geneva Bible was the more popular of the two. Known as "The Breeches Bible" because of its rendering of Genesis 3:7, "They sewed figge tree leaves together, and made themselves *breeches*," the Geneva translation enjoyed a circulation from Shakespeare's *desk* to the Mayflower's *deck*.

James' dissatisfaction with this translation was primarily over the Calvinistic marginal notes which naturally clashed ideologically with his Divine Right of Kings. He described these references as, "partial, untrue, and seditious, savouring too much of dangerous and traitorous conceits."[37] A typical example was the note at Exodus 1:19 where the midwives' disobedience to Pharaoh was termed "lawful."[38] Another bone of contention involved the story in II Chronicles 15:16 where King Asa is seen to spare the life of his idolatrous mother, Queen Maachah. The Geneva note reads, "Herein [Asa] showed that he lacked zeal: for she ought to have died . . . but he gave place to foolish pity."[39] This could hardly be acceptable to a son whose first order of business as England's newest monarch had included the honorable interment of his own mother's body in Westminster Abbey.[40]

James also realized that the foreign origin of the Geneva Bible afforded him with the propitious opportunity to provide his subjects with a Bible that would be truly *English*, being translated on English soil. And of course, the prestige gained from so noble a venture could only enhance his fledgling reign, the writer of Proverbs ensuring that, *"the throne is established by righteousness"* (Proverbs 16:12b). (In other words, unknown to James at the time was the naming, in 1607, of the first permanent settlement in America as "Jamestown" in his honor.)

The King had made his decision. With the prudent motive of uniting his nation behind a single English Bible (". . . *no man can serve two masters"*), James placed his official sanction on the proposal:

> That a translation be made of the whole Bible, *as consonant as can be to the original Hebrew and Greek*; and this to be set out and printed, *without any marginal notes*, and only to be used in all churches of England, in time of Divine service.[41]

In response to the pharisaical, nit-picking of 20th-century Nicolaitanes who would challenge the extent of James' actual endorsement (*"Strictly* speaking, the Authorized Version was never authorized." [Geisler and Nix][42]), we submit the contemporary testimony of Bishop Bancroft, whose initial resistance to the project has already been stated. Writing to an aide, Bancroft charged:

> I move you in his majesty's name that, agreeably to the charge and trust committed unto you, no time may be overstepped by you for the better furtherance of this holy work ... **You will scarcely conceive how earnest his majesty is to have this work begun!** [43]

Thus we observe that the Lord who delights in giving His children *"abundantly above all that we ask or think,"* (Ephesians 3:20), bestowed upon His beloved Tyndale a double portion of blessing. With the "attitude adjustment" of Henry VIII occurring in answer to the martyr's prayer, "Open the King's eyes," we stand in awe at God's moving of the apostrophe, three-quarters of a century later to, "Open the *kings'* eyes"!

XI

The Old Black Book

". . . purified seven times."
(Psalm 12:6)

In the months following Hampton Court, a diligent search was commissioned for men who had "taken pains in their private study of the Scriptures,"[1] so as to secure a qualified team of translators. By July, James had made public his personal selection of fifty-four of the kingdom's brightest intellects. By the time the project was formally begun in 1607, the number of participants had been reduced by seven.

The revisers were divided into six companies and assigned to three principal locations. In the famed Jerusalem Chamber at *Westminster*, ten men under the direction of the erudite Lancelot Andrews translated Genesis through II Kings, while William Barlow chaired a second company of seven to work with Romans through Jude.

At *Oxford*, John Harding led another seven men to labor on Isaiah through Malachi with the Greek committee of eight completing the Gospels, Acts and Revelation under the chairmanship of Thomas Ravis.

The *Cambridge* groups toiled exclusively from Hebrew; Edward Lively's team of eight rendering I Chronicles through Song of Solomon, while the remaining seven men worked with John Bois to translate the *Apocrypha*. (The manner in which the translaters handled the Apocrypha will be discussed later in this chapter.)

The church of Jesus Christ will be forever indebted to the following team of Spirit-filled scholars for giving us *The Old Black Book*:

Dr Lancelot Andrews, dean of Westminster.	(Westminster)
Dr John Overall, dean of St Paul's.	(Westminster)
Dr Hadrian de Saravia, canon of Canterbury.	(Westminster)
Dr Richard Clark, fellow of Christ's Coll., Camb.	(Westminster)
Dr John Layfield, fellow of Trin. Coll., Camb.	(Westminster)
Dr Robert Teigh, archdeacon of Middlesex.	(Westminster)
Mr Francis Burleight, Pemb. Hall, Camb., D.D.	(Westminster)
Mr Geoffrey King, fellow of King's Coll., Camb.	(Westminster)
Mr Thompson, Clare Hall, Camb.	(Westminster)
Mr William Bedwell, St John's Coll., Camb.	(Westminster)
Mr Edward Lively, fellow of Trin. Coll.	(Cambridge)
Mr John Richardson, aftrwds master of Trin. Coll.	(Cambridge)
Mr Laurence Chatterton, master of Emm. College	(Cambridge)
Mr Francis Dillingham, fellow of Christ's Coll.	(Cambridge)
Mr Thomas Harrison, vice-master of Trin. Coll.	(Cambridge)
Mr Roger Andrewes, afterwards master of Jesus Coll.	(Cambridge)
Mr Robert Spalding, fellow of St John's.	(Cambridge)
Mr Andrew Byng, fellow of St Peter's Coll.	(Cambridge)
Dr John Harding, pres. of Magd. Coll.	(Oxford)
Dr John Reynolds, pres. of Corpus Christi Coll.	(Oxford)
Dr Thomas Holland, afterwards rector of Ex. Coll.	(Oxford)
Dr Richard Kilbye, rector of Lincoln Coll.	(Oxford)
Dr Miles Smith, Brasenose Coll.	(Oxford)
Dr Richard Brett, fellow of Lincoln Coll.	(Oxford)
Mr Richard Fairclough, fellow of New Coll.	(Oxford)
Dr John Duport, master of Jesus Coll.	(Cambridge)
Dr William Branthwait, master of Caius Coll.	(Cambridge)
Dr Jeremiah Radcliffe, fellow of Trin. Coll.	(Cambridge)
Dr Samuel Ward, afterwards master of Sid. Coll.	(Cambridge)
Mr Andrew Downes, fellow of St John's Coll.	(Cambridge)
Mr John Bois, fellow of St John's Coll.	(Cambridge)
Mr Robert Ward, fellow of King's Coll.	(Cambridge)
Dr Thomas Ravis, dean of Christ Church.	(Oxford)
Dr George Abbot, dean of Winchester.	(Oxford)
Dr Richard Eedes, dean of Worcester.	(Oxford)
Dr Giles Thompson, dean of Windsor.	(Oxford)
Mr (Sir Henry) Saville, provost of Eton.	(Oxford)
Dr John Perin, fellow of St John's Coll.	(Oxford)
Dr Ravens, [fellow of St John's Coll.]	(Oxford)
Dr John Harmer, fellow of New. Coll.	(Oxford)
Dr William Barlow, dean of Chester.	(Westminster)
Dr William Hutchinson, archdeacon of St Albans.	(Westminster)
Dr John Spencer, pres. of Corp. Chr. Coll., Ox.	(Westminster)
Dr Roger Fenton, fellow of Pemb. Hall, Camb.	(Westminster)
Mr Michael Rabbett, Trin. Coll., Camb.	(Westminster)
Mr Thomas Sanderson, Balliol Coll., Oxford, D.D.	(Westminster)
Mr William Dakins, fellow of Trin. Coll., Camb.	(Westminster)[2]

James had requested the aid of "all our principal learned men within this our kingdom."[3] The excellent biographical sketches contained in Alexander McClure's *Translator's Revived* and *The Men Behind the King James Version* by Gustavus S. Paine confirm that this royal wish was *more* than realized!

In a *Moody Monthly* article entitled "The Bible That Bears His Name," Leslie Keylock wrote, "Because of the limitations of seventeenth-century scholarship, the KJV has major weaknesses"[4] and, "It was based on the best scholarship of its day."[5] Statements such as these reveal a deep-seated and often subconscious *Darwinian* influence.

Despite the inroads of theistic evolution, most professing Christians would be quick to decry the "Puddle to Paradise" approach when discussing the origin of man. However, these same Christians are inclined to believe that man's mental prowess is somehow on an upward climb. The facts of the matter indicate that quite the opposite is true. Notwithstanding the so-called blessings of "modern technology" (the inventions of which are controlled by a sovereign God and presently hastening the end-day apostasy—i.e., "Who needs God?", etc.), the average SAT scores confirm that man's intellectual faculties are in a state of decline commensurate with a deterioration of the English language in general. That these two are inseparably connected is borne out by the reality that we *think with words*. And is not this decline consistent with the second Law of Thermodynamics? Where are the modern scholars who can compete with the men of the 1611 committee? Dr. Sam Gipp writes:

> The men on the translation committee of the King James Bible were, without dispute, the most learned men of their day and vastly qualified for the job which they undertook. They were overall both academically qualified by their cumulative knowledge and spiritually qualified by their exemplary lives. Among their company were men who, academically, took a month's vacation and used the time to learn and master an entirely foreign language; wrote a Persian dictionary; invented a specialized mathematical ruler; one was an architect; mastered oriental languages; publicly debated in Greek; tutored Queen Elizabeth in Greek and mathematics; and of one it was said, "Hebrew he had at his fingers end."[6]

When John Bois was only five years old, his father taught him to *read* Hebrew. By the time he was six, he could not only *write* the same, but in a fair and elegant character. At age fifteen, he was already a student at St. John's College, Cambridge, where he was renowned for corresponding with his superiors in *Greek*.[7]

Though engulfed with his studies, Bois made time for his mother, frequently hiking some twenty miles just to have breakfast with her. He would read as he walked.[8]

His devouring of over sixty grammars[9] made him one of the most popular Greek professors at Cambridge with students attending his voluntary lectures as early as four a.m. Afterwards, he would remain with his books until eight p.m.,[10] studying on his feet and resting only on his knees.[11] Of the man destined to become the committee's final editor, McClure said, "He was so familiar with the Greek Testament that he could, at any time, turn to any word that it contained."[12] The secret to such a consecrated life can be summed up in the translator's own words who said, "There has not been a day for these many years in which I have not meditated at least once upon my death."[13]

Name the twentieth-century scholars who could shine the shoes of John Bois. Or what of Lancelot Andrews, chairman of the New Testament committee at Westminster, who was conversant in *fifteen* languages?[14] It was said of Miles Smith that he was "a very walking library."[15] For an attitude that was, "covetous of nothing but books,"[16] his was the privilege of writing the new Bible's preface. George Abbot entered Oxford at fourteen years of age and later became the Archbishop of Canterbury.[17] Andrew Downes was described by Milton as the "chief of learned men in England."[18] The literary accomplishments of Thomas Ravis (eventual successor to Bancroft, Bishop of London) at Oxford were representative of the translators as a whole: Bachelor of Arts, 1578; Master of Arts, 1581; Bachelor of Divinity, 1589; Doctor of Divinity, 1595.[19]

Having become a fellow at Corpus Christi College at age 17, Dr. John Rainolds was known as "a living library, a third university,"[20] Anthony Wood saying of him that he was "most prodigiously seen in all kinds of learning; most excellent in all tongues," as well as "a prodigy in reading, famous in doctrine, and the very treasure of erudition."[21]

In the Providence of God, however, the good Dr. Rainolds did not live through the project he initiated. When urged by his friends to ease up his strenuous schedule, he replied, "Non propter vitam, vivendi perdere causas,"—"for the sake of life, he would not lose the very end of living."[22] Expiring on the 21st of May, 1607, he was replaced as president of Corpus Christi College by another translator, John Spencer, who himself had been on the Greek faculty since nineteen years of age.

It should be noted that these amazing scholars were not just a bunch of dry theologues but accomplished preachers and balanced Christians as well. Although proficient in Latin, Greek, Hebrew, Chaldee, Arabic and several Ethiopic tongues, it was said of Richard Brett that:

> He was a most vigilant pastor, a diligent preacher of God's Word, a liberal benefactor to the poor, a faithful friend, and a good neighbor.[23]

Thomas Fuller says of Lancelot Andrews that he was:

> An inimitable preacher in his way; and such plagiarists as have stolen his sermons could never steal his preaching, and could make nothing of that, whereof he made all things as he desired.[24]

One of the eight translators whose responsibilities included the chapter on life's setting sun in Ecclesiastes 12 was Lawrence Chaderton, who himself lived to the ripe old age of one hundred three. Described as a "grave, pious and excellent preacher," McClure relates an incredible account of his pulpit power:

> It is stated on high authority, that while our aged saint was visiting some friends in his native country of Lancashire, he was invited to preach. Having addressed his audience for *two full hours* by the glass, he paused and said,—"I will no longer trespass on your patience." And now comes the marvel; for the whole congregation cried out with one consent,—"For God's sake, go on, go on!" He, accordingly, proceeded *much longer,* to their great satisfaction and delight.[25]

Not only are congregations such as these conspicuously absent in our present lukewarm age, but the fiery preaching which they heard is absent as well. Citing a sermon excerpt from Richard Kilby of the Oxford team (Old Testament), Paine records:

> Consider well what He hath done for you. He made you at the first like unto Himself, in wisdom and holiness, and when you were by sin made like the devil, and must therefore have been condemned to hell torments, God sent His only Son who taking unto him a body and soul, was a man and suffered great wrong and shameful death, to secure your pardon, and to buy you out of the devil's bondage, that ye might be renewed to the likeness of God . . . to the end ye might be fit to keep company with all saints in the joys of heaven.[26]

First and foremost, the translators were men of pronounced godliness and spiritual power. It was said that whenever Lancelot Andrews was near, King James "desisted from mirth and frivolity in his presence."[27]

The unusual diary entries of twenty-seven-year-old Samuel Ward, youngest of the translators, speak volumes. Condemning himself in the second person, he wrote:

> May 13, 1595, "Thy wandering regard in chapel at prayer time . . ." May 17th, "Thy gluttony the night before." May 23, "My sleeping without remembering my last thought, which should have been of God." May 26, "Thy dullness this day in hearing God's Word."[28]

Writing on the subject of divinity, Rainolds declared:

> Sith that divinity, the knowledge of God, is the water of life, the vessel must be cleansed that shall have God's holy spirit not only a guest but also a continual dweller within. God forbid that you should think divinity consists of words, as a wood doth of trees. Divinity without godliness doth but condemn consciences against the day of vengeance, and provide the wrath of the mighty Lord, and make more inexcusable before the seat of judgment . . . True divinity cannot be learned unless we frame our hearts and minds wholly to it.[29]

Now when the critics are not casting innuendos at the translators' personal qualifications, they will be seen questioning the available manuscripts at their disposal. Keylock's article continuing:

> Few Christians familiar with Biblical scholarship argue any longer that the KJV is either the most accurate or the most readable English translation. Scholars **now have** at their disposal a wealth of materials that the KJV translators knew **nothing** about . . . The Hebrew and Greek texts **now available** to Bible translators are far superior to what the KJV translators had.[30]

Referring to the discoveries of codices ℵ and B, this impressive sounding challenge is one of the most frequently used objections to the claimed superiority of the King James Bible. However, as we have already seen in previous chapters, it is also one of the weakest arguments when one realizes that these latent discoveries were indeed resting on the translators' table, in the text of the *Latin Vulgate*. That the King James men were more than adequately equipped was conceded even by F. F. Bruce who wrote:

> The Authorized Version was formally a revision of the 1602 edition of the Bishops' Bible. But all the existing English versions

lay before the translators, and every available foreign version, Latin translations, ancient **and recent**, the Targums and the Peshitta—all as aids to the elucidation of the Hebrew and Greek originals.[31]

Exasperated Nicolaitane scholars will then attempt to key in on this strength of available resources by challenging the traditional designation of the King James Bible as a *version* (instead of a translation). A typical example of such "gnat straining" is the statement by Geisler and Nix that:

> There is one fact that has often been overlooked by the adherents to the Authorized Version, namely, the Authorized Version is not really a version at all. Even the original title page of 1611 indicates that it is a translation, as it reads, "The Holy Bible, conteyning the Old Testament, and the New: *Newly translated out of the Originall* Tongues: and with the former Translations diligently compared and revised, by his Majesties speciall Commandement."[32]

These critics were apparently too incensed to realize that their challenge is, in itself, a tribute to the integrity of the Authorized Version. The incredible truth brought to light by their complaint is that the King James Bible is the result not of four years' effort, *but of an eighty-six-year process of scrutinizing revision beginning with William Tyndale* (or 229 years if we date from Wycliff).

With the numbers seven and eight representing "perfection" and "new beginnings" respectively, we marvel at the King James Bible being erected upon the sevenfold foundation of the Wycliff, Tyndale, Coverdale, Matthew, Great, Geneva, and Bishops' Bibles. Thus we find this spirit of humble appreciation expressed in the message from "The Translators to the Reader," that:

> Truly (good Christian reader) we never thought from the beginning that we should need to make a new translation nor yet to make of a bad one a good one, . . . but to make a good one better, or out of many good ones, one principal good one . . . To this purpose there were many chosen, that were greater in other men's eyes than in their own, and that sought the truth rather than their own praise.[33]

In another place, they acknowledged their sixteenth-century predecessors by saying:

> They deserve to be had of us and of posterity in everlasting remembrance . . . blessed be they, and most honoured be their name, that break the ice, and give the onset upon that which helpeth forward to the saving of souls.[34]

Such was the spirituality requisite for so vital an undertaking by so wide an array of intellects throughout such an extended period of time. In view of this unprecedented camaraderie, the committee's procedural guidelines were laced with wisdom.

Picking up McClure's informative report at the eighth rule we learn that:

> Each man in each company shall separately examine the same chapter or chapters, and put the translation into the best shape he can. The whole company must then come together, and compare what they have done, and agree on what shall stand. Thus in each company, according to the number of members, there would be from seven to ten distinct and carefully labored revisions, the whole to be compared, and digested into one copy of the portion of the Bible assigned to each particular company. The ninth rule directs, that as fast as any company shall, in this manner, complete any one of the sacred books, it is to be sent to each of the other companies, to be critically reviewed by them all. The tenth rule prescribes, that if any company, upon reviewing a book so sent to them, find anything doubtful or unsatisfactory, they are to note the places, and their reasons for objecting thereto, and send it back to the company from whence it came. If that company should not concur in the suggestions thus made, the matter was to be finally arranged at a general meeting of the chief persons of all the companies at the end of the work. Thus every part of the Bible would be fully considered, first, separately, by each member of the company to which it was originally assigned; secondly, by that whole company in concert; thirdly, by the other five companies severally; and fourthly, by the general committee of revision. By this judicious plan, each part must have been closely scrutinized at least *fourteen* times.[35]

Now when all of these intellectual attainments and operational precautions are considered, a startling statistic is discovered when their finished product is compared with the Tyndale Bible. According to a consensus of authorities, approximately 90 percent of Tyndale's words were left intact by the King James translators.[36] Foxe rendering tribute to Tyndale states:

> Before Tyndale's day the English versions of the Bible had been but translations of a translation, being derived from the Vulgate or older Latin versions. Tyndale, for the first time, went back to the original Hebrew and Greek. And not only did he go back to the original languages seeking for the truth, but he embodied that truth when found in so noble a translation that it has ever since been deemed wise by scholars and revisers to make but few changes in it; consequently every succeeding version is in

reality little more than a revision of Tyndale's. It has been truly
said that "the peculiar genius which breathes through the
English Bible, the mingled tenderness and majesty, the Saxon
simplicity, the grandeur—unequalled, unapproached in the
attempted improvements of modern scholars—all are here, and
bear the impress of the mind of one man, and that man William
Tyndale."[37]

For an illustration of Tyndale's enduring spiritual legacy,
consider the case of the Lord's Prayer in Matthew 6:9-10.

Tyndale (1526)
O oure father which arte in heven halowed be thy name Let thy
kyngdom come. Thy wyll be fulfilled as well in erth as it ys in
heven.

Coverdale (1535)
O oure father which art in heaven, halowed be thy name. Let thy
kyndome come. Thy wyll be fulfilled upon earth as it is in
heaven.

Great Bible (1539)
Oure father which art in heaven, halowed be thy name. Let thy
kingdome come. Thy will be fulfilled, as well in erth, as it is in
heaven.

Geneva Bible (1560)
Our father which art in heaven, halowed be thy Name. Thy
kingdome come. Thy will be done even in earth, as it is in
heaven.

Bishops' Bible (1568)
O our father, which art in heaven, halowed be thy name. Let thy
kyngdome come. Thy wyll be done, as well in earth, as it is in
heaven.[38]

For such a notable achievement, William Tyndale has been
justly designated as the "Father of the English Bible."[39]

As was to be expected, the attacks of the enemy were
immediately felt. While a marginal reference in the Douay Bible
(English translation for Catholics) predicted that the King James
revisers would "be abhorred in the depths of hell,"[40] a disgruntled
Protestant scholar, Dr. Hugh Broughton, said that he "had rather
be rent in pieces with wild horses than any such translation by
my consent should be urged upon poor churches."[41]

The complaints of today's lukewarm Nicolaitanes are
numerous and hypocritical. In addition to the many discussed
thus far, there is the demand of some for the italicized words to

be removed because they were added by the translators.

Anyone who is familiar with translation work is aware of the necessity for adding certain words to complete the sense of the new language. Italicized words are also needed because of the unique *idioms* of a given tongue. For instance, how would you translate the American idiom, "step on the gas" for a Spanish reader?

The pharisaism of their objection is seen not only from the fact that *all* translations contain some added words but that these words are not italicized in the modern versions. While Psalm 23:1 in the King James Bible reads, "The LORD *is* my shepherd," the New International Version reads, "The LORD is my shepherd." Thus, we conclude that the King James men have been assailed for displaying a superior integrity to modern translators. When attempting to remove some italicized words, many a reviser has opened a "Pandora's Box." A classic example of such nonsense is found in the New International Version's rendering of II Samuel 21:19, which reads:

> "In another battle with the Philistines at Gob, **Elhanan** son of Jaare-Oregim the Bethlehemite **killed Goliath** the Gittite, who had a spear with a shaft like a weaver's rod."

If you check the Authorized Version, you will see that the translators had enough sense to add the italicized words, *the brother of* before Goliath's name. Any Sunday school child could have told the NIV committee that it was *David* who slew Goliath!

Furthermore, Samuel Gipp has made the astute observation that the New Testament authors frequently incorporated such italicized words when quoting an Old Testament passage.

> First, take a Bible (King James, of course) and read Psalm 16:8. "I have set the LORD always before me: because *he is* at my right hand, I shall not be moved." You will notice that the two words "he is" are in italics. Yet when we find the Apostle Peter quoting this verse in the New Testament in Acts 2:25 we find it says: "For David speaketh concerning him, I foresaw the Lord always before my face, for he is on my right hand, that I should not be moved:" So here we find the Apostle Peter quoting Psalm 16:8 **italicized words and all**! You would almost believe that God wanted them in there wouldn't you?[42]

Other critics are so hard up that they take exception with the chapter and verse divisions, demanding to know if they are also inspired. Although Christians who love the King James Bible rarely spend much time thinking about such trivial matters, they are not unaware of the numerous blessings derived from such a study.

For example, an excellent case in point concerning the subject of chapter and verse divisions can be found in the book known as "the little Bible within the Bible." Convinced by a contrast of styles that Isaiah was penned by at least two human authors, the liberal school of higher criticism concurred in dividing the book at the conclusion of chapter 39! Although this *Deutero-Isaiah Theory* is refuted by our Saviour's attributing of *both* sections to the singular prophet (Matthew 12:17 and 13:14), the uncanny matchup of Isaiah's sixty-six chapters with each of the sixty-six books of Scripture is a little too heavy for the average "scholar" to handle.

Bible believers are not surprised to find the account of man's creation and fall alluded to in the opening verses of Isaiah, chapter one.

> *"Hear, O heavens, and give ear, O earth: for the LORD hath spoken, I have nourished and brought up children, and they have rebelled against me."* (Isaiah 1:2)

Can you think of anything that is found in the third chapter of Matthew's Gospel (the 40th book of the Bible) that parallels the material in Isaiah chapter 40, specifically the third verse which reads:

> *"The voice of him that crieth in the wilderness, Prepare ye the way of the LORD, make straight in the desert a highway for our God."* (Isaiah 40:3)

A reading of Isaiah 66 will disclose such similarities with the Bible's sixty-sixth book (Revelation) as:

> *"For, behold, the LORD will come with fire, and with his chariots like a whirlwind, to render his anger with fury, and his rebuke with flames of fire. For by fire and by his sword will the LORD plead with all flesh: and the slain of the LORD shall be many . . . For I know their works and their thoughts: it shall come, that I will gather all nations and tongues; and they shall come, and see my glory."* (Isaiah 66:15-16; 18)

Ask the critic who would question the chapter and verse divisions in the King James Bible if he can find anything particularly apocalyptic in verse 22.

> *"For as the new heavens and the new earth, which I will*
> *make, shall remain before me, saith the LORD, so shall your seed*
> *and your name remain."* (Isaiah 66:22)

Then there is the objection raised against the so-called archaic words of the Authorized Version, Keylock stating, "Many sentences in the KJV cannot be understood today unless the reader consults a good Bible commentary."[43] The highly regarded *Norton Anthology of World Masterpieces* (5th edition) would disagree with Keylock's contention. From the information contained on the inside jacket cover, we understand that the purpose of this work is to recommend to the student the most readable text of any number of literary works:

> Every selection, every text, every translation has been reexamined to ensure that the students of the 1980's have the fewest obstacles between them and the great masterpieces of the Western tradition.[44]

Much to the chagrin of critics like Keylock, the Norton editors selected the 1611 Authorized Version when printing both the Old and New Testaments of the Holy Bible! To complain about archaic words is to betray one's ignorance of the Bible's unique way of dealing with this subject. Once again, we are indebted to Dr. Gipp's valuable insight on this point. Commenting on I Samuel 9:1-11 with an emphasis on verse nine, he writes:

> Here, in the first eleven verses of I Samuel 9 we are not only confronted with an archaic word, but with the Bible **practice** for handling it. We find Saul and one of his father's servants searching for the asses that had run off (I Samuel 9:1-5). They decide to go to see Samuel the seer and enlist his help in finding the asses (Verses 6-8). In verse 11 we are going to run into an archaic word. But, before we do, God puts a parenthesis in the narrative (verse 9) to tell us about it. Notice that verse 9 states that *"he that is now called a **Prophet** was beforetime called a **Seer**."* Thus we see that, between the time that this event took place and the time that the incident was divinely recorded the word "Seer" had passed from common use to be replaced with "Prophet." "Seer" was now archaic. **BUT**, look carefully at **verse 11** where the archaic word appeared. *"And as they went up the hill to the city, they found young maidens going out to draw water, and said unto them, Is the **seer** here?"* Please note that the verse **retains** the outdated word "seer." It does **not** say "Is the prophet here?" Thus we see that **God Himself** through the

Divine inspiration of the Holy Spirit used verse 9 to **explain** the upcoming archaic words **but did not change the holy text.**[45]

The "archaic" words of the King James Bible have already been "updated" more than 100 times in as many years for an average of one modern version per year. *Now, who's kidding whom?* Can the English language be changing that fast?

Another area of gross inconsistency involves the accusation of incorrect grammar usage by the King James translators. Despite the occasional liberty afforded by the grammatical phenomenon known as anacoluthon ("A change from one grammatical construction to another within the same sentence, sometimes as a rhetorical device" [Webster's New World Dictionary]), those who would undermine the Authorized Version piously remonstrate against wrong tenses, improper treatment of the article and an overall refusal to translate literally.

However, when it suits *their* purposes, such critics will employ those very procedures in their own apostate versions. It is no secret that the translators for the modern English revisions, such as the New American Standard Version (NASV) and others, frequently refused to translate their *own* Greek articles. Conversely, they elected to insert the English article in numerous verses without the "authoritative" go-ahead of the corresponding Greek article. And the same hypocrites have been caught red-handed with respect to incorrect tense usage, adding words not found in *any* text.

> *"Therefore thou art inexcusable, O man, whosoever thou art that judgest: for wherein thou judgest another, thou condemnest thyself; for thou that judgest doest the same things."* (Romans 2:1)

Now of the many issues raised against the King James Bible, none is so hypocritical as that of the Apocrypha question. A typical example of Nicolaitane desperation is the sarcastic barb of Robert L. Sumner who wrote:

> It is also interesting—and perhaps you are not aware of it—that the early editions of the Authorized Version contained the Apocrypha. *Horrors!*[46]

Although it is *technically* correct that the first editions of the King James Bible contained the Apocrypha, the complete picture is rarely given. What Dr. Sumner conveniently failed to mention is that the translators were careful to set these spurious books apart from the inspired text by inserting them *between* the

Testaments. And to insure that there was no misunderstanding, they listed *seven* reasons why the apocryphal books were to be categorically rejected as part of the inspired canon.[47]

The only reason for their inclusion at all was due to their accepted *historical* value. Whereas our Scofield Reference Bible divides the testaments with an informative article entitled, "From Malachi to Matthew," the King James translators inserted the actual literature of that nebulous, intertestamental period.

Despite this historical contribution, the King's revisers were not about to endorse such recurrent nonsense as: the two books of Maccabees recounting the death of Antiochus Epiphanes *three* different times in as many places;[48] or the ridiculous account of Tobias being providentially blinded by falling sparrow droppings.[49]

For the record, the Roman Catholic Council of Trent (1545-1563) officially pronounced as *inspired* and *canonical* the books of: Tobit, Judith, Wisdom, Ecclesiasticus, Baruch, I and II Maccabees, and ancillary additions to Esther and Daniel.[50] The Vatican's latent appreciation for these works, *after seventeen centuries of obscurity (Apocrypha* meaning *the hidden things),*[51] was naturally connected to monetary gain. With the escalating denunciation against his "indulgence scam" threatening the building fund for St. Peter's Basilica, "His Holiness" (Pope Paul III, 1534-1549) was more than happy to embrace II Maccabees 12:46 as his new life's verse: "It is therefore a holy and wholesome thought to pray for the dead that they may be loosed from sin." (This would be especially timely in view of Henry VIII's 1534 suspension of the lucrative "Peter's Pence," an ecclesiastical tax paid to the Pope.) Once again, Tetzel's cruel proverb would ring out through the land, "As soon as the money in the coffer rings, the soul from purgatory's fire springs."[52]

Having supposedly secured an "instantaneous salvation" for his dying Protestant mother by "baptizing" her a Catholic, the extent of this author's indoctrination in II Maccabees 12:46 is evident by the double-jeopardy experience of his subsequent, repeated and costly purchase of superfluous Mass cards for her. (Grieving Catholics in need of a shepherd's compassion are frequently given their "Father's" price list which reads, "High Money=High Mass; Low Money=Low Mass; No Money=No Mass.")

What thousands of duped souls are never shown is another verse in II Maccabees which reveals the incredible lack of *final authority* for such a heresy. In contrast to the Apostle Paul who wrote,

"If any man think himself to be a prophet, or spiritual, let him acknowledge that the things that I write unto you are the commandments of the Lord." (I Corinthians 14:37)

. . . the author of II Maccabees concluded his book with the words:

I also will here make an end of my narration. Which if I have done well and as it becometh the history it is what I desired: but if not so perfectly it must be pardoned me. (II Maccabees 15:38-39)

As the personal embodiment of final authority, Rome's Pontifex Maximus ignored the obvious problems with these writings and went so far as to place a curse upon all who would reject the Apocrypha as inspired Scripture.[53] However, the "Holy Father" who claimed to be Christ's Vicar on earth was not nearly as hypocritical as professing Christians like Robert Sumner who questioned the King James translators' inclusion of the Apocrypha. Dr. Sumner also failed to tell you that the "careful translations" (New American Standard and New International) which he describes in his next paragraph as "honest, reliable works translated by competent, evangelical men"[54] trace their underlying Greek text to codices *Sinaiticus* and *Vaticanus*, which display the apocryphal books *interspersed throughout the inspired text.* **Horrors!**

Then, when all else fails, detractors of the King James Bible will invariably ask their despised opponents, *"Which* Authorized Version do you believe, the 1611, 1613, 1767 or perhaps the 1850?" And while their bewildered victims are pondering this troublesome innuendo (analogous to such nonsense as "Have you quit beating your wife lately?"), they are subjected to an array of staggering statistics. Citing the Evangelical scholar Jack Lewis, Keylock quotes him as stating:

Few people realize, for example, that thousands of textual errors have been found in the KJV. As early as 1659 William Kilburne found 20,000 errors in six KJV editions.[55]

Reckless statements such as Lewis' are incredibly misleading as the extent of these so-called "errors" are never explained to be primarily lithographical (printing) and orthographical (spelling) in nature. In 1611, the art of printing was an occupation of utmost drudgery. With every character being set by hand, a multitude of typographical mistakes was to be expected. And when the 1613 edition corrected many of these initial misprints, a crop of new ones was accidentally introduced. Sometimes words were inverted. Other times, a plural was written as a singular or vice versa. Occasionally, an entire word or phrase was left out.

A second classification of "printing changes" involves nothing more than a switch in respective *type styles*. The first edition of the King James Bible was printed in Gothic type. In 1612, the Roman type style was introduced and soon became the standard for all editions of the Authorized Version. If one examines a copy of an original 1611 edition, he will note that the Gothic "v" looks like a Roman "u" while the Gothic "u" looks like a Roman "v." The Gothic "j" resembles the Roman "i." Although the same in the upper case, the Gothic "s" in lower case looks like our "f." Such "changes" account for a significant percentage of the so-called "tens of thousands" of errors in the Authorized Version.

In addition to printing flaws, there was a continual change in spelling for which to care. Lewis did not inform his readers that there was no such thing as proper spelling in the seventeenth century. Even in Dr. Hort's biography by his son, we find his name spelled "Horte." Dr. David Reagan informs us:

> Most histories date the beginning of Modern English around the year 1500. Therefore, by 1611 the grammatical structure and basic vocabulary of present-day English had long been established. However, the spelling did not stabilize at the same time. In the 1600's spelling was according to whim. There was no such thing as correct spelling. No standards had been established. An author often spelled the same word several different ways, often in the same book and sometimes on the same page . . . Not until the eighteenth century did the spelling begin to take a stable form. Therefore, in the last half of the eighteenth century, the spelling of the King James Version of 1611 was standardized.[56]

A significant portion of these twenty thousand "textual errors" were in reality nothing more than changing "darke" to "dark" or "rann" to "ran." Who but a Nicolaitane priest would categorize as serious revisions the normal follow-up corrections of mistakes at the press?

It is impossible to overstate the duplicity of such critics who would weaken the faith of some with their preposterous reports of tens of thousands of errors in the Authorized Version. Although we cannot endorse every opinion of Dr. Scrivener (he was naive enough to be drawn into the Revision Committee of 1871-1881), we would recommend his data to *Moody Monthly*. In his Appendix A (List of wrong readings of the Bible of 1611 amended in later editions) of his informative work, *The Authorized Edition of the English Bible (1611), Its Subsequent Reprints and Modern Representatives*, Scrivener catalogued but a fraction of the inflated figures of modern scholarship.

Excluding marginal alterations and Apocrypha citings, this author has personally reviewed pages 147-194 and counted *less than 800 corrections*. And even this figure is misleading when you consider that many of the instances were repetitious in nature. (Six such changes involved the corrected spelling of "Nathanael" from the 1611's Nathaneel in John 1:45-49 and 21:2).

Whereas Geisler and Nix cited Goodspeed's denouncing of Dr. Blayney's 1769 Oxford edition for deviating from the Authorized Version in "at least *75,000 details*,"[57] Scrivener alludes to less than two hundred as noteworthy of mention.[58] Despite his own criticizing of Blayney's shortcomings (and those of Dr. Paris's edition of 1762), Scrivener states:

> It cannot be doubted that these two editors are the great modernizers of the diction of the version, from what it was left in the seventeenth century, to the state wherein it appears in modern Bibles.[59]

Other conscientious editions appeared in 1629, 1638, 1644, 1676, 1680, 1701, 1762, 1769, 1806, 1813, 1850 and 1852 changing legitimate human errors. An excellent sample of such "dangerous" alterations was extracted from Scrivener's work by Dr. Reagan (as cited by Gipp) and reads as follows:

> In order to be objective, the samples give the first textual correction on consecutive left-hand pages of Scrivener's book. The 1611 reading is given first; then the present reading; and finally, the date the correction was made.
>
> 1. this thing—this thing also (1638)
> 2. shalt have remained—ye shall have remained (1762)
> 3. Achzib, nor Helbath, nor Aphik—of Achzib, nor of Helbath, nor of Aphik (1762)
> 4. requite good—requite me good (1629)
> 5. this book of the Covenant—the book of this covenant (1629)
> 6. chief rulers—chief ruler (1629)
> 7. And Parbar—At Parbar (1638)
> 8. For this cause—And for this cause (1638)
> 9. For the king had appointed—for so the king had appointed (1629)
> 10. Seek good—Seek God (1617)
> 11. The cormorant—But the cormorant (1629)
> 12. returned—turned (1769)

13.   a fiery furnace—a burning fiery furnace (1638)
14.   The crowned—Thy crowned (1629)
15.   thy right doeth—thy right hand doeth (1613)
16.   the wayes side—the way side (1743)
17.   which was a Jew—which was a Jewess (1629)
18.   the city—the city of the Damascenes (1629)
19.   now and ever—both now and ever (1638)
20.   which was of our father's—which was of our fathers (1616)[60]

It is obvious to thinking people that such alterations as these were of a purely correctional nature. Why should anyone be surprised by a host of technical errors in the first *English Bibles* when Satan already set his precedent by pouncing on the earliest of the *Greek manuscripts* (II Corinthians 2:11)? Aided by such living legends as Dr. John Bois and Dr. Samuel Ward, over 72 percent of the textual variations were already cleared up by 1638.[61] (Remember our analogy of the flowing stream?)

That the true *text* of the A.V. 1611 had remained unaffected throughout these corrective stages was confirmed in a special report to the "Board of Managers" of the American Bible Society in 1852. The official findings of this committee of seven, chaired by Dr. James W. McLane, were as follows:

> The English Bible as left by the translators has come down to us unaltered in respect to its text . . . With the exception of typographical errors and changes required by the progress of orthography in the English language, the text of our present Bibles remains unchanged, and without variations from the original copy as left by the translators.[62]

At this juncture, it is imperative for the Bible believer to discern Satan's strategy through this myth of multiplied revisions. His sole objective has been to plant the subliminal suggestion that the various King James editions are to be associated with the modern English translations, *though predicated upon an entirely different Greek text!* People like the Thomas Nelson Publishing Company would lead you to believe that the genuine updating and revisions God allowed from men who *were faithful to the intentions of the original translators* has justified replacing the underlying Greek text with the corrupt readings of Alexandria. Dr. Reagan points out this ploy when commenting on the preface to the New King James Version which states:

> For nearly four hundred years, and throughout several revisions of its English form, the King James Bible has been deeply revered among the English-speaking people of the world.[63]

Today's Nicolaitanes would have you equate such changes as "thou shall kill" to *"thou shalt kill"* (Deuteronomy 12:21); "Abraham our father" to *"Abraham our father,"* (Romans 4:1); and "Jonas" to *"Jona"* (John 1:42) with those of the New American Standard Version that deny the incarnation (I Timothy 3:16), make Christ a sinner (Matthew 5:22), and attack the blood atonement (Colossians 1:14).

The sum total of all lithological errors in *any* edition of the Authorized Version would still produce a text that is superior to any of the modern revisions translated from the polluted text of Westcott and Hort. Is it any wonder that the NASV went bankrupt in only fifteen years?

Finding all exits blocked by the roaring lion of the Reformation, today's Nicolaitane scholars take their last stand behind Mother Teresa's skirts, invoking an old Jesuit charge that the Authorized Version is "the Paper Pope of the Protestants." When all else fails, accuse the Bible believer of being a "Bibliolator," accuse him of "worshiping a book." Perhaps it is time to leave the fellow with a smile of pity.

In all likelihood, the unfortunate wretch was denied a sound Bible education by attending a conservative, accredited seminary. How can we hold him responsible for ridiculing those of us who revere our Bibles when the "exegesis victim" never has been taught Hebrews 4:13a which says, *"Neither is there any creature that is not manifest in **his** sight"*? How could he know that the personal pronoun "his" is a reference to the *"word of God"* in verse twelve? His egotistical professors probably refused to show him Romans 9:17 where the Scripture is seen to be a talking entity and able to foresee the future. Can you imagine what would happen if our boy ever got hold of the fact that Moses wrote Exodus *after* his conversation with Pharaoh? And what would he do if he ever read Galatians 3:7-8 where the Scripture is spoken of as preaching the Gospel to Abraham *before* the writing of Genesis? Isn't it amazing how the Bible's writers equate the *Scriptures* with *God Himself*?

"For thou hast magnified thy word above all thy name."
(Psalm 138:2b)

XII

Sanctioned from on High

"For ever, O LORD thy word is settled in heaven."
(Psalm 119:89)

The completion of the King James Bible was in accord with the plan of God for English to become the end-day, universal language. With standardized time and location being determined in Greenwich, England, and even proper temperature readings established by British thermal units, men would henceforth look to this same island nation to secure the correct Bible!

Others more discerning than this author have inspired God's people by pointing out the symbolism inherent in the name *King James* which marvelously anticipated that Bible's ensuing track record for souls. For instance, if you count the number of letters in the words *King James* (or, for that matter, in *Holy Bible, Scripture,* or *Word of God*) you will find that the answer will equal the total of the individual numbers in 1611 added together.

Now isn't it a coincidence that according to Bible numerology, the number *nine* just happens to be God's number for *fruit bearing*? For example, in the *ninth* chapter of Genesis we read, *"And you, be ye **fruitful**, and multiply; bring forth abundantly in the earth, and multiply therein."* (Genesis 9:7)

How old was Abraham when he fathered Isaac, the seed of promise? Here we have a *double nine* to emphasize the miracle of such advanced fruit bearing. (By the way, how long does the gestation period last, anyway?) The chosen seed is then passed along to Jacob who *fathers* the twelve tribes of Israel. Remember that the name *Jacob* is the Old Testament equivalent of *James*.

Then there is the birth of Israel's throne in the *ninth* chapter of the *ninth* book of the Old Testament from which Jesus, the King of kings, will rule one day.

When we come to the parenthetical church age, we find that the pastor of the first local assembly is also named *James!* The conversion of the most productive soul winner of all time is recorded in Acts chapter *nine.* Do you suppose there is anything about fruit in the *ninth* book of the New Testament? How many types of fruit do you suppose will be found? (For a hint, count up the numbers in the reference Galatians 5:22.)

Although this may appear as unfounded speculation to some, the undeniable blessings of God which accompanied the preaching of the A.D. 1611 Authorized Version constitute the central, irrefutable argument for the superiority of our King James Bible. Church history confirms that the greatst period of revivalism and missionary activity prevailed when the Authorized Version reigned supreme in the land. Conversely, with the Revised Version of 1881 (and its American counterpart, the American Standard Version of 1901) signaling a clear repudiation of *final authority,* a new era of spiritual deterioration was inaugurated (e.g., the British Foreign Mission Society switched over to the Revised Version in 1904).

The major premise of this chapter is that *the King James Bible has already received the endorsement of God Himself through an unprecedented proliferation of over 900,000,000 copies, translated into at least 300 foreign languages.* Though the heathen continue to rage (Zondervan Corporation, Thomas Nelson Publishers, etc.), the Holy Spirit has personally answered the question of "Which Bible?" by honoring the Authorized Version with over three centuries of continuous usage. Notwithstanding the "scholar's" endless complaints regarding incorrect grammar, faulty translation, etc., our precious King James Bible has already been *sanctioned from on high!* Facts are stubborn things!

The translators themselves perceived the open door of opportunity before them, Miles Smith relaying their conviction in his preface, stating:

> And in what sort did these assemble? In the trust of their own knowledge, or of their sharpness of it, or deepness of judgment, as it were in an arm of flesh? At no hand. **They trusted in him that hath the key of David, opening and no man shutting;** they prayed to the Lord.[1]

For the skeptic who would challenge this analogy by insisting that the modern Bible movement has borne a similar amount of fruit, this author would respond with the words of Job 38:3–*"Gird up now thy loins like a man; for I will demand of thee, and **answer thou me**."*

• • •

Where are the preachers of Whitefield's stature who could address 100,000 people[2] *without a microphone* and remain audible for a phenomenal distance?[3]

• • •

When was the last time you saw refined New Englanders responding to a sermon by screaming *"Is there no way of escape?"* while clutching pews and pillars for fear that the ground itself would open beneath them?[4] Such was the case when Jonathan Edwards preached his famous sermon, "Sinners in the Hands of an Angry God" following an all-night prayer meeting. His sermons were described as "white heat."

• • •

How do today's scholars compare to men like John Wesley who found time to write *233* books and pamphlets while riding over *250,000* miles on horseback?[5]

• • •

Where are the prison ministry workers who would *lock themselves in overnight* with death row inmates and literally sing them into Heaven at the gallows like Charles Wesley did?[6] (The rats in England's prisons were so big that the guards were allowed to keep their dogs with them for protection.[7])

• • •

Can anyone name two modern songwriters who have composed nearly 17,000 *quality* songs between them as did Charles Wesley[8] and Fanny Crosby?[9]

• • •

How many Christian merchants do you know like John

Wanamaker who not only closed his stores on Sunday but *drew the curtains as well* to discourage window shopping? Having made enough time for God to superintend a Sunday school department of over 4,000 children, the retailing pioneer left an estate estimated to be $40,000,000.[10]

• • •

With hundreds of "Christian" organizations in operation today, where is the parallel to a sickly William Booth planting his Salvation Army in *58 countries* while preaching the Gospel in over *34 languages?*[11]

• • •

Where is the modern equivalent to the *staying power* of the preachers of yesteryear? Of all ministerial graduates of Yale from 1702-1775, 79 percent served *one* parish their entire life. Only 7 percent had more than two congregations and were reproachfully known as "ne'er-do-wells unable to maintain a continuing relationship with their people."

• • •

How many missionaries have you heard of like William Carey who taught himself six languages and stayed on the field for forty-two years *without a furlough* to translate the Scriptures into 44 languages and dialects?[12]

• • •

Do you know of a prayer warrior like George Mueller who without a single stewardship program, "Jesus First" pin, Giant Print Bible or 800-toll-free number prayed in $7.5 million dollars to feed 2,000 orphans daily, not to mention distributing 111 million Gospel tracts and 300,000 Bibles while supporting 163 missionaries as well? He also read the Bible through over 200 times and went on a nineteen-year, 200,000-mile evangelistic circuit *after* he was *seventy* years old.[13]

• • •

Would you prefer to discuss the subject of *Holy Spirit power?* In Charles Finney's day, sea captains testified that conviction broke out among passengers as their ships neared ports where revival was in progress.[14]

• • •

When did you last see figures like 50,000 souls out of a total New England population of only 300,000 coming to Christ during the Great Awakening of 1740-1770?[15]

• • •

How about 25,000 people travelling from 60 to 100 miles to the Cane Ridge camp meetings in August of 1801, when Kentucky's largest town of Lexington boasted only *1,800* inhabitants?[16]

• • •

D.L. Moody preached to 100,000,000 people[17] over a century ago with 1,000,000 professing Christ as Saviour. By comparison, Billy Graham's entire evangelistic team addressed only 53,561,970 listeners[18] from 1947-1977 when the world's population was significantly increased.

• • •

Over 10,000 residents of White Clay Creek, Pennsylvania, listened in profound silence to a Whitefield sermon for one and one-half hours *through a steady rain,* and in December no less![19] On a different occasion, 15,000 people assembled outside of Philadelphia for another Whitefield sermon, when the entire "city of brotherly love" claimed only 12,000 citizens![20] *Have you ever heard of such goings on?*

• • •

What can be said about the masses in excess of 6,000 that began assembling at *6:00 a.m.* for the first of *four* daily preaching services by Evangelist Sam Jones—*during the four consecutive weeks of his Nashville campaign?*[21] (There were over 10,000 additions to the area churches with the city's entire population numbering only 50,000.)

• • •

When was the last time you witnessed a church's teenage

department grow from 50 to 5,000 in its *first five weeks*? Having
survived an eighteenth-century mortality rate that claimed 74.5
percent of children of all classes before their fifth birthday,[22]
these grateful survivors were glad to attend Whitefield's Sunday
youth services, also conducted at 6:00 a.m.[23]

• • •

Have you ever observed a worldwide movement of God's power
resulting in 2.5 million legitimate conversions *without the
instrumentality of a big-name evangelist*? The Fulton Street
Prayer Revival (1857-1862) was started on September 23rd by
layman Jeremiah C. Lanphier (a Finney convert of 1842) as a
weekly prayer meeting with *six* in attendance. Less than six
months later over 10,000 Christians were praying daily! The
resultant harvest saw peak periods reaching *50,000 souls a
week!*[24] (Over 150,000 confederate troops or roughly one-third of
the total army were included in these figures.)

• • •

How would today's cream puff, Rolex watch-wearing
"reverends" compare with the caliber of their rugged
predecessors as epitomized by the following excerpt from an
anonymous Baptist circuit rider's correspondence in 1803:

> **Every day** I travel I have to swim through creeks or swamps,
> and I am wet from head to feet, and some days from morning to
> night I am dripping with water . . . I have rheumatism in all my
> joints . . . **What I have suffered in body and mind my pen is
> not able to communicate to you.** But this I can say: While my
> body is wet with water and chilled with cold my soul is filled with
> heavenly fire, and I can say with St. Paul: *"But none of these
> things move me, neither count I my life dear unto myself, so that
> I might finish my course with joy."*[25]

How do the "sermonettes" of today's NIV advocates compare
with the spiritual ultimatum issued by the fire-breathing
Jonathan Edwards in his sermon, "Sinners in the Hands of an
Angry God"?

> The God who holds you over the pit of Hell much in the same
> way as one holds a spider or some loathesome insect over the fire,
> abhors you and is dreadfully provoked. His wrath towards you
> burns like fire. He looks upon you as worthy of nothing else but

to be cast into the fire. He is of purer eyes than to bear to have you in His sight. You are ten thousand times more abominable in His eyes than the most hateful venomous serpent is in ours. You have offended Him infinitely more than ever a stubborn rebel did his prince; yet, it is nothing but His hand that holds you from falling into the fire every moment.

It is to be ascribed to nothing else that you did not go to Hell the last night; that you were suffered to awake again in this world after you closed your eyes to sleep; there is no other reason to be given why you have not dropped into Hell since you arose in the morning, but that God's hand has held you up. There is no other reason to be given, while you have been reading this address, but His mercy; yea, no other reason can be given why you do not this very moment drop down into Hell.

O sinner, consider the fearful danger you are in! It is a great furnace of wrath, a wide and bottomless pit, full of the fire of wrath that you are held over in the hand of that God whose wrath is provoked and incensed as much against you as against many of the damned in Hell. You hang by a slender thread, with the flames of divine wrath flashing about it and ready every moment to singe it and burn it asunder; and you have no interest in any Mediator, and nothing to lay hold of to save yourself, nothing to keep off the flames of wrath, nothing of your own, nothing that you have done, nothing that you can do, to induce God to spare you one moment.[26]

The unannounced arrival of evangelist George Whitefield would be certain to stir the countryside significantly. An illiterate farmer by the name of Nathan Cole has left us his personal account of such an experience. How does such a regard of an unsaved man for the preaching from an Authorized Version compare to today's "Christianettes" who get antsy after less than thirty minutes of dry exegesis from a NKJV?

> Now it pleased God to send mr whitefield into this land & . . . i longed to see & hear him . . . & then one morning all on a Suding there came a messanger & said mr whitefield . . . is to preach at middletown this morning at 10 o'clock i was in my field at work i dropt my tool that i had in my hand & run home and throu my house and bad my wife to get ready quick to go and hear mr whitefield preach at middletown & run to my pastire for my hors with all my might fearing i should be too late to hear him & took up my wife & went forward as fast as i thought ye hors could bear & when my hors began to be out of breth i would get down and put my wife on ye saddel and bid her ride as fast as she could & not Stop or Slack for me except i bad her & so i would run until

i was almost out of breth & then mount my hors again ... fearing we should be too late to hear ye Sarmon for we had twelve miles to ride dubble in little more than an our.

i saw before me a cloud or fog i first thought of from ye great river but as i came nearer ye road i heard a noise something like a low rumbling thunder & i presently found out it was ye rumbling of horses feet coming down ye road & this Cloud was a Cloud of dust made by the running of horses feet it arose some rods into ye air over the tops of ye hills and trees & when i came within about twenty rods of ye road i could see men and horses slipping along—it was like a steady streem of horses and their riders scarecely a hors more than his length behind another—i found a vacance between two horses to slip in my hors & my wife said law our cloaths will be all spoiled see how they look—& when we gat down to ye old meeting hous thare was a great multitude it was said to be 3 or 4000 & when i looked towards ye great river i see ye fery boats running swift forward and backward—when i see mr whitefield come up upon ye scaffold he looked almost angellical a young slim slender youth before thousands of people and with a bold undainted countenance & my hearing how god was with him everywhere as he came along it solemnized my mind and put me in a trembling fear before he began to preach for he looked as if he was Clothed with authority from ye great god and a sweet solemnity sat upon his brow and my hearing him preach gave me a heart wound & by gods blessing my old foundation was broken up & i see my righteousness would not save me.[27]

It was said that George Mueller read his Bible through over 200 times on his knees and knew of 50,000 specific answers to prayer. Can such a ministry of faith be rivaled by spiritual hucksters like Oral Roberts, who claimed God would kill him if he didn't raise several millions of dollars?

One morning the plates and cups and bowls on the table were empty. There was no food in the larder, and no money to buy food. The children were standing waiting for their morning meal, when Mueller said, 'Children, you know we must be in time for school.' Lifting his hand he said, 'Dear Father, we thank Thee for what Thou art going to give us to eat.' There was a knock on the door. The baker stood there, and said, 'Mr. Mueller, I couldn't sleep last night. Somehow I felt you didn't have bread for breakfast and the Lord wanted me to send you some. So I got up at 2 a.m. and baked some fresh bread, and have brought it.' Mueller thanked the man. No sooner had this transpired when there was a second knock at the door. It was the milkman. He announced that his milk cart had broken down right in front of the Orphanage, and he would like to give the chldren his cans of fresh milk so he could empty his wagon and repair it. No wonder, years later, when Mueller was to travel the world as an evangelist, he would be heralded as 'the man who gets things from God! '28

When Charles Finney would come to town, things would never be the same again. Do you know the modern factory owner who would interrupt *his* production schedule for a "talk" from the Living Bible?

An individual once went into a manufactory to see the machinery. His mind was solemn, as he had been where there was a revival. The people who laboured there all knew him by sight, and knew who he was. A young lady who was at work saw him, and whispered some foolish remark to her companion, and laughed. The person stopped and looked at her with a feeling of grief. She stopped; her thread broke—and she was so much agitated that she could not join it. She looked out at the window to compose herself, and then tried again; again and again she strove to recover her self-command. At length she sat down, overcome by her feelings. The person then approached and spoke with her; she soon manifested a deep sense of sin. The feeling spread through the establishment like fire, and in a few hours almost every person employed there was under conviction; so much so that the owner, though a worldly man, was astounded, and requested to have the works stopped and a prayer-meeting held; for he said it was a great deal more important to have these people converted than to have the works go on. And in a few days the owner and nearly all the persons employed in the establishment were hopefully converted. The eye of this individual, his solemn countenance, his compassionate feeling, rebuked the levity of the young woman, and brought her under conviction of sin; and probably in a great measure this whole revival followed from so small an incident.

The story is from Finney's own experience. The factory was 'on the Oriskany Creek, a little above Whitesborough.' The words of the gentleman who gave the order to close were: 'Stop the mill and let the people attend to religion; for it is more important that our souls should be saved than that this factory should run.' Accordingly the gates were closed, the factory stopped, and the meeting held forthwith. Finney's brother-in-law, who was superintendent of the factory, had invited the evangelist to the neighbourhood, and a crowded meeting had been held the previous night in the village school-house. Most of the young people from the factory had been present, and many had come under deep conviction. When, therefore, Finney visited the factory next morning they needed only a word to lead them to immediate decision for Christ. In a pamphlet issued by the minister of the Presbyterian Church at Whitesborough it was stated that the converts in the district, during the revival, numbered three thousand.[29]

These many examples of genuine Holy Ghost revivals shook up the world so profoundly that the theory of evolution was actually advanced as an explanation for the social improvements which followed. Yet, even the evolutionist was constrained to acknowledge a power higher than such foolish ideas as "natural selection," etc.

In 1833, Charles Darwin visited the South Sea island of Tierra del Fuego in search of his elusive "missing link." Upon observing the island's benighted inhabitants, Darwin concluded that he had indeed happened upon a lower stratum of humanity that would support his theory of evolution. Confident in his discovery, he wrote:

> The Fuegians are in a more miserable state of barbarism than I ever expected to have seen any human being.
> The expression of their faces is inconceiveably wild, and their tones and gesticulations are far less intelligible than those of domestic animals.[30]

However, after thirty-six years of gloating, Darwin made the mistake of returning to his "island of darkness." To his amazement, he found an entirely different community consisting of churches, schools, homes and every semblance of tranquility. The mystery was soon unraveled; *missionary John G. Paton had invaded the hellhole with the Word of God.* Showing more integrity than twentieth-century Nicolaitanes, Darwin was willing to give credit where credit was due, writing, "I certainly should have predicted that not all the missionaries in the world could have done what has been done."[31] The naturalist was so dumbfounded by what he witnessed that he made a generous contribution to the London Missionary Society.[32] (He also renounced his own theory later in life.)

As thrilling as this story appears, it is really quite the norm for nineteenth-century missionary activity. For instance, on the South Pacific island of Aneityum (New Hebrides) can be found the famous inscription to Dr. John Geddie which reads:

> When he landed here in 1848
> There were no Christians:

When he left here in 1872
There were no Heathen.[33]

Then there is that unbelievable account of revival which occurred on Pitcairn Island. Note with wonder what a single King James Bible can accomplish:

> The true story of the *Mutiny on the Bounty* has often been retold. One part that deserves retelling was the transformation wrought by one book. Nine mutineers with six native men and twelve native (Tahitian) women put ashore on Pitcairn Island in 1790. One sailor soon began distilling alcohol, and the little colony was plunged into debauchery and vice.
>
> Ten years later, only one white man survived, surrounded by native women and half-breed children. In an old chest from the *Bounty*, this sailor one day found a Bible. He began to read it and then to teach it to the others. The result was that his own life and ultimately the lives of all those in the colony was changed. Discovered in 1808 by the *U.S.S. Topas*, Pitcairn had become a prosperous community with no jail, no whisky, no crime and no laziness.[34]

When missionary Robert Moffat arrived in Capetown, South Africa, he was immediately warned about the demonic cannibal known as Africaner, chief of the Namaquas, the very tribe Moffat had come to evangelize. Dr. A.J. Gordon writes:

> It was said of him that he was such an incarnate fiend that he actually made a virtue of cruelty and a diversion of murder, killing men in order to make drum-heads of their skins and drinking-cups of their skulls. The audacity of his crimes created a reign of terror throughout the country where he dwelt, and neither savage chiefs nor colonial governments had found out any way to tame him. But Robert Moffat went to him in spite of the most earnest warnings to the contrary. He conquered him, not with carnal weapons, but with the living Word. The germ-principle of that Word being implanted in his heart, a whole harvest of sweet and Christlike virtues sprung up. The demon of cruelty became a meek disciple of Christ, and such a disciple that Moffat was able to say of him, concerning the whole time of his association with him after his conversion, "I do not once remember having occasion to be grieved with him or to complain of any part of his conduct: his very faults seemed to lean to virtue's side."[35]

When Moffat took his "trophy of grace" back to Capetown, the citizens were astonished, having given up the missionary for dead. After the colonial ruler observed the fierce headhunter transformed into a humble Christian, he exclaimed, *"This is the eighth wonder of the world!"*[36] Needless to say, *Africaner's* light was of a far greater brilliance than that *seventh* wonder of the world which illuminated the harbor at Alexandria!

Space will not permit this author to do justice to the many other thrilling occurrences of this time such as the sweat-drenched clothing of a travailing David Brainerd[37] (of whom it was said that his bended knees melted the snow around him); "Gypsy" Smith's forty-five transatlantic crossings in quest for souls;[38] C.T. Studd's conquering of China, India *and* Africa in *his* lifetime; Bunyan's *Pilgrim's Progress*; Borden of Yale; anxious seats and sawdust trails; "Tell Mother I'll Be There" and "Amazing Grace"; the Moravian prayer chain that continued unbroken for 100 years;[39] George Whitefield's swooning under the effect of his own sermons;[40] Voltaire's presses being sold to the Geneva Bible Society to print King James Bibles;[41] Peter Cartwright's legendary "dance hall" revival[42] and fearless remarks to Andrew Jackson;[43] the houses being disassembled *brick by brick* by enraged mobs while an undaunted Charles Wesley refused to curtail his sermon;[44] the dockside rocket attacks of drunken sailors against William Booth's courageous "lasses," *fired at point-blank range*;[45] the official autopsy report for the burdened "Praying Hyde" attributing his death to an unnatural shifting of his heart muscle by several inches;[46] or, for that matter, the shipment and ceremonious interment of David Livingston's body in Westminster Abbey on April 18, 1874, eleven months after his *heart* was buried under a mulva tree by the grieving African Christians for whom it had beaten so fervently.[47]

Perhaps the entire period could be summarized by the Moravian Coat of Arms which pictures an *ox* standing by an *altar* with a *plow* lying beside the altar. The German inscription translates, *"Ready for Either!"*

By contrast, what kind of fruit has the modern Bible movement produced? Oral Roberts' 900-foot Jesus? "Christian" heavy metal rock bands? Tammy Bakker's air-conditioned dog house? Reader's Digest Condensed Bibles? John MacArthur's theology on the blood? Theistic evolution offered in "Christian" colleges? "Sister" Amy Grant's smash hit "Baby, Baby"? Rev. Ike's prayer rugs and seed offerings? "Honk-if-You-Love Jesus" bumper stickers? "Christian" theme parks? "Roberta" Schuler's possibility thinking? Born-again athletes who rarely attend church? "Rev." Jesse Jackson's Rainbow Coalition? "Christian" aerobics? James Dobson's condoning of interracial marriages? Fundamental preachers kneeling beside Catholic priests in front of abortion clinics? The Reader's Digest "Fifty Beloved Songs of the Faith" including such classics as "Amazing Grace" by Willie Nelson, "Wings of a Dove" by Dolly Parton and "The Lord's Prayer" by the Mormom Tabernacle Choir? And last, but not least, Bible-totin', Southern Baptist, choir member Bill Clinton (a.k.a. "Slick Willie") campaigning on MTV, playing a saxophone on the Arsenio Hall Show and beginning his presidency by supporting queers in the military?

As everything reproduces after its own kind, should we be surprised that Billy Graham recently became the first of his profession to be honored with a star in Hollywood's Walk of Fame? Dr. Graham has also been listed in Gallup's "Ten Most Admired Men in the World" poll thirty times in thirty years, more than any other recipient. *"Woe unto you, when all men shall speak well of you!"* (Luke 6:26)

While pastoring in northern Idaho, this author clipped the following advertisement from the "personals" section of the local newspaper:

> Christian Mom, 22 years old, would like to meet a man who **also** lives for the Lord. I'm not into **worldly** things. I like Christian rock, bingo, boating, skiing, movies and **quiet** evenings at home. I am 5 feet 6 inches, 120 lbs, blue eyes and blond hair. Send name and photo to **Christian**, c/o (and the local P.O. box was given).

However, to gain the ultimate insight into such watered-down Christianity, consider the spiritual dilemma of "Concerned and Praying" as printed recently in Dear Abby's column. This one is really hard to beat!

> Dear Abby,
>   I am writing because I need some advice about myself spiritually. You see, I am a **topless dancer** and I also consider myself a **good Christian**. I don't want to change my job because I am a single parent and make a good living for myself and my family. This job allows me to spend time with my children, take classes at the university and live a **respectable life style**. I will eventually get my degree and pursue a career.
>   I believe in God, and live a **clean, virtuous life**. I go straight home after work at the club and do not accept invitations from

customers. Abby, do **you** think a person can dance topless and believe in God?

Concerned and Praying

The absurdity of the question was exceeded only by the absurdity of the answer!

Dear Concerned,
     Obviously a person can dance topless and believe in God, **because you do!**

So much for the wisdom of a liberal Jew!

With the greater proliferation of English versions occuring in the second half of this century, discerning believers have observed a distinct parallel between these new arrivals and the nation's growing ills. In the light of Psalm 33:12a, *"Blessed is the nation whose God is the LORD,"* don't you find it rather interesting that the blasphemous *Revised Standard Version* showed up in 1952, the same year the United Nations occupied its permanent headquarters in New York City? (This was also the same year that Dr. J. Frank Norris went to Heaven.) Elvis Presley would begin leading America's youth to destruction in another three years. Following the arrival of the *New American Standard Version* (1960) and the *New English Bible* (1961) came the Supreme Court ban on prayer (1962), the Beatles' appearance on the Ed Sullivan Show (1963), and the assassination of President Kennedy (1964).
     The *Good News for Modern Man* paraphrase (1966) spelled bad news for old-fashioned mothers with sons in *Vietnam*. And should we be surprised that *Roe vs. Wade* (1973) and *Watergate* (1973) just happened to occur in the same year that the *New International Version* hit the market? An insignificant notice which appeared in a 1961 edition of the *New York Times* speaks volumes, "The Fulton Street prayer meetings held during the noon hour for the past 103 years have been *shut down*."[48]

Having walked with the spiritual giants of yesteryear, Dr. Jack Hyles, pastor of the First Baptist Church of Hammond, Indiana concurs in this analysis:

> Check the history of Christianity in America, and see how well we've done without all these extra Bibles. Check the history of the church in America from 1950 back, before every little preacher had the misfortune to sit at the feet of a college theologian . . . Brother, it seems to me if there is any place in the world where

you ought to have your faith in the Bible stabilized, it's a Christian college or Christian seminary. However, the truth is that's where you get your faith shaken.[49]

With an ever-increasing hodge-podge of NIV-espousing Charismatics, Neo-Evangelicals, Southern Baptists and pseudo-Fundamentalists abandoning their soul-winning responsibilities, Dr. Hyles' phenomenal ministry remains the epitome of the King James Bible's fruit-bearing capacity.

Over 650,000 converts (approximately one out of every fourteen Chicago-area residents) have walked the aisles of First Baptist Church trusting Christ as their personal Saviour. You can be sure that each of these precious souls was dealt with out of the "Old Black Book"—the *only* Bible sanctioned from on high!

"And they that be wise shall shine as the brightness of the firmament; and they that turn many to righteousness, as the stars for ever and ever." (Daniel 12:3)

XIII

Enter, the Jesuits

". . . giving heed to seducing spirits, and doctrines of devils; Speaking lies in hypocrisy; having their conscience seared with a hot iron."
(I Timothy 4:1b, 2)

The central observation of our preceding chapter was that the perpetual fruit-bearing accomplishments of the King James Bible constitute an irrefutable argument for divine sanction. However, the god of this world was not about to surrender his kingdom of darkness without a struggle. Our present study will examine Satan's intense resistance to the A.D. 1611 Authorized Version as orchestrated through the "bloody whore" of Revelation chapter 17.

With the translation project of King James barely under way, an opening round of tremors was suddenly felt. On October 26, 1605, an unsigned letter was delivered to the Lord Chamberlain, Monteagle, warning him to stay away from the much-delayed opening session of Parliament on November 5th. On that occasion the King, Royal Family, and entire Parliamentary body were to assemble in Westminster Palace.

The portentous note was passed to the King's chief minister, Robert Cecil, first Earl of Salisbury, who in turn showed it to James at a special midnight audience. A major investigation was immediately launched.

Unbeknown to the King, a band of four Roman Catholics, Thomas Winter, Thomas Percy, John Wright and Guy Fawkes, led by another papist, Robert Catesby,[1] had taken an oath to assassinate him and the members of the House of Commons. Their pledge was sealed with a solemn communion service, served by a Jesuit priest, Father John Gerard.[2] Arms had been smuggled in from Flanders to facilitate an open revolt following the King's murder. These were purchased by a widening circle of conspirators which included Sir Edward Digby and Francis Tresham.[3]

Because history is *His Story*, a repeated postponement of the opening Parliamentary session began to unnerve the plotters, especially since a number of innocent victims were certain to perish in the attack. After conferring with two additional Jesuits, Father Oswald Greenway (via the confessional) and Father Henry Garnet, Provincial of the English Jesuits, a plan was decided upon to minimize unnecessary carnage. On the morning of the plot's unfolding, urgent messages were to be sent to the pro-Catholic members of Parliament calling them away from their unsuspecting presence in harm's way. Monteagle's note was one such warning and was sent by his Catholic relative, Francis Tresham.

At the stroke of midnight on November 5th, British security agents discovered the suspicious presence of Guy Fawkes (or, as he preferred, Guido Fawkes), a Catholic soldier of fortune, positioned outside the cellar door of Westminster Palace. A hurried inspection of the cellar's contents led to a hair-raising discovery.

Hidden beneath a large pile of faggots and coal and positioned beneath the very spot where James would be standing in only a few hours, *thirty-six barrels of gunpowder* were uncovered by the astonished members of the King's secret service. A tinder box and matches were found on Fawkes' person.[4] At one o'clock in the morning, Fawkes was summoned to face the council in the royal bedchamber at Whitehall Palace where he appeared unmoved, expressing as his only regret that he had "failed to blow the Scottish king and his Scottish followers back to Scotland where they belonged."[5]

During the ensuing trial on January 27, 1606, it was learned that the conspirators had secured a nearby house and had labored sixteen hours a day for nearly a year to dig a tunnel from their basement to that of the Palace. To their frustration, they discovered that the foundation walls under the House of Lords were nine feet thick. A secondary route of access was gained through an unsecured adjacent property.[6]

With their subsequent attempt to "shoot it out," Catesby, Percy and Wright were slain leaving Fawkes and three other collaborators to stand trial and be executed the same week in St. Paul's churchyard. ("Guy Fawkes Day" continues to be observed in England to this day.)

Three months later, the trial of the Jesuit, Henry Garnet, was convened. It is significant to note that "Father" Garnet (like Guy Fawkes) had been reared in the *Anglican Church*. Once again, a sentence of death was imposed. Note that the King James translators were caring of the *souls of men*. Paine picks up the somber commentary:

> At Garnet's hanging, May 3, in St. Paul's churchyard, John Overall, Dean of St. Paul's, took time off from his translating to be present. Very gravely and Christianly he and the dean of Winchester urged upon Garnet "a true and lively faith to God-ward," a free and plain statement to the world of his offense; and if any further treason lay in his knowledge, he was begged to unburden his conscience and show a sorrow and detestation of it. Garnet, firm in his beliefs, desired them not to trouble him. So after the men assigned to the gruesome duty had **hanged, drawn, and quartered the victim**, Dean Overall returned to St. Paul's and his Bible task.[7]

After viewing the macabre execution, Overall's Westminster Old Testament company went on to translate, among other verses, I Samuel 10:24, "God save the king"!

The application for today's Bible-believing pastor is all too clear. Any preacher who takes his stand for the King James Bible will *also* find thirty-six barrels of gunpowder under his feet, sooner or later. For the soul winner who would faithfully witness for Christ, there remains the warning of I Corinthians 16:9 – *"For a great door and effectual is opened unto me, and there are **many adversaries.**"*

God's men know from experience that the quickest way to draw the ire of their congregation is to criticize either the church of Rome or her polluted Bibles (i.e, the modern English translations based on *Vaticanus*). This is often due to the church member's unwillingness to acknowledge the lost condition of his or her Catholic acquaintances and to extend a personal witness. The courageous shepherd will ignore such threatenings, giving greater regard to his pastoral injunction in I Timothy 4:6 to *"put the brethren in remembrance of these things,"* (i.e., the presence of an evil church earmarked by doctrines of celibacy and fasting [I Timothy 4:3]).

The fact that such antagonism can be seen coming from the ranks of born-again people is highly significant. No greater evidence exists for our present-day apostasy than the growing acceptance of Roman Catholicism by professing blood-washed believers. Such open "mollycoddling" is a phenomenon unique to twentieth-century Christianity. When Dr. Thomas Holland, senior translator of the Oxford group, lay dying, his last words spoken in Latin were, "I commend you to the love of God, and to the *hatred of popery* and superstition."[8] The *Millenary Petition* itself had requested the suppression of "Popish usages" in the *Book of Common Prayer*.[9] With scattered references to "His Holiness" as the "man of sin," Dr. Miles Smith did not hesitate to warn the readers of his preface about the dangers of "Popish Persons."[10]

There never has been any love lost between the Catholic clergy and soul-winning Christians. When a priest asked John Wesley where *his* religion was before the Reformation, the no-nonsense Methodist replied, "In the same place your face was before you washed it—*behind the dirt!*"

Of course, believers such as these gained their inspiration from the writings of Luther who never could seem to hurl enough invectives at his former employer. He who would address "His Holiness" as "Your Hellishness" left no question as to the anti-Catholic spirit of his day, writing:

> Many think I am too fierce against popery; on the contrary I complain that I am, alas, too mild; I wish I could breathe out lightning against pope and popedom, and that every wind were a thunderbolt . . . I will curse and scold the scoundrels until I go to my grave, and never shall they have a civil word from me . . . For I am unable to pray without at the same time cursing. If I am prompted to say, "Hallowed be thy name," I must add, "Cursed, damned, outraged be the name of papists." If I am prompted to say, "Thy kingdom come," I must perforce add, "Cursed, damned, destroyed must be the papacy." Indeed, I pray thus orally every day and in my heart, without intermission . . . I never work better than when I am inspired by anger. When I am angry I can write, pray, and preach well, for then my whole temperament is quickened, my understanding sharpened.[11]

How does this clear line of demarcation compare with the Vatican's steady influx of evangelical and pseudo-fundamentalist endorsements? The same high-profile pastor who was cited in chapter one for his endorsement of *The Living Bible* was also quoted as saying, "Billy Graham and the Pope are great moral leaders and I'm honored to be in their presence."

And why would a heretic like Mother Teresa be promoted in Christian bookstores as a spiritual role model for Christian young people? Where are the Bible convictions of a person who would recommend a woman who declares:

> If in coming face to face with God we accept Him in our lives, then we . . . become a better Hindu, a better Muslim, a better Catholic, a better whatever we are . . . What God is in your mind you must accept.[12]

In his book *Global Peace and the Rise of the Antichrist*, Dave Hunt took exception with the so-called leading authority on the Christian family for running an article which identified Pope John Paul II as "the most eminent religious leader who names the name of Christ."[13] When this author contacted James Dobson's headquarters for an explanation, he was politely informed by the public relations department that "Dr. Dobson is a Christian *psychologist*, not a *theologian*." For the record, he is also a *dollar-conscious, pro-Vatican, end-day compromiser.*

This courting of Rome is especially disgraceful in light of the voluminous evidence documenting over fifteen centuries of Vatican-induced butchery. The caliber of material discussed in chapter nine is generally placed on the "back burner" by neo-evangelical scholarship.

For instance, we find the name *Torquemada* conspicuously absent in both the index and the ten-page section dealing with the Inquisition in the *Eerdmans' Handbook to the History of Christianity* (pages 314-323). Concerning these murders, it was stated, "Inquisitors were not all agitated zealots . . . Most were well-educated and devoted to what they considered their duty."[14]

To find out about these Catholic gangsters, one has to read Foxe:

> Torquemada was chief inquisitor until his death, and during the eighteen years he ruled the Holy Office, *ten thousand two hundred and twenty persons* were burned alive, and *ninety-seven thousand three hundred and twenty-two* punished with loss of property, or imprisonment—numbers so large as to seem incredible, but which are given by Llorente, the Spanish historian of the Inquisition, who was well qualified to judge of their accuracy.[15]

Similarly, the same neo-evangelical publication devotes an *entire page* to Pope John XXIII crediting him with, among other things, a "deep but traditional piety,"[16] while relegating the horrendous *St. Bartholomew's Day Massacre* to a mere *thirteen words* elsewhere.[17]

With at least two Catholic historians listed among the contributing editors, we are not surprised that the Eerdmans people would rather you read about Pope John's "kindliness and wit"[18] than the barbaric slaughter of over *ten thousand* Bible-believing Huguenots by bloodthirsty Roman Catholics on August 24, 1572.[19]

Of all the Pope's victims, it was the *Anabaptists* who generally suffered the most. In the year 1528, the fanatically Catholic Charles V, emperor of the Holy Roman Empire (1550-1558), issued an edict making "rebaptism" a *capital crime*. The Diet of Speyer (1529) sanctioned the Emperor's decree and ordered that such heretics should be deprived of any judiciary process and killed immediately like "wild beasts." An Anabaptist historian has left us this moving legacy:

> Some were racked and drawn asunder; others were burnt to ashes and dust; some were roasted on pillars or torn with red-hot pincers . . . Others were hanged on trees, beheaded with the sword, or thrown into the water . . . Some starved or rotted in darksome prisons . . . Some who were deemed too young for execution were whipped with rods, and many lay for years in dungeons . . . Numbers had holes burnt into their cheeks . . . The rest were hunted from one country and place to another. Like owls and ravens, which durst not fly by day, they were often compelled to hide and live in rocks and clefts, in wild forests, or in caves and pits.[20]

However, for the ultimate insight into the true demonic character of "Holy Mother Church," consider the treatment which she has bestowed upon *her own!* In the year 897, Pope Formosus was brought to trial by Pope Stephen VI on the charge of violating certain church laws. Because Formosus was not in a talkative mood, a deacon stood by answering the charges for the tight-lipped defendant. To be sure, this was not your everyday courtroom experience. One thing that made it unique was that the accused had been summoned from the papal *cemetery!* Hibbert informs us:

> The corpse was clothed in pontifical vestments, seated upon a throne and put on trial. Found guilty of all the offences with which it was charged it was stripped of its vestments; the three fingers on the right hand with which papal benediction was customarily bestowed were torn off; and the remains were thrown into the Tiber.[21]

When called on the carpet to account for these atrocities, Catholic apologists will invariably take cover behind such rhetoric

as, "the spirit of the times," or "the unfortunate acts of an
unenlightened age," etc. That this is pure nonsense can be easily
confirmed by a survey of Catholic bloodletting in the *twentieth*
century. Reference works such as *The Vatican's Holocaust* by
Avro Manhattan and *Convert . . . or Die!* by Edmond Paris
present the documented facts that the Catholic church liquidated
over *800,000* orthodox Serbians in Croatia, Yugoslavia, during the
years 1940-1945. That totals out to *40 times the fatality count of
the Inquisition and the St. Bartholomew's Day Massacre
combined*!

The next time some bigoted Catholic tries to dismiss his
murderous heritage as a "thing of the past," ask him to explain:
250 peasants buried alive in the Serbian district of Bjelovar;[22]
2,000 children gassed in the death camp at Bosanska Gradiska;[23]
a father and son crucified together and then burned in their own
home in Mliniste;[24] mothers and children (as young as three)
impaled on the same stake in Gorevac;[25] a mother forced to hold
the basin which caught the blood of her four sons as their throats
were slit in Kosinj;[26] an expectant mother having her unborn
child cut out of her womb and replaced by a cat in the death
camp at Jasenovac;[27] 1,360 prisoners having their throats cut in
a single night by one guard during a sadistic throat-cutting
contest (also at Jasenovac);[28] not to mention dismemberments;[29]
beheadings;[30] crowns of thorns;[31] "graviso" knives for specialized
throat cutting;[32] necklaces of human tongues and eyes;[33] the
confining of prisoners to rooms filled with blood to the ankles;[34]
and ten thousand other atrocities condoned by the Roman
Catholic Archbishop Aloysius Stepinac who prayed at the opening
of the Croatian Parliament in February of 1942, for ". . . the Holy
Ghost to descend upon the sharp knives of the Ustashi (Catholic
guerrilla army)."[35]

As discussed in previous chapters, the Papacy lost nearly half
of Europe to the arrival of Gutenberg's press. McClure
summarizes:

> The printing of the English Bible has proved to be by far the
> mightiest barrier ever reared to repel the advance of Popery, and
> to damage all the resources of the Papacy. Originally intended for
> the five or six millions who dwelt within the narrow limits of the
> British Islands, it at once formed and fixed their language, till
> then unsettled; and has since gone with that language to the isles
> and shores of every sea.[36]

Having held these invaluable real estate possessions for so
many long centuries, the Vatican was not about to give them up
without a fight. At stake was her perennial addiction to the
affairs of *this life* as depicted in Revelation 18:12-13.

> *"The merchandise of gold, and silver, and precious stones, and*
> *of pearls, and fine linen, and purple, and silk, and scarlet, and all*
> *thyine wood, and all manner vessels of ivory, and all manner*
> *vessels of most precious wood, and of brass, and iron, and marble,*
> *And cinnamon, and odours, and ointments, and frankincense, and*
> *wine, and oil, and fine flour, and wheat, and beasts, and sheep,*
> *and horses, and chariots, and slaves, **and souls of men.**"*

To regain her "corner on the market," Rome created an elite
para-military gestapo unit that would make Himmler's SS appear
like a Sunday school in comparison. Sparking what historians
have named the Counter-Reformation, the infamous *Society of
Jesus* was founded by Ignatius de Loyola in 1534. More commonly
known as the *Jesuits*, their avowed aim was to retrieve Rome's
wayward children by centering their attack on the *Textus
Receptus* and resultant English translations.

Because of his thirty plus years of soldiering, Ignatius insisted
on a regimented program of discipline, self-denial and above all
else, a blind loyalty to the Pope. Understandably, such a desired
result would be brought about by intensive degrees of
brainwashing. Boehmer writes:

> Ignatius understood more clearly than any other leader of men
> who preceded him that the best way to raise a man to a certain
> ideal is to become master of his imagination. We "imbue into him
> spiritual forces which he would find very difficult to eliminate
> later", forces more lasting than all the best principles and
> doctrines; these forces can come up again to the surface,
> sometimes after years of not even mentioning them, and become
> so imperative that the will finds itself unable to oppose any
> obstacle, and has to follow their irresistible impulse.[37]

The army that dedicated itself to destroying your King James
Bible did not pop up over night. Nearly five centuries ago, Loyola
embarked upon a program that would develop the *ultimate secret
agent*, far superior to anything that the world has ever seen.
Huber comments:

> Military obedience is not the equivalent of Jesuitic obedience;
> the latter is more extensive as it gets hold of the whole man and

is not satisfied like the other, with an exterior act, but requires the sacrifice of the will and laying aside of one's own judgment.[38]

Requiring all soldiers to repeat hundreds of times that their General (also called from his black cassock, the "Black Pope") is none other than Christ Himself, Ignatius was able to insist that his followers "must see black as white, if the church says so."[39]

Loyola's impressive new order provided Rome with the needed inspiration (muscle) to embark upon the historic *Council of Trent* (1545-1563). It was the Church's intention throughout this conference to reaffirm her most basic medieval theology while pronouncing anathemas upon any and all detractors. Some of the more noteworthy declarations concerned: recognition of the Old Testament Apocrypha as inspired, acceptance of Church traditions as equal in authority with Holy Scripture, official sanctioning of purgatory, and a renouncing of salvation by faith alone. An example of this last canon stated:

> If anyone saith, that by faith alone the impious is justified, in such wise as to mean, that nothing else is required . . . let him be anathema . . . If any one saith, that Christ Jesus was given of God to men, as a redeemer in whom to trust, and not also as a legislator whom to obey: let him be anathema.[40]

According to Ignatius, the purpose of his order was for the promotion of the "greater glory of God." This would translate to *the enslavement of an entire planet to the undisputed authority of the Roman pontiff.*

The Jesuits initiated their attempted world conquest by establishing "houses" in the nations still favorable toward Catholicism, such as Italy, Portugal and Spain. Having stabilized the home front, "missionaries" like Francis Xavier (1506-1552) launched out to the Orient and other distant lands as yet untouched by either faith.

However, the Jesuits' highest priority lay in recapturing those nations lost to the Protestant Reformation. The methods employed by this clandestine order are worthy of study as their ultimate target remains America and the despised Authorized Version.

The *modus operandi* for the Society of Jesus can be outlined by the following six stages: *education, indoctrination, infiltration, sedition, sedation and persecution.*

History confirms that a Jesuit takeover invariably begins with the establishment of colleges and universities sporting high academic standards to attract the aspiring scholars of a targeted nation. This inaugural stratagem of *education* cannot be overemphasized. *Apostasy is always conceived in the classroom.* Newman informs us:

> They early realized the vast importance of directing higher education as a means of gaining control of the lives of the ablest and best-connected young men and making trained intellect subservient to their purposes ... The marked ability of the Jesuit teachers, their unsurpassed knowledge of human nature, their affability of manners, and their remarkable adaptability to the idiosyncrasies and circumstances of each individual, made them practically irresistible when once they came into close relations with susceptible youth.[41]

The independent-minded Sir Francis Bacon (1565-1626) was so impressed with their schools that he said, "Such as they are, would that they were ours."[42]

Having lured the unsuspecting student by displaying a commitment to academic excellence, the Jesuit professors waste little time in shifting to their second stage of *indoctrination*. Newman states:

> It is probable that more time was employed in molding their religious and moral characters into complete harmony with the ideals of the society than in securing a mastery of the studies of the course ... Large numbers of the most desirable young men who entered their schools with no intention of becoming members of the society were won by the patient efforts of those in charge.[43]

With the natural turnover of several graduating classes, the inevitable third stage of *infiltration* begins. Because of their superior training and burning conviction, many of the best graduates are soon found occupying the leadership positions in government, commerce and the military. Newman continues:

> Their proselyting zeal led them to go forth into the surrounding regions and by personal effort to win back to the faith those that had become involved in heresy. Whole communities were often reconverted in an incredibly short time.[44]

This absorption into secular society has been facilitated by the Order's unique exemption from traditional clerical garb. Edmond Paris comments on this amazing secret order:

It is the same today; the 33,000 official members of the Society operate all over the world in the capacity of her personnel, officers of a truly secret army containing in its ranks heads of political parties, high ranking officials, generals, magistrates, physicians, Faculty professors, etc., all of them striving to bring about, in their own sphere, "l'Opus dei", God's work, in reality the plans of the papacy.[45]

The capacity for successful infiltration has been made possible by the all important fourth stage of *sedition*. A true Jesuit is the consummate embodiment of I Timothy 4:2, which says, "*Speaking lies in hypocrisy; having their conscience seared with a hot iron.*" Boettner has pointed out that the word *Jesuitical* has entered the dictionary as a synonym for that which is crafty or deceptive.[46]

Throughout the centuries, Jesuits have made it clear that they will stop at nothing to realize their purpose of global subjection to the Vatican. Because of their incredible doctrines of *mental reservation* (discussed in chapter two) and *probabilism* (an opinion is rendered "probable" if one authority can be found to support it), Jesuits can't be trusted as far as you can throw them. This deception was instilled early in their training when they were enjoined to:

> . . . hold their heads slightly down, without bending it to the left or right; they must not look up, and when they speak to someone, they are not to look them straight in the eyes so as to see them only indirectly.[47]

It is in the arena of world politics that the Jesuit is most adept. His reputation for subterfuge, espionage, subversion and worse is well-known to the serious student of history. Fifty-one documented expulsions from the governments of this world is a good indication that Jesuit missionaries do more than simply pass out tracts.[48]

In fact, the sons of Loyola are so diabolical that they have even been ousted from fanatically Catholic countries. On April 6, 1762, France gave them the boot describing their doctrines as:

> Perverse, a destroyer of all religious and honest principles, insulting to Christian morals, pernicious to civil society, hostile to the rights of the nation, the royal power, and even the security of the sovereigns and obedience of their subjects; suitable to stir up the greatest disturbances in the States, conceive and maintain the worst kind of corruption in men's hearts.[49]

The secret to the Jesuits' longevity in the face of such widespread resistance has been their willingness to continually reenter the various countries wherever and whenever possible. Lamenting such a resurgence of Jesuit activity, John Adams wrote to Thomas Jefferson, in 1816:

> I am not happy about the rebirth of the Jesuits. Swarms of them will present themselves under more disguises ever taken by even a chief of the Bohemians, as printers, writers, publishers, school teachers, etc. If ever an association of people deserved eternal damnation, on this earth and in hell, it is this Society of Loyola.[50]

Of their numerous sinister practices, none is as shocking to civilized men and women as the official Jesuit sanction for *political assassination*. A few lines from Suarez will shed light on the acrimony of Adams:

> It is permitted to an individual to kill a tyrant in virtue of the right of self-defense; for though the community does not command it, it is always to be understood that it wishes to be defended by every one of its citizens individually, and even by a stranger . . . Thus, after he has been declared to be deprived of his kingdom, it becomes legal to treat him as a real tyrant; and consequently any man has a right to kill him.[51]

It should be remembered that Suarez and his fellow Jesuits looked to the Pope and/or their General as having the right to declare *any* ruler deprived of his kingdom. Should a government head antagonize "His Holiness," a papal "thumbs down" would create a literal open season on the unfortunate official (referred to as "the minister of God" in Romans 13:4). This was precisely what precipitated the Jesuit attack on St. Bartholomew's Day. Admiral Coligny and Henry of Navarre did not appeal to the Pope, so he simply put out a "contract" on them. (Now you know why the Mafia comes from Italy.)

Closely related to *sedition* is the fifth stage of the Jesuit cycle—*sedation*. When one thinks of the reciprocal arrangement of these two concepts, he is reminded of the age-old question of "Which came first—the chicken or the egg?"

To ease the conscience of a *seditious* church member is one of the Jesuit's most invigorating means of perpetuating his own activities. This salving ministry has been carried out through the use of the *confessional booth*. The vicious cycle is seen when the freshly sedated conscience is thus incited to further sedition which requires additional sedation. Newman states:

> From the beginning they utilized the confessional to the utmost as a means of mastering the souls of men and women and gaining a knowledge of religious and political affairs that could serve the ends of the society. The sons and daughters of the rich and the noble they sought by every means to bring under their influence, and they were soon the favorite confessors in the imperial court and in many of the royal courts of Europe. It was their constant aim to make their confessional system so attractive to the rich and the noble that they would seek it of their own accord. To this end their casuistical system of moral theology was elaborated, whereby they were able to appease the consciences of their subjects in all kinds of wrong-doing.[52]

With these five steps in place, Loyola's henchmen would just about have the particular wayward nation back in the fold. There remained but the last stage of "tightening the screws" through *persecution.*

> When they had once molded a ruler to their will and made him the subservient instrument of their policy, they were ever at his side dictating to him the measures to be employed for the eradication of heresy and the complete reformation of his realm according to the Jesuit ideal, and they were ever ready, with full papal authority, to conduct inquisitorial work.[53]

While the Protestant factions became embroiled in an ever-widening circle of doctrinal disputes, the fresh troops of Loyola employed their sixfold plan successfully in one country after another.

In 1550 the Jesuit LeJay received permission from Ferdinand of Austria to establish a Jesuit college in Vienna. Within a year, fifteen Jesuit agents were roaming the countryside. Two years later, Ignatius installed a special college in Rome for the express purpose of training "missionaries" to Germany. By 1556, the universities at Ingolstadt and Cologne were overrun with Jesuit professors.[54]

Also in 1556, the King of Bohemia made the mistake of opening the door and Jesuit schools were immediately founded in Prague, Tyrnau, Olmütz and Brünn. The Jesuit work in Munich was so successful that the city was nicknamed "the German Rome."[55]

With dozens of other countries invaded (i.e., Austria, 1550; Sweden, 1568; Poland, 1569; Belgium, 1592, to name a few), the numbers began to tell their own story. By 1626 there was a total of 15,000 Jesuits, 476 colleges and 36 seminaries. By 1750, the numbers had jumped to 22,000 members, 669 colleges and 176 seminaries besides hundreds of lesser schools.[56]

For an excellent illustration of the havoc wrought by a Jesuit inroad, consider the case of the previously mentioned St. Bartholomew's Day Massacre. In 1551 the queen mother, Catherine de Medici, permitted the order to establish a house in a corner of Auvergne, known as Billom. Shortly thereafter, the *College of Clermont* was started in Paris.

On August 24, 1572, several thousand Huguenots (French Christians) descended on Paris to attend the wedding of the Protestant, Henry of Navarre (later King Henry IV), to Margaret of Valois. Over ten thousand of these loyal subjects of Henry were subsequently dispatched in a surprise nocturnal raid ordered by the Catholic, Charles IX, King of France. Manschreck cites the *Relation due massacre* by De Thou for the following eyewitness account.

> The streets were covered with dead bodies, the rivers stained, the doors and gates of the palace bespattered with blood. Wagon loads of corpses, men, women, girls, even infants, were thrown into the Seine . . . Spire Niquet, a poor bookbinder, who was the support of seven children, was slowly roasted over a bonfire of the books found in his house, and then pitched, half dead into the water . . . In the Rue St. Martin, another woman, about to be delivered, had taken refuge on the roof of her house, and after being killed, was ripped up and her infant dashed against the wall . . . One little girl was bathed in the blood of her butchered father and mother and threatened with the same fate if she ever became a Huguenot.[57]

At the instigation of Catherine, four different coins were minted to commemorate the ghastly slaughter, the first bearing the image of Pope Gregory XIII. Within two years, the deranged King (Catherine's son) died at but twenty-four, screaming from his deathbed, "What bloodshed, what murders! What evil counsel have I followed! O my God, forgive me! . . . I am lost!"[58]

With the growth of Jesuit power, the countries of Europe became embroiled in one religious war after another.

On October 11, 1531, a Catholic army of 8,000 crushed Zwingli's smaller force of 1,500 in the battle of Kappel. The body of the slain reformer was quartered and burned on a pyre of dung.[59]

With the death of Martin Luther in 1546, his spiritual descendants were set upon by a reviving Catholicism in the Schmalkald War of 1547. After suffering an initial defeat, the Protestant forces were rallied by Maurice of Saxony with the resultant Treaty of Passau (1552) temporarily securing Lutheran freedoms.[60]

The Huguenot Wars in France began in 1560 and raged intermittently until religious toleration was finally granted through the Edict of Nantes in 1598.

In 1567, the notorious Duke of Alva arrived in the Netherlands to suppress heresy on behalf of Philip II of Spain. The bloodletting of this campaign was so rampant that a houseful of Dutch Christians in Rotterdam was spared when one of their own created a ruse by slaying a goat and sweeping the blood underneath the bolted doors into the street.[61]

However, campaigns such as these were mere child's play when compared to the suffering of the Thirty Years' War (1618-1648). Fought mainly in Germany, the antagonists consisted of several German princes backed by the Protestant powers of Sweden, Denmark, France and England against the Catholic House of Hapsburg which controlled, in addition to The Holy Roman Empire, Spain, Austria, Bohemia, Hungary, most of Italy and the Southern Netherlands.

The ubiquitous "Jesuit Connection" was surmised by Newman who wrote:

> The house of Hapsburg, in its Austrian branch, by the close of the sixteenth century, had come strongly under the influence of the Jesuits. As Archduke of Styria (1596 onward), Ferdinand, who as emperor was to play so prominent a part throughout the Thirty Years' War, carried out remorselessly the Jesuit policy in which he had been schooled from infancy by prohibiting Protestant worship, banishing the Protestant clergy, and placing before Protestant laymen the alternative of conversion or exile.[62]

Throughout these intolerant years, Ferdinand's conscience was salved by his Jesuit confessor Viller.[63]

Although the historic *Peace of Westphalia*, concluded in 1648, was essentially a victory for Protestantism, the overall loss from war-related extractions was incalculable. Newman summarizes the Jesuit-induced holocaust:

> The extent of the destruction of life through the Thirty Years' War cannot be estimated. If we take into account the multitudes who died of starvation and exposure, the hundreds of thousands

of women and children who were slain in the sacking and
destroying of the towns and cities, the fearful waste of life that
must have been involved in camp—following, the deaths caused by
the war would amount to many millions. In Bohemia, at the
beginning of the war, there was a population of two million, of
whom about eight-tenths were Protestant; at the close of the war
there were about eight hundred thousand Catholics and no
Protestants. Taking Germany and Austria together, we may safely
say that the population was reduced by one-half, if not by two-
thirds. And the deaths were in most cases the result of untold
sufferings and as horrible as we can conceive. So far as the cities
and towns were not utterly destroyed, they were the mere
shadows of what they had been. Their buildings were dilapidated
and large numbers of them unoccupied. Business of all kinds had
been almost entirely destroyed. Agriculture had equally suffered.
Livestock had been almost exterminated; farming implements had
become scarce and rude. Desolation was everywhere.[64]

However, because of the inevitable westward expansion of
civilization, England's culture loomed ever larger as the Jesuits'
primary target of conquest. In 1569 the Vatican agent, William
Allen, established a college in Douai (then in the Spanish
Netherlands), and a second school in Rome ten years later for the
training of Jesuit missionaries to Britain. Allen set forth his goals
in a passionate manner:

> We make it our first and foremost study . . . to stir up in the
> minds of Catholics . . . zeal and just indignation against the
> heretics. This we do by setting before the eyes of the students the
> exceeding majesty of the ceremonial of the Catholic Church in the
> place where we live . . . At the same time we recall the mournful
> contrast that obtains at home: the utter desolation of all things
> sacred which there exists . . . our friends and kinsfolk, all our
> dear ones, and countless souls besides, perishing in schism and
> godlessness; every jail and dungeon filled to overflowing, not with
> thieves and villains but with Christ's priests and servants, nay,
> with our parents and kinsmen. There is nothing, then, that we
> ought not to suffer, rather than to look on at the ills that affect
> our nation.[65]

The capture of Douai by Calvinist troops in 1578 sent the
Jesuit College into exile in Reims until 1593. By the year 1585, a
total of 268 graduates had secretly infiltrated England.[66] The
leading personalities of this time were Jesuit agents Robert
Parsons and Edmund Campion who entered the country in 1580
disguised as English military officers. The only Gospel they

preached was the overthrow of Elizabeth! Boehmer states:

> Then, under diverse disguises, they spread from county to county, from country house to castle. In the evening, they would hear confession; in the morning, they would preach and give communion, then they would disappear as mysteriously as they had arrived.[67]

Green adds that their many disguises included "the cassock of the *English Clergy*."[68]

It has been estimated that they won over *20,000* converts[69] within a year of their arrival. However, their circulated literature encouraging the assassination of Elizabeth brought their English mission to an abrupt end. Although Parsons escaped to the Continent, "Father" Campion was captured and confined to the Tower, where he was "racked" severely to elicit the names of additional conspirators. On the following day when his jailor asked him how he felt, the exhausted Jesuit replied, "Not ill, because not at all."[70] On December 1, 1581, he and fourteen others were publicly hanged.

In 1583, Pope Gregory XIII formulated a plan to invade England with three armies at once—those of Ireland, France and Spain. Providentially, the Queen's agents discovered the plot and effective counter-measures caused a postponement of the attack.[71]

Three years later, another Jesuit, John Ballard, was arrested for conspiring to bring Mary Stuart to the throne via a general uprising of England's Catholics. He and thirteen others were hanged and then brought down from the gibbet *alive* to be dismembered and disemboweled (torn limb from trunk).[72] Sixty-one priests and forty-nine laymen would be hung for conspiracy over the next fifteen years.

With friends like these, Mary Stuart needed few enemies. The intensified Jesuit activity eventually cost the would-be queen her head in 1587. Only weeks after her momentous execution, Pope Sixtus V pledged 600,000 gold crowns to King Philip's military coffers for the financing of an immediate invasion of England. In the words of Cardinal Allen, Britain's "usurping, heretic, prostitute" queen must surely be deposed.[73]

On the morning of May 29, 1588, over 27,050 sailors and soldiers set sail from Lisbon's harbor aboard some 130 vessels sporting an average weight of 445 tons—the largest fleet in maritime annals to that time.

The destruction of the Protestant religion was perceived as an intensely spiritual mission. The campaign's official banner read, "Exurge, Domine, et Vindica Causam Tuam" – "Arise, O Lord, and vindicate thy cause."[74] Indeed, "revival" had broken out during the final stages of departure; prostitutes were expelled, gambling curtailed and profanity was reduced to a minimum. A high mass was celebrated and to a man, the Eucharist had been reverently received. Several hundred monks were among the passengers.[75]

On July 19th, the vanguard of Spain's invincible armada was spotted. A mere thirty-four warships and fifty-eight support vessels under the command of Charles, Lord Howard, assisted by Sir Francis Drake prepared to engage her. What happened next has constituted one of the most remarkable displays of Divine intervention in all of recorded history.

The year before, Drake had led a surprise attack on the Spanish ships in Cádiz Harbor and discovered firsthand the Armada's construction project. Having been reared in the home of a Puritan minister, the undaunted "P.K." assured his Queen:

> God increase your most excellent Majesty's forces both by sea and land daily, . . . for this I surely think: there was never any force so strong as there is now ready or making ready against your Majesty and true religion; but . . . **the Lord of all strengths is stronger and will defend the truth of his word.**[76]

Outmaneuvered by the smaller British vessels, the Spanish admiral, Medina-Sidonia, wrote in desperation:

> The enemy pursue me, they fire on me from morn till dark, but they will not grapple . . . There is no remedy, for they are swift and we are slow.[77]

Sustaining over 8,000 casualties on the twenty-seventh alone, Medina-Sidonia had had enough! However, the Northern seas would devour many thousands more along the stormy route of retreat. Twenty-three ships were wrecked off the rocky coast of Ireland alone. Over 1,100 drowned Spaniards were washed up on the beach of Sligo. And those who made it to the shore alive had their throats cut by the Kernes (poorer class of Irishmen).

Only fifty-one ships bearing 10,000 survivors were able to limp back to Spain. The Jesuit-educated Durant could only say that, "The winds favored Elizabeth."[78] However, a total count of English losses placed at *60 men and 0 ships* would divert the

attention of sober men to Him Who *"createth the wind."* (Amos
4:13) Not a single hole was made below any English waterline!

With the Armada's crushing defeat driving Philip into isolation
(a papal reneging on the 600,000 crowns not helping matters
any), a major Jesuit project would emerge as the Vatican's last
resort and ultimate secret weapon.

Heretofore, the success of English Protestantism had been
clearly attributable to her possession of God's Word in the
vernacular. In 1582, Rome gave tacit endorsement to the adage,
"If you can't beat them, join them" by producing her own
English version of the New Testament as rendered by the Jesuit
scholars at Reims (the Old Testament was completed in Douai
and published in 1610).

Such a proclivity for momentary pragmatism has remained one
of the Order's most distinguishable traits, Newman stating:

> As a means of winning back Protestant communities to the
> Catholic faith, they gave the utmost attention to the cultivation
> of the preaching gifts among the members and used every device
> suggested by Protestant worship or otherwise for the
> popularization of the church services.[79]

At this point, it is important to realize that the Pope's new
Bible was not issued to help Catholics, but rather to hurt
Christians. All good papists were still obliged to adhere religiously
to the official Tridentine Profession of Faith (1564) which read,
in part:

> I acknowledge the sacred Scripture according to that sense
> which Holy Mother Church has held and holds, to whom it
> belongs to decide upon the true sense and interpretation of the
> holy Scriptures, nor will I ever receive and interpret the Scripture
> except according to the unanimous consent of the fathers.[80]

As stated in an earlier chapter, it was this author's experience
to spend twenty-two years in the Catholic church (including
twelve years of parochial school) without ever reading a single
verse out of the church's official Bible.

The Douay-Rheims "Bible" was a translation of the Latin
Vulgate and therefore contained the multiplied perversities of
Vaticanus and *Sinaiticus*. With education as their forte, the
Jesuits would henceforth seek to undermine the Authorized
Version with an *appeal to superior manuscripts*, superior being
determined by *age*. Dr. Gipp writes:

The Jesuits' task was to entice Protestant scholarship back to Rome. They knew that they could not wean the leaders of Protestantism back into Rome as long as the stubborn "heretics" clung to the pure text of the Reformers. This Bible would have to be replaced with one which contained the pro-Roman Catholic readings of Jerome's Vulgate and the Jesuit translation of 1582. It would be necessary to "educate" the Protestant scholars to believe that their Reformation Text was unreliable and that their Authorized Version was "not scholarly." Once thus programmed, the egotistical scholars would spontaneously attack their own Bible and believe that they were helping God.[81]

The impressive-sounding designation conferred upon this process of scrutinizing the preserved Word of God became known as the "science of textual criticism." Contrary to common belief, higher criticism did not *begin* with German rationalists but with *Jesuit "fathers"*!

The first scholar to employ "scientific methods" to the so-called textual and literary problems of the Bible was a Catholic priest by the name of Richard Simon (1638-1712). The Oxford Dictionary states:

> Biblical scholar. From 1662 to 1678 he was a member of the French Oratory. His *Histoire Criticque du Vieux Testament* (1678), arguing from the existence of duplicate accounts of the same incident and variations of style, denied that Moses was the author of the Pentateuch. **He is generally regarded as the founder of Old Testament criticism.**[82]

Notice how the Oxford editors completely skirted Simon's *Catholic* credentials. For the record, "Father" Richard gained his liberal insights from the unsaved Jewish philosopher, Baruch Spinoza (1632-1677).

The next personality connected with the Catholic foundations for textual criticism was "Father" Jean Mabillon (1632-1707). Oxford bills him as, "the most erudite and discerning of all *Maurists* (a Benedictine order)."[83] In response to a controversy over the legitimacy of certain church documents, Mabillon published his work *Latin Paleography in Official Documents*. A second Benedictine, "Father" Bernard de Montfaucon (1655-1741), made a negative application of Mabillon's laws to the *Textus Receptus* entitled *Paleographic Gracea* and published it in Paris in 1708.

The Catholic physician/theologian Jean Astruc (1684-1766) was the next "critic" on the scene and decided that two different men wrote the Pentateuch! In his impressive-sounding *Conjectures sur les Mémoires originaux dont il paroît que moyse s'est servi pour composer le Livre de la Genèse* in 1753, Astruc maintained that Genesis had been pieced together from earlier documents.[84]

Throughout these turbulent years, the Jesuits made major inroads into the highest branches of government. In 1642, the pro-Vatican Charles I (1600-1649) plunged his nation into civil war. He was arrested, tried for treason, and on January 30, 1649, beheaded for his crime. Charles II was so fanatically Catholic that he had Oliver Cromwell's body dug up and decapitated in 1660.

Having set the science of textual criticism upon a solid footing, Rome passed the baton to the dead orthodox scholars of eighteenth-century Germany. Oxford says of Johann Salomo Semler (1725-1791), that:

> . . . he was one of the first German theologians to apply the critico-historical method to the study of the Bible, and he reached some novel and unorthodox conclusions.[85]

That special Jesuit school in Rome, *Collegium Germanicum*, founded for the training of "missionaries" to Germany had done its job well! "Father" Johann Adam Mohler (1796-1838), professor of history and theology at Tubingen and Munich (the "German Rome"), was the moving force of this time.

Clinging to the destructive tenets of higher criticism, one apostate Lutheran after another began questioning the "scientific accuracy" of the Holy Bible. A short list of such liberals would include: Ferdinand Christian Baur (1792-1860); Wilhelm Martin Leberecht DeWette (1780-1849); Johann Gottfried Eichhorn (1752-1827); Heinrich Georg August Ewald (1803-1875); Heinrich Friedrich Wilhem Gesenius (1786-1842); Johann Gottfried Herder (1744-1803); Hermann Hupfeld (1796-1866); Gotthold Ephraim Lessing (1729-1781); Johann David Michaelis (1717-1791); Herman Samuel Reimarus (1694-1768); Frederich Daniel Ernst Schleiermacher (1768-1834); and David Fredrick Strauss (1808-1874); and Julius Wellhausen (1844-1918).

With Martin Luther rolling over in his grave, the time had arrived for the Jesuits' final assault on the land of the Authorized Version. In preparation for the landmark Revision Committee of 1871-1881, Satan orchestrated a three-pronged attack against the English people which would, in time, affect the entire globe.

To eliminate the Biblical account of man's creation, the devil's first "S.W.A.T. team" of Charles Darwin (1809-1882) and Thomas Huxley (1825-1893) landed to revive the fourth-century evolutionary theories of Origen and company. Darwin's *The Origin of the Species* (1859) and *The Descent of Man* (1871) and Huxley's *Zoological Evidences as to Man's Place in Nature* (1863) and *The Physical Basis of Life* (1868) propagated the unscientific nonsense concerning matter and energy that the universe is *self-existing* and *eternal*. The concept of a non-created *anything* is, of course, a blatant rejection of the first and second laws of thermodynamics.

In the absence of a Supreme Being who alone could insist upon a code of moral absolutes, man chose to enthrone his own intelligence as *final authority*. The destructive philosophy of "situation ethics" was the natural outcome of this folly.

Having eliminated man's Divine origin, the next logical step called for a removal of his *means of livelihood*; enter Karl Marx (1813-1883) and Friedrich Engels (1820-1895). Given the fact that Marx never worked a day in his life, his trumpet blasts of "Workers and Farmers of the World Unite" rang out as a most "uncertain sound." In actuality, as a professional student and would-be journalist, Marx embodied the two great arms of Communism that would come to propagate his garbage—the *news media* and the *university*.

Basing his *Communist Manifesto* on Darwin's writings, Marx believed in the abolition of private property (Plato), the abolition of marriage and the family (Plato), and the abolition of the state government (Plato). The so-called equal distribution of wealth advocated in his *Das Kapital* could be reduced to the back-alley maxim of "Steal what you want." (Plato's *Republic*) Some of the more "positive" results of his *evolutionary economics* were: the graded income tax, gun control, compulsory education, classless societies, and the welfare state in general, not to mention the Taiping Rebellion (1850), the Crimean War (1853), the American Civil War (1861-1865), the Franco-Prussian War (1870) and two dozen other conflicts followed by two World Wars!

Someone has said that you cannot separate animal *origins* from animal *conduct*, and animal conduct must be controlled by a *zoo*. The unanswered question remains one of *final authority*; *who* will run the zoo? To paraphrase one of the ending sentences of *Animal Farm*, "Some animals are more equal than others."

The third line of attack centered on England's so-called

"Christian" universities. The leading culprits in this endeavor were Edward Bouverie Pusey (1800-1882) and Frederick Denison Maurice (1805-1872).

Pusey is credited (along with John Keble) with spearheading the pro-Catholic Oxford movement (also known as *Tractarianism*) within the Church of England. From his position as Regius Professor of Hebrew at Oxford and canon of Christ Church, Pusey sought to restore High Church polity and such Romanish doctrines as auricular confession and transubstantiation.[86]

Frederick Maurice was professor of theology at King's College until he was expelled for denying an eternal Hell in his *Theological Essays* (1853). He was later "picked up" by *Cambridge University* and installed as Knightsbridge Professor of Moral Philosophy!

Are you surprised that a school with the reputation of Cambridge should be interested in an avowed apostate like Dr. Maurice? You really shouldn't be, as decades of Jesuit infiltration had finally taken its toll.

One of the better-known Jesuit plants of this period was "Cardinal" John Henry Newman (1801-1890). His followers such as Frederick William Faber (1814-1863) had labeled the preaching of fellow Englishmen like Booth, Whitefield, and Wesley as "detestable and diabolical heresy." Of course, their influence had also spread to English politics. The Emancipation Act of 1829 made it legal for Roman Catholics to become elected to Parliament. After years of spreading pro-Vatican propaganda within the Church of England, the Oxford professor finally "jumped ship" and returned to Rome where he was given a Cardinal's hat in 1879. The sad part of the story is that within one year of his exodus, *over 150 clergy and laymen also crossed over to join him!*

By now, destructive textual critics were everywhere and permeating England with the question, *"Hath God said?"*

John William Colenso (1814-1883), Bishop of Natal, openly questioned the traditional authorship of the Pentateuch and Joshua. He also followed Maurice in denying eternal damnation.[87]

William Robertson Smith (1846-1894) was a Semitic scholar at the Free Church College in Aberdeen, Scotland. After being "shown the door" for his articles in the ninth edition of the Encyclopedia Britannica which opposed the doctrine of inspiration, he too was absorbed by Cambridge. He was also an advocate of J. Wellhausen's heretical position on the Pentateuch.[88]

Samuel Rolles Driver (1846-1914) was Regius Professor of

Hebrew in Oxford. His intellectual credentials led many to question the Mosaic authorship of Deuteronomy.[89]

Benjamin Jowett (1817-1893) was Master of Balliol College, also at Oxford. His essay on "The Interpretation of Scripture" in *Essays and Reviews* drew a storm of controversy from the orthodox faction at Oxford. His most important legacy was said to be his translation of Plato in 1871.[90]

Rowland Williams (1817-1870) was a noted Anglican Divine who was prosecuted for heterodoxy because of his articles on Biblical criticism in *Essays and Reviews*. Sentenced by the Court of Arches to a year's suspension, the sentence was later annulled by the pro-Jesuit Committee of the Privy Council in 1864.[91]

Henry Parry Liddon (1829-1890) was canon of St. Paul's and Dean Ireland professor of Exegesis at Oxford. A staunch supporter of the Tractarians, he spent a quarter of a century promoting Catholic dogma within the Church of England. His intense admiration for Pusey led him to write his biography.[92]

The Catholic most responsible for directing Protestant aggression against the Authorized Version was Cardinal Nicholas Patrick Stephen Wiseman (1802-1865). While rector of the English College at Rome, he studied under Cardinal Angelo Mai (1782-1854), prefect of the Vatican library and celebrated editor of the *Codex Vaticanus*. Wiseman himself was described as "a textual critic of the first rank."[93]

Among the many hundreds of English Protestants who were secretly weaned back to Rome by Wiseman, the three most injurious were Prime Minister William Gladstone (1809-1898); Archbishop Richard Chenevix Trench (1807-1886); and the previously mentioned Cardinal Newman.

Of course, many others could have been added to this list, but suffice it to say that the Society of Jesus was alive and well in what had been England's proudest bastion of orthodoxy. Instead of looking to the Holy Spirit for direction, these traitorous divines took their cues from the Vatican.

To be familiar with this survey of nineteenth-century apostasy within the Church of England is to understand the mindset of the forces who clamored for and participated in the Revision Committee of 1871-1881. Men such as Archbishop Trench and other Wiseman sympathizers labored for a decade to replace the readings of the King James Bible with those of the Jesuit Douay-Rheims version.

In fact, Cambridge University was so far gone by the time of the Revision Committee that they followed the lead of Karl

Marx—who had dedicated his *Das Kapital* to Charles Darwin—by conferring upon the unsaved naturalist *an honorary doctor's degree of their own!*[94]

As this chapter draws to a close, the reader naturally would be concerned about the extent of Jesuit influence in twentieth-century America, particularly in her centers of "conservative Christian scholarship." In chapter five we became acquainted with the critical views of Dr. Norman Geisler as evidenced by his rejection of Mark 16:9-20. In addition to co-authoring with William Nix *A General Introduction of the Bible,* Dr. Geisler has also taught systematic theology at the prestigious Dallas Theological Seminary as well as Liberty University. Obviously, the preference of this "Protestant" scholar for a "Catholic" text reflects a deep-seated, pro-Vatican mind set. Perhaps the fact that Dr. Geisler chose to enhance his evangelical training by earning his Ph.D. from *Loyola University,* one of the largest Jesuit schools in America, would be indicative of this predilection.[95] *Decide for yourself!*

XIV

Vessels of Dishonour

"But in a great house there are not only vessels of gold and of silver, but also of wood and of earth; and some to honour, and some to dishonour."
(II Timothy 2:20)

With essentially all modern translations being derived from the textual theories of Brooke Foss Westcott and Fenton John Anthony Hort, it would behoove God's people to thoroughly examine the ministerial character of these revisers in light of the Bible's charge to blamelessness. Even Dr. Hort would have concurred, having commented on the role of the clergyman that:

> He must have a desire to set forth the glory of God simply and directly, in those forms which show it forth most nakedly. He must not only act it out but speak of it, make men know it and consciously enter into it . . . He is not simply an officer or servant of God or workman of God, but His ambassador and herald to tell men about God Himself.[1]

Alarmingly, the average believer who uses an English translation other than the Authorized Version is completely unacquainted with the men who initiated it. This is a crucial issue, for one cannot endorse the modern Bible movement without tacitly ascribing a Divine sanction to the original Revision Committee. With the climacteric rescue of the Holy Scriptures at stake (according to Westcott-Hort theory), would it not be reasonable to expect that these self-appointed saviours should have displayed a minimum conformity to the verses which they "salvaged"?

*"But in a great house there are not only vessels of gold and of silver, but also of wood and of earth; and **some to honour, and some to dishonour**. If a man therefore purge himself from these, he shall be a vessel unto honour, sanctified, and meet for the master's use, and prepared unto every good work."* (II Timothy 2:20-21)

Having carefully read both the *Life and Letters of Brooke Foss Westcott* by his son Arthur Westcott (1903) and the *Life and Letters of Fenton John Anthony Hort* by his son Arthur Fenton Hort (1896), this author is firmly convinced that the celebrated Cambridge professors were anything *but* what they professed to be. It is the central premise of this chapter that Drs. Westcott and Hort were *a pair of unsaved liberals whose open Vatican sympathies cast them as the consummate Jesuit plants!*

By the completion of this dry collection of extant correspondence and biographical data, a most conspicuous impression is left upon the exhausted reader. Despite the Psalmist's injunction in Psalm 107:2 to *"Let the redeemed of the Lord say so,"* one will search in vain through nearly 1,800 pages of religious verbosity for a single, personal testimony of salvation by either man. The same goes for the conversion account of anyone else for that matter!

Although Westcott's first Cambridge address was 7 *Jesus* Lane and Hort's mourners sang *"Jesus* Lives" at his graveside service, it is significant that the Saviour's personal name was used only *nine times in both volumes!* A random inspection of *George Whitefield's Journals* disclosed the name of Jesus *36 times in 36 pages* (pages 328-364). Such a contrast will shed new light on the words of Jesus: *"And then will I profess unto them, I never **knew** you: depart from me, ye that work iniquity."* (Matthew 7:23)

The Nicolaitane apologist who would challenge this appraisal is referred to the testimony of those who knew the subjects best. While Arthur Westcott confirmed that such terms as "unsound," "shadowy" and "mystical" were frequently applied to the senior Westcott,[2] Arthur Hort brought in the most embarrassing evidence of all. Referring to his own grandmother, Annie (Collett) Hort, daughter of a Suffolk preacher, he wrote:

> Her religious feelings were deep and strong. Circumstances had made her an adherent of the Evangelical school . . . the Oxford Movement filled her with dread and anxiety as to its possible effect on her son. **She was unable to enter into his theological views, which to her school and generation seemed a desertion of the ancient ways**; thus, pathetically

enough, there came to be a barrier between mother and son. The close intercourse on subjects which lay nearest to the hearts of each was broken, to the loss and sorrow of both .... She studied and knew her Bible well, and her own religious life was most carefully regulated.[3]

Whereas Timothy owed his mother and grandmother a debt of gratitude for the Scriptural grounding he received at their knees, a rather pathetic allusion to Hort's misplaced values can be gleaned from a letter he wrote to *his* mother which read:

> I can assure you I do not forget how very much I owe both to you and to grandmamma, whether **in leading me to love plants** or in anything else.[4]

However, for the most convincing evidence of all, why not let the reprobates speak for themselves? Writing to Bishop Lightfoot, Westcott states:

> I intend to turn heresy-seeker. *The Churchman*(!) I see praises the book on the Canon as a necessary article in a clergyman's library. It is strange, but **all the questionable doctrines which I have ever maintained are in it.**[5]

And for an even more illuminating example of self-incrimination, consider the words of Hort as addressed to Reverend John Ellerton:

> Possibly you have not heard that I have become Harold Browne's Examining Chaplain. I have only seen him two or three times in my life, not at all intimately, and was amazed when he made the proposal, in the kindest terms. **I wrote to warn him that I was not safe or traditional in my theology, and that I could not give up association with heretics and such like.**[6]

With chapter fifteen covering the Revision Committee proper, the remainder of our present study will deal with the revisers themselves and will follow the threefold outline of: (1) their training, (2) their theology, and (3) their tomfoolery.

I. Their Training

Solomon wrote that, *"The glory of young men is their strength."* (Proverbs 20:29a) Despite Westcott's rescuing of a small boy from a bully and isolated references to his and Hort's occasional dabbling in sports, their childhood days were extremely wimpy to say the least. While Hort's boyhood letters to his younger brother Arthur (written from Rugby Boarding School) were almost weekly reports of his *flower tending*, Westcott was remembered by his brother-in-law, Reverend T.M. Middlemore-Whittard, who related:

> In those early days I cannot recollect that he had any school companions with whom he joined in boyish games. He used his leisure chiefly in **sketching**, and arranging his collections of **ferns** and **butterflies** and **moths**.[7]

Were Westcott alive today, he would likely be a part of the "Save the Whales" lobby, his son writing:

> He even later disapproved of his father's fishing excursions, because his sympathies were so entirely on the side of the fish. On one occasion, being then a little boy, he was carrying the fish-basket, when his father put a live fish into it, and late in life he used to declare that **he could still feel the struggles of that fish against his back**.[8]

Westcott's unhealthy insularity led to a myriad of philosophical rabbit trails including a study of Joseph Smith's writings. Arthur Westcott confirming:

> He took a strange interest . . . not very long after that time, especially in **Mormonism** . . . I recollect his procuring and studying the *Book of Mormon* about 1840.[9]

However, the most detrimental influence which they sustained during their formative, adolescent years, was an introduction to the world of *science*. Writing of his father, the younger Westcott stated, "His chief pastimes were, however, of a scientific kind."[10] In short order, both men would be hooked for life.

As early as 1847, a twenty-two-year-old Westcott acknowledged his inability to believe in Bible miracles.

> I never read an account of a miracle but I seem instinctively to feel its **improbability**, and discover some want of evidence in the account of it.[11]

Westcott paid a high price for allowing his intellect to call the shots.

> 19th October 1845
> How many are the difficulties I experience no one can tell. At least I trust I am teachable, and do sincerely desire to find the

truth, but I cannot acquiesce in that which I *hope* is true without I am also *convinced*.[12]

31st August 1847
    Oh, the weakness of my faith compared with that of others! So wild, so sceptical am I. I cannot yield.[13]

7th November 1847
    O Marie, as I wrote the last word, I could not help asking what am I? Can I claim the name of a believer?[14]

11th November 1847
    If I dare not communicate to you my own wild doubts at times, it is because I feel they are punishment for my own pride, and which I should tempt no one to share.[15]

6th January 1848
    It seems as if I am inclined to learn nothing; I must find out all myself, and then I am satisfied, but that simple faith and obedience which so many enjoy, I fear will never be mine.[16]

13th May 1849
    What a wild storm of unbelief seems to have seized my whole system. Literally to-day I feel "alone in the world" . . . I cannot describe the feeling with which I regard the hundreds I see around me who conform without an apparent struggle—who seem ever cheerful, ever faithful and believing.[17]

Westcott was so perplexed that he set his unbelief to verse:

> What is my task, O Lord? –
> For still, though fear and doubt oppress my heart,
> Dark doubt and unbelief,
> I feel that in Thy work I have a part.[18]

Although the scientific Westcott could not lower himself to accept the Bible's miracles, the healing powers of the Virgin Mary were quite another thing! One of the more ludicrous episodes of the professor's career occurred during a holiday excursion to the French town of LaSalette, near Grenoble. While visiting the sacred spring of Our Lady of LaSalette, Westcott was "blown away" by the "miraculous" healing of a particular Catholic girl. The flabbergasted tourist related:

> A written narrative can convey no notion of the effect of such a recital. The eager energy of the father, the modest thankfulness

of the daughter, the quick glances of the spectators from one to the other, the calm satisfaction of the priest, the comments of look and nod, combined to form a scene which appeared hardly to belong to the nineteenth century. An age of faith was restored before our sight in its ancient guise.[19]

When Westcott voiced his intention to write a paper on the subject, the prudent Dr. Lightfoot dissuaded his colleague from such a potentially damaging admission.[20] (Today's evangelical scholars are still trying to cover his tracks.) However, the healing pool of "Our Lady" would constitute but a mere drop in the bucket!

Our esteemed Cambridge professors were also known for dabbling in the *occult!* In the year 1851, Dr. Hort founded a society for the investigation and classification of ghosts and psychical phenomena in general. Westcott's own son described such practices as *spiritualism.*[21] Known as the *Ghostly Guild* by its membership, the more sensible citizens of English society sardonically referred to it as the "Bogie Club" or the "Cock-and-Bull Club." Notwithstanding the Bible's clear denunciation of such activity, Westcott wrote in his *Ghostly Circular*:

> The interest and importance of a serious and earnest inquiry into the nature of the phenomena which are vaguely called "supernatural" will scarcely be questioned. Many persons believe that all such apparently mysterious occurrences are due either to purely natural causes, or to delusions of the mind or senses, or to wilful deception. **But there are many others who believe it possible that the beings of the unseen world may manifest themselves to us in extraordinary ways,** and also are unable otherwise to explain many facts the evidence for which cannot be impeached. Both parties have obviously a common interest in wishing cases of supposed "supernatural" agency to be thoroughly sifted. If the belief of the latter class should be ultimately confirmed, the limits which human knowledge respecting the spirit-world has hitherto reached might be ascertained with some degree of accuracy. But in any case, even if it should appear that morbid or irregular workings of the mind or senses will satisfactorily account for every such marvel, still **some progress would be made towards ascertaining the laws which regulate our being,** and thus adding to our scanty knowledge of an obscure but important province of science.[22]

Thus far, we are to accept that the men God raised up to restore His Word were too "educated" to believe it but would marvel at "Our Lady's" holy water while seeking out "beings of the unseen world," so as to improve their knowledge of "the laws which regulate our being." Now *that* is a cock-and-bull story if ever such a one was told!

At this point, it is germane to our study to examine the array of liberal professors who carefully nurtured the seeds of unbelief in the youthful Westcott and Hort. Although some espoused philosophy or poetry and others theology, the unifying bond of all was their sustained determination to *Romanize the Church of England.* As mentioned previously, their activities came to be known as the *Oxford Movement.*

Arthur Hort points to the poet-philosopher *Samuel Taylor Coleridge* as one of the earliest influences on his father's life, stating matter of factly, "In undergraduate days, if not before, he came under the spell of Coleridge."[23] According to Dr. Gipp, Coleridge himself was under a "spell" or two. Citing the *New American Standard Encyclopedia,* he writes:

> Coleridge was the college drop-out whose drug addiction is an historical fact. "The opium habit, begun earlier to deaden the pain of rheumatism, grew stronger. After vainly trying in Malta and Italy to break away from opium, Coleridge came back to England in 1806."[24]

The aforementioned encyclopedia described Coleridge's main work, *Aids to Reflection,* with the words:

> Its chief aim is to harmonize formal Christianity with Coleridge's variety of transcendental philosophy. He also did much to introduce Immanual Kant and other German philosophers to English readers.[25]

Basically, Coleridge was your standard intellectual deadbeat, the *Dictionary of National Biography* stating:

> Coleridge was infirm of will, a dreamer of great schemes never to be fulfilled, diverted at any moment by his marvelous versatility from every path which he entered.[26]

During that same time, Westcott was becoming an avid reader of another apostate minstrel, *John Keble* (1792-1866), professor of Poetry at Oxford University. *The Concise Oxford Dictionary of the Christian Church* says of Keble:

> He took a leading part in the Oxford Movement, contributing

several of the *Tracts for the Times*. He co-operated closely with E. B. Pusey in keeping the High Church Movement steadily attached to the Church of England.[27]

Newman wrote in his *Apologia* that Keble was the "true and primary author of the Oxford Movement."[28] Westcott idolized Keble and read his poetry nearly every day. Writing to his fiancée, he stated:

> I am more fully convinced than ever that Keble has found the truest and noblest end of poetry—to calm and cheer and soothe and train the mind by the simple teaching of nature.[29]

What ever happened to finding "calm and cheer" in the Psalms? From the tone of their writings, Westcott and Hort never did show a preference for spiritual reading material. While the dying Scott had enough sense to ask for the "The Book," Professor Hort's last request, with but four days to live, was for a copy of *Ivanhoe*![30]

Continuing with the sequence of his father's philosophical digression, the younger Hort remarked:

> From Coleridge to Maurice the passage was natural. Maurice's teaching was the most powerful element in his religious development, satisfying many a want which had hitherto distressed him.[31]

You will recall from our previous chapter that Dr. Frederick Maurice was the avowed heretic who was dismissed from King's College for, among other things, denying the endlessness of future punishment. Dr. Hort confirms that it was Maurice who instilled in him a love for the homosexual Greek philosophers Plato and Aristotle:

> He urged me to give the greatest attention to the Plato and Aristotle, and to make them the central points of my reading, and the other books subsidiary.[32]

Accordingly we have the sick statement from Hort's confederate, Dr. Westcott, that:

> I can never look back on my Cambridge life with sufficient thankfulness. **Above all**, those hours which were spent over Plato and Aristotle have wrought that in me which I pray may never be done away.[33]

Their overall reading habits never did improve much. While Westcott's contemporary, the renowned Charles Haddon Spurgeon, testified to having read *Pilgrim's Progress* over *100* times,[34] we note that Bunyan's classic is not so much as even mentioned by either Westcott or Hort. Westcott does state that he took the time to read Dr. Thomas Arnold's *Life* 100 times through.[35] (Dr. Arnold was Hort's Headmaster at Rugby Boarding School.)

In another letter, Westcott relates having read Schiller's *William Tell* for the second time while stating in the very next paragraph, "I never read any of Fox's book."[36] Although he acknowledged the fame of *Fox's Book of Martyrs*, saying, "it was chained with the Bible to the reading desks in churches,"[37] the subtle effects of Keble's influence had already led Westcott to declare, "Poetry is, I think, a thousand times more true than History."[38]

Another ecumenical heretic who caught the attention of Westcott was Arthur Penrhyn Stanley, Dean of Westminster (1815-1881). Stanley had made an unsuccessful bid to convert the Abbey to a national shrine for all faiths. It was he who invited the Unitarian scholar, Dr. Vance Smith, to participate in a special communion service to inaugurate the Revision Committee labors. (See Chapter 15) Westcott's diary entry for 2nd January, 1848, reads: "Stanley's sermon on St. John, which I extremely admire, and yet it is called 'heresy' at Oxford."[39]

Westcott's admiration for the previously mentioned Edward Pusey was evidenced in a letter describing his first encounter with the Oxford Movement leader.

> Dr. Jeune introduced me to Dr. Pusey, one of the few men I was anxious to see . . . In the evening we had graver talk, and I was amazed at the acuteness and ready vigor of a man, near seventy I am told, who knows Homer and Horace better than I do.[40]

One would think that of these many veiled adversaries, a cut-and-dried case like that of the defector Newman would have surely been off limits. Unfortunately, such was not to be. Five years after the former Anglican joined ranks with the organization bent on the total liquidation of Protestantism (1850), Dr. Westcott went out to hear what he had to say. Writing to his fiancée, he said:

> Yesterday, as we intended, we went to the Corn Exchange to

hear Dr. Newman . . . My curiosity was, of course, intense, and
the appearance of the lecturer served to increase it. He looks
younger, more intellectual, but far less "pious" than I expected.[41]

After declaring that he wasn't buying Newman's views on
church tradition, he makes a statement that will come back to
haunt him in only two years:

> His mere rhetorical power is greater than I anticipated; his
> power of argument less; his capability of widely influencing
> English people, I think, absolutely nothing.[42]

Note with wonder how Newman's "inability" to influence the
English people was starting to work on Westcott himself after a
mere twenty-two months. Writing to the future Mrs. Westcott, he
confessed:

> To-day I have taken up *Tracts for the Times* and Dr. Newman.
> Don't tell me that he will do me harm. At least to-day he will, has
> done me good, and had you been here I should have asked you to
> read his solemn words to me.[43]

Such a reckless air of spiritual invincibility was characteristic
of the know-it-all professor. Commenting in another place on the
writer Carlyle, he asserted:

> What will you say to me for reading Carlyle? Will you quite
> despair? I don't think that I am likely to become too enthusiastic,
> though there is much in him which I like. Is it not right to learn
> even from a foe, as an old Latin proverb says?[44]

And again, "But from Cambridge days I have read the writings
of many who are called mystics with much profit."[45]

Less than five months after Westcott's second letter regarding
Newman, Hort also went off the deep end over the apostate.
Writing to Westcott in October of 1852, he declared, "Many of his
sayings and doings I cannot but condemn most strongly. But they
are not Newman; **and him I all but worship.**"[46]

This infatuation continued far beyond Newman's elevation to
Cardinal in 1879, Hort writing to his wife in 1890, "My own
personal feeling towards Newman has always included a large
share of **reverence.**"[47]

With so many Vatican sympathizers affecting the Cambridge
professors, it was inevitable that their writings would also begin

to exhibit a similar tone of betrayal. The results of Keble's pacifistic prose can be seen in a response by Westcott to a particular sermon preached against popery:

> As for Mr. Oldham's meetings, I think they are not good in their tendency, and nothing can be so bad as making them the vehicle of controversy. What an exquisitely beautiful verse is that of Keble's, "And yearns not her parental heart," etc. We seem now to have lost all sense of pity in bitterness and ill-feeling. **Should not our arm against Rome be prayer and not speeches**; the efforts of our inmost heart, and not the displays of secular reason?[48]

In another place, he wrote:

> Keble has lately published some sermons in which, as well as in a preface on "the position of Churchmen," I am afraid he will offend many. **I can in some measure sympathise with him**.[49]

The damage inflicted by Maurice, who was himself affected by Newman, is discernable from Westcott's diary entry for 8th May, 1846:

> See Maurice's new lectures, with a preface on Development written apparently with marvelous candour and fairness, and free from all controversial bitterness. He makes a remark which I **have often written and said, that the danger of our Church is from atheism, not Romanism**. What a striking picture is that he quotes from Newman of the present aspect of the Roman Church—as despised, rejected, persecuted in public opinion.[50]

Because "you are what you read," Hort's esteem for his own church was diminished after imbibing in Newman's autobiography.

> Newman certainly raises many thoughts. At present I have hardly got beyond the feeling of astonishment at our having the privilege of such an autobiography ... Anglicanism, though by no means without a sound standing, seems a poor and maimed thing beside great Rome.[51]

As to any personal comments regarding contemporary pontiffs, Dr. Hort makes mention of two, Pius IX (1846-1878) and Leo XIII (1878-1903). In defense of the former, he asked:

> **Must one hate the poor Pope** (who would like to be a good
> Italian) because one loves the cause of which Victor Emmanuel is
> the visible sign.[52]

On December 8, 1854, this "good Italian" announced his new
revelation of the *Immaculate Conception of the Blessed Virgin
Mary*. Basically, this means that despite Mary's own testimony
which contradicts this ridiculous view (Luke 1:47), the mother of
Jesus would henceforth be understood to have been miraculously
conceived without original sin. Also, he was so "pious" that in
July of 1870, he declared himself *infallible!*

Pius IX was succeeded by Leo XIII who elicited two remarks
from Dr. Hort. In a letter to his eldest daughter dated only two
weeks following Leo's installation service, he exclaimed:

> Mamma had the other day a long and interesting letter from
> Mrs. Luard, in which **she sent me a photograph of the new
> Pope, which I am very glad to have.** She and Mr. Luard are
> very fortunate to have been in Rome for the last few weeks. They
> could hardly have been there at a more interesting time.[53]

Six weeks after Dr. Hort hung Leo's "pontifical puss" on his
wall, "His Holiness" declared war on the concept of church-state
separation, rhetorically asking in his first encyclical *Inscrutabili*:

> Who will deny the service of the Church in bringing truth to
> the peoples sunk in ignorance and superstition? . . . If we compare
> the ages when the church was universally revered as a mother
> with our age, is it not beyond all question that our age is rushing
> wildly along the straight road to destruction? . . . It (the Papacy)
> is in very truth the glory of the Supreme Pontiffs that they
> steadfastly set themselves as a wall and bulwark to save human
> society from falling back into its former superstition and
> barbarism.[54]

Writing from Rome to his youngest daughter ten years later,
an ecstatic Hort described the "great excitement" he and Mrs.
Hort witnessed by a surprise Vatican announcement that Leo
would officiate at High Mass and give personal audiences as well.
(Oh, *goodie!*) Regretting that the audience notice was too short in
order to pull the right strings, Hort settled for a pair of tickets to
enjoy the gala Pontifical Mass.

The man who is credited (by the majority of born-again
Christians) with playing a leading role in the restoration of God's
Word nearly broke his neck leaving an hour-and-a-half early to

see a fellow man treated like a god, relating:

> The procession proper began to appear, and soon the Pope
> himself, carried high in his litter or chair, with a monster fan on
> each side of him. He came on slowly, turning his head from side
> to side and bowing, and giving blessings with his hand.[55]

Could you imagine Luther procuring seats for such a show? He
would have described *Leo* as the "monster" instead of the *fan*
while attaching the imposter's picture to his *dart board*.

For the record, the main objective of Hort's hero was the
suppression of all religious liberty in America. Expanding on the
standard Vatican policy that, "the State must not only have care
for religion, but must recognize the *true* religion," Manhattan
cites Leo's encyclical *Catholicity in the United States* and asks
alarmingly:

> What, then, should happen to American principles of liberty of
> conscience, of the individual, of religion, of opinion, and all those
> other aspects of freedom that are now an integral part of
> American life? And to take a particular sphere of society, the
> religious, what would happen if Catholicism assumed power?
> Since all religions, with the exception of Catholicism, are false,
> they cannot be allowed to pervert those who are in the fold of the
> Catholic Church. Hence all other religious denominations in the
> United States of America "might" be allowed to profess their
> faith and to worship only if such worship is "carried on within
> the family circle or in such inconspicuous manner as to be an
> occasion neither for scandal nor of perversion to the Faithful. . . ."
> Thus a Catholic United States of America would limit, and
> eventually even forbid, the practice of religious freedom, which
> automatically takes the Church into the cultural, social, and
> finally political, fields. This is based on the Catholic doctrine that
> "since no rational end is promoted by the dissemination of false
> doctrine, there exists no right to indulge in this practice." Why?
> Simply because the Pope states, and the leader of the American
> Catholics declares, that "error has not the same rights as
> truth."[56]

The average *Christian* student of American History is unaware
of how close Leo's predecessor came to dissolving the Union
during the Civil War years. For a sobering insight as to how the
Vatican can interfere with foreign governments, consider the
chaos incited by a single letter sent by Pius IX to Jefferson Davis
in 1863.

Responding to correspondence from Davis, dated 23rd September, 1863, the Pope's reply was formally addressed, "To Jefferson Davis, President of the **Confederate States of America**, Richmond."[57] This subtle salutation gave the Confederacy a badly needed vote of confidence from "His Holiness." What followed next is quite unnerving. Whereas the desertion rates of the Northern Armies showed 16 percent for Germans, 0.5 percent for native Americans, 0.7 percent for all others, **the Irish figures sky-rocketed to 72 percent!** Manhattan states:

> The above figures indicate **that out of every 10,000 Irish enlistees—almost all Catholics—there were over 33 times as many desertions as among all the other groups put together.** The point to be made here is not only the historical one—that the Vatican intervened in the agonies of the American Civil War—but that, in a different context and in a different way, it can do the same in today's conflicts, be they military or political. And even more so in the future.[58]

II. Their Theology

At this point, the reader should not be surprised to find Westcott and Hort defending a myriad of Catholic heresies.

Consider the doctrine of *Mariolatry*. Apparently, Westcott was already a little wacky prior to his encounter with "Our Lady of the Lagoon." Eighteen years earlier, Westcott accidentally stumbled upon another shrine to the Virgin after strolling through a *Carmelite Monastery* at Grâce Dieu. Westcott states:

> After leaving the monastery we shaped our course to a little oratory (private chapel) which we discovered on the summit of a neighbouring hill, and by a little scrambling we reached it. Fortunately we found the door open. It is very small, with one kneeling-place; and behind a screen was a "Piéta" the size of life (*i.e.*, a Virgin and dead Christ) . . . **Had I been alone I could have knelt there for hours.**[59]

With the proclamation by Pius IX regarding Mary's immaculate conception, Westcott's instability increased. While traveling in Dresden, Germany, in 1856 (two years after Mary's "promotion"), Westcott visited the Picture Gallery and became awestruck with the Sistine Madonna:

> It is smaller than I expected, and the colouring is less rich, but

in expression it is perfect. The face of the Virgin is unspeakably beautiful. I looked till the lip seemed to tremble with intensity of feeling.[60]

However, for the sickest account of Westcott's addiction to the Roman doctrine of Mariolatry, consider the revelation of Arthur that:

> My mother, whose name was Sarah Louise Whittard, was the eldest of three sisters. She afterwards, at the time of her confirmation, **at my father's request**, took the name of **Mary** in addition.[61]

Not to be outdone, Dr. Hort also stated:

> I am very far from pretending to understand completely the ever renewed vitality of Mariolatry ... I have been persuaded for many years that **Mary-worship and 'Jesus'-worship have very much in common** in their causes and their results.[62]

Although the King James translators were subject to many of the rubrical abuses of nineteenth-century Anglicanism, Westcott and Hort chose to align themselves with that Romanizing element bent on aggravating and expanding these weaknesses.

For instance, the central fallacy of Mariolatry is that it assigns to Mary an unscriptural role of mediator between God and man. Within Catholicism, the "Blessed Mother" is just one of many such go-betweens. In addition to a Catholic's option of praying to the departed saints, he is also a weekly beneficiary of an officiating priesthood. Westcott and Hort were the most stalwart supporters of this theological system within the Church of England.

Known as the doctrine of *sacerdotalism*, this tradition would eventually elevate the church and her sacraments above that of the Holy Scriptures in matters of *final authority*. In Dr. Westcott's thinking, (as also in the case of Leo XIII) conversion was synonymous with securing membership in the right church. While courting the Wesleyan Miss Whittard, he wrote:

> I feel sure (may I use the expression?) that you will be gathered again to **that Church** which is the object of my **devotion.**[63]

While contemporary father-and-son teams like William and Bramwell Booth labored tirelessly at winning souls to Jesus

Christ, Arthur Westcott said of his father:

> Many a time on a summer evening, after the Cathedral
> afternoon service, he would go out on his tricycle escorted by sons
> on bicycles, to visit and sketch neighbouring churches.[64]

While fellow Englishman G. Campbell Morgan was locking up
his books for seven years to study the Bible exclusively, Westcott
preferred to be edified by brick and mortar. With reference to the
ancient cathedrals, he wrote:

> It is by their buildings and by their sculpture that the men of
> the middle ages hold converse with us now. They wrote on
> parchment in a foreign language, but they wrote in a universal
> language on stone, as men cannot write now . . . The great
> churches are the sermons of the middle ages, and we shall do well
> to study them.[65]

Hort's devotion to the institutional church began with his
surrender to "Holy Orders." Writing to his parents to inform
them of his decision, he simply said, "You will at once perceive
that my choice is **the Church**."[66]

At the same time Booth was being assailed with rotten eggs,
human waste and burning sulphur while conducting outdoor
meetings in dancing saloons, stables, sheds, pig sties, theater
stages and circus rings, Arthur Hort said of his father:

> He was emphatically a churchman; he loved greatly the
> services of the Church of England, and cared much for a reverent
> observance of all matters of detail in worship.[67]

During the same years that C. H. Spurgeon was across town
imploring men and women to trust the *Saviour*, Hort was
affirming that:

> The Church is the only center of all our hopes, that only by
> clinging fast to her, by submitting to her mild and lawful
> authority, by shaping our ways according to her indications, and
> above all by venerating and upholding with gratitude and love,
> and leading others to venerate, those Holy Sacraments.[68]

In another place, Hort wrote, "Still we *dare* not forsake the
Sacraments, or God will forsake us."[69] And in another he stated,
"I am a staunch sacerdotalist."[70]

The Cambridge professor obviously despised Luther's

Reformation theology concerning the priesthood of the believers, Hort writing, "But this last error can hardly be expelled till Protestants unlearn the crazy horror of the idea of priesthood."[71]

With an elevated priesthood comes the inevitable Romanish doctrine of *Baptismal Regeneration.* The reason one cannot find Westcott and Hort referring to a single conversion account is because they didn't believe in such "nonsense." Writing to his wife, Westcott stated:

> I do think we have no right to exclaim against the idea of the commencement of a spiritual life, conditionally from Baptism, any more than we have to deny the commencement of a moral life from birth.[72]

In a letter to John Ellerton, Dr. Hort added:

> We maintain 'Baptismal Regeneration' as the most important of doctrines ... almost all Anglican statements are a mixture in various proportions of the true and the Romish view; 2nd, **the pure Romish view seems to me nearer, and more likely to lead to, the truth than the Evangelical.**[73]

To a lady convert to the Church of England, he wrote, **"Baptism assures us that we are children of God,** members of Christ and His body, and heirs of the heavenly kingdom."[74]

Writing to his eldest daughter on her confirmation, Hort stated:

> Our Confirmation points back to our Baptism, and ... without any act of ours, we are children of the great and gracious Heavenly Father; members, that is, as it were parts and limbs, of His blessed Son.[75]

And finally, to his eldest son on his confirmation, he wrote:

> **While yet an infant you were claimed for God by being made in Baptism an unconscious member of His Church,** the great Divine Society which has lived on unceasingly from the Apostles' time till now. You have been surrounded by Christian influences; taught to lift up your eyes to the Father in heaven as your own Father; to feel yourself in a wonderful sense a member or part of Christ, united to Him by strange invisible bonds; to know that **you have as your birthright a share in the kingdom of heaven** ... This is the privilege of a Christian, to know assuredly and clearly the facts which relate to all men.[76]

By now it should be clear to the reader that Westcott and Hort were nothing more than apostate Nicolaitanes who learned to lord over God's heritage by observing the Papacy. In a letter to his wife, Westcott remarked, "What marvellous power the organisation of the Roman Church gives to its leaders, and is it wrong?"[77]

For that matter, Westcott was also aware of the superior power of religious schools, writing to Hort in 1867 that:

> More and more I am convinced that the work of the Church must be done at the Universities—nay, at Cambridge. It is too late to shape men afterwards, even if they could be reached.[78]

Because apostasy always begins in the classroom, one of the most important ways Westcott believed in "shaping" the theological development of his students was to undermine the reliability of their Bibles. In the long run, this treachery was supposed to work to the priest's advantage, as a laity robbed of its Scripture would naturally look to the clergy for *final authority*.

Writing to Dr. Hort in 1860, Westcott declares his rejection of infallibility:

> I too "must disclaim setting forth infallibility" in the front of my convictions. All I hold is, that the more I learn, the more I am convinced that fresh doubts come from my own ignorance, and that at present I find the presumption in favour of the absolute truth—I **reject the word infallibility**—of **Holy Scripture overwhelming.**[79]

Hort writing to Lightfoot that same week warns:

> If you make a decided conviction of **the absolute infallibility of the N. T.** practically a *sine qua non* for co-operation, **I fear I could not join you,** even if you were willing to forget your fears about the origin of the Gospels.[80]

And then there is Hort's response to Westcott's letter:

> Your note came just as I was finishing a long letter to Lightfoot . . . **I am not able to go as far as you in asserting the absolute infallibility of a canonical writing** . . . If I am ultimately driven to admit occasional errors, I shall be sorry.[81]

Hort even went on record as mocking the nonconformists and

dissenters for their convicting example of Bible reading:

> The Bible then was closed, but now, thanks to Luther, it is
> open, and no power (unless it be the fanaticism of the bibliolaters,
> among whom reading so many 'chapters' seems exactly to
> correspond to the) Romish superstition of telling so many dozen
> beads on a rosary) can close it again.[82]

Having successfully questioned the reliability of the Scripture
itself, Nicolaitane scholarship will add insult to injury by
subjecting their "fallible text" to an *allegorical* interpretation.
When a certain student wrote to Hort for clarification on Article
IX of the Church's Thirty-nine Articles, he received the following
staggering reply:

> The authors of the Article doubtless assumed the strictly
> historical character of the account of the Fall in Genesis. This
> assumption is now, in my belief, no longer **reasonable**.[83]

Hort's rejection of the literal interpretation of Genesis was
fostered by his study of Darwin's works. Writing to Westcott in
1860, he declared:

> **Have you read Darwin?** How I should like a talk with you
> about it! In spite of difficulties, **I am inclined to think it
> unanswerable.** In any case it is a treat to read such a book.[84]

And in another letter to Ellerton, he wrote:

> But *the* **book which has most engaged me is Darwin.**
> Whatever may be thought of it, it is a book that one is proud to
> be contemporary with. I must work out and examine the
> argument more in detail, but at present **my feeling is strong
> that the theory is unanswerable.**[85]

Hort's conviction for evolution became so pronounced that he
recommended Darwin to his son[86] and became a student of
geology and an avid collector of fossils throughout the remainder
of his life.[87]

Westcott's "superior intellect" also prevailed upon him to
allegorize away a literal Heaven,[88] the second coming of Jesus
Christ,[89] and the millennial kingdom.[90]

Hort's theological hangups included: a denial of the Trinity's
oneness;[91] a doubting of the reality of angels;[92] belief in a ransom
paid to Satan;[93] a questioning of the soul's existence apart from

its body;[94] a suggestion of several degrees of salvation;[95] and a conviction that Christ's earthly ministry lasted but a year.[96]

Of the many doctrines rejected through an allegorical interpretation, it was Hort's disbelief in a literal devil which best explained his scientific approach to textual criticism. In a lengthy letter to Dr. Maurice in 1849, he stated:

> The discussion which immediately precedes these four lines naturally leads to another enigma most intimately connected with that of everlasting penalties, namely, that of the personality of the devil. It was Coleridge who some three years ago first raised any doubts in my mind on the subject—doubts which have never yet been at all set at rest . . . **Now if there be a devil**, he cannot merely bear a corrupted and marred image of God; he must be wholly evil, his name evil, his every energy and act evil. **Would it not be a violation of the divine attributes for the Word to be actively the support of such a nature as that?**[97]

By their elimination of a real devil, the revisers would be left with a non-threatened text. And such a text would require no supernatural preservation.

You will note that Dr. Hort made a connection between the existence of a literal devil and that of "everlasting penalties." In this same letter to Dr. Maurice, Hort joined his mentor in rejecting an eternal Hell in favor of a universal salvation, earned after a cleansing stint in the Catholic's purgatorial fires. Strangely enough, Hort claimed to have gained this insight from the New Testament writers:

> Not only are the Epistles almost free (as far as I can recollect) from allusions to everlasting torments, but their whole tone is such that the introduction of such a notion would seem to render it discordant and jarring. And little as I like to rest on isolated texts, I cannot get over the words, *"As in Adam all die, even so in Christ shall all be made alive."* St. Paul cannot mean merely the universal redemption, for he uses the future tense conformably to the whole tenor of the chapter, and is, moreover, speaking of the resurrection; further, the same universality is given to the one clause as to the other.[98]

Note how this self-proclaimed expert on the New Testament text was so willingly ignorant of the glorious doctrine of imputation. Continuing with his letter to Maurice, he says:

Nor, as far as I can recollect, have you anywhere written explicitly upon this point; even on the corresponding subject of vicarious righteousness I know only of two pages . . . and they have not been able to make me feel assured that the language of *imputation* is strictly true, however sanctioned by St. Paul's example. **The fact is, I do not see how God's justice can be satisfied without every man's suffering in his own person the full penalty for his sins.** I *know* that it *can*, for if it could not in the case of some at least, the whole Bible would be a lie; but if in the case *of some,* why not *of all?*[99]

Does this sound like the kind of man whom God would raise up to restore His Word—a theologian who cannot see how God's justice could be satisfied apart from the sinner's payment of his own debt? *Let the advocates of the New International Version hide their heads in shame for accusing our God of such nonsense!*

In another letter to John Ellerton, Hort summarized his position with a three-point outline:

(1) that eternity is independent of duration; (2) that the power of repentance is not limited to this life; (3) that it is not revealed whether or not all will ultimately repent.[100]

And in yet another place, he concludes:

But the idea of purgation, of cleansing as by fire, seems to me inseparable from what the Bible teaches us of the Divine chastisements; and, though little is directly said respecting the future state, it seems to me incredible that the Divine chastisements should in this respect change their character when this visible life is ended.[101]

Finally, Dr. Westcott puts his two cents in with a subtle endorsement for private prayers for the dead:

We agreed unanimously that we are, as things are now, forbidden to pray for the Dead apart from the whole Church *in our public Services.* No restriction is placed upon private devotions.[102]

Now as the revisers' disbelief in a real devil shaped their attitude toward the New Testament text, so it was that their rejection of an eternal Hell affected their opinion toward the lost sinner's plight. Thus, we begin the third division of our biographical study:

III. Their Tomfoolery

After persevering through nearly 1,800 boring pages of Westcott and Hort's biographies, the reader is left with a dull headache. His first impression is the unbelievable lack of spiritual fiber in both volumes. This is especially true if one is familiar with the revivalist heritage of the nation (Whitefield and Wesley) or the evangelistic giants of that day (Spurgeon, Booth and Mueller).

As a man's *theology* will dictate his *morality*, a pair of doctrinal statements void of "hellfire" ensured that Westcott and Hort's ministerial outreach would be characterized as wimpy, laid back and totally lacking in urgency. For example, whereas the Saviour commanded his preachers in Luke 14:21 to, *"Go out quickly into the streets and lanes of the city, and bring in hither the poor, and the maimed, and the halt, and the blind,"* Dr. Westcott preferred to spend his time promoting animal rights at the **Dicky Bird Society.**[103]

Although Jesus said in Luke 15:10 that *"there is joy in the presence of the angels of God over one sinner that repenteth,"* the aesthetic-minded Westcott testified, **"To hear a violin is about the greatest pleasure I know."**[104]

When a youthful William Booth first set eyes on the city of London in 1849, he exclaimed, "What a city to save!"[105] He would devote his entire life to accomplishing that burden. In 1882, the do-nothing Dr. Westcott spoke critically of General Booth after a two-hour discussion with him, relating, "Much he had evidently not thought out. I tried to make it clear that an army cannot be the final form of a kingdom."[106] Westcott's unsolicited advice was extended in 1882, the very year that Booth sent his first "soldiers" into India. (A total of 34 countries would eventually be so invaded.) In fact, by that time, the Salvation Army had 81 stations, 127 full-time evangelists (100 of whom were Booth's personal converts) and 75,000 services a year going on.[107] That's not bad for some "airhead" who had not thought out things!

Once his son found the aged General pacing the floor in the middle of the night. When asked, "What are you thinking about?", the old man sighed, "Ah, Bramwell, I'm thinking about the people's sin. What will people do with their sin?"[108] And in another place he broke down, crying out, "Oh, God, what can I say? Souls! Souls! Souls! My heart hungers for souls!"[109]

By comparison, Westcott's idea of a ministerial heartache was quite another matter. Writing to the Archbishop of Canterbury in

1887, he lamented, "I heard at a Chapter on Monday that the Queen proposes to come to the Abbey in a bonnet. It would be a national disaster."[110]

During a visit to Buckingham Palace in June of 1904 (three years after Victoria's death), King Edward asked Booth to comment on his favorite recreation. Writing in the royal autograph album, Booth replied:

> Your Majesty, some men's ambition is art, some men's ambition is fame, some men's ambition is gold, my ambition is the souls of men.[111]

How does this burden compare with the life's priorities of Westcott and Hort as reflected in their extant letters? With their city going to Hell, a sample of their weekly pursuits would include: flower shows, bird watching, art appreciation, fern arranging, theater going, stamp collecting, novel reading, fossil digging, architecture study, glee clubs, mountain climbing, sculpture, gardening, photography, sketching, poetry, concerts, marionettes and spiritism! *And modern Nicolaitane scholars want to suggest that King James projected homosexual tendencies?!*

Westcott and Hort knew nothing of soul winning, street preaching or prayer meetings. With absolutely no mention of such spiritual powerhouses as David Brainerd, George Whitefield, Jonathan Edwards, John Wesley, Charles Spurgeon, Gypsy Smith, William Carey, George Mueller and hundreds of others, the Cambridge professors chose to write about King Arthur, William Tell, Francis of Assisi, Confucius, Socrates, Homer, Shakespeare, Browning, DaVinci, Spinoza, Raphael, Dante, Mozart, Audubon, Wellington, Tennyson, Euripides, Mendelssohn, Byron, Sophocles, Wordsworth, Milton, Pascal, Comte, Gladstone, Horace, Disraeli, Madame Tussaud and "Uncle Tom."

It is interesting to note that Charles Spurgeon and Fenton Hort began their rural pastorates just five years apart. After being saved for only two years, a seventeen-year-old Spurgeon was called to pastor the Waterbeach Church of London in 1852. Using a King James Bible, the teenage pastor converted nearly his entire community. Reminiscing in his autobiography, the prince of preachers states:

> There went into that village a lad, who had no great scholarship, but who was earnest in seeking the souls of men. He began to preach there, and it pleased God to turn the whole place

upside down. In a short time, the little thatched chapel was crammed, the biggest vagabonds of the village were weeping floods of tears, and those who had been the curse of the parish became its blessing. Where there had been robberies and villainies of every kind, all around the neighbourhood, there were none, because the men who used to do the mischief were themselves in the house of God, rejoicing to hear of Jesus crucified. I am not telling an exaggerated story, nor a thing that I do not know, for **it was my delight to labour for the Lord in that village**. It was a pleasant thing to walk through that place, when drunkenness had almost ceased, when debauchery in the case of many was dead, when men and women went forth to labour with joyful hearts, singing the praises of the ever-living God; and when, at sunset, the humble cottager called his children together, read them some portion from the Book of Truth, and then together they bent their knees in prayer to God. I can say, with joy and happiness, that almost from one end of the village to the other, at the hour of eventide, one might have heard the voice of song coming from nearly every roof-tree, and echoing from almost every heart. I do testify, to the praise of God's grace, that it pleased the Lord to work wonders in our midst. **He showed the power of Jesu's name, and made me a witness of that gospel which can win souls,** draw reluctant hearts, and mould afresh the life and conduct of sinful men and women.[112]

In 1854, Spurgeon was called away to the New Park Street Church which was running a mere one hundred in attendance. Within three months, the twelve-hundred seat auditorium was packed and jammed and plans were immediately begun to construct the massive Metropolitan Tabernacle.

By comparison, Dr. Hort assumed his first "parochial ministry" in 1855 in the country village of St. Ippolyts at the age of twenty-nine. Whereas Spurgeon labored to "weed out" the sins in the lives of his people, Arthur said of his father:

He took up the charge with enthusiasm, and his interest in it never abated. The work itself was one for which he had definitely been preparing himself for years past; it was that which from his earliest days he had made his deliberate choice. His recreations also were just what he would have chosen; he loved the country and the simple living; **the garden was his constant delight**; it was wild and overgrown when he came, and many afternoons were given to felling and pruning, the planning of beds . . . **It was Hort's great delight to reduce it to order,** and preserve what he could of the original planting.[113]

While one man reduced a *garden* to order, the other restored a *village* to order. To be perfectly frank, the basic reason Hort experienced more success with his "pruning" than with his "preaching" was because he was the consummate **wimp**. Even his son admitted:

> The fact remains, however, that in the course of years the conviction grew on him that this was not his true sphere. His **extreme sensitiveness** and **shyness** were real hindrances, and he was well aware of the fact . . . he felt all along unable to speak to the people as he longed to do. He was and is regarded by them with reverent affection, but they must have felt, as he did, the barrier of his reserve.[114]

During Hort's first year at St. Ippolyts, England suffered a series of military disasters in India triggered by a particular mutiny. The government set aside Wednesday, October 7, 1857, for:

> A solemn fast, humiliation, and prayer before Almighty God: in order to obtain pardon of our sins, and for imploring His blessing and assistance on our arms for the restoration of tranquillity in India.[115]

Spurgeon got the nod for the central service to be held in the huge Crystal Palace. On the appointed day, 23,654 persons listened attentively to the twenty-three-year-old Spurgeon preach from the text, *"Hear ye the rod, and who hath appointed it."* (Micah 6:9b)

In Hort's first correspondence following this momentous service, a letter dated November 17, 1857, to the Reverend Gerald Blunt, he not only failed to mention the occasion but discussed instead *roses, squirrels, gooseberries* and the death of a *sick cat.*[116]

While Spurgeon used to say that his problem was not in writing a sermon but in choosing one, the younger Hort wrote of his father, **"It was in the production of sermons that the difficulty of finding expression for his thoughts was most felt."**[117]

Hort was always intimidated when confronted by a *real* preacher. Reference has already been made in chapter two to Hort's attendance at a Dwight Moody service on May 20th, 1875. His, ". . . but should not care to go again," speaks volumes of the Holy Ghost conviction in that meeting. The dry professor did admit to being a little bowled over by the crowds, writing, "Much the most remarkable thing is the congregation or rather audience."[118] This evangelist, described by Hort as "quite conventional and commonplace" and his song leader, Sankey, whose music Hort criticized as "inferior," had just wrapped up their two-year tour of the British Isles preaching to over 2½ million people in *285* meetings!

That Hort was irritated by these crowds can be seen in the opening line of his very next letter written to Reverend Charles Benson: "Our greatest want is of **theologians.**"[119]

Dr. Hort continued to be one giant contradiction. In a letter to Reverend Blunt, he specifically defines a minister's obligation to: "Tell men of God and Jesus Christ whom He has sent,—in a word, to preach the Gospel, that is, announce the Good Tidings."[120]

However, there is not a single recorded instance of any such activity in Hort's entire biography. (The same can be said for Westcott.) The non-soul-winning hypocrite would rather criticize such evangelistic dissenters as the Methodists for being, "worse than Popery, as being more insidious."[121] It is rather interesting that in the very year Hort made this insane comparison (1846), the sixty-year-old Methodist, Peter Cartwright, noted in his diary that, "I had to cross many ponds frozen over . . . my horse nearly worn down, and myself cold, hungry, and much fatigued."[122]

Westcott's preaching was not much better. The other Arthur had to also cover *his* father's dead sermonettes, writing:

> **It had always been a great physical effort to him to preach,** even in such a comparatively small building as the Harrow School Chapel, so that he was full of anxiety at the prospect of preaching from a Cathedral pulpit.[123]

The great "Doctor of Textual Criticism" was a weird duck, to say the least, Arthur relating:

> Many a time have I heard him remark that he could not fit the clown into his scheme of the universe, and have often wondered whether the very funniest of men could, if allowed a chance, have induced him to smile.[124]

In a rather sad note, the younger Westcott also remarked:

> In one of his letters my father says that nature had not endowed him with the gift of tears; but as he stood on the quay-side seeing that son off to Canada, the tears were pouring down his cheeks. That was the only occasion on which I ever saw him weep.[125]

The *sad* part of this story is that Westcott was not weeping for his son but for the boy's *dog*, "Mep," to which he had grown attached.

By contrast, the warmhearted Whitefield could hardly manage a sermon *without* tears, Pollock writing:

> "You blame me for weeping," he would say, "but how can I help it when you will not weep for yourselves although your immortal souls are on the verge of destruction, and for aught I know, you are hearing your last sermon and may never more have another opportunity to have Christ offered to you?"[126]

Westcott loved to talk about missions, but that's where it ended. It was perhaps a sore spot to him that two of the century's most productive missionaries, C.T. Studd and Dr. W.T. Grenfell, were saved and called to the field right out from under his nose at Cambridge—and through the instrumentality of D.L. Moody, no less. Studd gave away an inheritance to take the Gospel to China, India and Africa while Grenfell decided against a lucrative medical practice to become a missionary to Labrador. In his autobiography, Grenfell said that he had been converted through Moody's common sense. After a young minister turned the opening prayer into an "oratorical effort," young Grenfell grew bored and restless and decided to sneak out. Moody spotted him and interrupted the prayer with, "Let us sing a hymn while our brother finishes his prayer." Delighted at the remark, the Cambridge student dashed back to his seat and was soundly converted at the sermon's close.[127]

Westcott and Hort were Hell-bound impostors projecting a "form of godliness" who never gave a Gospel invitation, even under the most critical circumstances. Addressing a regiment of soldiers who stood on the brink of eternity, Dr. Westcott left them high and dry with the following lines of his letter which were read on parade:

> You will seek the blessing of God first, and then you will use to the uttermost with resolute courage the powers with which He has endowed you. In this spirit may you be enabled to meet hardships, privations, dangers, sufferings, the shadow of death, and feel the presence of God about you in every trial. May He keep you and bless you abundantly; and may you each, looking to Him, know in your own souls, as has been said by one of old time, that "The vision of God is the life of man."[128]

How cold and worthless can you get? Consider the appeal of his fellow Englishman, Gypsy Smith, in the same situation a generation later:

> I was talking behind the lines to some of the boys. Every boy in front of me was going up to the trenches that night. There were five or six hundred of them. It wasn't easy to talk. All I said was accompanied by the roar of guns, the crack of rifles, and the rattle of machine guns, and once in a while our faces were lit up by the flashes. I looked at those boys. I couldn't preach to them in any ordinary way. I knew, and they knew, that for many it was the last service for some on earth.
>
> I said, "Boys, you are going up to the trenches. Anything may happen there. I wish I could go with you. God knows I do. I would if they would let me, and if any of you fell, I would like to hold your hand and say something to you for your mother, for wife, and for lover, and for your little child. I'd like to be the link between you and home for just that moment—God's messenger for you. They won't let me go: but there is Somebody who will go with you. You know who that is." You should have heard the boys all over that hut whisper, "Yes, Sir, Jesus."
>
> "Well," I said, "**I want every man that is anxious to take Jesus with him into the trenches to stand.**" Instantly and quietly every man stood.[129]

The remainder of Westcott and Hort's ministries followed the typical liberal party line. There are numerous references in their letters to the merits of disarmament and pleas for world peace.[130] Both men despised the free enterprise system and promoted the benefits of communism,[131] with Westcott declaring bluntly, "**I suppose I am a communist by nature.**"[132] He claimed to abhor every luxury, and was so strange that he promoted the concept of communal living for years. He called this fantasy his *Coenobium.* The worthless project never got off the ground.[133]

Now, as these heresies have continued to surface, much of the support for Westcott and Hort has eroded. Robert L. Sumner made the insane statement that, "Westcott and Hort . . . were liberal in theology but were honest in seeking to restore the original text."[134]

Stewart Custer of Bob Jones University remains one of their staunchest defenders. Dr. Custer is chairman of the division of Bible and professor of graduate studies. In 1981, Dr. Custer authored a thirty-eight page pamphlet entitled *The Truth about the King James Version Controversy.* On page twenty-six, he states:

Most of the things quoted against Westcott and Hort come from their private correspondence. One of the damaging things quoted against Hort was written when he was 23 (1851). To quote a man's private correspondence and statements of **early years** when his theological position was still being formed is unfair at the very least. Especially when these men have written in their **mature years** book after book defending the conservative interpretation of Scripture, it is unjust to characterize their whole ministries by a few misinterpretations that they may have been guilty of.[135]

The reader will observe at least *seven* holes in Dr. Custer's remarks:

1. To insinuate a breach of ethics for exposing a man's private correspondence is ridiculous when one is dealing with a "wolf in sheep's clothing." The only way to catch a *liar* would be through his private correspondence.

2. Dr. Custer expects us to dismiss Westcott and Hort's early heresies because the professors were supposed to have gotten it straight in their older years. *Has the Chairman of Bible forgotten that it was in those early years (1853-1871)[136] that the heretical revisers were constructing their Greek New Testament?* As late as 1860, seven years into the Greek New Testament project, a thirty-three-year-old Hort complained to Dr. Lightfoot, "In our rapid correspondence about the N.T. I have been forgetting Plato."[137] And in the opening line of his very next letter (to Mr. A. Macmillan) he states, "About Darwin, I have been reading and thinking a good deal, and am getting to see my way comparatively clearly."[138] Would a conservative scholar sandwich God's Word in between *Plato and Darwin?*

3. You will note carefully that Dr. Custer gives us no information as to *when* Westcott and Hort were born again. One cannot mature until he is alive!

4. Dr. Custer seems to imply that a man can move gradually from being a heretic to a conservative. Charles Wesley would disagree: "Thine eye diffused a quick'ning ray, I woke, the dungeon flamed with light."

5. We are supposed to be assured because a number of

orthodox positions "... can be found" in the later works of Westcott and Hort. Liberals always talk out of both sides of their mouths. This is the very justification that is given for the modern English translations, despite their numerous heretical readings; i.e., "every major doctrine *can be found* therein."

6. As to Dr. Custer's impressive list of orthodox references from the late years, Dr. Donald Waite of *The Bible for Today* has already published a 182-page rebuttal of Custer's work entitled *Dr. Stewart Custer Answered on the Textus Receptus and the King James Version*. On pages 43 through 146, Dr. Waite demolishes the so-called "mature writings" of Drs. Westcott and Hort, as taken from their commentaries on John, Hebrews and I Peter.

7. Dr. Custer said that Westcott and Hort discarded their "few *misinterpretations*" (whatever that means) when they reached their mature years. *When* does Dr. Custer believe the golden years begin?

> "No one now, I suppose, holds that the first three chapters of Genesis, for example, give a literal history—I could never understand how anyone reading them with open eyes could think they did."[139]
>
> Dr. B. F. Westcott
> 4th March, 1890
> Age 65 years

His *eulogy*, eleven years later, read in part: "His earnest desire and endeavour were to promote the highest welfare of the human family by proclaiming the Fatherhood of God and the brotherhood of man."[140] *How much more mature can a guy get?*

XV

Behind Closed Doors

"But it is happened unto them according to the true proverb, The dog is turned to his own vomit again."
(II Peter 2:22a)

One of the clearest signs of papal affinity with Westcott and Hort was their shared abhorrence for democracy in all its forms. Like their Vatican counterpart, the Cambridge duumvirate disguised their private campaign against the free enterprise system with a bleeding-heart intercession on behalf of the poor. Dr. Hort writes:

> Surely every man is meant to be God's steward of every blessing and 'talent' (power, wealth, influence, station, birth, etc. etc.) which He gives him, for the benefit of his neighbors ... To be without responsibility, to be in no degree our 'brother's keeper,' would be the heaviest curse imaginable ... **I cannot at present see any objection to a limit being placed by the State upon the amount of property which any one person may possess** ... *I* would say that—the co-operative *principle* is a better and a mightier than the competitive *principle*.[1]

Occasionally, they would let down their guard with such candor as Hort's, "I ... cannot say that I see much as yet to soften my **deep hatred of democracy in all its forms.**"[2] In conjunction with the Vatican's avowed purpose of global conquest, Westcott and Hort were unalterably committed to *the destruction of the United States of America*, Hort admitting:

I care more for England and for Europe than for

America, how much more than for all the niggers in the world! and I contend that the highest morality requires me to do so. Some thirty years ago Niebuhr wrote to this effect: Whatever people may say to the contrary, **the American empire is a standing menace to the whole civilization of Europe,** and sooner or later one or the other must perish. Every year has, I think, brought fresh proof of the entire truth of these words. American doctrine . . . destroys the root of everything vitally precious which man has by painful growth been learning from the earliest times till now, and tends only to reduce us to the gorilla state. The American empire seems to me mainly an embodiment of American doctrine, its leading principle being lawless force. Surely, if ever Babylon or Rome were rightly cursed, **it cannot be wrong to desire and pray from the bottom of one's heart that the American Union may be shivered to pieces.**[3]

Dr. Westcott devoted many years of his life to an ingenious plan for betraying both America and his native England to the bondage of Rome. By expanding the standard liberal party line of the brotherhood of men to its wider application of a brotherhood of *nations,* Westcott led an impassioned lobby for a precedent-setting arbitration treaty between the United States and her mother country. Should America and Great Britain make the first move for world peace with a simultaneous disarmament, the Catholic nations of Europe would be only too happy to follow suit. Westcott, fantasizing in 1889:

The United States and England are already bound so closely together by their common language and common descent, that an Arbitration Treaty which shall exclude the thought of war—a civil war—between them seems to be within measurable distance. When once the great principle of arbitration has been adopted by two great nations, it cannot but be that the example will be followed, and then, at last, **however remote the vision may seem,** disarmament will be a natural consequence of the acceptance of a rational and legal method of settling national disputes.[4]

Fortunately, President Benjamin Harrison wasn't very impressed with Westcott's pipe dream.

However, where the Cambridge "peace-niks" failed at getting America and England to disarm *militarily,* they were successful in orchestrating a far deadlier *spiritual* disarmament. For their ultimate conformity to Roman dogma, the respectable professors introduced their private rendition of the Jesuit Douay-Rheims

Version of the Bible into the ranks of unsuspecting Protestantism.

The treacherous mission had its beginning in the opening months of 1853 when Westcott and Hort decided upon a joint revision of the text of the Greek New Testament. Although the idealistic Dr. Hort expressed the hope that "we may perhaps have it out in little more than a year,"[5] this opening phase of the overall project would drag on for seventeen years (to be followed by the formal Revision Committee [1871-1881]).

This naiveté on the part of Hort can be traced to his self-proclaimed ignorance of manuscript evidences. Writing in 1850, the twenty-one-year-old would-be reviser lamented, "**But I am so ignorant of** Hebrew and, what is worse, of **the Greek text of the N. T.,** that I have all but discarded them."[6]

As for Dr. Westcott's expertise, he was no Dr. John Bois, declaring a full nineteen years after the publication of the Revised Version, "I cannot speak of the Old Testament with adequate knowledge."[7]

However, what these young men lacked in knowledge, they more than made up for in prejudice against the Reformation text. With an incredible reiteration of his textual shortcomings, Dr. Hort says on the eve of his epoch-making project:

> I had no idea till the last few weeks of the importance of texts, having read so little Greek Testament, and dragged on with the villainous *Textus Receptus* . . . **Think of that vile *Textus Receptus* leaning entirely on late MSS.;** it is a blessing there are such early ones.[8]

Isn't it amazing what a few weeks of study can do for a neophyte scholar? And Westcott, at twenty-nine, was no less blasphemous, declaring, "I feel most keenly the disgrace of circulating what I feel to be falsified copies of Holy Scripture."[9]

The reader is reminded that Dr. Custer enjoins tolerance for these young whippersnappers as their orthodoxy did not evolve until much later. The inference is that the Westcott and Hort Greek Testament should be above suspicion—despite the fact that it was constructed during the professors' "pre-orthodox" years—because every "fundamental of the faith" can be found therein.

The cause for the revisers' animosity toward the *Textus Receptus* was no different than the problem modern Nicolaitanes have with the King James Bible today. Westcott and Hort could not and would not submit to *final authority*. Westcott wrote:

> I do in my heart believe that every syllable of Holy Scripture,

as Origen said, has its work; but I hope I may be saved from the presumption of saying, "It is this, this only."[10]

Hort's rebellion can also be seen in his words to Dr. Rowland Williams in a letter dated October of 1858:

> I have a deeply-rooted agreement with High Churchmen as to the Church, Ministry, Sacraments, and, above all, Creeds ... The positive doctrines even of the Evangelicals seem to me perverted rather than untrue. **There are, I fear, still more serious differences between us on the subject of authority, and especially the authority of the Bible.**[11]

It is rather fitting that II Thessalonians 2 constitutes one of the first passages to stump the revisers, Hort writing to Westcott:

> I *am* sticking at II Thessalonians 2 . . . That troublesome chapter has occupied many hours, but it is a great satisfaction that at last I have gained some light upon the matter, though a great deal remains to be cleared up.[12]

Little did they realize how their project would be used of Satan to usher in the very apostasy predicted in these verses. Writing to his wife years later to acknowledge his acceptance of a revision appointment, he stated:

> I have just written to Ellicott to accept! This makes it a memorable day; **the beginning of one knows not what changes or events in one's life, to say nothing of public results.** It is no longer a secret.[13]

With Hort's allusion to his and Westcott's Greek work having been completed in secret, we reapply the central premise of our previous chapter. There the reader was encouraged to decide for himself whether the revisers exhibited a spiritual walk consistent with "the Book" they had volunteered to improve. The challenge is now extended for a scrutiny of the revision itself.

Deceit was their *modus operandi* throughout every stage. Hort wrote to a Reverend Gerald Blunt in November of 1853:

> We came to a distinct and positive understanding about our Gk. Test. and the details thereof. **We still do not wish it to be talked about,** but are going to work at once.[14]

Being the apostates that they were, Westcott and Hort were frequently suspicioned by their peers for a variety of heresies. Arthur Westcott confirms that as early as 1861, his father was charged with being "unsafe" and of "Germanising."[15]

Continuing with his father's saga, the younger Westcott added:

> My father's orthodoxy was again called in question two years later. In 1867 he wrote a tract entitled *The Resurrection as a Fact and a Revelation*, the substance of which was derived for the most part from his essay on *The Gospel of the Resurrection*. This tract was accepted by the Society for Promoting Christian Knowledge, and was already in type, when one of the Society's episcopal referees detected heresy in it. The writer was unable to omit the suspected passage, as he held it to be essential to his argument, and consequently 'his valuable pamphlet' was suppressed.[16]

Westcott had earlier solicited Dr. Lightfoot's council for the above-mentioned tract, acknowledging his less-than-blameless theology:

> My dear Lightfoot—As you are the judge of my orthodoxy—a perilous office, I fear, in these days—I must ask you whether you think the title of my essay may be 'The Gospel of the Resurrection: Thoughts on its relation to Reason and History'?[17]

Accusations such as these kept the Cambridge duo in a constant state of paranoia lest their true beliefs should leak out. In a letter to a colleague, Hort cautioned against rocking the boat with a hasty push for High Church, Romanish polity:

> The errors and prejudices, which we agree in wishing to remove, can surely be more wholesomely and also more effectually reached by individual efforts of an **indirect kind** than by combined open assault. At present very many orthodox but rational men are being unawares acted on by influences which will assuredly bear good fruit in due time, **if the process is allowed to go on quietly**; but I cannot help fearing that a premature crisis would frighten back many.[18]

In 1861, Westcott and Hort were debating whether to publish some of their heresies in the liberal *Essays and Reviews*. They finally came to the conclusion that the anticipated fallout would impair the credibility of their Greek New Testament. Writing to Westcott, Dr. Hort reasons:

Also—but this may be cowardice—I have a sort of craving that our text should be cast upon the world before we deal with matters likely to brand us with suspicion. I mean, a text, issued **by men already known for what will undoubtedly be treated as dangerous heresy**, will have great difficulties in finding its way to regions which it might otherwise hope to reach, and whence it would not be easily banished by subsequent alarms.[19]

As one surveys the letters of Westcott and Hort which were written throughout their revision of the *Textus Receptus*, the Holy Spirit becomes conspicuous by His absence. Writing in 1859, the superstitious Dr. Hort remarks:

St. Mark is frightfully slow to get through, nearly every word wanting rigid scrutiny. St. Luke will, I hope, be decidedly easier, and the rest quite another thing. It is really very **lucky** that we did not do it a year or two ago, so much fresh light comes from Tregelles and the new Tischendorf.[20]

In addition to leaning on "Lady Luck," their rationale was that of the natural man. Writing to his eldest son after the printing of the Revised Version, Hort asserts smugly:

It is impossible not to hope that there are multitudes of quiet people who will be able to read their Bible a little more **intelligently** now.[21]

In the previous chapter, we learned that Dr. Hort sandwiched his New Testament work in between *Plato* and *Darwin*. He even had the audacity to say, "**In our rapid correspondence about the N. T. I have been forgetting Plato.**"[22]

A good bit of the revisers' time was also spent at the "feeding trough" of third-century Alexandria. With reference to his father's articles to the *Dictionary of Christian Antiquities*, Arthur Westcott states:

My father's promised contributions, however, were completed, the most important being his articles on the Alexandrian Divines, including Clement, Demetrius, Dionysius, and, greatest of all, Origen. **For many years the works of Origen were close to his hand**, and he continually turned to them at every opportunity.[23]

In fact, Hort's infatuation with Alexandria was so intense that he even dug up and translated the "Candlelight Hymn" of the

Alexandrian Church.[24] Can you imagine how dead that number must have been?

Understandably, the influence of the Hamite capital would incite a "scholarly prejudice" for Codex B. Arthur Hort relates:

> The nearest approach to such a character is made by the great Vatican Codex, the readings of which were till recently made inaccesible by Papal jealousy. Though, however, it is not entirely free from the characteristics of the less pure types of text, it is regarded by Hort as a first-rate authority; even when it stands alone, its evidence is regarded as of very high value, while, when it agrees with some other of certain selected good manuscripts, especially with Tischendorf's Sinai Codex, **their joint testimony is accepted as almost decisive.**[25]

With over 3,000 disagreements between ℵ and B in the Gospels alone, one would question what kind of "joint" young Arthur was smoking when he praised their "joint testimony" as decisive!

By the opening days of 1870, the remonstrative pressure from various pseudo-Anglican scholars (Jesuit agents) had prevailed upon the Church of England for a conservative revision of the 1611 Authorized Version. It was no accident that this "decision" just happened to coincide with the completion of the Westcott and Hort Greek Text. Dr. Gipp sets the scene:

> In 1870, the Convention of the Church of England commissioned a revision of the Authorized Version. A gleam of hope shone in the eye of every Roman Catholic in England and the Continent. An eager anticipation filled every Jesuit-inspired, Protestant scholar in England. Although it was meant to correct a few supposed "errors" in the Authorized Version, the textual critics of the day assured themselves that they would never again have to submit to the Divine authority of the Universal Text.[26]

On the dates of February 10th, May 3rd, and 5th, 1870, the Church's Southern Convocation passed formal resolutions to that effect with the strongest possible language, limiting revision activity to "PLAIN AND CLEAR ERRORS."[27]

With their work scheduled for the historic Jerusalem Chamber, the eventual number of participating scholars would peak at ninety-nine. However, only forty-nine of these would be Anglican clergymen with the remainder comprising an ecumenical mish-mash.[28] Although the Roman Catholic Cardinal Newman politely refused his invitation to contribute, Dr. Vance Smith, pastor of

St. Stephen's Gate **Unitarian** Church, did not.

On June 22nd, Dr. Smith joined the other revisers for a special inaugural communion service officiated by Dean Stanley. After kneeling at the grave of Edward VI, the entourage moved into Henry VII's chapel to receive the elements. Dr. Hort reported to a friend that:

> The Communion in Henry VII's chapel was one of those few great services which seem to mark points in one's life. There was nothing to disturb its perfect quietness and solemnity ... The two sessions of work which followed carried on, rather than disturbed, the impression. The tone was admirable. It became evident that we could work with thorough harmony, notwithstanding differences of all kinds.[29]

While Westcott and Hort were kneeling alongside the Christ-rejecting Smith at Edward VI's grave, the "Pious Josiah" was probably rolling over down below at the hypocritical proceedings. As it turned out, the Unitarian minister had more conviction than the rest, declaring on the following day that he had received the Sacrament without "joining in the Nicene Creed" and without "compromise of his principles as a Unitarian."[30]

Within days of this outrage, several thousand Anglican divines affixed their signatures to a solemn protest which resulted in the following resolution being passed by the Upper House:

> That it is the judgment of this House that no person who denies the Godhead of our Lord Jesus Christ ought to be invited to join either company to which is committed the Revision of the Authorized Version of Holy Scripture: and that it is further the judgment of this House that any such person now on either Company should cease to act therewith.[31]

Dr. Westcott came to Smith's aid threatening to "quit and take his ball home" if the Unitarian was forced to resign. Writing to Dr. Hort, his exact words were:

> I never felt more clear as to my duty. If the Company accept the dictation of Convocation, my work must end. I see no escape from the conclusion.[32]

Unfortunately, the Convocation backed down and Smith remained on the committee. The truth is that Westcott would have come to the aid of *any* religionist, writing in 1851:

I give the title "Rev." to all recognised religious teachers—to a Rabbi, an Iman, or even to as uncertain a lecturer as E. Dawson, if he desired it.[33]

Dr. Hort was ecstatic over Smith being allowed to remain on the committee. Writing to Westcott in August, he said:

There is the strangest blindness about the Unitarian position, and the moral damage that would have been done to the acceptance of the Revision by the laity if Unitarians had been outlawed as such.[34]

And in another letter to Lightfoot:

It is, I think, difficult to measure the weight of acceptance won beforehand for the Revision by the single fact of our welcoming an Unitarian, if only the Company perseveres in its present serious and faithful spirit.[35]

But note further how Dr. Hort openly acknowledges this Christ-rejecting heretic as a Christian brother:

So far the angry objectors have reason for their astonishment. But it is strange that they should not ask themselves what other alternatives were preferable, and what is really lost to any great interest by the union, for once, of **all English Christians** around the altar of the Church.[36]

When the Revised Version was eventually released to the English people in 1881, one of the more shocking discoveries was the "revised" reading of I Timothy 3:16. Where the Holy Spirit had led Paul to write, *"God was manifest in the flesh,"* the new "Bible" read, **"who** was manifest in the flesh." Would you like to guess the identity of the one most responsible for such an attack on Christ's Deity? In the words of the Unitarian himself:

The old reading is pronounced untenable by the Revisers, as it has long been known to be by all careful students of the New Testament . . . It is in truth another example of the facility with which ancient copiers could introduce the word God into their manuscripts,—a reading which was the natural result of the growing tendency in early Christian times . . . to look upon the humble Teacher as the incarnate Word, and therefore as 'God manifest in the flesh.'[37]

The Communion controversy surrounding Dr. Smith was not

the only bad omen to surface. Although accepting their invitation to join the committee, several key participants went on record as being totally opposed to the prospect of any revision. No less of a distinguished personage than the committee chairman himself, Bishop Charles Ellicott, had remarked in 1861:

> It is my honest conviction that for any authoritative REVISION, we are not yet mature; *either in Biblical learning or Hellenistic scholarship.* There is good scholarship in this country, . . . but *it has certainly not yet been sufficiently directed to the study of the New Testament* . . . to render any national attempt at REVISION either hopeful or lastingly profitable.[38]

And only days before the project's convening, Ellicott voiced concern over the prospect of going too far with the work. To the Bishop's way of thinking, "too far" would involve alterations in the underlying Greek text. The Chairman warned:

> What course would revisers have us to follow? . . . Would it be well for them to agree on a Critical Greek Text? *To this question we venture to answer very unhesitatingly in the negative.*
> Though we have much critical material, and a very fair amount of critical knowledge, *we have certainly not yet acquired sufficient critical judgment* for any body of revisers hopefully to undertake such a work as this . . . Nothing is more satisfactory at the present time than the evident feelings of veneration for our Authorized Version, and the very generally-felt desire for *as little change as possible.*[39]

In an earlier speech to the Convocation in February of that year, Bishop Ellicott summarized his conviction with the words, "We may be satisfied with the attempt to correct *plain and clear errors* but *there it is our duty to stop.*"[40]

It is vital for the reader to understand that Ellicott's concern was a reflection of the directives laid down by the Convocation itself. In no uncertain terms, the revisers were enjoined to limit their alterations to *an absolute minimum.* Dean Burgon commented:

> The Authors of this new Revision of the Greek have either entitled themselves to the Church's profound reverence and abiding gratitude; or else they have laid themselves open to her gravest censure, and must experience at her hands nothing short of stern and well-merited rebuke. No middle course presents itself; since assuredly *to construct a new Greek Text* formed no

part of the Instructions which the Revisionists received at the hands of the Convocation of the Southern Province. Rather were they warned against venturing on such an experiment; the fundamental principle of the entire undertaking having been declared at the outset to be—That 'a Revision of *the Authorized Version*' is desirable; and the terms of the original Resolution of Feb. 10th, 1870, being, that the removal of 'PLAIN AND CLEAR ERRORS' was alone contemplated,—'whether in the Greek Text originally adopted by the Translators, or in the Translation made from the same.' Such were in fact *the limits formally imposed by Convocation*, (10th Feb. and 3rd, 5th May, 1870,) *on the work of Revision*. Only NECESSARY changes were to be made. The first Rule of the Committee (25th May) was similar in character: viz.—'*To introduce as few alterations as possible into the Text of the Authorized Version*, consistently with faithfulness.'[41]

Another critical injunction (Rule IV of Convocation) concerned the procedure to be followed whenever it was deemed necessary to make a change in the Greek itself. Whereas the majority of anticipated changes would be in the *English*, resulting from assumed translation improvements from the *Textus Receptus*, a limited percentage was also expected in the underlying Greek text. Because such changes would be undetected by the average layman, a precautionary proviso was inserted to guard against unnecessary license by the revisers. Burgon continues:

> The condition was enjoined upon them that whenever '*decidedly preponderating evidence*' constrained their adoption of some change in 'the Text from which the Authorized Version was made,' *they should indicate such alteration in the margin.*[42]

As we shall presently see, the revisers did not even come *close* to observing either one of these mandates. Both were entirely ignored! One could see the handwriting on the wall from the very first session. Hort's son tells us of the unusual surprise which greeted the naive revisers:

> Each member of the Company had been supplied with a private copy of Westcott and Hort's Text, but the Company did not, of course, in any way bind itself to accept their conclusions.[43]

Although the astonished participants were not bound "to accept their conclusions" (ten years of intimidation by Dr. Hort would take care of that), they were obligated to a vow of secrecy as to the existence of the new Greek text. Dr. Fuller citing

Wilkinson:

> When the English New Testament Committee met, it was immediately apparent what was going to happen. Though **for ten long years the iron rule of silence kept the public ignorant** of what was going on behind closed doors, the story is now known.[44]

To buy as much time as possible, the new Greek Text was purposefully withheld from the publishers, being released on May 12th, only five days before the Revised Version's debut. Had this not been done, reviewers such as Dean Burgon would have torpedoed the proceedings.

Unbeknown to the company of revisers, Westcott and Hort had been plotting an immediate takeover of the proceedings. Their preliminary collusion is now an established fact. Westcott wrote to Hort saying, "The rules though liberal are vague, and the interpretation of them will depend upon action at the first."[45] With reference to their third collaborator, the influential Bishop Lightfoot, Westcott writes to Hort on May 28, 1870:

> Your note came with one from Ellicott this morning . . . Though I think that Convocation is not competent to initiate such a measure, yet I feel that as **'we three' are together** it would be wrong not to 'make the best of it' as Lightfoot first says . . . There is some hope that alternative readings might find a place in the margin.[46]

The conniving Westcott wrote to Lightfoot on June 4th:

> Ought we not to have a conference **before** the first meeting for Revision? There are many points on which it is important that we should be agreed.[47]

In a second letter to Hort dated July 1, 1870, Westcott sheds further light on how the chairman himself was being drawn into these unethical maneuvers.

> The Revision on the whole surprised me by prospects of hope. I suggested to Ellicott a plan of tabulating and circulating emendations **before** our meeting, which may in the end prove valuable.[48]

And a third letter to Hort the following week confirmed:

The Bishop of Gloucester (Ellicott) seems to me to be quite capable of accepting heartily and adopting personally a thorough scheme.[49]

Dr. Hort pretty well summed up the Jesuit mentality of the conspirators with his own principles (as cited by Wilkinson): "I am rather in favor of **indirect** dealing."[50] Should we really be surprised? Remember the *trampoline*?

The atmosphere of entrapment was accentuated by the revisers' frustration at being ill-equipped to contribute substantially to the proceedings. Skilled in linguistics, these men came prepared to analyze the translation proper. However, what Westcott and Hort were advocating—a substantial overhauling of the Greek Text—required a rare expertise in the field of manuscript evidences. Burgon highlighted the basic problem:

> It can never be any question among scholars, that a fatal error was committed when a body of Divines, appointed *to revise the Authorized English Version* of the New Testament Scriptures, addressed themselves to the solution of an entirely different and far more intricate problem, namely *the re-construction of the Greek Text.*[51]

With the exception of Westcott, Hort, and Lightfoot, the only committee member with a significant background in New Testament manuscripts was Dr. Frederick Scrivener. As alluded to previously, Prebendary Scrivener became the chief spokesman for the minority party of conservatives. Bishop Ellicott reported afterwards that the proceedings were, "often a kind of critical duel between Dr. Hort and Dr. Scrivener."[52]

The methodology of these two men was as different as day and night. Dr. Hort perfected what has been called the "eclectic" method because of its unscholarly emphasis on the reviser's personal caprice when "feeling his way through" the limited and overrated selection of "internal evidence" as contrasted with the painstaking investigation of the wider array of "external evidence," such as fathers, versions, etc.

Arthur Hort described his father's approach thusly:

> The obvious method of deciding between variant readings, is for the critic to ask which the author is most likely to have written, and so to settle the question **by the light of his own inner consciousness.**[53]

Referring to Hort's "Let-your-conscience-be-your-guide" approach to the study of the Bible, Burgon states:

> The only indication we anywhere meet with of the actual *ground* of Dr. Hort's certainty, and reason of his preference, is contained in his claim that,—"Every binary group [of MSS.] *containing* B is found to offer a large proportion of Readings, which, on the closest scrutiny, have THE RING OF GENUINENESS: while it is difficult to find any Readings so attested which LOOK SUSPICIOUS after full consideration."[54]

Burgon's analysis follows:

> And thus we have, at last, an honest confession of the ultimate principle which has determined the Text of the present edition of the N.T. *"The ring of genuineness"*! *This* it must be which was referred to when *"instinctive processes of Criticism"* were vaunted; and the candid avowal made that "the experience which is their foundation needs perpetual correction and recorrection."
>
> "We are obliged" (say these accomplished writers) "to *come to the individual mind at last."*
>
> And thus, behold, at last we *have* reached the goal! . . . *Individual idiosyncrasy,—not* external Evidence:—Readings *"strongly prefered,"—not* Readings *strongly attested:—*"personal discernment" (self! still self!) *conscientiously exercising itself upon Codex B;* this is a true account of the Critical method pursued by these accomplished Scholars. They deliberately claim *"personal discernment"* as "the surest ground for confidence." Accordingly, they judge of Readings by their *looks* and by their *sound.* When, in *their* opinion, words "look suspicious," words are to be rejected. If a word has "the ring of genuineness,"—(i.e. *if it seems to them* to have it,)—they claim that the word shall pass unchallenged.[55]

As a classic example of the prideful license of Westcott and Hort, consider the following example of such Nicolaitane madness:

> Are there, as a matter of fact, places in which we are *constrained by overwhelming evidence* to recognize the existence of Textual error in *all* extant documents? To this question, we have no hesitation in replying in the affirmative.[56]

Here the "good doctors" flatter themselves with being able to throw out **all** extant evidence as per their own professional opinion. (The critic is politely *"headed off at the pass"* concerning Erasmus and the *Johannine Comma* as the textual liberty under discussion was, for Westcott and Hort, the rule and not the exception. See *The King James Version Defended* by Edward Hills, pp. 209-213.)

Being the liberals that they were, Westcott and Hort were constrained to cut corners by the social demands of the *Dicky Bird Society* and other such "high-priority" activities. Where Westcott preferred the *violin* as his greatest pleasure on earth, men of the "old school" like Scrivener and Burgon chose the dreary *study* instead. Burgon relates:

> What compels me to repeat this so often, is the impatient self-sufficiency of these last days, which is for breaking away from the old restraints; and for erecting the individual conscience into an authority from which there shall be no appeal. I know but too well how laborious is the scientific method which *I* advocate. A long summer day disappears, while the student—with all his appliances about him—is resolutely threshing out some minute textual problem. Another, and yet another bright day vanishes. Comes Saturday evening at last, and a page of illegible manuscript is all that he has to show for a week's heavy toil. *Quousque tandem?* And yet, it is the indispensable condition of progress in an unexplored region, that a few should thus labour, until a path has been cut through the forest,—a road laid down,—huts built,—a *modus vivendi* established.[57]

Dr. Scrivener's lot became one of increasing frustration. As the days dragged on, more of the committee came under the control of the domineering Westcott and Hort, described by Wilkinson as **"constantly at their elbow."**[58] Especially mesmerizing was the pontificating Dr. Hort, Hemphill relating:

> Nor is it difficult to understand that many of their less resolute and decided colleagues must often have been completely carried off their feet by the persuasiveness and resourcefulness, and zeal of Hort, backed by the great prestige of Lightfoot, the popular Canon of St. Paul's, and the quiet determination of Westcott, who set his face as a flint. In fact, it can hardly be doubted that Hort's was the strongest will of the whole Company, and his adroitness in debate was only equaled by his pertinacity.[59]

Arthur Hort does not attempt to dispute this point and even cites the flowery testimony of Dr. William Moulton, himself a committee member:

> By tacit consent Dr. Scrivener and Dr. Hort were respectively the exponents and advocates of the opposing principles. I well

remember the deep impression made on me from the first by Dr. Hort's exposition of what he held to be the true method of criticism, especially his care in tracing the various streams of evidence, and the cogency of his argument from the convergence of different streams in favour of particular readings. So complete was his success in convincing the Company as to the general soundness of his **theory**, that Dr. Scrivener in later meetings very often contented himself with the bare mention of the less conspicuous readings advocated by Dr. Hort's school, assuming that they would certainly be accepted by the Company; though he was always ready for a battle on points of special moment . . . Many, no doubt, differed from him, but his noble simplicity of character raised him above all temptation to argue for aught but the true, or to look at counter arguments otherwise than as they bore upon the true.[60]

Another opponent who was less impressed with Dr. Hort's "noble character" related:

Dr. Hort advocated his own peculiar views in the Jerusalem Chamber with so much volubility, eagerness, pertinacity, and plausibility, that in the end . . . **his counsels prevailed.**[61]

This same unnamed detractor (cited by Arthur Hort) calculated that, **"Dr. Hort talked for three years out of the ten!"**[62]

The reader may be interested to know that these mind-bending techniques were developed in adolescence. Speaking of Dr. Hort when he was an eleven-year-old student, his teacher, the Rev. John Buckland perceived him to be "somewhat overbearing with other boys."[63] Dr. Westcott was also an intellectual bully in his youth, personally testifying that, "I was as proud and overbearing as a little fellow well could be."[64] Apparently thirty years had not changed much, Westcott writing to his wife, 24th May, 1871, "We have had **hard fighting** during these last two days, and a **battle-royal** is announced for tomorrow."[65]

These fully developed strong-arm tactics would consign the 1611 Authorized Version to a decade of reproachful interrogation. As the *living* Word was abused by the likes of Caiaphas, Herod and Pilate, the *written* Word came under the same abuse from Westcott, Hort and Lightfoot. In the face of conflicting witnesses, both would be victimized by the mockery of a majority vote. Two thousand years ago, the jury was asked, *"Whether of the twain will ye that I release unto you?"* with their response being, *"Barabbas."* (Matthew 27:21) Another reviser, Dr. Newth, relates the nineteenth-century version of this kangaroo-court scenario (as cited and commented on by Philip Mauro in *True or False?*):

> This was the mode: A passage being under consideration, the Chairman asks, 'Are any Textual changes proposed?' If a change be proposed then 'the evidence for and against is briefly stated.' This is done by 'two members of the Company—Dr. Scrivener and Dr. Hort.' And if those two members disagree 'The vote of the Company is taken, and the proposed Reading accepted or rejected. The Text being thus settled, the Chairman asks for proposals on the Rendering' (i.e., the Translation).
> *Thus it appears that there was no attempt whatever on the part of the Revisionists to examine the evidence bearing upon the many disputed readings. They only listened to the views of two of their number.*[66]

With the **Majority Text** being systematically removed by a **majority vote**, a number of the committee members either attended spasmodically or resigned altogether. Dr. Newth describes the fallout from Hort's overbearing presence at 88 percent[67] of the sittings:

> The average attendance was *not so many as sixteen,*— concerning whom, moreover, the fact has transpired that some of the most judicious of their number often *declined to give any vote at all*—is by no means calculated to inspire any sort of confidence.[68]

The distinguished Richard Chenevix Trench, Archbishop of Dublin attended only 63 sessions in ten years, complaining of the translation's "not unfrequent sacrifice of grace and ease to the rigorous requirements of a literal accuracy . . . pushed to a faulty excess."[69]

In fact, the committee's original chairman, Samuel Wilberforce, Bishop of Oxford, relinquished his prestigious appointment after only *one* meeting, bemoaning to an associate, **"What can be done in this most miserable business?"**[70]

On May 17, 1881, the long-awaited Revised Version of the English New Testament was released amidst much fanfare upon a gullible nation. (The Old Testament was completed in 1885.) Dean Burgon spent that entire summer poring over the celebrated arrival and published his first of three scholarly rejoinders in the October issue of the *Quarterly Review*. With the inclusion of his 150-page letter of protest to the turncoat, Bishop Ellicott, (96 pages of which dealt with I Timothy 3:16) the eventual page count of Burgon's incomparable masterpiece swelled to over *500 pages!*

Burgon devoted the very first page of his *Revision Revised* to listing the four summary complaints Prebendary Scrivener posed against the "system" on which Drs. Westcott and Hort had constructed their revised Greek text of the New Testament (1881). These remarks were cited in Scrivener's own massive protest of 506 initial pages, (920 pages eventually), entitled *A Plain Introduction to the Criticism of the New Testament* (1883):

1. There is little hope for the stability of their imposing structure, if *its foundations have been laid on the sandy ground of ingenious conjecture.* And, since barely the smallest vestige of historical evidence has ever been alleged in support of the views of these accomplished Editors, their teaching must either be received as intuitively true or *dismissed from our consideration as precarious and even visionary.*

2. Dr. Hort's System *is entirely destitute of historical foundation.*

3. We are compelled to repeat as emphatically as ever our strong conviction that the Hypothesis to whose proof he has devoted so many laborious years, *is destitute not only of historical foundation, but of all probability, resulting from the internal goodness of the Text which its adoption would force upon us.*

4. 'We cannot doubt' (says Dr. Hort) 'that S. Luke 23:34 comes from an extraneous source.' [*Notes* p. 68.]– *"Nor can we, on our part, doubt,"* (rejoins Dr. Scrivener,) *"that the System which entails such consequences is hopelessly self-condemned."*[71]

The most significant observation for the Bible believer to make is that *the esteemed revisers completely forsook their sacred trust.* With impunity did they violate rules one and four of the Convocation's mandate. It was soon revealed by Scrivener that the underlying Greek of the *Textus Receptus* was changed by the Westcott and Hort text in approximately 5,337 instances.[72]

In our generation, Dr. D.A. Waite made a careful study of the Nestle/Aland 26th edition Greek Testament (the present repository of the basic Westcott and Hort text) and found 5,604 alterations. Dr. Waite writes:

Of these **5,604** CHANGES, I found **1,952** to be OMISSIONS (35%), **467** to be ADDITIONS (8%) and **3,185** to be CHANGES

(57%). In these **5,604** places that were involved in these CHANGES, there were **4,366** more words involved, making a total of **9,970** Greek words that were involved. This means that in a Greek Text of 647 pages, this would average **15 words per page** that were CHANGED from the RECEIVED TEXT.[73]

By now, the reader is aware that the single Vatican Codex B was responsible for the great majority of these perturbations. However, the fiasco was aggravated still further by the total disregard of rule four of the Convocation which read:

> That the Text to be adopted be that for which the evidence is decidedly preponderating; and that when the Text so adopted differs from that from which the Authorized Version was made, *the alteration be indicated in the margin.*[74]

Of the 5,000-plus changes, **not a single one was so noted.** Their only defense was that the prospect "proved inconvenient."[75]

However, as if all of this were not bad enough, the revisers added insult to injury by invading the margins with a host of disconcerting jargon. It was the committee's decision to use this space for the branding of multiplied passages as being suspect, though they were allowed to remain in the text. Burgon stating:

> Will it be believed that, this notwithstanding, *not one* of the many alterations which have been introduced into the original Text is so commemorated? On the contrary: singular to relate, the Margin is disfigured throughout with ominous hints that, had 'Some ancient authorities,' 'Many ancient authorities,' 'Many very ancient authorities,' been attended to, a vast many more changes might, could, would, or should have been introduced into the Greek Text than have been actually adopted. And yet, this is precisely the kind of record which we ought to have been spared.[76]

To cite but a few examples, the King James reading for Matthew 1:18 states, *"Now the birth of Jesus Christ was on this wise."* The RV's accompanying marginal note says, "Some ancient authorities read 'of the Christ'." Mark 1:1 in the Authorized Version reads, *"The beginning of the gospel of Jesus Christ, the Son of God,"* while the RV marginal note states, "Some ancient authorities omit 'the Son of God'." For the Island of Melita in Acts 28:1, the RV note reads, "some ancient authorities read Militene." And for the well-known "666" of Revelation 13:18, the reference states, "Some ancient authorities read six hundred and sixteen."

But there were marginal references far more confusing than these. The note for Romans 9:5 reads:

> Some modern Interpreters place a full stop after *flesh*, and translate, *He who is God over all be* (is) *blessed for ever*: or, *He who is over all is God, blessed for ever*. Others punctuate, *flesh, who is over all. God be* (is) *blessed for ever*.[77]

Dean Burgon addressing the marginal problem:

> What else must be the result of all this but general uncertainty, confusion, distress? A hazy mistrust of all Scripture has been insinuated into the hearts and minds of countless millions, who in this way have been *forced* to become doubters,— yes, doubters in the Truth of Revelation itself. One recalls sorrowfully the terrible woe denounced by the Author of Scripture on those who minister occasions of falling to others:—'It must needs be that offences come; but woe to that man by whom the offence cometh!'[78]

Not only did the revisers abuse *rule four*, but they totally ignored *rule one* as well, which enjoined the members, "to introduce *as few alterations as possible* into the Text of the Authorized Version consistently with faithfulness."[79]

When the dust finally settled, it was determined that the committee had changed the Authorized Version in some **36,191** places.[80] Having understood the charge to limit changes to PLAIN AND CLEAR ERRORS only, the chairman had assured England in 1870, that:

> We do not contemplate any new Translation, *or any alteration of the language*, EXCEPT WHERE, in the judgment of the most competent Scholars, SUCH CHANGE IS *NECESSARY*.[81]

They furthermore avowed:

> If the meaning was fairly expressed by the word or phrase that was before us in the Authorized Version, we made no change, even where rigid adherence *to the rule of Translating, as far as possible, the same Greek word by the same English word* might have prescribed some modification.[82]

Dean Burgon isolated a number of these "necessary" alterations:

Now it is idle to deny that this fundamental Principle has been utterly set at defiance. To such an extent is this the case, that even an unlettered Reader is competent to judge them. When we find *'to'* substituted for 'unto' (*passim*):– *'hereby'* for 'by this' (I Jo. 5:2):–'all that *are,*' for 'all that be' (Rom. 1:7): *'alway'* for 'always' (II Thess. 1:3):–'we *that,*' 'them *that,*' for 'we *which,*' 'them *which,*' (I Thess. 4:15); and yet 'every spirit *which,*' for 'every spirit that' (I Jo. 4:3) and 'he *who* is not of GOD,' for 'he that is not of GOD' (ver. 6,–although 'he *that* knoweth GOD' had preceded, in the same verse):–*'my* host' for 'mine host' (Rom. 16:23); and *'underneath'* for 'under' (Rev. 6:9):–**it becomes clear that the Revisers' notion of NECESSITY is not that of the rest of mankind.**[83]

At this point we are reminded of our chapter's central premise: would God lead His servants to consistently defy their human authorities for the restoration of His Word? Are revisers above the Bishops' charge to *blamelessness?*

When we turn to a consideration of the English employed in the Revised Version, we arrive at quite a paradox. After a decade of "doing their own thing," the revisers have been judged to be miserable failures in the only area of responsibility they were given. One of the truly sick statements found in Dr. Hort's biography was made by young Arthur who said:

> But I am unable to say whether or no he was altogether satisfied with the revisers' English, which is generally considered the most vulnerable part of their work.[84]

That statement makes about as much sense as an automobile salesman telling a prospective customer that *apart from the fact that the car doesn't run, it is a pretty good buy!* Furthermore, Arthur's candor is the understatement of the century.

Although Bishop Ellicott became a staunch defender of the Revised Version, his remarks of 1870 have come back to haunt him and expose the project for the flop that it was:

> No Revision in the present day *could hope to meet with an hour's acceptance* if it failed to preserve the tone, rhythm, and diction of the present Authorized Version.[85]

An analogy by Bishop Wordsworth depicting one's transition from the King James to the Revised Version has a timely application to Ellicott's prediction.

To pass from the one to the other, is, as it were, to alight from a well-built and well-hung carriage which glides easily over a macadamized road,—and to get into one *which has bad springs or none at all*, and in which you are *jolted in ruts with aching bones over the stones of a newly-mended and rarely traversed road*, like some of the roads in our North Lincolnshire villages.[86]

Dean Burgon holds the revisers' feet to the fire in no uncertain terms:

As Translators, full two-thirds of the Revisionists have shown themselves singularly deficient,—alike in their critical acquaintance with the language out of which they had to translate, and in their familiarity with the idiomatic requirements of their own tongue. They had a noble Version before them, which they have contrived to spoil in every part. Its dignified simplicity and essential faithfulness, its manly grace and its delightful rhythm, they have shown themselves alike unable to imitate and unwilling to retain. Their queer uncouth phraseology and their jerky sentences:—their pedantic obscurity and their stiff, constrained manner:—their fidgetty affection of accuracy,—and their habitual achievement of English which fails to exhibit the spirit of the original Greek;—are sorry substitutes for the living freshness, and elastic freedom, and habitual fidelity of the grand old Version which we inherited from our Fathers, and which has sustained the spiritual life of the Church of England, and of all English-speaking Christians, for 350 years. Linked with all our holiest, happiest memories, and bound up with all our purest aspirations: part and parcel of whatever there is of good about us: fraught with men's hopes of a blessed Eternity and many a bright vision of the never ending Life;—the Authorized Version, wherever it was possible, *should have been jealously retained.* But on the contrary. Every familiar cadence has been dislocated: the congenial flow of almost every verse of Scripture has been hopelessly marred: so many of those little connecting words, which give life and continuity to a narrative, have been vexatiously displaced, that a perpetual sense of annoyance is created. The countless minute alterations which have been needlessly introduced into every familiar page prove at last as tormenting as a swarm of flies to the weary traveller on a summer's day. To speak plainly, the book has been made *unreadable.*[87]

Anyone familiar with Burgon's exhaustive treatise knows that the Dean was not "blowing smoke." His illustrations are numerous:

Thus, in ver. 2, the correct English rendering *'we have seen'* is made to give place to the incorrect **'we saw** his star in the east.' – In ver. 9, the idiomatic *'when they had heard the king,* they departed,' is rejected for the unidiomatic 'And they, **having heard the king,** went their way.' – In ver. 15, we are treated to *'that it might be fulfilled which was spoken by the Lord **through the prophet saying, out of Egypt did I call** my son.'* And yet who sees not, that in both instances the old rendering is better? . . . Note how infelicitously, in S. Matth. ii. 1, *'there came wise men from the east'* is changed into **'wise men from the east came.**" – In ver. 4, the accurate, *'And when [Herod] had gathered together'* . . . is displaced for the inaccurate, 'And **gathering together'** . . . In ver. 6, we are presented with the unintelligible, 'And thou **Bethlehem, land of Judah:'** while in ver. 7, 'Then Herod **privily called** the wise men and **learned of them carefully,'** is improperly put in the place of *'Then Herod, when he had privily called the wise men, enquired of them diligently'* . . . – In ver. 11, the familiar *'And when they were come into the house, they saw'* is needlessly changed into, 'They **came into the house,** and saw:' while *'and when they had opened . . . their treasures,'* is also needlessly altered into 'and **opening** their treasures.'[88]

And then there is the pharisaical rigidity which they employed concerning the use of the definite article. Burgon continues:

'**The** sower went forth to sow' (Matth. xiii. 3). – 'It is greater than **the** herbs' (ver. 32). – 'Let him be to thee as **the** Gentile and **the** publican' (xviii. 17). – 'The unclean spirit, when he is gone out of **the** man' (xii. 43). – 'Did I not choose you **the** twelve?' (Jo. vi. 70). – 'If I then, **the** Lord and **the** master' (xiii. 14). – 'For **the** joy that a man is born into the world' (xvi. 21). – 'But as touching Apollos **the** brother' (1 Cor. xvi. 12). – '**The** Bishop must be blameless . . . able to exhort in **the** sound doctrine' (Titus i. 7, 9). – '**The** lust when it hath conceived, beareth sin: and **the** sin, when it is full grown' (James i. 15). – 'Does **the** fountain send forth from the same opening sweet water and bitter?' (iii. 11). – 'Speak thou the things which befit **the** sound doctrine' (Titus ii. 1). – 'The time will come when they will not endure **the** sound doctrine' (2 Tim. iv. 3). – 'We had **the** fathers of our flesh to chasten us' (Heb. xii. 9). – 'Follow after peace with all men, and **the** sanctification' (ver. 14). – 'Who is **the** liar but he that denieth that Jesus is the Christ' (1 Jo. ii. 22). – 'Not with **the** water only, but with **the** water and with **the** blood.' (v. 6). – 'He that hath the Son hath **the** life: he that hath not the Son of God hath not **the** life' (ver. 12.).[89]

Other idiomatic inaccuracies would include:

John 17:24a

"Father, I will that they also, whom thou hast given me, be with me where I am." (King James)

Father, that which thou hast given Me I will that, where I am, they also may be with Me. (Revised Version)

Luke 4:1b & 2a

"And was led by the Spirit into the wilderness, Being forty days tempted of the devil." (King James)

. . . Was led by the Spirit in the wilderness during forty days. (Revised Version)

II Corinthians 12:7

"And lest I should be exalted above measure through the abundance of the revelations, there was given to me a thorn in the flesh . . ." (King James)

And by reason of the exceeding greatness of the revelations— wherefore, that I should not be exalted overmuch there was given to me a thorn in the flesh.[90] (Revised Version)

Burgon did not have much patience for the revisers' use of prepositions either.

II Peter 1:5-7

"And beside this, giving all diligence, add to your faith virtue; and to virtue knowledge; and to knowledge temperance; and to temperance patience; and to patience godliness; and to godliness brotherly kindness; and to brotherly kindness charity." (King James)

Yea, and for this very cause adding on your part all diligence, in your faith supply virtue; and in your virtue knowledge; and in your knowledge temperance; and in your temperance patience; and in your patience godliness; and in your godliness love of the brethren; and in your love of the brethren love.[91] (Revised Version)

The good Bishop Wordsworth had that jolting wagon ride pegged correctly. However, it is when we hit the various heresies of the Revised Version that we are *thrown completely from the carriage!*

The evolutionary beliefs of Westcott and Hort can be seen in their "revising" of Colossians 1:16. Where the King James reads *"all things were created by him, and for him"* (in perfect harmony with John 1:3, 10), the Revised Version says, "all things were created **through** him." The same switch is made in I Corinthians 8:6, and Hebrews 1:2.[92]

The professors' hang-up with inspiration was more noticeable in the RV's rendering of II Timothy 3:16 which says, "Every scripture **given by God** is inspired."

Dr. Westcott never did get around to believing the miracles in "the Book" he was supposed to have salvaged. Note how subtly the change is made from "miracle" to "sign" in John 2:11 and 4:54: "This beginning of **his signs** did Jesus,"—"this is again the **second sign** that Jesus did." Burgon adds that this exchange can be found in twenty references.[93]

And then there was the problem the Cambridge professors had with *everlasting punishment.* Would you believe that they changed *everlasting* to *eternal* in every place it occurs except for Romans 1:20 and Jude 6?[94]

Finally, there was Burgon's pet peeve concerning the butchery of the Lord's Prayer in Matthew's Gospel. By removing the Doxology—(*"for thine is the kingdom, and the power and the glory for ever, Amen."*) and substituting "evil one" for "evil," the Nicolaitane perverts have actually *inserted **Satan** into the Lord's Prayer!* Imagine beginning such a sacred reading with *"Our Father"* only to conclude it with the *"Evil One"!* (That's not bad for a liberal who did not even believe in a "real devil.")

Space does not permit our extended comments on: the revisers' elimination of *chapter headings* and *verse divisions* (to make their product conform more to the appearance of a secular book); or the endless substitutions which smack of futility—"robbers" for *"thieves"* (Matthew 27:38), "a soldier of his guard" for *"an executioner"* (Mark 6:27), "the twin brothers" for *"Castor and Pollux"* (Acts 28:11), "fluteplayers" for *"minstrels"* (Matthew 9:23), "shuddering devils" for *"devils"* (James 2:19), "he is epileptic" for *"he is lunatick"* (Matthew 17:15), "horses' bridles" for *horses "bits"* (James 3:3), "the pods of the carob tree" for *"the husks that the swine did eat"* (Luke 15:16); general changes such as "love" for *"charity"* and "Holy Spirit" for *"Holy Ghost"*; the host of new words added (after being charged "to introduce as few alterations" as possible), such as—"assassin," "apparition," "boon," "disparagement," "divinity," "effulgence," "epileptic," "fickleness," "gratulation," "irksome," "interpose," "pitiable," "sluggish," "stupor," "surpass," "tranquil," and a host of additional problems which fill Burgon's and Scrivener's 1,300-plus pages!

When we look to the revisers themselves for an accounting of their deeds, we are met with additional hypocrisy. While Westcott's letters make reference to his conviction for the reading exhibiting an "obvious preponderance of evidence,"[95] Arthur Hort informs us that his father was:

> . . . greatly disturbed because an accent was unaccountably missing in the final proof, which he could prove had been present in the previous one; the thin projection of the type had broken off in the printing.[96]

In Burgon's opinion, the Scripture which most accurately exemplified the revisers' accomplishments was II Peter 2:22a — *"But it is happened unto them according to the true proverb, The dog is turned to his own vomit again."* Referring to their resuscitation of the heretofore discarded rendering of II Timothy 3:16, he declared:

> May we be permitted to say without offence that, in our humble judgment, if the Church of England, at the Revisers' bidding, were to adopt this and thousands of other depravations of the sacred page, — with which the Church Universal was once well acquainted, but which in her corporate character she has long since unconditionally condemned and abandoned, — she would deserve to be pointed at with scorn by the rest of Christendom? Yes, and to have *that* openly said of her which St. Peter openly said of the false teachers of his day who fell back into the very errors which they had already abjured. The place will be found in 2 S. Peter 2:22. So singularly applicable is it to the matter in hand, that we can but invite attention to the quotation on our title-page and p. 1.[97]

Dr. Hort's consternation over Burgon's assault was evidenced in a pair of whimpering letters to his wife. Writing on January 30th, 1882, he states:

> Dr. Moulton has now sent me out the new number of the *Quarterly*. It is (Dean Burgon's article, I mean) poor, sorry, and acrid stuff, duller than the last article, and no better. As I expected, he returns often to the charge about our text; but there is no sign that he has *read* five pages of either 'Introduction' or 'Appendix,' though he is supposed to have demolished us.[98]

And again on February 2nd, 1882.

> A kind note, with interesting enclosures, has come from Dr. Moulton, who seems terribly pressed for time. He is still uneasy about the bad impression produced by the *Quarterly Review*; but

I confess I am much easier now that I have seen that very significant paragraph in the *Guardian*, calling attention to the article in the *Church Quarterly* which I wanted you to find out about. Apparently it is very favourable. The *Guardian* and the *Church Quarterly* together may do a good deal towards preventing the Revised Version from being damaged by Dean Burgon's nonsense.[99]

Dr. Westcott's letter of 28th October, 1881, gives us the impression that the "shook up doctor" was in desperate need of a good tricycle ride somewhere:

My dear Hort—I cannot read Burgon yet. A glance at one or two sentences leads me to think that his violence answers himself.[100]

Hort's son was also quite upset with Burgon, writing:

The *Revision Revised* is a portly volume, full of the raciest English, with the literary flavour of methods of controversy usually regarded as obsolete. Westcott and Hort are therein treated as the chief authors of all the mischief of the Revision, and their text is throughout regarded as the work of a picturesque imagination. But it would be unprofitable to quote at length, or in any way to revive unnecessarily a somewhat hopeless controversy.[101]

As previously mentioned, Burgon's work included a stinging 150-page missive to Chairman Ellicott as a formal denunciation of the committee's liberal faction. The letter was also a reply to Ellicott's anemic pamphlet defending the paranoid professors. As expected, his diatribe was filled with, "poor," "sorry," and "acrid" stuff, not to mention a whole lot of "violence":

The task of laboriously collating the five "old uncials" throughout the Gospels, occupied me for five-and-a-half years, and taxes me severely. But I was rewarded. I rose from the investigation profoundly convinced that, however important they may be as instruments of Criticism, codices א B C D are among the most corrupt documents extant. It was a conviction derived from exact *Knowledge* and based on solid grounds of *Reason*. You, my lord Bishop, who have never gone deeply into the subject, repose simply on *Prejudice*. Never having at any time collated codices א A B C D for yourself, you are unable to gainsay a single statement of mine by a counter-appeal to *facts*. Your textual learning proves to have been all obtained at second-hand, — taken on trust. And so, instead of marshalling against me a corresponding array of ANCIENT AUTHORITIES, — you invariably attempt to put me down by an appeal to MODERN OPINION.[102]

While Westcott and Hort dragged their feet, Burgon concluded his work with the challenge:

> Here I lay down my pen,—glad to have completed what (because I have endeavoured to do my work *thoroughly*) has proved a very laborious task indeed. The present rejoinder to your Pamphlet covers all the ground you have yourself traversed, and will be found to have disposed of your entire contention.
>
> I take leave to print out, in conclusion, that it places you individually in a somewhat embarrassing predicament. For you have now no alternative but to come forward and disprove my statements as well as refute my arguments: or to admit, by your silence, that you have sustained defeat in the cause of which you constituted yourself the champion. You constrained me to reduce you to this alternative when you stood forth on behalf of the Revising body, and saw fit to provoke me to a personal encounter.
>
> But you must come provided with something vastly more formidable, remember, than denunciations,—which are but wind: and vague generalities,—which prove nothing and persuade nobody: and appeals to the authority of 'Lachmann, Tischendorf, and Tregelles,'—which I disallow and disregard. You must produce a counter-array of well-ascertained facts; and you must build thereupon irrefragable arguments. In other words, you must conduct your cause with learning and ability. Else, believe me, you will make the painful discovery that 'the last error is worse than the first.' You had better a thousand times, even now, ingenuously admit that you made a grievous mistake when you put yourself into the hands of those ingenious theorists, Drs. Westcott and Hort, and embraced their arbitrary decrees,—than persevere in your present downward course, only to sink deeper and deeper in the mire.[103]

Arthur Hort tells the rest of the story:

> **There were some, doubtless, who wished that the two Cambridge Professors had publicly defended themselves against the attack** . . . When the *Quarterly* articles appeared, it does not seem that either collaborator was much upset by them; the only fear was lest those unacquainted with textual criticism should be misled by the reviewer's "formidable array of 'authorities.' " **Still silence seemed best, and it has been justified** . . . He (Dr. Hort) did indeed read and annotate carefully his copy of the *Revision Revised*, but decided eventually to leave the issue to time.[104]

Arthur Westcott brings our chapter to a close with the following ignoble lines about "John (Burgon) of Chichester":

My father could never be persuaded to treat Dean Burgon's criticisms seriously. He was, I believe, amused by the following lines sent to him by a friend:

For private circulation only.
VERSES—"MORE BURGONENSIUM"

Says the Dean to himself as he penned his retort,
"I *think* I've exhorted my friend Dr. *Hort*
And as for poor *Westcott,* I've well warmed his jacket
With a nut hard to crack—let us hope he may crack it.
My logic, as clear and unyielding as crystal,
Has boycotted *Ellicott* clean out of Bristol.
So now we may trust that each reckless Reviser,
'Taught' by me to be sadder, may learn to be wiser.
Henceforth I alone represent Convocation;
Henceforth I alone am the Voice of the Nation;
Henceforth, if I choose to condemn 'Sinaiticus,'
My fiat's as plain as the Law in Leviticus.
If B, C, and D I condemn as unsound,
No critic to quote them I ween will be found.
My praise is a proof, and my blame is subversive
Of versions and codices, uncial or cursive.
Henceforth when I speak let the critics be mum;
Let Tischendorf tremble and Durham be dumb.
Let no waistcoat, no cassock, no gaiters, no breeches stir,
Without leave of license from me, John of Chichester.
                    P.S.
If the claims of Greek Testament critics be reckoned,
I think Canon Scrivener's certainly—*second.*
But the work which *one* critic has done, and done well,
'*The Author alone of his Being can tell.*'
His learning and manner are truly patristic;
His style, as a critic, decidedly fistic.
My modesty will not allow me to name
This writer—though Europe re-echoes his fame.
But cease, O ye sons of the Church, to despair,
While I, Johnny Burgon, my fisticuffs square!"[105]
                    3rd January, 1884

"Blessed are ye when men shall revile you . . ."
(Matthew 5:11)

XVI

The Midnight Hour

"For the time will come when they will not endure sound doctrine." (II Timothy 4:3a)

It was with great foreboding that Dean Burgon spent the remaining years of his life warning his beloved nation of the inevitable storm clouds ahead. Speaking of codices ℵ and B, he prophesied, "Those two documents are caused to cast their sombre shadows a long way ahead and to darken all our future."[1]

Of his church in particular, he said:

> Who will venture to predict the amount of mischief which must follow, if the *'New Greek Text'* which has been put forth by the men who were appointed to *revise the English Authorized Version,* should become used in our Schools and in our Colleges,—should impose largely on the Clergy of the Church of England?[2]

And again:

> It would ill become such an one as myself to pretend to skill in forecasting the future. But of *this* at least I feel certain:—that if, in an evil hour, (quod absit!), the Church of England shall ever be induced to commit herself to the adoption of the present Revision, she will by so doing expose herself to the ridicule of the rest of Christendom, as well as incur irreparable harm and loss. And such a proceeding on her part will be inexcusable, for she has been at least faithfully forewarned. Moreover, in the end, she will most certainly have to retrace her steps with sorrow and confusion.[3]

Though "the sun never set on the British Empire" in Burgon's day, an English embracing of the Revised Version triggered an eclipse that has lasted for a century: tribal spears from the Boer War; mustard gas and V2 rockets from World Wars I and II; the sinkings of the *Titanic* and *Lusitania*; socialism; tabloids; punk rockers; IRA bombings; three-day work weeks, and *a present national church attendance of only 3 percent.*

Perhaps Dr. Hort's words were the most portentous of all: "It is, one can hardly doubt, the beginning of a **new period** in Church history."[4]

Wilkinson concurred, writing:

> Because of the changes which came about in the nineteenth century, there arose a new type of Protestantism and a new version of the Protestant Bible. This new kind of Protestantism was hostile to the fundamental doctrines of the Reformation. Previous to this there had been only two types of Bibles in the world, the Protestant and the Catholic. **Now Protestants were asked to choose between the true Protestant Bible and one which reproduced readings rejected by the Reformers.**[5]

Hort's "prayer burden" for America's destruction was cited in our last chapter. Because he believed in putting feet to his prayers, two U.S. committees (one for each of the Testaments) were assembled in New York to serve as special reviewing bodies. Although the American committees had no deciding vote on points of revision, they were expected to forward their editorial recommendations to the mother committee for further consideration.

Dr. Philip Schaff of Union Theological Seminary in New York City was selected as chairman for both of the stateside committees. Because this inconspicuous effort was destined to become the fountainhead for dozens of polluted American revisions, the reader would do well to take a good look at the esteemed Dr. Schaff.

Without question, Schaff was regarded as one of the country's leading theological liberals. Wilkinson said of him, "Dr. Schaff ... was to America what Newman was to England."[6] Expanding on Schaff's *pantheism* ("the totality of the universe is God"), he states:

> False science teaches the origin of the universe by organic development without God, and calls it evolution. German philosophy early taught the development of humanity through the self-evolution of the absolute spirit. The outstanding advocates of

this latter philosophy, Schelling and Hegel, were admitted pantheists. Their theory was applied to theology in the hands of Schleiermacher whose follower was Dr. Schaff, and whom Dr. Schaff characterizes as 'the greatest theological genius' since the Reformation. He also said, 'There is not to be found now a single theologian of importance, in whom the influence of his great mind is not more or less traced.' The basis of Schleiermacher's philosophy and theology was acknowledged by such men as Dorner to be 'thoroughly pantheistic.'[7]

Among his numerous works, Schaff wrote the massive eight-volume *History of the Christian Church*, published by Eerdmans. A careful reading of the entire set demonstrated to this author that Schaff was pro-Catholic, anti-*Receptus*, and decidedly ecumenical. In a limp attempt at defending Rome's historic suppression of Scripture, he wrote:

> The Roman Church, while recognizing the Divine inspiration and authority of the Bible, prefers to control the laity by the teaching priesthood, and allows the reading of the Scriptures in the popular tongues only under certain restrictions and precautions, from fear of abuse and profanation. Pope Innocent III. was of the opinion that the Scriptures were too deep for the common people, as they surpassed even the understanding of the wise and learned.[8]

That Schaff held Dr. Hort's prejudice for "that vile *Textus Receptus* leaning entirely on late mss." can be seen from such statements as:

> The science of textual criticism was not yet born, and the materials for it were not yet collected from the manuscripts, ancient versions, and patristic quotations. Luther had to use the first printed editions (by Erasmus). He had no access to manuscripts, the most important of which were not even discovered or made available before the middle of the nineteenth century.[9]

Schaff's Jesuit philosophy of an ultimate return to Rome can be found in "the chairman's" own words:

> Such a personage as Augustine, still holding a mediating place between the two great divisions of Christendom, revered alike by both, and of equal influence with both, is furthermore a welcome pledge of the elevating prospect of a **future reconciliation of Catholicism and Protestantism** in a higher unity, conserving

all the truths, losing all the errors, forgiving all the sins, forgetting all the enmities of both.[10]

Wilkinson gives us this additional glimpse into Schaff's twisted ecumenicism:

> Dr. Schaff sat in the Parliament of Religions at the Chicago World's Fair, 1893, and was so happy among the Buddhists, Confucianists, Shintoists, and other world religions, that he said he would be willing to die among them.[11]

By contrast, while Schaff was "meditating with the mystics" in the Parliament of Religions, D.L. Moody and a host of soul winners were laying siege to the Fairground and its environs with 125 daily Gospel meetings! Describing the World's Fair as "the opportunity of a century," Moody also was burdened for the international religionists in attendance, his son Will relating:

> Chicago at all times is a cosmopolitan city, and this was, of course, especially apparent during that notable season. Strangers from all parts of the world came by thousands, and it was Mr. Moody's purpose, as far as possible, to reach all people and all nations.[12]

Whereas the chairman of the American Revision Committee expressed his willingness to "die *among* them," Moody used a King James Bible to inform the same of One Who had already died *for* them! An observer describes a Sunday morning service which was so characteristic of this "One Bible" era:

> The surroundings were the usual circus furniture—ropes, trapezes, gaudy decorations, etc., while in an adjoining canvas building was a large menagerie, including eleven elephants. Clowns, grooms, circus-riders, men, women, and children, eighteen thousand of them, and on a Sunday morning, too! Whether the Gospel was ever before preached under such circumstances I know not, but it was wonderful to ear and eye alike.
>
> When that mighty throng took up the hymn, 'Nearer, my God, to Thee,' a visible sense of awe fell upon the multitude. After an hour of singing and prayer Mr. Moody rose to preach, his text being, *"The Son of Man is come to seek and to save that which was lost."* The Spirit of God was present. The hush of Heaven was over the meeting.[13]

Unlike the *Greek* scholar Schaff, Moody chose to build his

ministry on the *English* Bible instead. Will stating:

> He devoted himself to an intense study of it, and from it got
> two things: In the first place, he gained that clear-cut, plain,
> simple Anglo-Saxon of the King James version, that gave him
> such an immense power over people everywhere. In the second
> place, he gained an arsenal and armament of promise and
> warning, which he used through all his life with such magnificent
> power. There was something wonderful about his simple
> directness. I could give by the hour instances of the clear way in
> which he went directly to a point.[14]

Moody was probably unaware of the approaching midnight
hour and the role his fellow World's Fair attendee would play in
its encroachment. Schaff's committees had forwarded a minimum
of recommendations to Ellicott's attention. With the May, 1881,
publication of the Revised Version in England, the U.S. team
entered into its agreed-upon waiting period of twenty years before
releasing their own product to the American market. (Apparently
"profit" was more important than "souls.") It was during this
interim that Schaff would have viewed "Crazy" Moody's tireless
soul-winning marathon. With his life's work behind him, Schaff's
desire to die among the "gurus" was realized that same year
when he beat them all to their shared fate of a Christ-rejecter's
Hell. In this case, the eleven circus elephants that "heard" Moody
preach showed more sense than the renowned seminary
professor!

With Moody's death in December of 1899, more than just a
century had ended. The release by Thomas Nelson Publishers of
the *American Standard Version* in 1901 ushered in an age when
Americans would grow to learn the meaning of the question,
"Which Bible?" As Dr. Hort prophesied, it was "the beginning of
a new period in Church history."

At the time when the highly publicized ASV was trotted out,
the Lion of the Protestant Reformation had already been roaring
for 290 years. It would not be much of a contest. Surprisingly
enough, the ASV was able to survive for all of twenty-three years
before *going broke in 1924*. Like a flock of circling vultures, the
National Council of Churches purchased the ASV's copyright with
plans for a future resuscitation.

Though short-lived, its accomplishments were impressive and
the resultant judgment devastating: the moral decline of the "gay
nineties"; President McKinley's assassination (1901); Hollywood's

first film (1911); hundreds of returning American "doughboys" being quarantined for venereal diseases (1919); an influenza epidemic killing 500,000 Americans (1918-1919); Al Capone and the entire Roaring 20's!

Following the ASV's collapse after only twenty-three years of "Holy Spirit preservation," a number of optimistic replacements were sent in from the bench: Weymouth's New Testament in Modern Speech (1902); The New Testament, an American Translation, by Edgar Goodspeed (1923); The New Testament, A New Translation, by James Moffatt (1924); The New Testament in Modern English, by Helen Barrett Montgomery (1924); The New Testament: a Translation in the Language of the People, by Charles B. Williams (1937); The Holy Bible, the Berkeley Version in Modern English, by Gerrit Verkuyl (1945); The Four Gospels, Translated, by E.V. Rieu (1953); The New Testament in Modern English, by J.B. Phillips (1960); The Amplified New Testament, by the Lockman Foundation (1958); The New English Bible, by the Oxford University and Cambridge Press (1961); The New Testament, A New Translation, by Olaf M. Norlie (1961); Living Letters, by Kenneth Taylor (1962) and The New Testament, in the Language of Today, by William F. Beck (1963). These represent but a sample of the nearly 100 such perversions in our century.[15]

Burton cites an article in *Christianity Today* by Dr. Gordon D. Fee of Wheaton College which confirms the common denominator of these multiplied revisions:

> The contemporary translations as a group have one thing in common: **they tend to agree against the KJV** . . . in omitting hundreds of words, phrases, and verses.[16]

That these counterfeit Bibles were void of Holy Spirit endorsement is revealed by their conspicuous absence in the "Christian" bookstores of our day.

As the American public continued to be harangued by these so-called improvements, a host of consequential developments began their erosive activity. Newspapers and magazines started replacing God's Word as the primary reading material in the home. Radio drove the wedge still deeper. The "one-room schoolhouse" was supplanted by the progressive education espoused by pragmatist John Dewey (1859-1952).

In addition to a multitude of cults, the tongues speakers and faith healers established a sustained track record of confusion through such standard-bearers as Aimee Semple McPherson, Rex Humbard, Kathryn Kuhlman, and Oral Roberts.

After repealing Prohibition, Franklin Roosevelt inaugurated the modern welfare state with his New Deal policies, while forcing the taxpayers to exchange their gold for silver certificates (worth about one-half of the gold). "The Fed" would later confiscate the silver certificates and replace them with paper notes (1960-1980).

The nation's moral decline was hastened further by an invasion of African music. The songs of Zion were successfully challenged by the blues, jazz, ragtime, and big band sound. America's "love affair with the automobile" is legendary, but unfortunately, so is the vehicle's latent reputation among our youth as a "motel on wheels." And of course, how does one estimate the damage caused by the television with its daily access to the "light of the body"?

However, of these multiplied encroachments on American society, the most pernicious of all has been the sustained growth of *Vatican infiltration*. For instance, the scariest episode in the Nixon administration was not the Watergate scandal, but rather the fact that the President's official speech writer for three years was the Reverend John McLaughlin, *a Jesuit priest*. The government servant known as "Tricky Dicky" personally hired "Father John" at an annual salary of $32,000.[17]

With the readings of her "Bible" receiving an unprecedented endorsement by evangelical scholars (through the ASV and subsequent replacements), it was only natural that "Holy Mother Church" would gain a greater base of power within the United States.

When the average Christian meets a Catholic on the street, he basically perceives him to be a fellow American with a different religious affiliation. In actuality, this is far from the case. According to the dictates of his faith, that Catholic's *first* allegiance is not to the United States Constitution, or even to the Catholic *church* per se but to the *Vatican State*, a foreign government holding full diplomatic recognition by the State Department as initiated by President Reagan, December 14, 1981.[18] (See also, *Time Magazine*, 24 February, 1992, cover story entitled "The Holy Alliance" pp. 28-35 for a full exposé of the secret Washington-Vatican league between Pope John Paul II and President Reagan.) Avro Manhattan comments on the danger of this global monstrosity:

> Thus, whereas, the USA has a mere 250 million citizens and the Soviet Union about 300 million, the Vatican, via the Catholic

Church, can influence, between 800 and 1000 million Catholics. These . . . have no frontiers whatsoever . . . and can be made to operate, independently of their own administrations, governments or regimes. A Catholic citizen, therefore, . . . can and often is influenced in his social and ideological attitudes by those taken by the Vatican, acting as the political facet of the Catholic Church.[19]

While Christian scholars were influencing God's people to exchange their King James Bibles for a Jesuit counterfeit, the Catholic Church in America became a force with which to be reckoned—a veritable nation within a nation. Manhattan citing population statistics:

Total Catholic membership in 1890 was eight million, nine hundred nine thousand. By 1900 it had grown to twelve million, by 1910 to sixteen million, by 1920 to twenty million, by 1930 to twenty-three million, by 1945 to twenty-four million, by 1950 to twenty-eight million. When, in 1776, the American Declaration of Independence was made, there were thirty thousand Catholics in the American population of three million. In the opening years of the second half of this century there were approaching thirty million in a population of one hundred fifty million—one out of every five. In 1988 there were over 60 million in a population of two hundred sixty to two hundred seventy million.[20]

Now you know why "conservative" Catholics have always opposed abortion! What they really oppose is the killing of their own so they can one day outnumber and kill YOU!

With their increase in numbers has come an incredible financial clout. Manhattan summarizes the church's wealth in this country:

By June, 1965, the Catholic Church had accumulated a minimum of $80 billion in real estate of the total 325 billion dollars' worth of privately owned real estate in the U.S. And that is 25 percent of all privately owned land. Of this, 56 percent is held in trust for the Vatican. By 1972, the combined assets of the U.S.'s five largest industrial corporations totalled about $46.9 billion. Those of the Catholic Church between $80 and $100 billion.[21]

Believe it or not, the Jesuit Order is one of the largest stockholders in the Boeing, Lockheed, Douglas and Curtis-Wright aircraft corporations.[22]

One must remember that these billions are but a fraction in the Vatican's worldwide coffers. It is little wonder that the U.S.

government, presently in arrears of $4,500,000,000,000.00, can be seen courting the favor of the Roman Curia. When asked to guess at the total Vatican wealth, a church official replied, "Only God knows."[23]

Thus far we have observed that America's loss of vitality has kept abreast with her penchant for Bible revision. An all time low was reached in 1952 with the release of the Revised Standard Version (the New Testament being completed in 1946). Billed as a "revived" version of the American Standard Version, the work was done by a committee of 95 scholars assembled by the National Council of Churches. *Thirty of the men had Communist affiliations with at least 90 different Communist front organizations!*

The next eight years must have seen a major change in the English language because another timely revision appeared in 1960 entitled the New American Standard Version. We do not know how many of these translators may have been Communists because the publishers (Lockman Foundation) elected to keep their identities anonymous.[24]

On the front flap of the jacket of their New Testament (second edition) are the words, "The Literary Masterpiece of the Coming Generations." Above this phrase, one will find the official stamp of the Roman Catholic Church—the "Rho" "Chi" resembling a "P" with an elongated stem, crossed by an X. This is the very sign that is presently affixed to the robes that bishops wear when saying mass in the Vatican.

Continuing with our observations, the preface to the NASV contains some really humorous promotion. You would never think that the publishers believed the ASV to have been the preserved word of God:

> The producers of this translation were imbued with the conviction that interest in the American Standard Version 1901 should be renewed and increased . . . Perhaps the most weighty impetus for this undertaking can be attributed to **a disturbing awareness that the American Standard Version of 1901 was fast disappearing from the scene.** As a generation 'which knew not Joseph' was born, even so a generation unacquainted with this great and important work has come into being. Recognizing a responsibility to posterity, THE LOCKMAN FOUNDATION felt an urgency **to rescue this noble achievement from an inevitable demise,** to preserve it as a heritage for coming generations, and to do so in such a form as

the demands of passing time dictate.[25]

Can you imagine such a sales pitch being made to the body of Christ? If the ASV was such a "great and important work," why was it discovered to be "fast disappearing from the scene" to an "inevitable demise"? *Since when is the true Word of God ever in danger of an "inevitable demise"?* More ridiculous than this is the Christian public who would buy such a perversion. Worse still are the Christian centers of higher education who would promote it with a straight face.

This brings us to the all-important *motive* behind the proliferation of modern English versions in the latter half of the twentieth century. The following article appeared in the *Wall Street Journal,* November 16, 1978, and dealt with the initial success of the New International Version. The story was entitled "Zondervan, Blessed with Bible Contract, Lists Profit Forecast," with the sub-title reading, "Church Leaders' Endorsement Aids Sales of New Version; Initial Press Run Sold Out."

> Grand Rapids, Mich.—Zondervan Corp. believes it has struck a new vein of gold in an ancient and well-mined lode: the Bible. Accordingly, it told analysts here, it raised its already-gleaming sales and earning forecasts.
> Zondervan, a publisher of religious books and music, has been blessed with a 30-year exclusive contract to publish the New International Version of the Bible, translated and edited by the New York International Bible Society. After the version was endorsed by a number of church leaders, the initial press run of 1.2 million copies sold out before the book went on sale Oct. 27, the company said.
> Thus, Zondervan raised its earnings prediction 10 cents a share, to $1.85, and its sales prediction $3 million, to $41 million, for the year. In 1977, the concern earned $1.5 million, or $1.41 a share, on sales of $32.7 million.
> 'Bibles are always a much-wanted item at Christmas,' commented Peter Kladder Jr., president. Noting that a second printing will bring the total of New International Version Bibles in print at year-end to 1.6 million, he said he isn't sure stores will be able to meet customer demand.
> The executive prophesied that sales of the Bible will rise in 1979 and 1980, then remain on a 'high plateau' because 'the sales pattern for a well-accepted version of the Bible tends to continue years longer than other best-selling books.'[26]

So there you have it. All one has to do is to find a "well-accepted version of the Bible" and the sales will hit a "high plateau." These are the types of folks Jesus booted out of the Temple for making it *"an house of merchandise."*

But for the classic example of "Bible-thumping" hypocrisy, consider the following contrast in marketing approaches. In the preface to the Revised Standard Version, we read:

> Yet the King James Version has grave defects. By the middle of the nineteenth century, the development of Biblical studies and the discovery of many manuscripts more ancient than those upon which the King James Version was based, made it manifest that these defects are so many and so serious as to call for revision of the English translation . . . **The King James Version of the New Testament was based upon a Greek text that was marred by mistakes, containing the accumulated errors of fourteen centuries of manuscript copying . . . We now possess many more ancient manuscripts of the New Testament,** and are far better equipped to seek to recover the original wording of the Greek text.[27]

When we come to the New King James Version, we find that *its* promoters took an entirely *opposite* position. Singing the praises of the *Textus Receptus*, the NKJV preface reads:

> Along with this awakened concern for the classics came a flourishing companion interest in the Scriptures, an interest that was enlivened by the conviction that the manuscripts were providentially handed down and were a trustworthy record of the inspired Word of God . . . Other manuscript differences, regarding the omission or inclusion of a word or a clause, and two paragraphs in the Gospels, should not overshadow the overwhelming degree of *agreement* which exists among the ancient records. Bible readers may be assured that the most important differences in the English New Testament of today are due, not to manuscript divergence, but to the way in which translators view the task of translation . . . The manuscript preferences cited in many contemporary translations of the New Testament are due to recent reliance on a relatively few manuscripts discovered in the late nineteenth and early twentieth centuries. Dependence on these manuscripts, especially two, the Sinaitic and Vatican manuscripts, is due to the greater age of these documents. **However, in spite of their age, some scholars have reason to doubt their faithfulness to the autographs, since they often disagree with one another and show other signs of unreliability.** The Greek text obtained by using these sources and related papyri is known as

the Alexandrian Text.

On the other hand, the great majority of existing manuscripts are in substantial agreement. Even though many are late, and none are earlier than the fifth century, most of their readings are verified by ancient papyri, ancient versions, and quotations in the writings of the early church fathers ... The New King James New Testament has been based on this Received Text.[28]

Thus the public is presented with two emotional appeals: one for the *Alexandrian* text of ℵ and B and the other for the *Textus Receptus*. Both sides are to be credited for their clear, no-nonsense approach. While the RSV's publishers declared that the *Textus Receptus* was "marred by mistakes," publishers for the NKJV chose to indict the Egyptian manuscripts, "since they often disagree with one another and show other signs of unreadability."

"So, which is the true representative of *final authority*?" you ask. The answer may be found by considering the respective publishers. For the Revised Standard Version, it is Thomas Nelson Publishers, while for the New King James Version, it is—Thomas Nelson Publishers. The same publisher prints two versions that are totally incompatible! How's *"filthy lucre"* for an underlying motive? After all, one generic counterfeit is as good as another.

Having promoted a loser back in 1901 (ASV), the Nelson people were taking no chances in our day, pushing *simultaneously* the most suspect of the versions (RSV) as well as the most acclaimed (NKJV). Such a strategy was especially needful to prevent Zondervan from "cornering the market" with the NIV.

The lying hypocrites tried to cover their tracks by blaming their "Johnny-come-lately" support for the NKJV on "recent studies" (the same justification used for the RSV). If Thomas Nelson Publishers *really* believed their own spiel, why would they continue to market the "unreliable" RSV? Do you think that it is a coincidence that I Timothy 6:10, *"For the love of money is the root of all evil,"* has been watered down in the NKJV to, "for the love of money is **a** root of all **kinds of** evil"? (Is this less corrupt than Reverend Ike's rendition of, "the **lack** of money is the root of all evil"?) Nor is it a coincidence that the King James Bible's, *"For we are not as many, which corrupt the word of God ... "* (II Corinthians 2:17) was changed in the NKJV to read, "For we are not, as so many, **peddling** the word of God."

A *Newsweek* article about Nelson's president, Sam Moore, entitled, "He Reaps What He Sows" was "right on the money."

The business is blessed by its recession-proof nature. Unlike other products, the Good Book sells particularly well in tough economic times. And Nelson, which distributes its Bibles largely through Christian bookstores, has left no page unturned. **The company publishes seven of the nine major translations of the Bible** and presents them in 650 different styles—including study Bibles, bride's Bibles, giant-print Bibles, gift Bibles and even a baby's Bible called "Precious Moments." A special version titled "The Businesswoman's Bible" contains short readings on management tied to relevant Biblical verses. It warns, for example, of the temptations on the way up the corporate ladder, recommending "consistent fellowship with the same sex" and "minimizing coed [business] travel" to guard against adultery.

Of course, even the Scripture business cannot bring eternal rewards. Sales in the Bible unit are not expected to increase as rapidly as in the past. Thus, Moore is focusing on secular offerings, including what one employee calls a "touchy-feely" line of calendars, baby books, photo albums, audio tapes and other gifts marketed through stores like Wal-mart. In addition to titles like "How to Rescue the Earth Without Worshiping Nature" ("Save Water in the Name of Jesus" it advises), Nelson is promoting Zig Ziglar's books on salesmanship and records by (Amy) Grant, a darling on the pop, as well as gospel, circuit. It's all in keeping, he says, with his mission to "honor God, serve humanity—and enhance shareholder value." As Wall Street might say, Amen.[29]

The basic difference between the King James Bible and all modern facsimiles can be determined by the presence (or absence) of that little ⊚ meaning copyright. This author is aware of the crown copyright laws of England which governed the King James translation. These seventeenth-century conditions cannot be compared to those of a nation predicated on the free enterprise system as well as a *separation of church and state*. He is also cognizant of the fact that copyrights do not pertain to material produced before the year 1900, as such works (Beethoven, Byron, etc.) are in the public domain. The burden of ethics, therefore, rests squarely upon the Sam Moores of this age who would dare to place what they purport to be the very words of God under human copyright.

Although our entire century has been inundated by over 100 versions and revisions (more than one for each year), the degree of their acceptance has undergone a marked increase in recent years. As we discovered in chapter one, a submission to affluence renders one incapable of pursuing spiritual priorities. With the closing quarter of this century earmarked by a rise in materialism, an unprecedented number of affected Christians were suddenly drawn to the prospect of abandoning *final authority*.

Whereas their grandparents survived the depression years by relying on a King James Bible, despite the availability of Weymouth, Goodspeed, Moffatt, etc., a new age of yuppie grandchildren have pursued their freedom in the *Bible-of-the-Month Club*. Where Billy Sunday would have never dreamed of taking on a "wet" community with *The New Testament in Modern English* by Helen Barrett Montgomery (1924), today's reformers have tried to build their "Moral Majorities" after morning devotions with the Living Bible.

With the dust settled, three front-runners appear to have pulled away from the rest of the pack. These are the two previously mentioned New International and New King James versions joined by the New Scofield Reference Edition of 1966, published by Oxford Press. The remainder of this chapter will deal with the NIV; chapter 17 will analyze the New King James and the New Scofield.

The New International Version

At the outset of this study, one must be reminded of the underlying purpose for all such revision work. It is the obsession of conservative Christian scholars to convince the man in the pew that his AV 1611 has enough errors in it to need the revisers' expertise. When brother "So-and-So" becomes intimidated by the professor's technical vocabulary, Dr. "Big Bottom" will have succeeded in enthroning his conservative scholarship as *final authority*. The preface to the NIV makes it clear that the common man will never be free of his need for the scholar: "There is a sense in which the work of translation is **never** wholly finished."[30]

This pious statement was followed by the "encouraging" news that numerous suggestions for correction and revision followed hard on the NIV's initial release in 1973. And then their concluding paragraph begins:

> Like all translations of the Bible, made as they are by imperfect man, this one undoubtedly falls short of its goals. Yet we are grateful to God for the extent to which he has enabled us to realize these goals and for the strength he has given us and our

colleagues to complete our task.[31]

Spoken in the spirit of II Maccabees 15:38-39, the committee members resign themselves to a faulty product and then have the audacity to give God the credit for their workmanship!

However, the subtle point in all of this is that the Nicolaitane's unwillingness to accept a mere translation as *final authority* will extend even to his *own* revision activity. This is the same defensive play the convicted sinner will throw at the soul winner: "I will respect your religion and I expect you to respect mine, etc."

The NIV claims to be an entirely new translation produced by a nonsectarian committee of over one hundred scholars. Although they assure the reader that they used "the best current printed texts of the Greek New Testament,"[32] they never make it clear as to what text they mean. However, they do let the cat out of the bag with:

> Where existing manuscripts differ, the translators made their choice of readings according to accepted principles of New Testament textual criticism.[33]

In his book, *God Wrote Only One Bible*, Jasper Ray compared 45 Bible versions against 162 test Scriptures to determine how many times a departure from the *Textus Receptus* had occurred. The results of his study were enlightening.

Whereas the Douay Version (Catholic) showed changes in 75 of these verses; the Living New Testament, 114; the Revised Version, 135; the American Standard Version, 135; Good News for Modern Man, 145; and the Jehovah's Witnesses' New World Translation, 145, – the New International Version (success story of Wall Street) was declared guilty in *160*[34] *out of the possible 162 verses for a 98.7 percent departure factor!*

An April, 1991, *Moody Monthly* ad for the NIV, sporting a rusty sickle, stated:

> Open an NIV Bible and you'll see how it separates the wheat from the chaff, cutting through outdated words and obscure meanings of older versions.[35]

Upon examining an NIV, the reader will discover that Zondervan Corp. excluded a significant portion of God's Word from the barn. Having been relegated to mere chaff, the following whole verses have been omitted from the NIV text:

"Howbeit this kind goeth not out but by prayer and fasting." (Matthew 17:21) *"For the Son of man is come to save that which was lost."* (Matthew 18:11) *"Woe unto you, scribes and Pharisees, hypocrites! for ye devour widows' houses, and for a pretence make long prayer: therefore ye shall receive the greater damnation."* (Matthew 23:14) *"If any man have ears to hear, let him hear."* (Mark 7:16) *"Where their worm dieth not, and the fire is not quenched."* (Mark 9:44) *"Where their worm dieth not, and the fire is not quenched."* (Mark 9:46) *"But if ye do not forgive, neither will your Father which is in heaven forgive your trespasses."* (Mark 11:26) *"And the scripture was fulfilled, which saith, And he was numbered with the transgressors."* (Mark 15:28) *"Two men shall be in the field; the one shall be taken, and the other left."* (Luke 17:36) *"(For of necessity he must release one unto them at the feast.)"* (Luke 23:17) *"For an angel went down at a certain season into the pool, and troubled the water: whosoever then first after the troubling of the water stepped in was made whole of whatsoever disease he had."* (John 5:4) *"And Philip said, If thou believest with all thine heart, thou mayest. And he answered and said, I believe that Jesus Christ is the Son of God."* (Acts 8:37) *"Notwithstanding it pleased Silas to abide there still."* (Acts 15:34) *"But the chief captain Lysias came upon us, and with great violence took him away out of our hands,"* (Acts 24:7) *"And when he had said these words, the Jews departed, and had great reasoning among themselves."* (Acts 28:29) *"The grace of our Lord Jesus Christ be with you all. Amen."* (Romans 16:24) *"For there are three that bear record in heaven, the Father, the Word, and the Holy Ghost: and these three are one."* (I John 5:7)

The Nicolaitane propensity for confusion is also exemplified by a break in consecutive verse numbering which corresponds to the excluded Scriptures. Such incongruity bears witness to the submission required of all modern challengers to the enduring standard of 1611; in this case, it is submission to the chapter and verse arrangement.

This is an understandable sore spot to the would-be usurpers of God's *final authority*, Keylock citing Lewis:

> Many people believe that the KJV is *the* Bible against which all new translations are to be measured . . . these assumptions need critical evaluation.[36]

The standard scholarly prejudice that Lewis holds against the Authorized Version can be seen in the chapter titles of his book, *The English Bible from KJV to NIV.* With chapters 4 through 14 simply named after the Bible being discussed (i.e., Chapter 4, The

American Standard Version, etc.), chapter 3 is entitled "Doctrinal Problems in the King James Version." Why, even the Jehovah's Witness Bible (Chapter 10) was spared from such a negative billing![37] (Lewis wrote 33 pages deprecating the King James Bible [pp. 35-68], while devoting only 7 [pp. 229-235] to a critical analysis of the Jehovah's Witnesses' New World Translation.)

The Zondervan reapers have also excised considerable *portions* from 147 other verses:

Matthew 5:44; 6:13; 15:6, 8; 19:9; 20:7, 16, 22, 23; 25:13; 27:35; 28:9; Mark 1:42; 6:11, 33; 7:8; 8:26; 9:38, 45, 49; 10:21, 24; 11:8, 10, 23; 12:23, 29, 30, 33; 13:14; 14:19, 27, 68, 70; Luke 1:28; 4:4, 8, 18; 5:38; 7:31; 8:43, 45, 48, 54; 9:54, 55, 56; 11:2, 4, 11, 44, 54; 17:9; 18:24; 19:45; 20:23, 30; 22:64, 68; 23:23, 38; 24:1, 42; John 1:27; 3:13, 15; 5:3, 16; 6:11, 22, 47; 8:9, 10, 59; 10:26; 11:41; 12:1; 16:16; 17:12; 19:16; Acts 2:30; 7:37; 9:5, 6; 10:6, 21, 32; 13:42; 15:18, 24; 18:21; 20:15; 21:8, 22, 25; 23:9; 24:6, 8, 26; 26:30; 28:16; Romans 8:1; 9:28; 10:15; 11:6; 13:9; 14:6, 21; 15:24; I Corinthians 6:20; 10:28; 11:24; Galatians 3:1; Ephesians 3:14; 5:30; Philippians 3:16; Colossians 1:2, 14; 3:6; I Thessalonians 1:1; I Timothy 3:3; 6:5, 7; Hebrews 2:7; 3:6; 7:21; 8:12; 10:30; 11:11, 13; 12:20; I Peter 4:14; I John 4:3; 5:13; Revelation 1:8, 11; 5:14; 11:1, 17; 14:5; 15:2; 21:24.[38]

Having limited this survey to the New Testament alone, the cited passages constitute a total omission of 1,284 words. The imagery of the Zondervan ad would consign these eternal words of the Living God to unquenchable fire. The day is surely coming when the NIV Committee, Zondervan's cooperating bookstores and their apostate customers will give an accounting for their actions in light of Revelation 22:19.

*"And if any man shall **take away** from the words of the book of this prophecy, God shall take away his part out of the book of life, and out of the holy city, and from the things which are written in this book."*

When we come to an analysis of the NIV's individual renderings, we are confronted by an unscholarly license throughout. And yet, this very thing was to be expected in light of the revisers' own admission:

The first concern of the translators has been the accuracy of the translation and its fidelity to the **thought** of the biblical writers. They have weighed the significance of the lexical and grammatical details of the Hebrew, Aramaic and Greek texts. At the same time, they have striven for more than a word-for-word translation. Because thought patterns and syntax differ from language to language, faithful communication of the meaning of the writers of the Bible demands frequent modifications in sentence structure and constant regard for the contextual meanings of words.[39]

Basically, this would break down in layman's terminology to a "doing of one's own thing." With a higher regard for the "thoughts" of the Biblical writers (as opposed to their actual words), the revisers would be foreordained to employ a host of such "frequent modifications in sentence structure." As we shall presently see, having "striven for more than a word-for-word translation," they got exactly what they wanted! The following observations are not unique to this author.

For over three-and-a-half centuries, God's people have understood Genesis 24:22 to represent Abraham's servant giving Rebekah several gifts including a *"golden earring."* With the *African* manuscripts א and B as their guide, the NIV revisers came up with an *African* reading: "When the camels had finished drinking, the man took out a gold **nose ring.**" How's *that* for more than a word-for-word translation?!

In Exodus 3:13, Moses asked God for the correct reply to the question he anticipated his people asking, *"What is his name?"* The King James rendering of Exodus 3:14 reads, *"And God said unto Moses, I AM THAT I AM,"* stressing the Divine eternality. The NIV changed this to the nonsensical "I AM **WHO** I AM." Can't you see the Jews reply—"Well, *who* exactly is 'I AM **WHO** I AM'?" This is about as scholarly as "Who's on first, what's on second, etc."

When Jesus began His public ministry, John the Baptist immediately identified Him as *"the Lamb of God"* in John 1:29. A junior-age Sunday school child knows that the Passover lamb was a type of the Saviour. NIV scholarship changes the King James reading in Exodus 12:5 of *"your lamb"* to "the **animals** you choose."

These examples are only three of the hundreds of others that appear to be randomly scattered throughout the corrupt NIV. However, upon closer examination, we discover that these changes tend to follow a pattern similar to the revisers' biographical outline as given in chapter fourteen.

For instance, the Westcott and Hort Greek Text has come to

be represented in what is called the Nestle's Greek Text. Originally edited in Germany by Dr. Eberhard Nestle and most recently by his son, Dr. Ervin Nestle, and Dr. Kurt Aland, these readings have passed through 26 editions to date. The flaws of this text, as exhibited in the NIV and other English revisions, show an uncanny parallel to the hang-ups of Westcott and Hort themselves.

As the Cambridge professors were trained in the finest of liberal traditions, we are not surprised to discover NIV readings which promote a permissive approach to education. The reader is acquainted with the infatuation these scholars had for Greek philosophy. Accordingly, where the King James Bible warns, *"Beware lest any man spoil you through philosophy"* (Colossians 2:8), the NIV qualifies this to, "see to it that no one takes you captive through **hollow and deceptive** philosophy." Thus, the NIV would allow our young people to read all the Greek philosophy they want, so long as it's not "hollow and deceptive."

Westcott and Hort were also committed to the world of science as the ultimate panacea for man's woes. The NIV protects this end-day sacred cow by changing the word *science* to **knowledge** in I Timothy 6:20, the Bible's only reference to and clear warning on the subject in question.

When a man becomes puffed up by his knowledge of *philosophy and science,* an addiction to CULTure is right around the corner. With its emphasis on refinement, social graces and aesthetic values, culture salves the rebel's conscience while he enthrones his own intellect as *final authority.* However, it is the consistent testimony of history that a society's surrender to the authoritative dictates of culture will inevitably lead to that society's demise. While culture is elevating man's "nobler qualities" via art appreciation, classical music, excessive etiquette, etc., it is also enslaving his individuality by forcing him to conform to the social mores of the majority. This is the essence of peer pressure.

The Bible is very clear in its denunciation of this smooth-talking crowd (Zondervan, etc.) who, *"by good words and fair speeches* deceive the hearts of the simple."* (Romans 16:18) The man God used to write this very Scripture was the antithesis of culture. Could you imagine Paul speaking to the *Dicky Bird Society?* By his own testimony, the undignified apostle was *"rude in speech."* (II Corinthians 11:6) The NIV has Paul saying instead, "I may not be a **trained speaker.**" Well, neither is Mother Teresa, but who would accuse *her* of rudeness? (Certainly not James Dobson!)

Paul had also referred to his speech as being *"contemptible."* (II Corinthians 10:10) Of course, this was another "no-no" for the "culture vultures," so their NIV simply changed it to, "his speaking amounts to nothing."

These are the types of Christians who are always stressing the love of God to the exclusion of His justice. A good illustration of this is the NIV's rendering of Psalm 136. Because the word *mercy* can imply negative undertones (i.e., the recipient's state *before* receiving mercy), the modern version inserts the word *love* in its place. After three centuries of assurance that *"his mercy endureth for ever,"* the church must now content itself with "His **love** endures for ever"—*in all twenty-six verses.* In view of the Bible's warning that *"whom the Lord loveth he chasteneth"* (Hebrews 12:6), the Bema-bound believer would be more encouraged in knowing that *"His mercy endureth for ever."*

Having supplanted the Father, Son and Holy Ghost with Science, Philosophy and Culture, the end-day apostate has now become his *own* final authority! An examination of his methods of textual criticism gives credence to the adage, "Power corrupts and absolute power corrupts absolutely."

Consider the well-known botching of Mark 1:2 by nearly all of the modern versions, including the "Zondervan Sickle."

Mark 1:2
*"As it is written in the **prophets**, Behold, I send my messenger before thy face, which shall prepare thy way before thee."* (KJV)

It is written in **Isaiah the prophet**: 'I will send my messenger ahead of you, who will prepare your way.' (NIV)

Dr. Gipp cites the manuscript evidence for this verse:

The phrase, 'Isaiah the prophet' appears in the Hesychian (Local Text) family represented primarily by B, C, and Aleph. The problem arises when you *read* the remainder of verse two and then verse three, the Old Testament quote in verse two is *NOT* from Isaiah! It is quoted from Malachi 3:1. Verse *three* is from Isaiah. (Isaiah 40:3) Malachi plus Isaiah does *not* equal 'Isaiah the prophet;' it equals 'the prophets.'

The reading 'the prophets' is found in W along with the *Textus Receptus* (Universal Text) which is represented by E, F, G, and H in the gospels. It is also found in the *majority* of witnesses. Also it was cited in 202 A.D., 150 years before Vaticanus or Sinaiticus.[40]

The NIV people (like the NASV, RSV and numerous others before them) would rather perpetuate an unquestionable error than admit their "oldest is best" theory *stinks*.

A second illustration of Nicolaitane indifference will suffice:

James 5:16

*"Confess your **faults** one to another, and pray one for another, that ye may be healed. The effectual fervent prayer of a righteous man availeth much."* (KJV)

Therefore confess your **sins** to each other and pray for each other so that you may be healed. The prayer of a righteous man is powerful and effective. (NIV)

Dr. Gipp comments:

> Confession of *sins* has been a teaching of the Roman Catholic Church for centuries. The Greek word for "faults" (paraptomata) is found in MSS E, F, G, H, S, V, Y, and Omega, plus the rest of the Receptus family and the *greater* number of all remaining witnesses. Nestle's text inserts "sins" (taxamartias) with *NO* manuscript authority . . . Perhaps there are more Jesuits lurking in the shadows than we think! Anyone accepting an alternate reading with *no evidence* CANNOT be credited with acting ethically or scholarly.[41]

As Westcott and Hort's liberal *training* led to their liberal *theology*, a "Bible" that encourages intellectual freedom (philosophy, science and culture) will also be found to espouse numerous doctrinal heresies.

In order to protect his self-appointment as the believer's *final authority*, the "Christian" scholar must work overtime at undermining the authority of his two major rivals—the written Word and the Living Word.

Reference has already been made to the NIV's altering of Psalm 12:7 from *"thou shalt keep **them**"* (the *"words of the Lord"* in verse six) to ". . . you will keep **us** safe." With one stroke of the sickle they have eliminated the Bible's most important reference on Divine preservation.

According to Psalm 138:2, the doctrine of Holy Scripture tops God's priority list, David declaring, *"thou hast magnified thy word above all thy name."* The *final authority* of Nicolaitane scholarship decided to change this to, "for you have exalted above all things your name *and* your word."

Having attacked both the *preservation* and *priority* of God's

Word, the NIV also maligned the most informative verse regarding proper Bible study. In II Timothy 2:15, we have the only command in Scripture to *study* the Word of God. The King James rendering also instructs the believer as to *how* he is to study—by *"rightly dividing the word of truth."* Because "all of the Bible was written *for* you, but not *to* you," an ability to differentiate between Jews, Gentiles and Christians (I Corinthians 10:32) constitutes the very foundation of conservative hermeneutics.

That the Bible student could actually be weaned from his oppressive teacher posed a serious threat to the *final authority* of Nicolaitane scholars. The NIV saved the day by removing "study" from the text and by changing *"rightly dividing the word of truth"* to the nebulous, **"correctly handles** the word of truth." There is no commandment in any English Bible anywhere in the universe for a believer to *study* the word of truth, unless he has a 1611 Authorized Version. If he has an NIV, he will read, "Do your best to **present yourself."**

When we come to the NIV's treatment of the Lord Jesus Christ, we are outraged to say the least. You will recall that the extant correspondence of Westcott and Hort contained the Lord's personal name "Jesus" only nine times in almost eighteen hundred pages! Accordingly, we discover that *"the name which is above every name"* has been stricken from the following verses of the NIV:

> Matthew 8:29; 13:36; 15:30; 16:20; 17:11, 20; 18:2; 24:2; Mark 5:13; 6:34; 11:14; Luke 7:22; John 4:16, 46; 8:20; Acts 3:36; 9:29; 19:10; Romans 1:16; 15:8; 16:18; I Corinthians 5:5; 16:22; II Corinthians 4:6; 5:18; Galatians 6:15; Ephesians 3:9, 14; Colossians 1:2, 28; II Timothy 4:22; Philemon 6 and I Peter 5:10, 14.

In John 9:35 of a King James Bible, Jesus asks the blind man, *"Dost thou believe on the **Son of God**?"* The NIV changes this to "Do you believe in the **Son of Man?**" Dr. Gipp cites the existing manuscript evidence:

> The word for "God" (Theou) is found in MSS E, F, G, H, S, V, Y, Omega, Theta, the majority of the remaining minuscules, most of the remaining witnesses, plus the entire Latin tradition. The Greek word "man" (anthropouo) is upheld by **one Twentieth Century Greek scholar.**[42]

Realizing that the Saviour's acceptance of worship was a tacit admission of Deity (Matthew 4:10; Acts 10:25-26; Revelation 22:8-9), the NIV revisers altered the King James reading of *"there came a certain ruler, and worshipped him"* in Matthew 9:18 to "a ruler came and **knelt before him.**" The same was done in Matthew 20:20 and Mark 5:6. Kneeling is not the same thing as worshiping. One can bow respectfully before royalty without rendering worship.

Then there is the infamous corruption of I Timothy 3:16 from *"God was manifest in the flesh"* to "**He** appeared in a body." According to the NIV's rendering of Micah 5:2, Christ was not eternal: "out of you will come for me one who will be ruler over Israel, whose **origins** are from old, from ancient times." The "blood" is removed by NIV revision in Acts 17:26 and Colossians 1:14. Blood and culture cannot coexist!

The King James Bible reading for Matthew 5:22 states, *"whosoever is angry with his brother **without a cause** shall be in danger of the judgment."* By omitting the qualifying *"without a cause,"* the NIV strips Christ of His sinlessness, Bruce Lackey commenting:

> The phrase *"without a cause"* is omitted. These two pronouncements are quite different. The NIV would condemn all anger, and in so doing, would condemn Christ, or rather, would have Christ contradicting Himself. In Mark 3:5, Christ looked *"round about on them with anger,"* but He clearly was not doing this *"without a cause,"* since the verse goes on to say, *"being grieved for the hardness of their hearts."* And the NIV points this out also. If the phrase *"without a cause"* be omitted, we would have the Saviour breaking His own command and thus would not be sinless.[43]

About this time, the Nicolaitane apologist will be found retreating to his favorite defensive posture. When confronted by these departures from orthodoxy, he will begin by assuring us that these "unfortunate renderings" constitute a small percentage of the entire Bible, Bernard Ramm stating:

> The number of really important textual variations of the New Testament that cannot be settled with our present information is very small.[44]

And in another place, he "encourages" us with, "Hort claims that less than one-thousandth of the New Testament text is corrupt."[45]

The next argument of conservative scholarship is that the

particular truth in question can still be found in a great majority of passages. He would reason that although *"the Son of God"* has been downgraded to "the Son of **man**" in John 9:35, the doctrine of Christ's Deity is retained elsewhere. Thus he confidently asserts that each of the "Historical Fundamentals of the Faith" can be found in even the weakest of conservative translations.

Stewart Custer believes that all manuscript families are "theologically conservative" stating:

> Each one sets forth an accurate gospel of the Lord Jesus Christ, His deity, the personality and deity of the Holy Spirit, the blood atonement, justification by faith, and the other major doctrines of the faith. Not one of these texts can be called heretical or apostate . . . In the Alexandrian text Jesus Christ is called "Lord" some 749 times. The deity of Christ is taught as well in 161 verses in the Gospels and Acts; in the Thessalonians and Corinthian epistles it is taught in 57 more verses; in Romans and Galatians it is taught in 40 more verses. The deity of Christ is not found in just a few proof texts; it is woven into the very structure of the New Testament. It does not matter at all which of these types of texts you examine—all of them set forth the deity of Christ hundreds and hundreds of times. Every one of the major doctrines of the faith is found in each kind of text. There is no attempt to twist or to disparage any of the great doctrines of the faith. Someone will say, "Does not the Alexandrian text omit the title 'Lord' in some passages?" It is not that the Alexandrian text is deliberately omitting the title. Rather, the manuscripts from which the Alexandrian text was copied did not have it in them. That still does not alter a single doctrine.[46]

Where in the world does Dr. Custer believe the corrupt exemplar, from which the Alexandrian copies were made, originated? Has the chairman of the BJU Bible Department ever heard of an *Egyptian* heretic named *Origen*?

There are a number of serious problems with Dr. Custer's argument. First, it is a direct contradiction of the Bible's teaching on false doctrine. According to Matthew 16:12, *leaven* as a corrupting agent is a type of heretical doctrine: *"Then understood they how that he bade them not beware of the leaven of bread, but of the doctrine of the Pharisees and of the Sadducees."* The Apostle Paul made it clear that "one rotten apple will spoil the whole barrel" writing in Galatians 5:9 that, *"A **little** leaven leaveneth the whole lump."* For Dr. Custer to imply that *any* text is acceptable so long as one can find the desired doctrine somewhere within is utterly preposterous. Someone has said that finding a dollar bill in a trash can does not make the trash can a bank! From a standpoint of Biblical typology, the corrupting agent of leaven is to bread what fermentation is to wine. Neither were permitted in the elements which pictured our Lord's perfect body and blood. To allow "some" leaven (false doctrine) in the *written* Word, is to allow "some" leaven (sin) in the *living* Word. Of course, such an indirect challenge to the sinlessness of Christ is consistent with the NIV's removal of *"without a cause"* in Matthew 5:22.

Second, Dr. Custer's position is inconsistent with the pretended Nicolaitane justification for revision in the first place. With the goal of making our Bible more readable, "conservative Christian scholars" have produced nearly 100 revisions in as many years. Would someone tell this author why such revision has been necessary when *"no fundamental doctrines of the faith were affected?"* Why the double standard?

Third, despite these assurances of minimum theological alterations, there are some instances where the NIV "bakers" have added *more* than a little leaven. The doctrine of Hell is an excellent case in point. Whereas Custer speculated that the Alexandrian manuscripts omitted the title Lord in only 20 out of 769 places,[47] he did not tell you that the NIV removed the word *Hell* in 40 out of the 53 places (75%) it is found in the King James Bible.

Believing that "the customer is always right," Zondervan created a product that would appeal to the refined sensibilities of their targeted market; i.e., the "born-again yuppie." The NIV replaced "Hell" in the following verses with the accompanying generic substitutions:

Deuteronomy 32:22, death; II Samuel 22:6, grave; Job 11:8, grave; Job 26:6, death; Psalm 9:17, grave; Psalm 16:10, grave; Psalm 18:5, death; Psalm 55:15, grave; Psalm 86:13, grave; Psalm 116:3, grave; Psalm 139:8, depths; Proverbs 5:5, grave; Proverbs 7:27, grave; Proverbs 9:18, grave; Proverbs 15:11, death; Proverbs 15:24, grave; Proverbs 23:14, death; Proverbs 27:20, destruction; Isaiah 5:14, grave; Isaiah 14:9, grave; Isaiah 14:15, grave; Isaiah 28:15, grave; Isaiah 28:18, death; Isaiah 57:9, grave; Ezekiel 31:16, grave; Ezekiel 31:17, grave; Ezekiel 32:21, grave; Ezekiel 32:27, grave; Amos 9:2, grave; Jonah 2:2, grave; Habakkuk 2:5, grave; Matthew 11:23, depths; Matthew 16:18, Hades; Luke 10:15, depths; Acts 2:27, grave; Acts 2:31, grave; Revelation 1:18, Hades; Revelation 6:8, Hades; Revelation 20:13, Hades; and Revelation 20:14, Hades.

Notice how this watered-down position on Hell has been articulated by the senior statesmen of evangelicalism, Dr. Billy Graham:

> The only thing I could say for sure is that hell means separation from God. We are separated from his light, from his fellowship. That is going to be hell. **When it comes to a literal fire, I don't preach it because I'm not sure about it.** When the Scripture uses fire concerning hell, that is possibly an illustration of how terrible it's going to be—not fire but something worse, a thirst for God that cannot be quenched.[48]

The colorful evangelist, Sam P. Jones, once stirred an entire community to revival after having his door-to-door visitation teams greet the unsuspecting residents with the blunt announcement, "You are going to Hell."[49] Were he alive today, this fearless preacher would have no doubt rebuked Custer, Graham, Zondervan and the entire NIV committee with a similar frankness for their reprehensible adulteration of Holy Scripture.

When Drs. Westcott and Hort persuaded themselves against the doctrine of everlasting punishment, their lifestyles became centered around temporal priorities. Once again, this spirit may be seen in the pages of the NIV.

Having downgraded the Bible's central exposé of man's money-hungry nature to being "**a** root of all **kinds of** evil" (I Timothy 6:10), the NIV gets down to business by giving its "health and wealth" readership exactly what they want. In the King James Bible we read, "*Commit thy works unto the Lord, and thy thoughts shall be established.*" (Proverbs 16:3) This has been changed to, "Commit to the Lord whatever you do, and **your plans will succeed**." (i.e., "Something good is going to happen to you!")

The NIV's rendering of Ecclesiastes 10:10 informs these positive thinkers that the key ingredient for success is no longer the spiritual advantage of "*wisdom*" (King James Bible) but rather, "**skill** will bring success."

Everyone would agree that the television industry sets the pace for our nation's materialistic philosophy. With multiplied millions of Americans glued to "the box" by the hour, the NIV would have to make an unusual alteration in the 33rd chapter of Numbers. Here we find the preserved account of God's instructions to His people concerning separation from heathen influences. The King James Bible reads, "*Then ye shall drive out all the inhabitants of the land from before you, and **destroy all their pictures**.*"

(Numbers 33:52a) Of course, this would never do in the twentieth century, so the NIV simply substituted "carved images" for *"pictures."* We wouldn't want to lose the amazing influence of "Christian" television programming (Jim and Tammy, Oral Roberts, The 700 Club, etc.).

Should any of the "brethren" get to wondering whether his worldly testimony might be damning some neighbor or loved one, the NIV is there to relieve his conscience by altering *"Abstain from all **appearance** of evil."* (I Thessalonians 5:22) The NIV says, "Avoid every **kind** of evil."

However, as "everything rises and falls on leadership," it would be in the area of pulpit supply that the NIV would minister to lukewarm believers best. Because *"no man can serve two masters,"* materialistic Christians will be continually drawn to a host of non-convicting, teaching ministries which put more emphasis on *overhead projectors* than *altar calls.* With a "we-aim-to-please" attitude, the NIV-Zondervan team has twice replaced "the preacher" with "the teacher" in their back-to-back renderings of Ecclesiastes 12:9-10. *How convenient!*

Now although our survey of the NIV is finished, no such end appears in sight for future revisions. In his epilogue, Lewis states:

> A translation starts to become outdated from the moment it is completed. Information from new manuscript materials, new insights into the languages in which the Bible was first written, and new data concerning biblical history need to be communicated to the reader. Changing ideas about translations and changes in the English language itself all outdate a version, thus preparing the way for the process to be started all over again.[50]

However, even Lewis is willing to concede the true motive behind all the "helpful revisions":

> If one should ask if there are too many translations, the reply must be that the question is really irrelevant. The translations are here; they are not going away; and they must be dealt with. To hide one's head in the sand will not make the translations disappear; it will not bring back the so-called "good old days" when everyone read one translation. **As long as there is financial gain in it, publishers will push translations, old or new.**[51]

We will now proceed to a review of the New King James Version and the New Scofield Bible.

XVII

The Cutting Edge of Apostasy

". . . and his hand clave unto the sword."
(II Samuel 23:10a)

In our last chapter, we examined the many weaknesses of the New International Version (1973). However, as bad as the NIV was seen to be, it has actually been sandwiched in between a pair of even greater imposters—the New Scofield Reference Edition (1967) and the New King James Version (1984).

The single factor which makes these recent versions so dangerous is that they are promoted as being authentic King James Bibles with only a minimum of cosmetic improvements. That this is far from the truth shall be demonstrated by the following survey beginning with the NKJV.

The New King James Version is particularly deceptive because it uses the name "King James" in its title. This exclusive claim to King James legitimacy was based upon a *professed* return to the *Textus Receptus*. After 75 years of publishing Bibles from the corrupt texts of Alexandria, Thomas Nelson would have you believe that they have suddenly seen a giant *"TR"* in the sky!

The editors piously relate:

> In the early 1970's, there appeared to be a growing concern over the fact that the revisions of 1881, 1901, and 1952 had used a Greek text that largely ignored the great majority of biblical manuscripts. Some were concerned that the words of men had begun to change the Word of God, even if only in subtle ways.
>
> In 1975 Thomas Nelson Publishers, successor to the British firm that had first published the English Revised Version (1885),

the American Standard Version (1901), and the Revised Standard Version (1952), determined to assess the depth of this concern.

Because any revision of the Scriptures must meet the needs of public worship, Christian education, personal reading and study, leading clergymen and lay Christians were invited to meetings in Chicago, Illinois, and Nashville, Tennessee, in 1975, and in London, England, in 1976, to discuss the need for a new revision. Almost one hundred church leaders from a broad spectrum of Christian churches attended those meetings.

The expression of concern which Nelson Bible editors had been hearing for several years was confirmed by those in attendance. And there was a strong sentiment that the King James Bible should once more be sensitively revised in a way that would retain everything that could be retained of the text and language of that historic translation.[1]

This "broad spectrum" of scholars included charismatics, neo-evangelicals, Southern Baptists and pseudo-Fundamentalists, none of whom believed he possessed a copy of the inspired, inerrant Word of God. With militant conviction, it was announced:

Each of the selected scholars signed a statement of faith, declaring his belief that the Scriptures in their entirety are the uniquely inspired Word of God, *free from error in the original autographs.*[2]

Now although Nelson Publishers did not believe that their finished product constituted the very words of God, they did believe that their NKJV would make a nifty Christmas present, an early advertisement in *Moody Monthly* concluding:

A $1 million ad campaign–scheduled to be launched this summer–will make the New King James Version the ideal gift for holidays and other special occasions.[3]

With the holiday season fast approaching, the November *Moody Monthly* (1982) ran the following bizarre endorsement of the NKJV from Kenneth Taylor, editor of *The Living Bible*:

I'm happy to tell you how much I like the New King James Version. It is always a pleasure to me when new Bible translations come out because a certain number of people are particularly helped by each one. I'm sure this will be especially true of the New King James. There are so many millions of people who, like myself, have found the old King James difficult to read and understand. Now in God's Providence, we have a new edition of the King James edition that is much easier to understand because of the updating of the language. I hope that some organizations that put Bibles in hotels and prisons will use the NKJV because those who are unfamiliar with the Bible are going to find it much easier to read. I congratulate and thank Thomas Nelson Publishers for the New King James Version of the Bible.[4]

Don't you find it rather odd that a revision committee which professed to be "concerned that the words of men had begun to change the Word of God" would court the patronage of some *nut* who would speak of God's Son as participating in a "brawl" in violation of I Timothy 3:3? (The same could be said for Taylor's exegesis of Baal's "potty break.")

Incidentally, the most outstanding advocate of the NKJV just happens to be the brother referred to in chapter one who claimed to be jump-started each morning by this same Living Bible! Preferring either of these polarized perversions is bad enough, but how could anyone be taken seriously who would recommend *both* at the same time?

The NKJV was not only deceptive in name, but in the way it was marketed to the public, with special emphasis on the campuses of colleges and universities. Every effort was made to equate the Thomas Nelson "revisions" of 1979-1982 with the legitimate proofreading editions of the 1611 Authorized Version discussed in chapter eleven.

Among the propaganda ploys of this time was a color brochure, circulated by a leading "Christian" university, displaying a page from the original 1611 edition. Their motive was to convince the young person that since his King James Bible was not an exact match of the original 1611, the NKJV could be passed off as just another revision.

The preface to the NKJV conveys this theme of "legitimized revision" from the opening paragraph:

In the Preface to the 1611 edition, the translators of the Authorized Version, known popularly as the King James Bible, state that it was not their purpose "to make a new translation ... but to make a good one better." Indebted to the earlier work of William Tyndale and others, they saw their best contribution to consist in revising and enhancing the excellence of the English versions which had sprung from the Reformation of the sixteenth century. In harmony with the purpose of the King James scholars, the translators and editors of the present work have not pursued a goal of innovation. They have perceived the Holy Bible, New King James Version, as a continuation of the labors of the earlier translators, thus unlocking for today's readers the spiritual treasures found especially in the Authorized Version of the Holy Scriptures.[5]

And again:

Students of the Bible applaud the timeless devotional character of our historic Bible. Yet it is also universally understood that our language, like all living languages, has undergone profound change since 1611. Subsequent revisions of the King James Bible have sought to keep abreast of changes in English speech. The present work is a further step toward this objective.[6]

Note the inculcation of this idea in their media advertising, a June, *Moody Monthly* ad stating:

The World's #1 Best Seller Born Again August 2nd. The New King James Version. The most significant publishing event since 1611. In the entire history of the world the King James Version has repeatedly outsold any other book ever published. Why? Because people trust the King James. It's the Bible for all who love God's Word.

Since 1611 four major editions of the KJV have been published. And now Thomas Nelson—the world's leading Bible publisher—is pleased to present the 5th major edition of this magnificent translation, the New King James Version.[7]

Having reviewed the material in chapter eleven, the reader is aware of the inaccuracy of Nelson's comparison. The changes made in editions subsequent to the 1611 original were orthographical (spelling) and lithographical (printing) in nature. Neither of these concerns was addressed in the NKJV preface.

Instead, other inane priorities were voiced, such as:

In addition to the pronoun usages of the seventeenth century, the *-eth* and *-est* verb endings so familiar in the earlier King James editions are now obsolete. Unless a speaker is schooled in these verb endings, there is common difficulty in selecting the correct form to be used with a given subject of the verb in vocal prayer. That is, should we use *love, loveth,* or *lovest? do, doeth, doest* or *dost? have, hath* or *hast?*[8]

With such deception receiving an unprecedented endorsement from the "Christian right" (pseudo-Fundamentalist colleges and universities), it was not unnatural for naive believers to begin expressing doubt. The natural question would be, "If the NKJV is indeed the first modern revision translated from the correct Greek Text, could this not be the work of the Lord?"

It is the contention of this author that were the NKJV what it claims to be (WHICH IT IS **NOT**, as we shall presently discover), the principles contained in Scripture would still negate such a possibility of Divine sanction.

In II Samuel 23:9-10 and I Chronicles 11:12-14, we have the brief account of Eleazar's engagement with the Philistines. While Chronicles details the *spoil* of Eleazar's victory—*"a parcel of ground full of barley,"* Samuel divulges the *secret* of his success— *"and his hand clave unto the sword."*

From 1611 to 1881, God's foot soldiers wielded KJV swords while defending spiritual barley fields against Jesuits armed with Douay-Rheims Versions. Their grip grew tighter from 1881-1974 as one Alexandrian imposter after another was driven from the field.

Suddenly, a profit-oriented corporation (the same crowd who manufactured the *enemies'* swords) would prevail upon the church to believe that the Holy Spirit had abruptly ordered a *weapon change—in the very heat of the battle!* Their corrupt rendering of Romans 1:25 says it best. Instead of the KJV's *"changed"* we read, "who **exchanged** the truth of God for a lie." A true Bible believer will never exchange his KJV for a NKJV. The reason for this resistance is the same today as it was in Bible days. With his very life at stake, the grip of the ancient warrior was so intense that warm water was often needed at battle's end to literally pry the weapon from his cramped hands. A person with an ounce of spiritual discernment can see that he who *"is not the author of confusion"* would *never* pick such timing to introduce yet another English revision! The outstanding distinctive of a spiritual warrior will *always* be that, *"his hand clave unto the sword."*

The NIV committee claims to be in harmony with the original King James translators. If this be so, where is the editor's identification of Pope John Paul II as *the man of sin?* Can the "burden" of a secular corporation compare with a royal authorization (Ecclesiastes 8:4)? If Nelson Publishers really want to *harmonize*, why don't they take off that little ℗ on page two?

The truth of the matter is that the New King James Version represents Satan's ultimate deception to oppose God's remnant in the closing days of the New Testament age. Having enlisted the lukewarm materialist with his NIV, the devil sets a trap for the diligent soul winner with the NKJV. Although his worldly counterpart embraced the "oldest is best" theory of manuscript evidences, the true Bible believer refused to abandon the Majority Text, retaining the Divine commendation of, *"thou hast kept my word."* Thus we find Satan attempting to wean him away from his Authorized Version with the deceitful *half-step* of a generic look-alike, **TRANSLATED FROM THE TRUSTWORTHY** *TEXTUS RECEPTUS!*

Now, although the Nelson Company pitched their Bible on the strength of the Received Text, they were soon caught talking out of both sides of their mouths. When a study is made of the footnote section in the NKJV, one discovers a classic example of compromise. Understanding the self-centered nature of today's carnal believers, Nelson Publishers decided to let their customers have a literal choice between *three different Greek readings!* With the main English Scripture **supposedly** translated from the traditional *Textus Receptus*, 774 instances appear where two alternative Greek texts are presented for consideration.[9] These are the old Westcott and Hort readings, perpetuated by the Nestle's/United Bible Societies text, designated as "NU" and the Hodges-Farstad-Nelson Majority Greek text, denoted by "M" in the footnotes.[10]

For the most unbelievable illustration of end-day compromise, consider the following announcement in the NKJV preface:

> It was the editors' conviction that the use of footnotes would encourage further inquiry by readers. They also recognized that it was easier for the average reader to delete something he or she felt was not properly a part of the text, than to insert a word or phrase which had been left out by the revisors.[11]

Can you imagine the confusion being wrought among laypeople as they suddenly discover their new responsibilities to become *textual critics*? However, to find the greatest problem with the NKJV, the reader is directed to the English text itself. The Nelson ad campaign assured us of a conservative translation format:

> Every word of the New King James Version has been checked against the original in light of increasing knowledge about the Greek and Hebrew languages. **Nothing has been changed except** to make the original meaning clearer.[12]

Whereas Ezra 8:36a reads in the Authorized Version, *"And*

they delivered the king's commissions unto the king's lieutenants,"
the NKJV alters this to, "And they delivered the king's orders to
the king's **satraps** . . ." Does "satraps" make the original
meaning *clearer?*

Yet in their preface one discovers a significant loophole. Like
the NIV committee before them, the NKJV editors gave fair
warning of a shaky venture at best. Commenting on their eclectic
translation procedures, they stated, "A special feature of the New
King James Version is its conformity to the **thought flow** of the
1611 Bible."[13]

This unscholarly and unreliable practice which supposedly
equipped the translator to perceive the "thought flow" (whatever
that is) of the King James Bible, is known as "dynamic
equivalence." Basically this means that the scholar can take
whatever license he desires. *Conservative estimates of the total
translation changes in the NKJV are generally put at over
100,000!* (This is an average of 82 changes for each of the 1219
pages in the NKJV.)[14]

Along this line of abuse, the most shocking revelation about
the "New" King James Version is that it is literally laced with
"old" readings from the Revised Standard and New American
Standard Versions. This revival of Alexandrian readings is one of
the best-kept secrets of the decade.

Whenever there is a marked departure from the text of the
KJV, the alternate reading is frequently taken from either the
RSV, NASV, or oftentimes, both. For instance, in the first chapter
of John's Gospel, there are 51 verses. Of this total, 45 (or 88%)
have been altered by the NKJV. Among this number, 34 (75%)
exhibit a distinct RSV or NASV reading while 6 show a partial
reading. Only 5 (15%) appear unique to the NKJV.

By way of illustration, the KJV rendering of Job 17:1a is, *"My
breath is corrupt."* The NKJV, RSV and NASV combine to read
"My spirit is broken." Psalm 19:6a in the Authorized Version
reads, *"His going forth is from the end of the heaven."* This time,
all three agree to the pronoun switch of, "its rising is from . . ."
While the KJV reads in Psalm 22:21b, *"for thou hast heard me
from the horns of the unicorns,"* the NKJV, RSV and NASV unite
with, "from the horns of the wild oxen."

The following 36 cases from the Song of Solomon represent
some of the more pronounced examples of NKJV affinity with the
RSV and NASV:

Song of Solomon 1:4

"the upright love thee."	(King James Version)
"rightly do they love you."	(New King James Version)
"rightly do they love you."	(Revised Standard Version)
"rightly do they love you."	(New American Standard Version)

Song of Solomon 1:6

"my mother's children"	(KJV)
"my mother's sons"	(NKJV)
"my mother's sons"	(RSV)
"my mother's sons"	(NASV)

Song of Solomon 1:7

"that turneth aside"	(KJV)
"who veils herself"	(NKJV)
"who wanders"	(RSV)
"who veils herself"	(NASV)

Song of Solomon 1:10

"Thy cheeks are comely with rows of jewels,"	(KJV)
"Your cheeks are lovely with ornaments."	(NKJV)
"Your cheeks are comely with ornaments."	(RSV)
"Your cheeks are lovely with ornaments."	(NASV)

Song of Solomon 1:11

"borders of gold"	(KJV)
"ornaments of gold"	(NKJV)
"ornaments of gold"	(RSV)
"ornaments of gold"	(NASV)

Song of Solomon 1:14

"My beloved is unto me as a cluster of camphire"	(KJV)
"My beloved is to me a cluster of henna blooms."	(NKJV)
"My beloved is to me a cluster of henna blossoms."	(RSV)
"My beloved is to me a cluster of henna blossoms."	(NASV)

Song of Solomon 2:5

"Stay me with flagons, comfort me with apples:"	(KJV)
"Sustain me with cakes of raisins, refresh me with apples"	(NKJV)
"Sustain me with raisins, refresh me with apples"	(RSV)
"Sustain me with raisin cakes, refresh me with apples"	(NASV)

Song of Solomon 2:7

"by the roes,"	(KJV)
"by the gazelles"	(NKJV)
"by the gazelles"	(RSV)

"by the gazelles" (NASV)

Song of Solomon 2:9
"My beloved is like a roe or a young hart:" (KJV)
"My beloved is like a gazelle or a young stag" (NKJV)
"My beloved is like a gazelle or a young stag" (RSV)
"My beloved is like a gazelle or a young stag" (NASV)

Song of Solomon 2:16
"he feedeth among the lilies." (KJV)
"he feeds his flock among the lilies" (NKJV)
"he pastures his flock among the lilies" (RSV)
"he pastures his flock among the lilies" (NASV)

Song of Solomon 2:17
"be thou like a roe or a young hart" (KJV)
"be like a gazelle or a young stag" (NKJV)
"be like a gazelle or a young stag" (RSV)
"be like a gazelle or a young stag" (NASV)

Song of Solomon 3:2
"in the broad ways" (KJV)
"in the squares" (NKJV)
"in the squares" (RSV)
"in the squares" (NASV)

Song of Solomon 3:9
"King Solomon made himself a chariot" (KJV)
"Solomon the King made himself a palanquin" (NKJV)
"King Solomon made himself a palanquin" (RSV)
"King Solomon made for himself a sedan chair" (NASV)

Song of Solomon 4:1
"within thy locks:" (KJV)
"behind your veil" (NKJV)
"behind your veil" (RSV)
"behind your veil" (NASV)

Song of Solomon 4:3
"thy speech is comely:" (KJV)
"your mouth is lovely" (NKJV)
"your mouth is lovely" (RSV)
"your mouth is lovely" (NASV)

Song of Solomon 4:5
"like two young roes that are twins," (KJV)

"like two fawns, twins of a gazelle" (NKJV)
"like two fawns, twins of a gazelle" (RSV)
"like her fawns, twins of a gazelle" (NASV)

Song of Solomon 4:9
"with one of thine eyes," (KJV)
"with one look of your eyes" (NKJV)
"with a glance of your eyes" (RSV)
"with a single glance of your eyes" (NASV)

Song of Solomon 5:2
"my undefiled:" (KJV)
"my perfect one" (NKJV)
"my perfect one" (RSV)
"my perfect one" (NASV)

Song of Solomon 5:5
"with sweet smelling myrrh," (KJV)
"with liquid myrrh" (NKJV)
"with liquid myrrh" (RSV)
"with liquid myrrh" (NASV)

Song of Solomon 5:12
"as the eyes of doves" (KJV)
"like doves" (NKJV)
"like doves" (RSV)
"like doves" (NASV)

Song of Solomon 6:2
"to feed in the gardens," (KJV)
"to feed his flock in the gardens" (NKJV)
"to pasture his flock in the gardens" (RSV)
"to pasture his flock in the gardens" (NASV)

Song of Solomon 6:7
"within thy locks" (KJV)
"behind your veil" (NKJV)
"behind your veil" (RSV)
"behind your veil" (NASV)

Song of Solomon 6:8
"threescore queens, and fourscore concubines," (KJV)
"sixty queens and eighty concubines" (NKJV)
"sixty queens and eighty concubines" (RSV)
"sixty queens and eighty concubines" (NASV)

Song of Solomon 6:12

"chariots of Ammi-nadib"	(KJV)
"chariots of my noble people"	(NKJV)
"chariot beside my prince"	(RSV)
"chariots of my noble people"	(NASV)

Song of Solomon 6:13

"As it were the company of two armies."	(KJV)
"As it were the dance of the double camp?"	(NKJV)
"As upon a dance before two armies"	(RSV)
"As at the dance of the two companies"	(NASV)

Song of Solomon 7:1

"shoes,"	(KJV)
"sandals"	(NKJV)
"sandals"	(RSV)
"sandals"	(NASV)

Song of Solomon 7:4

"fishpools"	(KJV)
"pools"	(NKJV)
"pools"	(RSV)
"pools"	(NASV)

Song of Solomon 7:5a

"Thine head upon thee is like Carmel,"	(KJV)
"Your head crowns you like Mount Carmel"	(NKJV)
"Your head crowns you like Carmel"	(RSV)
"Your head crowns you like Carmel"	(NASV)

Song of Solomon 7:5b

"held in the galleries."	(KJV)
"held captive by its tresses"	(NKJV)
"held captive in the tresses"	(RSV)
"captivated by your tresses"	(NASV)

Song of Solomon 7:7

"and thy breasts to clusters of grapes."	(KJV)
"and your breasts like its clusters"	(NKJV)
"and your breasts are like its clusters"	(RSV)
"and your breasts are like its clusters"	(NASV)

Song of Solomon 7:8

"the smell of thy nose"	(KJV)
"the fragrance of your breath"	(NKJV)
"the scent of your breath"	(RSV)

"the fragrance of your breath"   (NASV)

Song of Solomon 7:9
"goeth down sweetly,"   (KJV)
"goes down smoothly"   (NKJV)
"goes down smoothly"   (RSV)
"goes down smoothly"   (NASV)

Song of Solomon 7:12
"flourish,"   (KJV)
"budded"   (NKJV)
"budded"   (RSV)
"budded"   (NASV)

Song of Solomon 8:1
"sucked the breasts of my mother!"   (KJV)
"nursed at my mother's breasts"   (NKJV)
"nursed at my mother's breast"   (RSV)
"nursed at my mother's breasts"   (NASV)

Song of Solomon 8:9
"palace of silver:"   (KJV)
"battlement of silver"   (NKJV)
"battlement of silver"   (RSV)
"battlement of silver"   (NASV)

Song of Solomon 8:10
"favour."   (KJV)
"peace"   (NKJV)
"peace"   (RSV)
"peace"   (NASV)

Such evidence as this makes it clear that the NKJV is a far cry from the 1611 Authorized Version. In reality, it is nothing more than a resuscitated African Bible from the hand of Origen.

The lovely Rebekah, as a type of Christ's Bride, is *still* cast as a borderline *cannibal*: "So I put the *nose ring* on her **nose** and the bracelets on her wrists." (Genesis 24:47, NKJV)

Nelson Publishers had promised that the NKJV would be "unlocking for today's readers the spiritual treasures found especially in the Authorized Version."[15] At this point, we would ask, "Where is this treasure?" So far, all that we have seen is a rehash of Westcott and Hort.

The NKJV rendering of II Corinthians 2:17 is *still* the corrupt, "For we are not as so many, **peddling** the word of God." The word "appearance" is *still* missing in I Thessalonians 5:22. The word "knowledge" continues to hide the sacrosanct "science" in I Timothy 6:20. We *still* cannot find the command to "study" God's Word (II Timothy 2:15). The underlying motive of this mess continues to be clouded with, "For the love of money is **a** root of all **kinds of** evil." (I Timothy 6:10, NKJV) And today's "liberated" believers continue to be appeased by such anti-authoritative nonsense as the ERA reading of Genesis 2:18 in the NKJV: "And the LORD God said, It is not good that man should be alone; I will make him a helper **comparable** to him." New? Yes! A King James Version? *Absolutely not!*

Now when the faithful soul winner is not being pressed to exchange his KJV for a NKJV, he will frequently be offered a New Scofield Reference Bible instead. Satan wants the Lord's barley field and will stop at nothing to disarm its defenders. The NSRB is another dangerous option because it too is passed off as a legitimate Authorized Version.

A May, 1982, ad in *Moody Monthly* read:

> Here the King James Version text, with word changes to help the reader, is illuminated by authoritative study aids, a Bible printed and bound with the superb craftsmanship you expect from Oxford.[16]

Dean Burgon would have described the opening phrase of this ad as "an excursion into cloud land." How could the NSRB be the King James Version text if it has been altered by various word changes? And yet, this is precisely what is claimed in the frontispiece of the NSRB:

> Holy Bible, Authorized King James Version with introductions, annotations, subject chain references and such word changes in the text as will help the reader.[17]

With all due respect to the body of Christ, this is the kind of sales pitch that only a *Christian* could swallow! A lost man would laugh at the suggestion that a particular text could be promoted as the same text with even *one* alteration. Name the courtroom where such foolishness would be tolerated. When such religious "meatballs" tried the patience of Gallio, he "*drave them from the judgment seat.*" (Acts 18:16) Such would be the case today.

The very margins themselves display glaring testimony that the text of the NSRB is not the same as the Authorized Version. Whenever a King James word was "exchanged" in the NSRB, the

Authorized reading was noted in the margin along with the designation "KJV."

As a follow-up to our NKJV study of the Song of Solomon, the NSRB replaced 42 original King James words with 37 generic replacements! Of course, most of the "helpful" additions can be found in the RSV and NASV.

If the reader took the time to examine every margin in the NSRB, he would discover that approximately *6,560* words have been removed from the true Authorized Version and replaced with their generic equivalents. This total is roughly equal to the five entire books of II Peter, I, II, and III John and Jude, plus the first three chapters of Revelation.

Included in this list are 1,234 proper noun changes that the editors themselves acknowledge on pages 1388-1392. Not even Deuteronomy 4:2 was spared in the NSRB, confirming that *nothing* is sacred to Nicolaitane scholarship:

> Ye shall not add unto the word which I command you, neither shall ye diminish **anything** *(ought* in the KJV) from it, that ye may keep the commandments of the Lord your God which I command you.

Can you imagine such a thing being presented to thinking people—"the King James Version text *with word changes*"? Could not a first grader see the difference? Consider Genesis 49:6b:

> *"For in their anger they slew a man, and in their selfwill they digged down a wall."* (KJV)

> "For in their anger they slew a man, and in their self-will *they* **hamstrung oxen.**" (NSRB)

Since when is an *oxen* and a *wall* the same thing?! And then there is Exodus 2:25:

> *"And God looked upon the children of Israel, and God had respect unto them."* (KJV)

> "And God looked upon the children of Israel and God **knew their plight.**" (NSRB)

Did the changes in Joshua 12:8a "help the reader" understand any better?

> *"In the mountains, and in the valleys, and in the plains, and*

in the springs, and in the wilderness, and in the south country."
(KJV)

"In the mountains, and in the **Shephelah,** and in the **Arabah,** and in the springs, and in the wilderness, and in the **Negev.**" (NSRB)

Not only does the NSRB alter existing pronouns in the Authorized Version, but they create new ones out of thin air as well! This is what they mean by "The King James Version text, with word changes." (i.e., a square–circle; black–white, etc.)

As was the case with the NIV and the NKJV, the promoters behind the NSRB were well aware of the need to make some concession to the culture and refinement of their targeted market share. Where Jacob told his sons, *"Ye have troubled me to make me to **stink** among the inhabitants"* (Genesis 34:30, KJV), the Oxford people water this down to, "Ye have troubled me to make me **odious.**" (NSRB) The KJV rendering of *"**whorish** woman"* in Proverbs 6:26 has been altered to an "**unchaste** woman." (NSRB) And **"refuse"** has replaced *"**dung**"* in Philippians 3:8.

The next time some Nicolaitane priest tries to get you to switch swords, ask him to explain the NSRB reading at I Samuel 13:1. The Authorized Version states:

> *"Saul reigned one year; and when he had reigned two years over Israel, Saul chose him . . ."*

How is this NSRB selection for "helping the reader," especially a new convert:

> "Saul was . . . years old and when he had reigned two years over Israel, Saul chose him . . ."

Confused? Wait till you read the footnote!

> The Hebrew text states "Saul was . . . years old," giving Saul's age. Obviously the numeral before "years" was lost. Conjectures of thirty or forty years have been made.[18]

That **blank** between the words "was" and "years" represents the mentality of a money-hungry publishing company that would induce its customers to put more faith in "human conjectures" than in "Divine preservation."

The justification for these hundreds of "helpful changes" can be found in the *Introduction to the 1967 Edition* by E. Schuyler English. The opening lines are meant to establish an immediate impression that the original "Old Scofield" of 1909 was itself later "revised" in 1917. The naive believer is about to be set up in classic Nicolaitane style:

> The origin of the Scofield Reference Bible has been explained by Dr. C. I. Scofield in his Introduction to the 1909 Edition (see p. viii), and his reason for making certain changes eight years later is stated in the Preface to the 1917 Edition (p. ix). In Scofield's own words, he was "solicitous that . . . he might find his opportunity to add, here and there, such further help as experience has shown to be desirable."[19]

Can you see it coming? English is about to equate the changes of his committee in 1967 with those of Dr. Scofield's in 1917. The hypocrisy of the modern Bible revision movement gets worse all the time. Of course, English fails to inform his readers that Dr. Scofield limited his changes to his own *personal notes*. Scofield never dreamed of altering the inspired text in any way!

English continues:

> More than a half century has passed since the first edition of this Reference Bible was issued. Just as there was need for improvement eight years after the original publication of this work, so today a revision is past due, with improvements and further helps to the reader—not that the Bible has changed but that additional light has been thrown upon the Scriptures by textual scholarship, archaeological discoveries, and developments on a world-wide scale in the light of Bible prophecy.[20]

Did you notice how English never said one word about Scofield's changes being restricted to his *notes*? The sales pitch then acknowledges:

> Among the changes and improvements in this edition are: important word changes in the text to help the reader.[21]

And then on the *same page* he adds:

> This revision, like the 1909 and 1917 editions, is printed in the text of the Authorized King James Version of 1611.[22]

The pathetic thing is that the Oxford Press would desecrate the memory of a dead man to make a fast buck! Although Dr.

Scofield was deceived by some of the claims of the emerging yet unproven ASV (as were many godly men such as R.A. Torrey, etc.) his opinions *never* went further than his notes!

Unlike the charlatans who would misrepresent his life's work posthumously, C.I. Scofield was a rare specimen of courage, devotion, and integrity. Scofield was a man's man who fought and survived *eighteen* Civil War battles. At age *twenty*, he earned the Confederate Cross of Honor in the Battle of Antietam, the bloodiest day of fighting in U.S. military history (over 20,000 casualties). Can you imagine a grizzled veteran like this being "bothered" by such words as "dung," "whorish," and "stink"?

After the war, Scofield became a successful attorney but soon succumbed to the stranglehold of liquor. A soul-winning YMCA worker by the name of Thomas McPheeters changed all that by winning him to Christ in his own law office. However, Satan was not about to surrender this intellectual trophy without a fight. Four years after his conversion, Scofield's Catholic wife divorced him over religious conflicts. In the face of this reproach, Scofield determined to fulfill what he perceived to be the will of God for his life. (Scofield's mother died during his birth, but not before claiming him for the ministry.) Beale writes:

> When Scofield had been a Christian for only four years, his unconverted Roman Catholic wife filed for a divorce. She would no longer tolerate his new lifestyle. Scofield objected to the divorce, but she filed again and succeeded in 1883. The following year, Scofield, on the basis of I Corinthians 7:15, married Hettie Van Wark, who remained his companion until his death.[23]

Although scorned by some, Scofield was later recommended to the pulpit of the Congregational Church at East Northfield, Massachusetts, in 1895 by D.L. Moody. He remained Moody's pastor until the latter's death in 1899.

In the summer of 1901, Scofield shared with his friend, A.C. Gaebelein, his burden to produce a reference Bible. He labored on the notes for this proposed study from 1902-1909. With the financial sponsorship of John T. Pirie (owner of Carson, Pirie, Scott and Company) and others, the original Scofield Reference Bible was released on January 12, 1909. Over two million copies were sold within two years.[24]

Although the notes of the Scofield Bible are far from inspired (only a fool would expect such from a mere man), the work went on to become the most popular study Bible on the market. *However, this was not to be the case for the New Scofield Reference Bible.* In the 1909 and 1917 editions, Scofield's *fallible notes* were juxtapositional with an *infallible text!* The generic substitute of 1967 altered this infallible text, thereby forfeiting a "sanction from on high." Beale conceding:

> A new and slightly revised edition appeared in 1917, and this became the standard "old" Scofield Bible. Although the New Scofield Reference Bible of 1967 admirably revised many of the old notes, that edition never gained a comparable acceptance. This was due perhaps to its altering of the seventeenth-century archaic or obsolete words and expressions, **so that it deviates a great deal from the actual King James Version that it claims to be.**[25]

This author feels little compulsion to bore the reader further: Rebekah *still* has, "the ring in her nose" (Genesis 24:47); Numbers 33:52 *still* has "stone idols" for pictures; science is *still* called "knowledge" (I Timothy 6:20); etc., etc., etc. And don't forget that a great percentage of the NSRB's readings can also be found in the RSV, NASV or both. A random survey of the NSRB margins in Philippians alone revealed a total of 29 changes from the King James Bible. Of these, twenty-one (72%) were traced to either the RSV or NASV. The skeptic can check it out for himself: Philippians 1:7, 8, 23, 27; 2:1, 15, 25, 27, 28; 3:1, 8, 17, 19, 20, 21; 4:3, 6, 14, 15, 21 and 22.

Now as we conclude our chapter on *"The Cutting Edge of Apostasy,"* a final warning is given concerning the hidden "Vatican Connection" in all weapons exchange offers. This time, the Catholic doctrine of Rome is found in the footnotes. The note for Acts 8:12 concerning the baptism of the Ethiopian reads:

> Baptism has, since the apostolic age, been practiced by every major group in the Christian church and, in Protestant communions, is recognized as one of two **sacraments** – the other being the Lord's supper.[26]

Who ever heard of a Bible-believing Christian referring to the *ordinance* of baptism as a *sacrament?* "His Holiness" is after your sword – don't let him have it! If you stay in the barley field a little while longer, the Saviour *Himself* will pour the warm water over your cramped hands. The wait *will* be worth it.

> *"His lord said unto him, Well done, thou good and faithful servant: thou hast been faithful over a few things, I will make thee ruler over many things: enter thou into the joy of thy lord."* (Matthew 25:21)

XVIII

Preservation for Propagation

"Understandest thou what thou readest? And he said,
How can I, except some man should guide me?"
(Acts 8:30b, 31a)

We have now arrived at the subject which Satan hates the most. Were the sole accomplishment of this book to be an enhanced regard for the Authorized Version, this author would consider his labor to have been in vain.

The average King James Bible advocate betrays his ignorance of the very purpose for its preservation by a life that is void of *personal soul winning*. Chapters one through seventeen of *Final Authority* reach their culmination in the singular theme of this concluding chapter. That is to say, *the King James Bible has been preserved by God to be propagated by man!*

That the Holy Spirit applied the term "Scripture" to copies has been previously established by such passages as Acts 8:27-35. A "1611 man" would be quick to connect II Timothy 3:16 with the eunuch's *copy* of Isaiah, but he will often miss "the forest for the trees"; although the Queen's treasurer possessed a preserved copy of the prophet's work, he was still in need of a *soul winner's guidance*. While Bible believers take *their* militant stand for the 1611 Authorized Version, many a benighted Ethiopian returns home in darkness as *they'll only wait so long!*

'Tis sad but true: the more we learn, the less we do. Striking a proper balance between *zeal* and *knowledge* continues to plague the people of God. The question has often been asked, "When was the last time you saw a *theologian* who could preach or an *evangelist* who could read and write?" However, even though this is true, the conviction of *preservation* for *propagation* has a consistent, historic tradition. Dr. Hills pointed out that the assurance of Divine preservation can be found in the Great Commission itself.

> In the concluding verses of the Gospel of Matthew we find His "Great Commission" not only to the twelve Apostles but also to His Church throughout all ages, *go ye therefore and teach all nations.* Implied in this solemn charge is the promise that through the working of God's providence the Church will always be kept in possession of an infallible record of Jesus' words and works.[1]

We have already seen that the first translations were occasioned by an impassioned missionary outreach. The man known as "Little Wolf" (Ulfilas) spent a lifetime propagating the preserved Word of God among his Gothic followers. As quickly as England received her first preserved readings via the Wycliff translation, the Good News was propagated by soul-winning Lollards. Having preserved the Word of God in his native German tongue, Martin Luther defined the Gospel as "The preaching and crying of the grace of God," and stated that it "stood not in books and letters but more in oral preaching."

In chapter thirteen, reference was made to John Overall's unsuccessful attempt to win the condemned "Father" Garnet to Christ as he stood upon the gallows. Despite their Calvinistic theology, the King James translators were aggressive "propagators." Paine tells us that John Rainolds wrote a report *six hundred pages long* documenting his effort "to turn from popish ways, a young man confined to the Tower of London." A former Catholic himself, the kindly Rainolds implored his prospect:

> God give you both a soft heart and an understanding mind that you may be able wisely to discern and gladly to embrace the truth when you shall hear it.[2]

As is the case with all soul-winning Christians, Rainolds had his share of persecution. In 1602, as he walked in London's Finsbury Fields, an arrow "fell upon his breast but entered not his body."[3] God was at work protecting the man who would move "his Majestie, that there might bee a newe translation of the Bible."

It is fitting that the most fruitful of the "soul-winning translators" was none other than William Tyndale, the "Father of the English Bible." Foxe tells us that, despite his confinement to a damp and dark dungeon:

> Such was the power of his doctrine, and the sincerity of his life, that during the time of his imprisonment (which endured a year and a half), he converted, it is said, his keeper, the keeper's daughter, and others of his household.[4]

And yet, prior to this Acts 16 experience, Tyndale was the means of conversion for another individual who would accomplish more for God than the combined efforts of the entire Revised Version committee put together! Before *John Rogers* became the godly translator of the Matthew Bible, he was the official Roman Catholic Chaplain of Antwerp. "What happened?" you ask? "Why, he met Tyndale the soul winner, of course!"[5] Little did Tyndale realize that the man he was leading to Jesus Christ would become his trusted co-laborer, preserving his eleventh-hour translation of Joshua through II Chronicles.

With Japheth's enlargement, the *preservation* for *propagation* concept was as strong as ever. In November of 1620, the Mayflower, with 102 passengers on board, dropped anchor in Cape Cod Harbor. Although it would be a few more years before their weaning from the Geneva Bible, the opening lines of the Mayflower Compact left no doubt as to their views on *propagation*. Before taking so much as one step off ship, they wrote:

> In ye name of God Amen. We whose names are underwritten, the loyall subjects of our dread soveraigne **Lord King James** by ye grace of God of Great Britain, France and Ireland king, defender of ye faith, and having undertaken, for ye glorie of God, and **advancement of ye Christian faith** and honor of our king and countrie, a voyage to plant ye first colonie in ye Northerne part of Virginia.[6]

America was founded by a band of soul-winning Christians, committed to the "advancement of ye Christian faith." Like their spiritual ancestors of sixteen centuries, they believed that *preservation* was for *propagation*. Seeking the souls of men has always constituted the highest calling for spiritual Christians. Although one may believe in preservation without practicing propagation, he cannot propagate a message that he does not believe is preserved. The Divine order from hindsight is *revelation, inspiration, illumination, preservation,* and *propagation.*

The problem in our day is that most Christians have exchanged *propagation* for *saturation*—as in the deeper-life movement.

While they can see a backslidden America in such texts as Amos 7:10, *"the land is not able to bear all his words,"* they sadly miss the weightier verses such as Joel 1:17a, which reads, *"The seed is rotten under their clods, the garners are laid desolate."*

Time is surely running out on our nation. As this book was going to press, a *USA Today* article reported that the *American Bible Society* had just released an "MTV-like" video entitled *"Out of the Tombs."* Under the heading of "Behold, rap Bible stories are born on video," a portion of the story reads:

> In *Out of the Tombs,* a linguistically direct translation of Mark 5:1-20, Jesus appears in a dark jacket and T-shirt to battle a drooling, baseball cap wearing demon. The desert scenes, flowing robes and stentorian voices of most Bible films have been traded in for gritty urban landscapes, street garb and rap-like narration.
>
> *Out of the Tombs* is the first in the society's new multimedia translations that use fast-paced, MTV-like images and contemporary music to tell Bible stories. "We targeted music videos as a way to reach younger people," says Fern Lee Hagedorn, director of the multimedia translations department. "The American Bible Society would be the last to advocate not *reading* the Bible, but our mandate to make the scriptures available to every man, woman and child wouldn't be fulfilled unless we used new forms of communication."
>
> The $14.95 video is paired with a 20-page instructional booklet . . . Next on tape: the story of the Prodigal Son and the virgin birth story.[7]

However, the strongest evidence that Jesus will return in our lifetime (and you can bet that He won't be wearing any T-shirt!) is related to the push-button technology of today's modern society. For twelve hundred years, our Bible-believing forefathers evaded papal armies by hiding in such out-of-the-way places as the Swiss, French and Italian Alps, their legacy being "A Trail of Blood." Upon the Mayflower's landing in Cape Cod, an aquatic barrier of over 3,000 miles gave the church unprecedented protection and liberty. Because of this, the victories that would follow Hampton Court were right around the corner.

However, as the twentieth century draws to its climactic end, this same Atlantic Ocean can be crossed in only three hours. The truism, "it's a small world" has a sober application to the modern-day Christian. Concerning our age-old enemy, "the Bloody Whore," there is literally now *nowhere to run!*

At the present time, there are one hundred forty-one Roman Catholics seated in Congress, constituting the largest denomination in that legislative body (more than twice as many as the second place United Methodist total of sixty-five).[8] With a dozen plus Catholic governors added to these and several more in the Cabinet and Supreme Court, not to mention the thousands spread throughout the FBI, CIA and Pentagon, the Church of Jesus Christ is in dire need of One greater than Sir Francis Drake.

Until we hear His trumpet sound (I Thessalonians 4:16), we must not only believe the King James Bible is the preserved Word of God, but we must also win every man, woman, boy, and girl to Christ while there is still time.

As America's young people are seen walking to school wearing bullet-proof vests, exchanging serial-killer cards during recess, shooting one another in the bathrooms and gang-raping their teachers after school, the time has come for fundamental Christians to be not only right on *preservation* but on *propagation* as well!

We must "get the seed out of the barn." *We must reach them while we can!*

What is needed is a school that teaches the whole English Bible. What is needed is a school that will take men from the engine cab, from between the plowshares and teach them the Bible. What is needed is a school that is free from modernism. What is needed is a school that will teach a man how to go out with the Bible under his arms, faith in his heart, and in the power of the Holy Spirit begin in a vacant lot and build a church to the glory of God.

J. Frank Norris

Glossary of Terms

Alexandrian Text – The corrupt manuscript tradition which can be traced to the Alexandrian father, Origen Adamantius (c. 185-254). Codices *Vaticanus* (B) and *Sinaiticus* (א) are the standard-bearers for this text type.

allegorical – The liberal method of hermeneutics, pioneered by Philo and Origen, which would assign a mystical or subjective meaning to Scripture in favor of the normally intended *literal* interpretation.

amanuensis – Akin to a scribe, but more specifically, one who takes dictation, as with *Tertius* in Romans 16:22.

anacoluthon – A phenomenon of Greek syntax which allows for a switch from one grammatical construction to another within the same sentence as a rhetorical device.

ante-Nicene – The era of church history which predates the watershed Council of Nicea in A.D. 325.

Apocrypha – From the Greek *apokryphos* meaning "obscure"; those writings of dubious authenticity belonging to the pre-Christian era, yet excluded from the Old Testament text. Although declared inspired and canonical by the Roman Catholic *Council of Trent* in 1546, the Apocrypha has remained unacceptable to Bible-believing Christians. Significantly, these dozen plus books can be found scattered throughout the *text* of codices *Vaticanus* (B) and *Sinaiticus* (א).

autographs – The original manuscripts of Scripture that were produced by either the Divinely-appointed writer himself or his amanuensis.

canonicity – The Spirit-led process by which God's people were able to differentiate non-inspired writings (pseudepigrapha) from those of Divine authority.

catechetical school (of Alexandria) – The mysterious "Christian" school of Alexandria, founded by Philo, an apostate, Platonic Jew and eventually superintended by the self-emasculated Origen Adamantius, who taught, among other things, that the stars were living creatures. Hailed by modern scholars as the pioneer of textual criticism, Origen was a rabid allegorist and is credited with the majority of textual corruptions associated with the "Alexandrian text type," specifically, codices *Vaticanus* and *Sinaiticus*.

chirography – The handwriting or penmanship style of an individual scribe or manuscript era.

codex – A manuscript in traditional book form (as opposed to one composed of cumbersome scrolls) produced by first-century soul winners to facilitate their Gospel outreach.

colophon – A collection of scribal notes placed at the end of a manuscript containing pertinent information regarding the transcription.

cursive manuscript (or "minuscule") – From the Medieval Latin *cursiuus*, literally "running," the form of manuscript written (as opposed to printed) in a free or "running hand style" employing lower case letters (prompting the additional designation of minuscule from the Latin *minusculus* meaning "small"). Developed by the scribes of Charlemagne, this format was utilized from the ninth to the sixteenth century.

Douay-Rheims Bible – Jesuit translation of the Latin Vulgate constituting Rome's first official "Bible" for English-speaking Catholics. Unleashed as a major stratagem of the Vatican's *Counter Reformation*, the New Testament was published in Rheims (1582), with the Old Testament completed in Douay (1610).

eclecticism – The liberal method of textual criticism which enjoins its adherents to select one manuscript reading over another solely on the basis of the highly subjective criteria of *internal evidence*. This unscholarly rejection of the more conclusive body of *external evidence* – i.e., multiplied manuscripts, lectionaries, versions and patristic testimony – was the *modis operandi* behind the Westcott and Hort Greek New Testament. The eclectic method is to textual criticism what the allegorical school is to hermeneutics.

English Revision of the Authorized Version, 1881-1885 – The project sanctioned by the Convocation of Canterbury in 1870 to revise the Authorized Version, which produced the Revised New Testament in 1881 with the Old Testament following in 1885. With Drs. Westcott and Hort at the helm, the "esteemed" committee completely ignored the Convocation's directive to "introduce as few alterations into the text of the A.V. as possible . . ." to the tune of over 30,000 changes.

extant – In a state of current existence as opposed to that which is lost or perished.

fathers – The venerated leaders of ancient Christendom whose extant writings containing numerous Scriptural citings provide an invaluable witness to the prevailing text of their day.

Gunpowder Plot – Jesuit-inspired assassination attempt against England's James I. The plot was foiled by royal agents on November 5, 1605, less than 24 hours before the convening of Parliament when Guy Fawkes was caught superintending 36 barrels of gunpowder in that assembly's basement.

Hampton Court Conference – The historic gathering in 1604 of Puritan and high church leaders convened by James I which provided the impetus for the A.D. 1611 Authorized Version.

hermeneutics – From the Greek *hermeneuein*, "to interpret," the principles or methodology one follows when attempting to interpret scripture; the two major schools being the *literal* (conservative) and the *allegorical* (liberal).

Hexapla – Origen's highly overrated manuscript consisting of six parallel columns displaying as many Greek and Hebrew translations of the Old Testament.

idiom – From the Latin *idioma*, for "individual peculiarity of language," a phrase that is exclusive either syntactically or in possessing a definition that cannot be extracted from the combined meanings of its word parts.

illumination – The doctrine that man is incapable of comprehending Divine revelation apart from Holy Spirit enlightenment. (Psalm 119:18)

inspiration – From the Greek *theopneustos*, literally, "God-breathed," the Biblical usage of this term centers on the very breath of the Almighty as it enters and quickens that which he has *already* fashioned: human bodies (Genesis 2:7); dry bones (Ezekiel 37:10); prophetic utterances (II Peter 1:21); and written Scripture (II Timothy 3:16) among others. More specifically with application to the Bible, that supernatural influence upon the sacred writers which enabled them to receive and record, with preciseness, the Divine revelation. By virtue of the eternality of God, inspiration (as the veritable "breath of God") cannot be divorced from Holy Ghost preservation (Psalm 12:6-7). See also Job 32:8, 33:4.

interpolation – An unauthorized insertion of a word or words into the text of any document.

itacism – The misspelling of a word in an ancient manuscript, especially by an interchanging of vowels.

Itala Bible (or, *Old Latin*) – A second-century version of the Bible in Latin, the readings of which agree frequently with the King James Bible against those of the modern versions based on codices *Vaticanus* (B) and *Sinaiticus* (‎ℵ) dated mid-fourth century.

italicized words – Those necessary English words (without an equivalent in the Hebrew or Greek manuscripts) inserted by the King James translators for clarity's sake (i.e., as in the case of idioms—"step on the gas," etc.). Although this practice is common to all modern translators, the Authorized Version is unique in its usage of italics to indicate the extent of such activity.

Jesuits – See *Jesus, Society of*

Jesus, Society of – Fanatical order of Catholicism known as the *Jesuits*, established by Ignatius de Loyola between 1534-1539 for the sole purpose of reintroducing papal authority to the "wayward" nations of Protestantism.

lectionaries – Books containing selected passages of Scripture employed by the ancient assemblies for congregational reading. Lectionaries prescribing a weekly lesson were called *Synaxaria* while those consisting of readings for special days such as Easter, Christmas, etc., were called *Menologion*.

lithographic errors – Pertaining to *printing* errors within the earliest editions of the King James Bible.

Latin Vulgate – Jerome's fourth century "revision" of the *Itala Bible* (or *Old Latin*) using the *Vaticanus* readings as his standard. Responsible for ushering in the Dark Ages, the *Latin Vulgate* became Rome's official Bible throughout this benighted period.

Lollards – Followers of John Wycliff; known as the "poor priests" who suffered great persecution for their Bible distribution and street preaching.

Lucianic Recension (or "Antiochian") – Dr. Hort's desperate conjecture that the *Textus Receptus* readings received an official, empire-wide sanction at two church councils between A.D. 250-350 at Antioch. Despite speculation that one *Lucian* (d. 312) led in this venture, the theory remains destitute of any historical corroboration.

Majority Text – See *Textus Receptus*

manuscript – Any portion of a literary work that has been handwritten as opposed to a copy printed from moveable type.

manuscript evidences – The true or conservative mode of textual criticism which would seek to establish the correct text on the basis of all available data, such as the whole body of cursive manuscripts, lectionaries, ancient versions and the writings of the church fathers.

Mariolatry – An excessive and unnatural veneration of the Virgin Mary. Drs. Westcott and Hort were guilty of this Romanish obsession.

mental reservation – Jesuit doctrine of deceit that allows a person to profess one thing while secretly believing something different.

Millenary Petition – Religious petition containing nearly one thousand ministerial signatures which was presented to James I in 1603 by a Puritan delegation incensed with increased Catholic-inspired formalism within the Church of England.

Nestle-Aland Greek Text – Named after the German scholar Eberhard Nestle, this text represents the major adversary of the *Textus Receptus* in our day, being used in most colleges and seminaries. Despite a periodic fluctuation throughout its twenty-six editions, the Nestles's Greek Text is basically the Westcott and Hort text of 1881. The committee for the twenty-sixth edition comprised several unbelievers including Rev. Carlo M. Martini, a Roman Catholic cardinal.

Nicolaitanes – From the Greek compound *Nikao*, "to conquer," and *laos*, "the people" or "laity"; a first-century sect which anticipated Rome's priesthood by dividing God's people into an unscriptural *clergy-laity* relationship.

orthographic discrepancies – Pertaining to *spelling* discrepancies within the various editions of the 1611 Authorized Version.

Oxford Movement – A fruition of the earlier *Tractorian* controversy (1833-1841) which aimed at restoring high church principles within the Church of England. Orchestrated by secret Vatican sympathizers, this effort exerted considerable influence on Drs. Westcott and Hort.

papyrus – A primitive paper fashioned by cross-weaving the dried, flattened stems of the reed-like papyrus plant.

parchment – An ancient writing material prepared from the skins of sheep or goats.

patristic – Of or pertaining to the church fathers or their extant writings.

Peshitta – Ancient version of the Scriptures translated into Syriac about A.D. 145 (antedating *Vaticanus* and *Sinaiticus* by over two centuries) with most of its extant readings agreeing with the King James Bible against those of the modern versions.

plenary inspiration – The doctrine which attributes inspiration to *all* parts of Scripture, thus holding the Bible's declarations on science as being equally authoritative and infallible with those of a theological nature.

post-Nicene – The period of church history which commences with the landmark Council of Nicea in A.D. 325.

preservation – The supernatural conveyance of the inspired text throughout all ages without loss or error.

probabilism – A Jesuit doctrine that regards an opinion as *probable* even if only one theologian can be found in support of its acceptance. Thus, any single Jesuit allied *with* the Pope can make a majority.

pseudigrapha – From the Greek *pseudepigraphos* for "falsely ascribed"; the non-canonical books of spurious authorship composed between B.C. 200-A.D. 200. Whereas the Old Testament Apocrypha gained a limited acceptance, the pseudigrapha writings have been rejected by all, Eusebius calling them "totally absurd and impious."

Puritans – The "purifying" element within the Church of England, occasioned by the political laxity of Elizabeth I, which committed itself to restoring an intolerance of Catholic encroachments, particularly in the areas of formalism and ritual.

revelation – The communication of a truth from God to man that is not discernable by the unaided human intellect.

scribe – One who transcribes manuscripts in a professional or official capacity.

scriptorium – A special room set aside for scribes to use when copying their manuscripts.

Sinaiticus (or "Aleph") – The fourth-century manuscript rescued by Count Tischendorf from a trash can of St. Catherine's monastery (situated at the base of Mt. Sinai) which is second only to the famed *Codex Vaticanus* as a cited witness against the Authorized Version. The pair of "ancient authorities" disagree with each other in over 3,000 places in the Gospels alone.

soul winning – The *propagation* of the *preserved* Gospel.

textual criticism – Theoretically, the scholastic discipline that would employ manuscript evidences to determine the correct Scriptural text. Although the concept of *Biblical criticism* per se has maintained a traditional distinction between the higher (liberal) and lower (orthodox) schools, the latter body is in need of yet a further division. The truly conservative view will prefer *external* evidence (the whole spectrum of multiplied copies, lectionaries, patristic testimony and ancient versions) over *internal* testimony (caprice, conjecture, eclecticism).

Textus Receptus – The predominant Greek tradition of the manuscript era and underlying text for most of the Authorized Version. The honored designation of *Textus Receptus* (for "received text") was first used by the Elzevir brothers in the introduction to their second edition of 1633. Although some technical disagreements exist among scholars, other accepted names for this text would include *Majority, Traditional, Byzantine* and *Antiochian.*

Tractarianism – See *Oxford Movement*

Traditores – Christians who surrendered the Scriptures and or names of fellow believers to the Roman authorities during seasons of imperial persecution.

translation – The rendering of a literary work from one language into another as opposed to the more definitive term of *version* which constitutes a translation from the original tongue.

transmission – The providentially guarded process by which the Scriptures have been reproduced down through the ages.

uncial manuscript (or "majuscule") – Derived from the Latin *uncia* for "twelfth part" (indicating that such characters occupied roughly one-twelfth of a line of print), *uncials* has come to depict the style of ancient printing employing "inch high" (one twelfth) letters. Majuscule, a diminutive of *major,* (from the Latin *majusculus* for large) refers to the exclusive usage of "upper case" type. These block capital letters of such manuscripts as *Vaticanus* and *Sinaiticus* were positioned together with no break between the words. In English, this would be comparable to GODISNOWHERE or perhaps ISAWABUNDANCEONTHETABLE.

universalism – The theological position that all men will eventually be saved. Espoused by liberals in every age (i.e., Origen, Westcott, Peale, etc.) this doctrine denies the endlessness of future punishment. A final restoration of Lucifer himself is also maintained by some.

Vaticanus (or "B") – The fourth-century manuscript named after its Vatican guardianship which remains the catalyst for all modern revisions of the King James Bible. Although joining the celebrated *Codex Sinaiticus* as Alexandrian in origin, *Vaticanus* is found to disagree with this depraved contemporary in over 3,000 instances in the Gospels alone.

vellum – The finest, most expensive parchment material made from antelope or calf skin.

verbal inspiration – The theological position that ascribes Divine authority to the very words of Scripture as opposed to the mere thoughts of the writer.

version – The translation of a literary composition from its original tongue into a second language.

Glossary of Proper Names

Andrews, Lancelot (1555-1626) – Chairman of the Old Testament committee at Westminster who was conversant in fifteen languages. It was said that whenever the godly Lancelot was near, King James "desisted from mirth and frivolity in his presence."

Astruc, Jean (1684-1766) – Roman Catholic physician and textual critic who developed the theory that the Pentateuch was authored by at least two different men, neither of whom was Moses.

Bede, the Venerable (673-735) – British scholar known as "The Father of English Church History," who crowned his literary career with a deathbed translation of the Gospel of John into Middle English.

Beza, Theodore (1519-1605) – Swiss reformer and successor to John Calvin who produced ten editions of his pro-*Textus Receptus* Greek New Testament. He was also a major contributor to the translation committee for the *Geneva Bible* in 1560.

Bois, John (1560-1643) – One of the final editors for the King James translation who may have been the most accomplished scholar of them all. As a child, he was reading Hebrew at age five and writing the same at six. As a student, he corresponded with his teachers in Greek. As a professor, he taught and studied sixteen hours a day, studying on his feet and resting only on his knees. During his career, he mastered sixty Greek grammars.

Burgon, Dean John William (1813-1888) – Outstanding conservative scholar of 19th century Anglicanism whose literary works in defence of the A.D. 1611 Authorized Version have never been refuted. They include: *The Revision Revised; The Traditional Text of the Holy Gospels Vindicated and Established; The Causes of the Corruption of the Traditional Text of the Holy Gospels;* and *The Last Twelve Verses of Mark.*

Campion, Father Edmund (1540-1581) – Former Protestant who turned Jesuit agent; arrested in England for conspiracy and executed in 1581.

Chrysostom, John (345-407) – Bishop of Constantinople recognized as the first historical personality to refer to Scripture as "the Bible." Name means "golden-mouthed."

Clement of Alexandria (150-215) – Successor to Pantaenus as headmaster of Alexandria's catechetical school of theology and philosophy. Among his many doctrinal heresies, Clement believed that Plato's writings were inspired and that the stars were to be worshiped. Origen succeeded him in 202.

Coleridge, Samuel Taylor (1772-1834) – Pro-Vatican poet-philosopher who composed numbers of his works under the "inspiration" of a lingering opium habit. Arthur Hort, writing of his father, stated, "In undergraduate days, if not before, he came under the spell of Coleridge."

Constantine the Great (d. 337) – First of the so-called "Christian" emperors, who commissioned Eusebius of Caesarea to transcribe fifty new Bibles in the aftermath of the Diocletian-Galerius persecution. Most scholars believe codices *Vaticanus* and *Sinaiticus* are two of these fifty copies.

Coverdale, Miles (1488-1568) – Cambridge scholar who produced the first complete English Bible printed in 1535, called *The Coverdale Bible,* as well as *The Great Bible* three years later. The indefatigable reformer was also a part of the translation committee that issued the *Geneva Bible* in 1560.

Diocletian, Emperor Valerius (245-313) – Roman emperor who initiated the tenth and worst of the Imperial persecutions against organized Christianity (303-313). After only two years of bloodletting, Diocletian "lost his marbles" and abdicated his throne to plant cabbages in Dalmatia. The widespread incineration of Holy Scripture carried on by Diocletian's successor-nephew Galerius prompted the "converted" Constantine to later procure fifty new Bibles for his realm.

Edward VI, King (1537-1553) – Pious son of England's Henry VIII (by the Protestant Jane Seymour), whose brief reign of six years was characterized by an unprecedented proliferation of Bibles throughout the land.

Elzevir, Bonaventure (c. 1546-1617) – Dutch printer, whose Leiden publishing house produced seven editions of the Greek New Testament between 1624-1787. His 1633 second edition introduced the term *Textus Receptus* in the preface with the words "Textum Ab Omnibus receiptum" meaning "You have therefore the text now received by all."

Ellicott, Bishop Charles John (1819-1905) – Chairman of the British New Testament Revision Committee (1871-1881) who sided with Drs. Westcott and Hort in their undermining of the Authorized Version.

Erasmus, Desiderius (1469-1536) – Dutch intellectual known as the "journalist of scholarship" credited with producing the world's first printed Greek New Testament. His decided preference for the readings of the *Textus Receptus* over those of *Codex Vaticanus* (as supplied to him by the Catholic Sepulveda) found its fruition in the adage, "Erasmus laid the egg and Luther hatched it."

Eusebius of Caesarea (260-340) – Ancient scholar known as the "Father of Church History," who was commissioned by Emperor Constantine to procure fifty new Bibles in the wake of Diocletian's decade-long persecution. Many believe codices *Vaticanus* and *Sinaiticus* are two of these fifty copies.

Fawkes, Guy (1570-1606) – Catholic soldier of fortune caught superintending thirty-six barrels of gunpowder in the basement of Parliament only hours before the convening of that assembly. Executed in 1606, the would-be assassin of James I continues to be burned in effigy each *Guy Fawkes Day* in Britain.

Garnet, Father Henry (1555-1606) – Superior general of the Jesuit House in England who was hanged, drawn and quartered for his role in the foiled *Gunpowder Plot* of 1605.

Hort, Fenton John Anthony (1828-1892) – Unsaved Cambridge professor who joined Brooke Westcott in producing a Greek New Testament built upon the *Codex Vaticanus*. During the ensuing Revision Committee of 1871-1881, Dr. Hort took the lead in cramming this corrupt text down the throats of his fellow committee members. The end result was the equally perverted Revised Version New Testament of 1881.

Ignatius de Loyola (1491-1556) – Fanatical founder of *The Society of Jesus* (more commonly known as the Jesuits) in 1534. The avowed purpose of his mission was to recapture those "wayward" nations lost to the Protestant Reformation.

Irenaeus (130-200) – Bishop of Lyons and one of several Ante-Nicene fathers whose extant writings contain quotations from Mark 16:9-20. He cites Mark 16:19 in his polemical treatise entitled *Irenaeus Against Heresies,* penned in approximately 177 A.D. (over a century and a half *before Vaticanus* and *Sinaiticus*).

James I, King (1566-1625) – Formerly James VI of Scotland (through the Catholic, Mary, Queen of Scots), his English reign was distinguished by the authorized translation of the Bible which bears his name.

Jerome (342-420) – Catholic scholar who produced the Latin Vulgate by "revising" the Itala version (or, *Old Latin*) according to the readings of *Codex Vaticanus*.

Keble, John (1792-1866) – Professor of Poetry at Oxford, and co-laborer with E.B. Pusey in the pro-Vatican Oxford Movement. This apostate minstrel exercised a strong influence on Dr. Westcott.

Lucian of Antioch (250-312) – The purported catalyst behind Dr. Hort's unfounded conjecture regarding an empire-wide sanction of the *Textus Receptus* readings at two church councils between A.D. 250-350 at Antioch.

Luther, Martin (1483-1546) – Father of the European Reformation who employed Erasmus' second edition Greek text for his epochal German translation of the Bible in 1534. He also provided the protection and encouragement for the exiled William Tyndale to print and smuggle into England his first 3,000 English New Testaments in 1525.

Mabillon, Father Jean (1632-1707) – Benedictine priest whose work *Latin Paleography in Official Documents* helped lay the earliest foundations of textual criticism using the scientific method.

Marcion the Heretic (d. 160) – Ancient enemy of the church known for his repeated mutilation of the New Testament scriptures.

Mary, Queen (1516-1558) – Also known as Bloody Mary. Fanatical Catholic daughter of Henry VIII (by Catherine of Aragon) whose five-year reign of terror caused the deaths of over three hundred English Christians including John Rogers, John Hooper, Hugh Latimer, Nicholas Ridley and Thomas Cranmer.

Matthew, Thomas – see *Rogers, John*.

Maurice, Frederick Denison (1805-1872) – Anglican scholar expelled from King's College in London for denying the endlessness of future punishment. Appointed Knightsbridge Professor of Moral Philosophy at Cambridge in 1866, he impressed upon Dr. Hort an appreciation for the writings of Plato and Aristotle.

Miller, Edward (19th century) – Faithful friend and editorial assistant to Dean John William Burgon. His own literary works include *A Guide to the Textual Criticism of the New Testament*.

Nestle, Eberhard (1851-1913) – German scholar whose initial Greek New Testament of 1898 has undergone twenty-six editions to date. Used in the majority of Bible colleges and seminaries, the Nestle's text is basically identical with the text of Westcott and Hort.

Newman, Cardinal John Henry (1801-1890) – Early leader within the Oxford Movement whose *Tract 90* (written in 1841) evoked a major controversy for attempting to interpret the Church of England's 39 Articles as consistent with Catholicism. The apostate Anglican revealed his true pro-Vatican sympathies by converting to Rome in 1845. Seven years later, Dr. Westcott wrote "and him I all but worship." Newman was elevated to Cardinal in 1879.

Origen, Adamantius (185-254) – One-time headmaster of Alexandria's catechetical school of theology and philosophy. Hailed as the Church's first textual critic, this apostate African denied the existence of Hell and believed that the stars were living creatures in possession of souls for which Christ died. After his Alexandrian excommunication for castrating himself, Origen took his mutilated manuscripts and migrated to Caesarea where he set up another school. Expiring in 254, he bequeathed his library to his favorite pupil Pamphilus. Upon his own death in 309, Pamphilus passed the corrupted readings of Origen on to Eusebius.

Pamphilus (240-309) – Little-known personality representing the central link between the corrupting hand of Origen and modern English Bibles. Before his death in 254, Origen passed his contaminated manuscripts and leadership of his catechetical school on to his favored pupil Pamphilus. Upon his own death in 309, Pamphilus did the same with the church historian Eusebius. With his charge from Constantine to produce fifty new Bibles, Eusebius would have naturally directed his scribes to employ the readings of Origen as their exemplar.

Pantaenus (d. 190) – The first supposedly Christian headmaster of Alexandria's catechetical school of theology and philosophy, referred to by Clement as "the deepest Gnostic."

Philo (20 B.C.-50 A.D.) – Apostate Jewish intellectual who founded Alexandria's infamous catechetical school of science, theology and philosophy. He is also credited with pioneering the allegorical mode of hermeneutics.

Plato – Unsaved, queer Greek philosopher.

Pusey, Edward Bouverie (1800-1882) – Apostate leader of the pro-Vatican Oxford Movement who exerted considerable influence over Dr. Westcott.

Rainolds, John (1549-1607) – Leader of the four-man Puritan delegation at Hampton Court who struck a royal nerve with his request for a new English Bible. Despite his reputation for being "a living library" and "a third university," the good doctor did not live through the project he initiated, expiring in the Providence of God on May 21, 1607.

Rogers, John (1500-1555) – Tyndale's faithful assistant who incorporated his master's "dungeon works" of Joshua through II Chronicles into his own translation under the pseudonym of Thomas Matthew. Rogers was the first of Bloody Mary's victims, being burned at the stake in the presence of his wife and eleven children.

Schaff, Philip (1819-1893) – Ecumenical church historian and professor at the apostate Union Theological Seminary selected by the English Revision Committee to chair their American advisory board.

Scofield, Cyrus Ingerson (1843-1921) – Civil War veteran and accomplished attorney led to Christ by Y.M.C.A. soul winner, Thomas McPheeters. With the financial backing of John T. Pirie, Scofield published his famous reference Bible in 1909. The New Scofield Reference Bible released in 1967 makes the insane claim of using the King James text while noting in the margins over six thousand departures from the same.

Scrivener, Prebendary Frederick H.A. (1813-1893) – Conservative Anglican scholar who contested with Dr. Hort for the *Textus Receptus* readings throughout the decade of work done by the Revision Committee of 1871-1881. His literary works include *A Plain Introduction to the Criticism of the New Testament for the Use of the Biblical Student* and *The Authorized Edition of the Bible (1611), Its Subsequent Reprints and Modern Representatives.*

Semler, Johann Salomo (1725-1791) – One of the earliest of the German theologians to apply the liberal critico-historical method of scientific Bible study to Scripture.

Sepulveda (16th century) – Catholic scholar cited by Tregelles for his correspondence with Erasmus over the purported merits of *Codex Vaticanus.*

Simon, Father Richard (1638-1712) – Catholic priest credited with being the founder of Old Testament criticism. Using the scientific methods, Simon rejected the traditional Mosaic authorship of Genesis through Deuteronomy.

Smith, Miles (1554-1624) – King James translator who was "covetous of nothing but books." In addition to being selected to join the final review board, he was also appointed to write the new Bible's preface entitled *Translators to the Reader.*

Smith, Vance (19th century) – Pastor of St. Saviour's Gate *Unitarian* Church whose participation in the Revision Committee of 1871-1881 evoked bitter controversy, especially with regard to the role he played in removing the word *God* from I Timothy 3:16.

Stanley, Dean Arthur Penrhyn (1815-1881) – Ecumenical Dean of Westminster who created a stir by inviting the Unitarian Vance Smith to the Revision Committee Communion service of 1871. He also made an unsuccessful bid to convert the Abbey into a national shrine for all faiths. Dr. Westcott wrote of him admiringly as early as 1848.

Stephanus, Robert (1503-1559) – Also known as Robert Estienne, or Robert Stephen. French scholar and printer, raised up after the death of Erasmus, who published four editions of the Greek New Testament in 1546, 1549, 1550 and 1551.

Tertullian (160-225) – Ante-Nicene father whose treatise *On Persecution Against Heretics* (A.D. 208) makes reference to the Apostles' autographs as being extant in his day.

Tischendorf, Count Constantin (1815-1874) – German textual critic who discovered Codex א in a trash can at St. Catherine's Monastery in 1844.

Tregelles, Samuel Prideaux (1813-1875) – English scholar who spent forty-two hours examining *Codex Vaticanus*. His own Greek New Testament published in 1870 was decidedly anti-*Receptus*.

Tyndale, William (1494-1536) – British scholar who gave his beloved countrymen their first printed English New Testament in 1525. Possessing the courage of his convictions, he was strangled and burned at Vilvorde (Belgium), his last words being the prayer, "Open the King of England's eyes." With 90 percent of the Tyndale New Testament preserved in our Authorized Version, the pioneer translator has been duly honored as the "Father of the English Bible."

Weldon, Anthony (d. 1650) – Former confidant to James I whose abeyant resentment over being dismissed from the royal inner circle evoked retaliatory accusations of homosexuality against the defenseless king twenty-five years after his decease.

Westcott, Brooke Foss (1825-1901) – Liberal Anglican scholar who conspired with Dr. Fenton Hort from 1853-1871 to produce a radical Greek New Testament predicated on *Codex Vaticanus*. Their corrupt text then became the catalyst for the English Revision Committee of 1871-1881 which resulted in the equally corrupt Revised Version New Testament of 1881.

Wiseman, Cardinal Nicholas Patrick Stephen (1802-1865) – Rector
of the Vatican's English College at Rome from 1828-1840 who returned
to England to become Archbishop of Westminster and a cardinal in
1850. Among the hundreds of English Protestants who were secretly
weaned back to Catholicism by this persuasive papist were Prime
Minister William Gladstone, Archbishop Richard Chevenix Trench and
John Henry Newman.

Wycliff, John (1330-1384) – English Patriot and reformer known as
"The Morning Star of the Reformation" for producing the first entire
Bible in English. The one-hour rental fee for a hand-copied Wycliff Bible
was an entire load of hay. Despised by the Pope, Wycliff's body was
eventually unearthed and burned.

Endnotes

Introduction

[1] David Otis Fuller, D.D., *Which Bible?*, 5th ed., rev. (Grand Rapids, Mich.: Grand Rapids International Publications, 1975), 153.

[2] Robert L. Sumner, *Bible Translations* (n.p.: Biblical Evangelist, 1979), 26.

[3] *Ibid.*, 30.

[4] Ed Reese, *The Life and Ministry of Gipsy Smith (1860-1947)*, Christian Hall of Fame Series, no. 1 (Glenwood, Ill.: Fundamental Publishers, 1975), 12.

[5] Ed Reese, *The Life and Ministry of Reuben Torrey (1856-1928)*, Christian Hall of Fame Series, no. 8 (Glenwood, Ill.: Fundamental Publishers, 1975), 6.

[6] Roger Martin, *R.A. Torrey, Apostle of Certainty* (Murfreesboro, Tenn.: Sword of the Lord Publishers, 1976), 61.

[7] Louis Gaussen, D.D., *Divine Inspiration of the Bible*, trans. David D. Scott (Grand Rapids, Mich.: Kregel Publications, 1841), 25.

[8] Lewis Sperry Chafer, *Major Bible Themes*, rev. (Grand Rapids, Mich.: Zondervan Publishing House for Academie Books, 1974), 17.

[9] Henry Clarence Thiessen, B.D., Ph.D., D.D., *Introductory Lectures in Systematic Theology* (Grand Rapids, Mich.: Wm. B. Eerdmans Publishing Co., 1949), 107.

[10] Harold Lindsell, *The Battle for the Bible* (Grand Rapids, Mich.: Zondervan Publishing House, 1976), 34.

[11] Unpublished Prepared Class Notes: Biblical Introduction Extension Class, "Inspiration" (Philadelphia, Pa.: Philadelphia College of the Bible, 1970), 10.

Chapter II

[1] David Otis Fuller, D.D., ed., *True or False?* (Grand Rapids, Mich.: Grand Rapids International Publications, 1973), 6.

[2] Alexander McClure, *Translators Revived,* with a Foreword and Update by R.E. Rhoades (Litchfield, Mich.: Maranatha Bible Society, 1858), 40.

[3] Arnold Dallimore, *George Whitefield, The Life and Times of the Great Evangelist of the Eighteenth Century*, vol. 1 (Edinburgh, Scotland: Banner of Truth Trust, 1970), 1:500-501.

[4] Alexander Roberts, D.D. and James Donaldson, LL.D., eds., *The Ante-Nicene Fathers*, vol. 7, *Fathers of the Third and Fourth Centuries* (Grand Rapids, Mich.: Wm. B. Eerdmans Publishing Co., 1989), 136.

[5] C.I. Scofield, ed., *The Scofield Study Bible* (New York: Oxford University Press, 1945), 1332.

[6] W.L. Watkinson, *The Life of John Wicklif* (Litchfield, Mich.: Maranatha Bible Society, n.d.), 164-65.

[7] Wilbur N. Pickering, *The Identity of the New Testament Text*, rev. (Nashville, Tenn.: Thomas Nelson Publishers, 1980), 83.

[8] Stewart Custer, *The Truth About the King James Bible Controversy*

(Greenville, S. C.: Bob Jones University Press, 1981), Introduction and 16.

[9] Cindy Lafavre Yorks, "McChurch," *Daily Courier News, U.S.A. Weekend,* 13-15 April 1990, 4.

[10] *Ibid.*

[11] John R. Kohlenberger III, "Which Translation Is Best for Me?", *Moody Monthly,* May 1987, 17.

[12] Norman L. Geisler, *Decide for Yourself: How History Views the Bible* (Grand Rapids, Mich.: Zondervan Corp., 1982), 115.

[13] Arthur Fenton Hort, *Life and Letters of Fenton John Anthony Hort,* (London: Macmillan & Co., 1896), 2:207.

Chapter III

[1] Robert L. Sumner, *Bible Translations* (n.p.: Biblical Evangelist, 1978), 10.

[2] David Otis Fuller, D.D., ed., *Which Bible?,* 5th ed., rev. (Grand Rapids, Mich.: Grand Rapids International Publications, 1975), 101.

[3] Samuel C. Gipp, Th.D., *An Understandable History of the Bible* (Macedonia, Ohio: Bible Believer's Baptist Bookstore, 1987), 119.

[4] Wilbur N. Pickering, *The Identity of the New Testament Text,* 1st. ed., rev. (Nashville, Tenn.: Thomas Nelson Publishers, 1980), 32.

[5] *Ibid.*

[6] Arthur Fenton Hort, *Life and Letters of Fenton John Anthony Hort,* (London: Macmillan & Co., 1896), 1:122-23.

[7] Paul Lee Tan, *Encyclopedia of 7,700 Illustrations* (Rockville, Md.: Assurance Publishers, 1979), 184-85.

[8] "Advertisement," *Saturday Evening Post,* March 1991, inside back cover.

[9] "George Burns Celebrates Eighty Years in Show Business," N.B.C. telecast, 19 September 1983. Host, John Forsythe.

[10] Sumner, *Bible Translations,* 19-20.

[11] Robert L. Sumner, "Dear Abner! ," review of *Dear Abner, I Love You, Joab,* by Dr. Roy L. Branson, in the *Biblical Evangelist,* 1 November 1992, 21.

[12] Alexander Roberts, D.D. and James Donaldson, LL.D., ed., *The Ante-Nicene Fathers,* vol. 3, *Latin Christianity: Its Founder, Tertullian* (Grand Rapids, Mich.: Wm. B. Eerdmans Publishing Co., 1989), 261.

[13] Sumner, *Bible Translations,* 13.

[14] Unpublished Prepared Class Notes: Biblical Introduction Extension Class, "Inspiration," (Philadelphia, Pa.: Philadelphia College of the Bible, 1970,) 10.

Chapter IV

[1] David Otis Fuller, D.D., ed., *Which Bible?,* 5th ed., rev. (Grand Rapids, Mich.: International Publications, 1975), 26.

[2] F.F. Bruce, *The New Testament Documents* (Leicester, England: Inter-Varsity Press, 1943), 16.

[3] Wilbur N. Pickering, *The Identity of the New Testament Text,* 1st. ed., rev. (Nashville, Tenn.: Thomas Nelson Publishers, 1980), 114.

[4] Fuller, *Which Bible?,* 26.

[5] Pickering, *Identity,* 118.

[6] Fuller, *Which Bible?*, 37.

[7] *Ibid.*

[8] Alexander Roberts, D.D. and James Donaldson, LL.D., eds., *The Ante-Nicene Fathers*, vol. 1, *The Apostolic Fathers with Justin Martyr and Irenaeus* (Grand Rapids, Mich.: Wm. B. Eerdmans Publishing Co., 1989), 34.

[9] Pickering, *Identity*, 108.

[10] Alexander Roberts, D.D. and James Donaldson, LL.D., eds., *The Ante-Nicene Fathers*, vol. 3, *Latin Christianity: Its Founder, Tertullian* (Grand Rapids, Mich.: Wm. B. Eerdmans Publishing Co., 1989), 260.

[11] Alexander McClure, *Translators Revived* (Litchfield, Mich.: Maranatha Bible Society, 1858), 39-40.

[12] John William Burgon, B.D., *The Revision Revised*, with a Foreword and Update by R.E. Rhoades (Paradise, Pa.: Conservative Classics, 1883), 257.

[13] Pickering, *Identity*, 37.

[14] *Ibid.*

[15] John William Burgon, B.D., *The Traditional Text of the Holy Gospels*, ed. Edward Miller (London: George Bell & Sons, 1896), 56.

[16] Edward F. Hills, *The King James Version Defended*, 4th ed. (Des Moines, Iowa: Christian Research Press, 1984), 174.

[17] Webb Garrison, *Strange Facts About the Bible* (Nashville, Tenn.: Abingdon Press, 1968), 219.

[18] Fuller, *Which Bible?*, 208.

[19] Burgon, *Traditional Text*, 91.

[20] *Ibid.*, 118-21.

[21] *Ibid.*, 116.

[22] *Ibid.*, 57.

[23] Edward F. Hills, *Believing Bible Study*, 2d. ed. (Des Moines, Iowa: Christian Research Press, 1977), 40.

[24] John William Burgon, B.D., *The Causes of the Corruption of the Traditional Text of the Holy Gospels*, ed. Edward Miller (London: George Bell & Sons, Publishers, 1896), 68-69.

[25] Hills, *Believing Bible Study*, 100.

[26] Burgon, *Revision Revised*, 292-93.

[27] *Ibid.*, 293.

[28] Roberts and Donaldson, *Ante-Nicene Fathers*, 3:261.

Chapter V

[1] C.I. Scofield, ed., *The Scofield Study Bible* (New York: Oxford University Press, 1945), 1069.

[2] Norman L. Geisler and William E. Nix, *A General Introduction to the Bible* (Chicago: Moody Press, 1968), 372.

[3] *Ibid.*

[4] *Ibid.*

[5] Herman C. Hoskier, *Codex B and Its Allies*, vol. 2, *Chiefly Concerning ℵ, but covering three thousand differences between ℵ and B in the Four Gospels.* (London: Bernard Quaritch, Publisher, 1914), 1.

[6] Geisler and Nix, *Introduction to the Bible*, 372.

[7] David Otis Fuller, *True or False?* (Grand Rapids, Mich.: International Publications, 1973), 95.

[8] Jay P. Green, ed., *Unholy Hands on the Bible*, vol. 1, *An Understanding to Textual Criticism, Including the Complete Works of John W. Burgon, Dean of Chichester* (Lafayette, Ind.: Sovereign Grace Trust Fund, 1990), c40-c41.

[9] Geisler and Nix, *Introduction to the Bible*, 372.

[10] Edward F. Hills, *Believing Bible Study*, 2d. ed. (Des Moines, Iowa: Christian Research Press, 1977), 133.

[11] *Ibid.*

[12] Geisler and Nix, *Introduction to the Bible*, 372.

[13] Alexander Roberts, D.D. and James Donaldson, LL.D., eds., *The Ante-Nicene Fathers*, vol. 2, *Fathers of the Second Century* (Grand Rapids, Mich.: Wm. B. Eerdmans Publishing Co., 1989), 192.

[14] Earle E. Cairns, *Chrisitianity Through the Centuries, A History of the Christian Church*, 1st. ed., rev. (Grand Rapids, Mich.: Zondervan Publishing House for Academie Books, 1981), 112.

[15] J.G. Davies, *The Early Christian Church, A History of Its First Five Centuries* (Grand Rapids, Mich.: Baker Book House, 1965), 124.

[16] Colm Luibheid, *The Essential Eusebius* (n.p.: Mentor Omega Book for New American Library, 1966), 213.

[17] Edward F. Hills, *The King James Version Defended*, 4th. ed. (Des Moines, Iowa: Christian Research Press, 1984), 165.

[18] Geisler and Nix, *Introduction to the Bible*, 372.

[19] Frederick H.A. Scrivener, M.A., D.C.L., LL.D., *A Plain Introduction to the Criticism of the New Testament for the Use of the Biblical Student*, ed. Edward Miller (London: George Bell & Sons, 1894), 2:342.

[20] John William Burgon, B.D., *The Revision Revised* (Paradise, Pa.: Conservative Classics, 1883), 422-23.

[21] Alexander Roberts, D.D. and James Donaldson, LL.D., eds. *The Ante-Nicene Fathers*, vol. 1, *The Apostolic Fathers with Justin Martyr and Irenaeus* (Grand Rapids, Mich.: Wm. B. Eerdmans Publishing Co., 1989), 426.

[22] Burgon, *Revision Revised*, 40.

[23] Geisler and Nix, *Introduction to the Bible*, 372-73.

[24] *Ibid.*, 373.

[25] Hills, *King James Version Defended*, 163.

[26] John William Burgon, B.D., *The Causes of the Corruption of the Traditional Text of the Holy Gospels*, ed. Edward Miller (London: George Bell & Sons, Publishers, 1896), 68.

[27] Hills, *King James Version Defended*, 160-61.

[28] Green, *Unholy Hands*, 1:c49.

[29] John William Burgon, B.D., *The Traditional Text of the Holy Gospels Vindicated and Established*, ed. Edward Miller (London: George Bell & Sons, Publishers, 1896), 298-99.

[30] Scrivener, *Criticism of the New Testament*, 2:337.

[31] Burgon, *Traditional Text*, 299.

[32] Green, *Unholy Hands*, 1:c117.

[33] Burgon, *Causes of Corruption*, 70-71.

[34] Green, *Unholy Hands*, 1:c124.

[35] *Ibid.*, c129-30.

[36] *Ibid.*, c26.

[37] *Ibid.*, c124.

[38] *Ibid.*, c130.

[39] Eusebius Pamphilus, *The Ecclesiastical History of Eusebius Pamphilus*, trans. Dr. Hanmer (Grand Rapids, Mich.: Baker Book House, 1989), 65.

[40] *Ibid.*

[41] *Ibid.*

[42] F.F. Bruce, *The Canon of Scripture* (Downers Grove, Ill.: InterVarsity Press, 1988), 302.

[43] Daniel Theron, *Evidence of Tradition* (Grand Rapids, Mich.: Baker Book House, 1958), 69.

[44] Bruce, *Canon of Scripture*, 309-10.

[45] Will Durant, *The Story of Civilization,* vol. 5, *The Renaissance* (New York: Simon & Schuster, 1953), 427.

[46] Christopher Hibbert, *Rome, The Biography of a City* (New York: W.W. Norton & Co., 1985), 135.

[47] Durant, *Story of Civilization*, 5:411.

[48] J.N.D. Kelly, *The Oxford Dictionary of Popes* (Oxford: Oxford University Press, 1986), 254.

[49] Durant, *Story of Civilization*, 5:433.

[50] *Ibid.*

[51] *Ibid.*, 434.

[52] Hills, *Believing Bible Study,* 139.

[53] *Ibid.*, 141.

[54] Daniel G. Reid, *Dictionary of Christianity in America* (Downers Grove, Ill.: InterVarsity Press, 1990), 241.

Chapter VI

[1] John William Burgon, B.D., *The Causes of the Corruption of the Traditional Text of the Holy Gospels*, ed. Edward Miller (London: George Bell & Sons, Publishers, 1896), 40-67.

[2] David Otis Fuller, ed., *True or False?* (Grand Rapids, Mich.: International Publications, 1973), 284.

[3] E.C. Colwell, *"The Origin of Text-types of New Testament Manuscripts,"* in *Early Christian Origins*, ed. Allen Wikgren (Chicago: Quadrangle Books, 1961), 138.

[4] Frederick H.A. Scrivener, *A Plain Introduction to the Criticism of the New Testament for the Use of the Biblical Student*, ed. Edward Miller (London: George Bell & Sons, 1894), 2:264-65.

[5] Arthur Fenton Hort, *Life and Letters of Fenton John Anthony Hort* (London: Macmillan & Co., 1896), 2:228.

[6] Jack Moorman, ed., *Forever Settled* (Collingswood, N. J.: Bible for Today, 1985), 75-76.

[7] Wilbur N. Pickering, *The Identity of the New Testament Text*, 1st. ed., rev. (Nashville, Tenn.: Thomas Nelson Publishers, 1980), 123.

[8] *Ibid.*, 123-24.

[9] *Ibid.*, 125.

[10] *Ibid.*

[11] John William Burgon, B.D., *The Traditional Text of the Holy Gospels Vindicated and Established,* ed. Edward Miller (London: George Bell & Sons, Publishers, 1896), 84.

[12] John William Burgon, B.D., *The Revision Revised* (Paradise, Pa.: Conservative Classics, 1883), 30-31.

[13] Pickering, *Identity*, 125-26.

[14] Fuller, *True or False?*, 271.

[15] John William Burgon, B.D., *The Causes of the Corruption of the Traditional Text of the Holy Gospels*, ed. Edward Miller (London: George Bell & Sons, Publishers, 1896), 13.

[16] *Ibid.*, 212-13.

[17] *Ibid.*, 212.

[18] Pickering, *Identity*, 32.

[19] Scrivener, *Criticism of New Testament*, 2:259.

[20] George Park Fisher, D.D., LL.D., *History of Christian Doctrine* (New York: Charles Scribner's Sons, 1896), 19.

[21] Eusebius Pamphilus, *The Ecclesiastical History of Eusebius Pamphilus*, trans. Dr. Hanmer (Grand Rapids, Mich.: Baker Book House, 1989), 160.

[22] Alexander Roberts, D.D. and James Donaldson, LL.D., eds., *The Ante-Nicene Fathers*, vol. 3, *Latin Christianity: Its Founder, Tertullian* (Grand Rapids, Mich.: Wm. B. Eerdmans Publishing Co., 1989), 262.

[23] Pamphilus, *Ecclesiastical History*, 142.

[24] Alexander Roberts, D.D. and James Donaldson, LL.D., eds., *The Ante-Nicene Fathers*, vol. 1, *The Apostolic Fathers with Justin Martyr and Irenaeus* (Grand Rapids, Mich.: Wm. B. Eerdmans Publishing Co., 1989), 352.

[25] Pamphilus, *Ecclesiastical History*, 215-16.

[26] Burgon, *Revision Revised*, 324.

[27] Hort, *Life and Letters of Hort*, 1:211.

[28] Pamphilus, *Ecclesiastical History*, 110.

[29] Norman L. Geisler and William E. Nix, *A General Introduction to the Bible* (Chicago: Moody Press, 1968), 200-201.

[30] Burgon, *Traditional Text*, 11-12.

[31] Fuller, *Which Bible?*, 99.

[32] *Ibid.*, 92.

[33] Edward F. Hills, *The King James Version Defended*, 4th. ed. (Des Moines, Iowa: Christian Research Press, 1984), 110-11.

[34] Fuller, *True or False?*, 86-87.

Chapter VII

[1] Will Durant, *The Story of Civilization*, vol. 3, *Caesar and Christ* (New York: Simon and Schuster, 1944), 499-500.

[2] Durant, *Story of Civilization*, 3: 500.

[3] Albert Henry Newman, D.D., LL.D., *A Manual of Church History*, vol. 1, *Ancient and Medieval Church History (To. A.D. 1517)*, 1st. ed., rev. (Valley Forge, Pa.: Judson Press, 1933), 59-60.

[4] Alfred Edersheim, *The Life and Times of Jesus the Messiah* (Grand Rapids, Mich.: Wm. B. Eerdmans Publishing Co., 1971), 43.

[5] Edersheim, *Jesus the Messiah*, 40.

[6] Durant, *Story of Civilization*, 3:501.

[7] Edersheim, *Jesus the Messiah*, 40

[8] *Ibid.*, 61.

[9] Gerritt P. Judd, *A History of Civilization* (New York: Macmillan Co., 1966), 62.

[10] Will Durant, *The Story of Civilization,* vol. 2, *The Life of Greece* (New York: Simon & Schuster, 1939), 592.

[11] Judd, *History of Civilization,* 83.

[12] Edersheim, *Jesus the Messiah,* 60.

[13] Durant, *Story of Civilization,* 3:499.

[14] Edersheim, *Jesus the Messiah,* 60.

[15] *Ibid.*

[16] Durant, *Story of Civilization,* 2:601.

[17] *Ibid.,* 3:500.

[18] *Ibid.,* 2:608.

[19] H.G. Wells, *The Outline of History,* rev. (Garden City, N. Y.: Garden City Books, 1961), 305.

[20] Will Durant, *The Story of Civilization,* vol. 4, *The Age of Faith* (New York: Simon & Schuster, 1950), 282.

[21] Edersheim, *Jesus the Messiah,* 59.

[22] Durant, Story of Civilization, 2:593.

[23] *Ibid.*

[24] *Ibid.,* 3:500.

[25] Will Durant, *The Story of Civilization,* vol. 1, *Our Oriental Heritage* (New York: Simon & Schuster, 1935), 137.

[26] *Ibid.,* 3:498.

[27] *Ibid.,* 2:596-97.

[28] Madeleine S. Miller and J. Lane Miller, *Harper's Encyclopedia of Bible Life,* 3d rev. ed. (San Francisco, Calif.: Harper & Row, Publishers, 1978), 84.

[29] Durant, *Story of Civilization,* 2:609.

[30] Chester G. Starr, *The Roman Empire, 27 B.C.-A.D. 476* (New York: Oxford University Press, 1982), 119.

[31] Reader's Digest Association, *Quest for the Past* (Pleasantville, N. Y.: Reader's Digest Association, 1984), 120.

[32] Durant, *Story of Civilization,* 4:123.

[33] *New Standard Encyclopedia,* 1990 ed., *s.v.* "Alexandria, Egypt."

[34] *Ibid.*

[35] Durant, *Story of Civilization,* 4:282-83.

[36] *Ibid.,* 283.

[37] Elizabeth A. Livingstone, ed., *The Concise Oxford Dictionary of the Christian Church* (Oxford: Oxford University Press, 1977), 94.

[38] Alexander Roberts, D.D. and James Donaldson, LL.D., eds., *The Ante-Nicene Fathers,* vol. 2, *Fathers of the Second Century* (Grand Rapids, Mich.: Wm. B. Eerdmans Publishing Co., 1989), 165.

[39] Newman, *Manual of Church History,* 1:272.

[40] George Park Fisher, D.D., LL.D., *History of Christian Doctrine* (New York: Charles Scribner's Sons, 1896), 39.

[41] Roberts and Donaldson, *Ante-Nicene Fathers,* 2:165.

[42] Newman, *Manual of Church History,* 1:273.

[43] Charles J. Thynne, ed., *Church Leaders in Primitive Times,* 2d ed. (London: Wycliffe House, 1896), 286.

[44] Fisher, *Christian Doctrine,* 94.

[45] Philip Schaff, *History of the Christian Church,* vol. 2, *Ante-Nicene Christianity, A.D. 100-325* (Grand Rapids, Mich.: Wm. B. Eerdmans Publishing Co., 1910), 779.

[46] *New Standard Encyclopedia,* 1990 ed., *s.v.* "Alexandria, Egypt."

[47] John William Burgon, *The Traditional Text of the Holy Gospels Vindicated*

and Established, ed. Edward Miller (London: George Bell & Sons, Publishers, 1896), 234.

[48] Norman L. Geisler and William E. Nix, *A General Introduction to the Bible* (Chicago: Moody Press, 1968), 274.

[49] F.F. Bruce, *The Canon of Scripture* (Downers Grove, Ill.: InterVarsity Press, 1988), 69-70.

[50] Frederick H.A. Scrivener, M.A., D.C.L., LL.D., *A Plain Introduction to the Criticism of the New Testament for the Use of the Biblical Student,* ed. Edward Miller, 4th ed. (London: George Bell & Sons, 1894), 1:104.

[51] Ibid, 99.

[52] Bruce, *Canon of Scripture,* 188.

[53] Schaff, *History Christian Church,* 2:779.

[54] Bruce, *Canon of Scripture,* 311.

[55] Roberts and Donaldson, *Ante-Nicene Fathers,* 2:191.

[56] *Ibid.,* 192.

[57] *Ibid.*

[58] Thynne, *Church Leaders,* 283.

[59] *Ibid.*

[60] Bruce, *Canon of Scripture,* 186.

[61] Durant, *Story of Civilization,* 2:520.

[62] *Ibid.,* 521.

[63] Reader's Digest Association, *Quest,* 58.

[64] Durant, *Story of Civilization,* 2:520-21.

[65] Reader's Digest Association, *Quest,* 113.

[66] Roberts and Donaldson, *Ante-Nicene Fathers,* 2:215.

[67] *Ibid.,* 305.

[68] Newman, *Church History,* 1:278.

[69] Roberts and Donaldson, *Ante-Nicene Fathers,* 1:217.

[70] Schaff, *History Christian Church,* 2:172.

[71] Roberts and Donaldson, *Ante-Nicene Fathers,* 2:204.

[72] *Ibid.,* 221.

[73] Williston Walker, *A History of the Christian Church,* 4th ed. (New York: Charles Scribner's Sons, 1918), 89.

[74] Roberts and Donaldson, *Ante-Nicene Fathers,* 2:204.

[75] Thynne, *Church Leaders,* 281.

[76] Schaff, *History Christian Church,* 2:783.

[77] Roberts and Donaldson, *Ante-Nicene Fathers,* 2:307.

[78] Thynne, *Church Leaders,* 292.

[79] Roberts and Donaldson, *Ante-Nicene Fathers,* 2:249.

[80] *Ibid.,* 253.

[81] *Ibid.*

[82] *Ibid.,* 259.

[83] *Ibid.,* 257.

[84] *Ibid.*

[85] *Ibid.,* 270.

[86] *Ibid.,* 275.

[87] *Ibid.*

[88] *Ibid.,* 282.

[89] *Ibid.,* 283.

[90] *Ibid.,* 289.

[91] *Ibid.,* 253.

[92] Schaff, *History Christian Church,* 2:783.

[93] Burgon, *Traditional Text,* 151.
[94] Schaff, *History Christian Church,* 2:790.
[95] Dr. Tim Dowley, ed., *Eerdmans' Handbook to the History of Christianity* (Grand Rapids, Mich.: Wm. B. Eerdmans Publishing Co., 1977), 104.
[96] Alexander Roberts, D.D. and James Donaldson, LL.D., eds., *The Ante-Nicene Fathers,* vol. 4, *Fathers of the Third Century* (Grand Rapids, Mich.: Wm. B. Eerdmans Publishing Co., 1989), 226.
[97] Durant, *Story of Civilization,* 3:613.
[98] *Ibid.,* 614.
[99] Schaff, *History Christian Church,* 2:786.
[100] Roberts and Donaldson, *Ante-Nicene Fathers,* 4:360.
[101] Wilbur N. Pickering, *The Identity of the New Testament Text,* rev. (Nashville, Tenn.: Thomas Nelson Publishers, 1977), 108-9.
[102] Roberts and Donaldson, *Ante-Nicene Fathers,* 4:235.
[103] *Ibid.,* 253.
[104] Allen Menzies, D.D., *The Ante-Nicene Fathers,* vol. 10, *Original Supplement to the American Edition,* 5th ed. (Grand Rapids, Mich.: Wm. B. Eerdmans Publishing Co., 1990), 328.
[105] Roberts and Donaldson, *Ante-Nicene Fathers,* 4:240.
[106] *Ibid.,* 347.
[107] *Ibid.,* 261.
[108] *Ibid.,* 275.
[109] *Ibid.,* 261.
[110] *Ibid.,* 260.
[111] Menzies, *Ante-Nicene Fathers,* 10:340.
[112] Fisher, *Christian Doctrine,* 68.
[113] Earle E. Cairns, *Christianity Through the Centuries, A History of the Christian Church,* rev. (Grand Rapids, Mich.: Zondervan Publishing House, 1954), 112.
[114] Herbert A. Musurillo, *Fathers of the Primitive Church* (New York: New American Library, 1966), 198.
[115] Cairns, *Christianity Through Centuries,* 112.
[116] Fisher, *Christian Doctrine,* 112.
[117] Roberts and Donaldson, *Ante-Nicene Fathers,* 4:365.
[118] Menzies, *Ante-Nicene Fathers,* 10:389-91.
[119] *Ibid.,* 402-6.
[120] Durant, *Story of Civilization,* 3:614.
[121] Menzies, *Ante-Nicene Fathers,* 10:391-95.
[122] Roberts and Donaldson, *Ante-Nicene Fathers,* 4:386.
[123] *Ibid.,* 359.
[124] *Ibid.,* 386-87.
[125] Menzies, *Ante-Nicene Fathers,* 10:383.
[126] Roberts and Donaldson, *Ante-Nicene Fathers,* 4:263.
[127] Menzies, *Ante-Nicene Fathers,* 10:293.
[128] *Ibid.,* 318.
[129] *Ibid.,* 318-19.
[130] *Ibid.,* 343.
[131] Thynne, *Church Leaders,* 324.

Chapter VIII

[1] Herman C. Hoskier, *Codex B and Its Allies,* vol. 1, *A Study and An*

Indictment (London: Bernard Quaritch, Publisher, 1914), *vi*.

[2] David Beale, *A Pictorial History of Our English Bible* (Greenville, S. C.: Bob Jones University Press, 1982), 48.

[3] Herman C. Hoskier, *Codex B and Its Allies*, vol. 2, *Chiefly Concerning ℵ, but covering three thousand differences between ℵ and B in the Four Gospels.* (London: Bernard Quaritch, Publisher, 1914), 1.

[4] Norman L. Geisler and William E. Nix, *A General Introduction to the Bible* (Chicago: Moody Press, 1968), 273.

[5] John William Burgon, B.D., *The Revision Revised* (Paradise, Pa.: Conservative Classics, 1883), 319.

[6] *Ibid.*, 75.

[7] Beale, *Pictorial History*, 52-53.

[8] *Ibid.*, 54.

[9] John William Burgon, *The Traditional Text of the Holy Gospels Vindicated and Established,* ed. Edward Miller (London: George Bell & Sons, Publishers, 1896), 159.

[10] Frederick H.A. Scrivener, M.A., D.C.L., LL.D., *A Plain Introduction to the Criticism of the New Testament for the Use of the Biblical Student,* ed. Edward Miller, 4th ed. (London: George Bell & Sons, 1894), 1:112.

[11] David Otis Fuller, ed., *Which Bible?*, 5th ed., rev. (Grand Rapids, Mich.: Grand Rapids International Publications, 1975), 108.

[12] Geisler and Nix, *General Introduction*, 271.

[13] Fuller, *Which Bible?*, 108.

[14] *Ibid.*

[15] Beale, *Pictorial History*, 52.

[16] Burgon, *Traditional Text*, 159-60.

[17] Scrivener, *Plain Introduction*, 2:283.

[18] David Otis Fuller, ed., *True or False?* (Grand Rapids, Mich.: Grand Rapids International Publications, 1973), 74-75.

[19] *Ibid.*, 75.

[20] *Ibid.*

[21] *Ibid.*, 77.

[22] *Ibid.*

[23] Scrivener, *Plain Introduction*, 2:267-68.

[24] Beale, *Pictorial History*, 51-52.

[25] Scrivener, *Plain Introduction*, 1:120.

[26] *Ibid.*

[27] Fuller, *True or False?*, 77.

[28] Scrivener, *Plain Introduction*, 1:120.

[29] Fuller, *Which Bible?*, 127.

[30] Scrivener, *Plain Introduction*, 1:120.

[31] *Ibid.*

[32] Burgon, *Revision Revised*, 12.

[33] Hoskier, *Codex B*, 1:i.

[34] *Ibid.*, 1-2.

[35] *Ibid.*, 2.

[36] Fuller, *True or False?*, 98.

[37] Wilbur N. Pickering, *The Identity of the New Testament Text*, rev. (Nashville, Tenn.: Thomas Nelson Publishers, 1980), 146.

[38] *Ibid.*

[39] Geisler and Nix, *General Introduction*, 273.

[40] *Ibid.*, 274.

[41] Eusebius Pamphilus, *The Ecclesiastical History of Eusebius Pamphilus*, trans. Dr. Hanmer (Grand Rapids, Mich.: Baker Book House, 1989), 319, 348.

[42] Elizabeth A. Livingstone, ed., *The Concise Oxford Dictionary of the Christian Church* (Oxford: Oxford University Press, 1977), 408.

[43] Philip Schaff, *History of the Christian Church*, vol. 3, *Nicene and Post-Nicene Christianity, From Constantine the Great to Gregory the Great, A.D. 311-600*, 5th ed., rev. (Grand Rapids, Mich.: Wm. B. Eerdmans Publishing Co., 1910), 875-76.

[44] Burgon, *Traditional Text*, 163.

[45] Beale, *Pictorial History*, 54.

[46] Burgon, *Traditional Text*, 161.

[47] *Ibid.*, 163.

[48] *Ibid.*, 234-35.

[49] Frederick Nolan, *An Inquiry into the Integrity of the Greek Vulgate, or Received Text of the New Testament* (London: F.C. & J. Rivington, Publishers, 1815), 83-84.

[50] Scrivener, *Plain Introduction*, 2:266.

[51] Burgon, *Traditional Text*, 167.

[52] Beale, *Pictorial History*, 48.

[53] Robert L. Sumner, "Dear Abner!," review of *Dear Abner, I Love You, Joab*, by Dr. Roy L. Branson, in *The Biblical Evangelist*, 1 November 1992, 21-22.

[54] Scrivener, *Plain Introduction*, 1:109.

[55] Geisler and Nix, *General Introduction*, 385.

[56] Hoskier, *Codex B*, 10.

[57] *Ibid.*

[58] Burgon, *Traditional Text*, 166.

[59] *Ibid.*, 169.

[60] *Ibid.*, 164-65.

[61] Hoskier, *Codex B*, 10-11.

Chapter IX

[1] John Fox, *Fox's Book of Martyrs*, ed. William Byron Forbush (Grand Rapids, Mich.: Zondervan Publishing House, 1969), 212.

[2] *Ibid.*, 214.

[3] *Ibid.*, 215.

[4] F.F. Bruce, *The Books and the Parchments*, 3d ed., rev. (Westwood, N. J.: Fleming H. Revell Co., 1950), 219.

[5] The Venerable Bede, *The Ecclesiastical History of England*, ed. Cecil Jane (Mobile, Ala.: R.E. Publications, n.d.), 12.

[6] Philip Schaff, *History of the Christian Church*, vol. 4, *Medieval Christianity, From Gregory I to Gregory VII, A.D. 590-1073* (Grand Rapids, Mich.: Wm. B. Eerdmans Publishing Co., 1910), 46.

[7] *Ibid.*, 32.

[8] *Ibid.*, 33.

[9] *Ibid.*, 36.

[10] Bede, *Ecclesiastical History*, 93.

[11] Bruce, *Books and Parchments*, 220.

[11] Bruce, *Books and Parchments*, 220.

[12] Norman L. Geisler and William E. Nix, *A General Introduction to the Bible* (Chicago: Moody Press, 1968), 399-401.

[13] Webb Garrison, *Strange Facts About the Bible* (Nashville, Tenn.:Abingdon Press, 1968), 218.

[14] Alexander McClure, *Translators Revived*, with a Foreword and Update by R.E. Rhoades (Litchfield, Mich.: Maranatha Bible Society, 1858), 12.

[15] Geisler and Nix, *General Introduction*, 401-2.

[16] Dr. Tim Dowley, ed., *Eerdmans' Handbook to the History of Christianity* (Grand Rapids, Mich.: Wm. B. Eerdmans Publishing Co., 1977), 269.

[17] Philip Schaff, *History of the Christian Church*, vol. 6, *The Middle Ages, from Boniface VIII, 1294, to the Protestant Reformation, 1517* (Grand Rapids, Mich.: Wm. B. Eerdmans Publishing Co., 1910), 309.

[18] *Ibid.*, 319.

[19] *Ibid.*, 316.

[20] Will Durant, *The Story of Civilization*, vol. 6, *The Reformation* (New York: Simon & Schuster, 1957), 30.

[21] *Ibid.*, 34.

[22] *Ibid.*

[23] J.R. Green, M.A., *A Short History of the English People* (New York: Harper & Bros. Publishers, 1884), 253.

[24] *Ibid.*, 249.

[25] W.L. Watkinson, *The Life of John Wicklif* (Litchfield, Mich.: Maranatha Bible Society, n.d.), 165.

[26] R.W. Thompson, *Footprints of the Jesuits* (Cincinnati, Ohio: Cranston & Curtis Publishing Co., 1894), 342.

[27] David Beale, *A Pictorial History of Our English Bible* (Greenville, S. C.: Bob Jones University Press, 1982), 10.

[28] McClure, *Translators Revived*, 15.

[29] *Ibid.*

[30] John Foxe *et al.*, *Foxe's Christian Martyrs of the World* (Westwood, N. J.: Barbour & Co., 1985), 346.

[31] McClure, *Translators Revived*, 71.

[32] Dowley, *Handbook to Christianity*, 339.

[33] Beale, *Pictorial History*, 10.

[34] McClure, *Translators Revived*, 15-16.

[35] Watkinson, *John Wicklif*, 195-96.

[36] Schaff and Schaff, *History Christian Church*, 6:314.

[37] Barbara W. Tuchman, *A Distant Mirror* (New York: Alfred A. Knopf, 1978), 469.

[38] William L. Sachse, ed., *English History in the Making*, vol. 1, *Readings from the Sources, to 1689* (Lexington, Mass.: Xerox College Publishing, 1967), 137.

[39] McClure, *Translators Revived*, 14.

[40] Green, *English People*, 357.

[41] Foxe *et al.*, *Christian Martyrs*, 345.

[42] *Ibid.*

[43] Schaff and Schaff, *History Christian Church*, 6:353.

[44] *Ibid.*, 356.

[45] Foxe *et al.*, *Christian Martyrs*, 345-46.

[46] Schaff and Schaff, *History Christian Church*, 6:358.

[47] *Ibid.*, 370-71.

48 *Ibid.*, 381.
49 Thomas Armitage, *Bright Lights in Dark Times* (Oak Park, Ill.: Bible Truth Publishers, 1978), 321.
50 Schaff and Schaff, *History Christian Church,* 6:689.
51 *Ibid.*, 687.
52 *Ibid.*, 703.
53 *Ibid.*, 699.
54 McClure, *Translators Revived,* 15.
55 *Ibid.*, 16.
56 Schaff and Schaff, *History Christian Church,* 6:722.
57 Durant, *Story of Civilization,* 6:320.
58 *Ibid.*, 276.
59 *Ibid.*, 285.
60 Owen Chadwick, ed., *The Pelican History of the Church,* vol. 3, *The Reformation,* rev. (Middlesex, England: Penguin Books, 1972), 39.
61 McClure, *Translators Revived,* 22-23.
62 *Ibid.*, 23.
63 *Dictionary of National Biography,* 1921-1922 ed., *s.v.* "William Tyndale."
64 Foxe *et al., Christian Martyrs,* 351.
65 McClure, *Translators Revived,* 30.
66 Lars P. Qualben, *A History of the Christian Church,* rev. (New York: Thomas Nelson & Sons, 1936), 319.
67 Durant, *Story of Civilization,* 6:349.
68 Green, *English People,* 357.
69 Chadwick, *Pelican History,* 3:61.
70 McClure, *Translators Revived,* 27-28.
71 Philip Schaff, *History of the Christian Church,* vol. 7, *Modern Christianity, The German Reformation* (Grand Rapids, Mich.: Wm. B. Eerdmans Publishing Co., 1910), 350.
72 Schaff and Schaff, *Christian Church,* 6:726.
73 Foxe *et al., Christian Martyrs,* 353.
74 *Ibid.*, 357.
75 *Ibid.*, 353.
76 Beale, *Pictorial History,* 20.
77 McClure, *Translators Revived,* 47.
78 Foxe *et al., Christian Martyrs,* 358.
79 *Ibid.*, 354.
80 *Ibid.*, 359-60.
81 McClure, *Translators Revived,* 29.
82 Bruce, *Books and Parchments,* 9.
83 Fox, *Book of Martyrs,* 184.
84 McClure, *Translators Revived,* 32.
85 Beale, *Pictorial History,* 25.
86 *Ibid.*, 27.
87 Bruce, *Books and Parchments,* 224.
88 McClure, Translators Revived, 43-44.
89 *Ibid.*, 44.
90 Foxe *et al., Christian Martyrs,* 422-23.
91 Green, *English People,* 372.
92 *Ibid.*
93 Fox, *Book of Martyrs,* 191.
94 *Ibid.*, 251.

⁹⁵ *Ibid.*, 227.

⁹⁶ *Ibid.*, 194.

⁹⁷ *Ibid.*

⁹⁸ *Ibid.*, 255-56.

⁹⁹ Jim Vineyard, *Great Preachers and Their Preaching*, vol. 1, *John Knox* (Hammond, Ind.: First Baptist Church of Hammond, 1975), 38-39.

¹⁰⁰ Fox, *Book of Martyrs*, 263-64.

Chapter X

¹ Albert Henry Newman, D.D., LL.D., *A Manual of Church History*, vol. 2, *Modern Church History (A.D. 1517-1932)* rev. (Valley Forge, Pa.: Judson Press, 1931), 266-67.

² Alexander McClure, *Translators Revived*, with a Foreword and Update by R.E. Rhoades (Litchfield, Mich.: Maranatha Bible Society, 1858), 56.

³ Kenneth Scott Latourette, *A History of Christianity* (New York: Harper & Bros. Publishers, 1953), 810.

⁴ Norman L. Geisler and William E. Nix, *A General Introduction to the Bible* (Chicago: Moody Press, 1968), 411.

⁵ J.R. Green, M.A., *A Short History of the English People* (New York: Harper & Bros. Publishers, 1884), 468-70.

⁶ Newman, *Church History*, 2:288.

⁷ Ariel Durant and Will Durant, *The Story of Civilization*, vol. 7, *The Age of Reason Begins* (New York: Simon & Schuster, 1961), 130.

⁸ Joseph R. Strayer and Hans W. Gatzke, *The Mainstream of Civilization, to 1715*, 3d. ed. (New York: Harcourt Brace Jovanovich Publishing Co., 1979), 424.

⁹ Durant and Durant, *Story of Civilization*, 7:131, 136.

¹⁰ George Park Fisher, D.D., LL.D., *History of the Christian Church* (New York: Charles Scribner's Sons, 1887), 396.

¹¹ *New Standard Encyclopedia*, 1990 ed., *s.v.* "James I."

¹² Durant and Durant, *Story of Civilization*, 7:136.

¹³ Samuel C. Gipp, Th.D., *The Answer Book* (Shelbyville, Tenn.: Bible & Literature Missionary Foundation, 1989), 9.

¹⁴ Karen Ann Wojahn, "The Real King James," *Moody Monthly*, July-August 1985, 87.

¹⁵ William L. Sachse, ed., *English History in the Making*, vol. 1, *Readings from the Sources, to 1689* (Lexington, Mass.: Xerox College Publishing, 1967), 237-38.

¹⁶ Durant and Durant, *Story of Civilization*, 7:136.

¹⁷ Wojahn, *Moody Monthly*, 87.

¹⁸ *Ibid.*, 88.

¹⁹ *Ibid.*, 87.

²⁰ Nancy Scott Anderson and Dwight Anderson, *The Generals, Ulysses S. Grant and Robert E. Lee* (New York: Alfred A. Knopf, 1987), 205.

²¹ Arthur Fenton Hort, *Life and Letters of Fenton John Anthony Hort* (London: Macmillan & Co., 1896), 1:345.

²² *Ibid.*, 62.

²³ Hort, *Life and Letters of Hort*, 2:11.

²⁴ Wojahn, *Moody Monthly*, 87.

²⁵ Gipp, *Answer Book*, 9-10.

[26] Gustavus S. Paine, *The Men Behind the King James Version* (Grand Rapids, Mich.: Baker Book House, 1959), 7.
[27] *Dictionary of National Biography*, 1960 ed., *s.v.* "James I."
[28] Wojahn, *Moody Monthly*, 88.
[29] McClure, *Translators Revived*, 57.
[30] Paine, *King James Version*, 2.
[31] McClure, *Translators Revived*, 57.
[32] Strayer and Gatzke, *Mainstream of Civilization*, 424.
[33] Sachse, *English History*, 247.
[34] Paine, *King James Version*, 4.
[35] *Ibid.*, 1.
[36] Green, *English People*, 455-57.
[37] David Beale, *A Pictorial History of Our English Bible* (Greenville, S. C.: Bob Jones University Press, 1982), 39.
[38] *Ibid.*
[39] *Ibid.*
[40] Paul Lee Tan, *Encyclopedia of 7,700 Illustrations* (Rockville, Md.: Assurance Publishers, 1979), 860-61.
[41] McClure, *Translators Revived*, 59.
[42] Geisler and Nix, *General Introduction*, 419.
[43] Paine, *King James Version*, 11.

Chapter XI

[1] Gustavus S. Paine, *The Men Behind the King James Version* (Grand Rapids, Mich.: Baker Book House, 1959), 12-13.
[2] *The Encyclopedia Brittanica*, 11th ed., *s.v.* "English Bible."
[3] Paine, *King James Version*, 13.
[4] Leslie R. Keylock, "The Bible that Bears His Name," *Moody Monthly*, July-August 1985, 89.
[5] *Ibid.*
[6] Samuel C. Gipp, Th.D., *The Answer Book* (Shelbyville, Tenn.: Bible & Literature Missionary Foundation, 1989), 61.
[7] Alexander McClure, *Translators Revived*, with a Foreword and Update by R. E. Rhoades (Litchfield, Mich.: Maranatha Bible Society, 1858), 200.
[8] Paine, *King James Version*, 65.
[9] *Ibid.*, 67.
[10] McClure, *Translators Revived*, 201.
[11] Paine, *King James Version*, 67.
[12] McClure, *Translators Revived*, 206.
[13] *Ibid.*, 207.
[14] *Ibid.*, 87.
[15] *Ibid.*, 143.
[16] *Ibid.*, 142.
[17] *Ibid.*, 152-53.
[18] *Ibid.*, 199.
[19] *Ibid.*, 148-49.
[20] Paine, *King James Version*, 22.
[21] McClure, *Translators Revived*, 132.
[22] *Ibid.*, 131-32.

[23] *Ibid.*, 144.

[24] *Ibid.*, 85.

[25] *Ibid.*, 115.

[26] Paine, *King James Version,* 48.

[27] McClure, *Translators Revived,* 82.

[28] Paine, *King James Version,* 62.

[29] *Ibid.*, 84.

[30] Keylock, *Bible Bears Name,* 89.

[31] F.F. Bruce, *The Books and the Parchments,* 3d rev. ed. (Westwood, N. J.: Fleming H. Revell Co., 1950), 229.

[32] Norman L. Geisler and William E. Nix, *A General Introduction to the Bible* (Chicago: Moody Press, 1968), 419.

[33] Paine, *King James Version,* 174.

[34] Bruce, *Books and Parchments,* 229.

[35] McClure, *Translators Revived,* 68-69.

[36] Dr. Tim Dowley, ed., *Eerdmans' Handbook to the History of Christianity* (Grand Rapids, Mich.: Wm. B. Eerdmans Publishing Co., 1977), 370.

[37] John Foxe *et al., Foxe's Christian Martyrs of the World* (Westwood, N. J.: Barbour & Company, 1985), 362.

[38] Charles C. Ryrie, "Before the King James," *Moody Monthly,* May 1987, 23.

[39] Dowley, *Handbook to Christianity,* 370.

[40] McClure, *Translators Revived,* 88.

[41] Bruce, *Books and Parchments,* 229.

[42] Gipp, *Answer Book,* 54.

[43] Keylock, *Bible Bears Name,* 89.

[44] Maynard Mack *et al.,* eds., *The Norton Anthology of World Masterpieces,* vol. 1, *Literature of Western Culture Through the Renaissance* (New York: W.W. Norton & Co., 1985), 18-64; 958-72.

[45] Gipp, *Answer Book,* 12-13.

[46] Robert L. Sumner, *Bible Translations* (n.p.: Biblical Evangelist, 1979), 9.

[47] Gipp, *Answer Book,* 99-100.

[48] *Ibid.*, 100.

[49] Tob. 2:11, *Apocrypha.*

[50] Edward F. Hills, *Believing Bible Study,* 2d ed. (Des Moines, Iowa: Christian Research Press, 1977), 15.

[51] Elizabeth A. Livingstone, ed., *The Concise Oxford Dictionary of the Christian Church* (Oxford: Oxford University Press, 1977), 27-28.

[52] Will Durant, *The Story of Civilization,* vol. 6, *The Reformation* (New York: Simon & Schuster, 1957), 339.

[53] Edward F. Hills, *The King James Version Defended,* 4th ed. (Des Moines, Iowa: Christian Research Press, 1984), 96.

[54] Sumner, *Bible Translations,* 9.

[55] Keylock, *Bible Bears Name,* 89.

[56] Gipp, *Answer Book,* 20-21.

[57] Geisler and Nix, *General Introduction,* 422.

[58] Frederick H.A. Scrivener, M.A., D.C.L., LL.D., *The Authorized Edition of the Bible (1611), Its Subsequent Reprints and Modern Representatives* (London: Cambridge University Press, 1884), 31-34.

[59] *Ibid.*, 30.

[60] Gipp, *Answer Book,* 22.

[61] *Ibid.*, 18.

[62] *Report of the Committee on Versions to the Board of Managers of the*

American Bible Society, Rev. James W. McLane, chairman (New York: n.p. 1852), 7, 11.
[63] Gipp, *Answer Book*, 26.

Chapter XII

[1] Gustavus S. Paine, *The Men Behind the King James Version*, (Grand Rapids, Mich.: Baker Book House, 1959), 176.
[2] James Gilchrist Lawson, *Deeper Experiences of Famous Christians* (Anderson, Ind.: Warner Press, 1911), 135.
[3] Arnold Dallimore, *George Whitefield, The Life and Times of the Great Evangelist of the Eighteenth-Century Revival* (Edinburgh, Scotland: Banner of Truth Trust, 1970), 1:439.
[4] Fred Barlow, *Profiles in Evangelism* (Murfreesboro, Tenn.: Sword of the Lord Publishers, 1976), 69.
[5] Keith J. Hardman, *The Spiritual Awakeners* (Chicago: Moody Press, 1983), 93.
[6] Arnold A. Dallimore, *A Heart Set Free* (Westchester, Ill.: Crossway Books, 1988), 71.
[7] Dallimore, *George Whitefield*, 1:27.
[8] Dallimore, *Heart Free*, 212.
[9] Paul Lee Tan, *Encyclopedia of 7,700 Illustrations* (Rockville, Md.: Assurance Publishers, 1979), 237.
[10] *Ibid.*, 1374.
[11] Ed Reese, *The Life and Ministry of William Booth (1829-1912)*, Christian Hall of Fame Series, no. 6 (Glenwood, Ill.: Fundamental Publishers, 1975), 4.
[12] George Smith, *A Short History of Christian Missions* (London: T.T. Clark Publishers, 1902), 167.
[13] Elmer L. Towns, *The Christian Hall of Fame* (Grand Rapids, Mich.: Baker Book House, 1971), 108.
[14] Ed Reese, "History of Evangelism and Evangelists," Unpublished lecture notes, Hyles-Anderson College, n.d., 15.
[15] Charles L. Thompson, D.D., *Times of Refreshing, A History of American Revivals from 1740 to 1877, with their Philosophy and Methods* (Chicago: M.W. Smith & Co., 1877), 64.
[16] Hardman, *Spiritual Awakeners*, 136-37.
[17] Tan, *7,700 Illustrations*, 1317.
[18] *Ibid.*, 1318.
[19] Dallimore, *George Whitefield*, 1:441.
[20] *Ibid.*, 1:481.
[21] Mrs. Sam P. (Laura) Jones and Walt Holcomb, *Life and Sayings of Sam P. Jones*, 2d ed., rev. (Atlanta, Ga.: Franklin-Turner Co., Publishers, 1907), 145.
[22] Hardman, *Spiritual Awakeners*, 76.
[23] Dallimore, *George Whitefield*, 1:266.
[24] Hardman, *Spiritual Awakeners*, 187-88.
[25] Henry C. Vedder, *A Short History of the Baptists* (Valley Forge, Pa.: Judson Press, 1907), 322.
[26] Jonathan Edwards, *Sinners in the Hands of an Angry God* (Murfreesboro, Tenn.: Sword of the Lord Publishers, n.d.), 13-14.
[27] Dallimore, *George Whitefield*, 1:540-41.
[28] Ed Reese, *The Life and Ministry of George Mueller (1805-1898)*, Christian Hall of Fame Series, no. 23 (Glenwood, Ill.: Fundamental Publishers, 1975), 9-10.

[29] Charles G. Finney, *Revival Lectures, Revivals of Religion* (n.p.: Fleming H. Revell Co., n.d.), 10-12

[30] A.J. Gordon, D.D., *The Holy Spirit in Missions* (New York: Fleming H. Revell Co., 1893), 150.

[31] *Ibid.*

[32] Tan, *7,700 Illustrations*, 395.

[33] Gordon, *Missions*, 152.

[34] Tan, *7,700 Illustrations*, 275.

[35] Gordon, *Missions*, 125-26.

[36] Tan, *7,700 Illustrations*, 275.

[37] Gordon, *Missions*, 209.

[38] Ed Reese, *The Life and Ministry of Gypsy Smith (1860-1947)*, Christian Hall of Fame Series, no. 1 (Glenwood, Ill.: Fundamental Publishers, 1975), 12.

[39] Dallimore, *George Whitefield*, 1:171.

[40] John Pollock, *George Whitefield and the Great Awakening* (Tring, Herts, England: Lion Publishing, 1972), 148-49.

[41] James C. Hefley, *What's So Great About the Bible,* rev. (Elgin, Ill.: David C. Cook Publishing Co., 1973), 76.

[42] W.P. Strickland, ed., *Autobiography of Peter Cartwright, The Backwoods Preacher* (New York: Carlton & Porter Publishers, 1857), 207-8.

[43] *Ibid.*, 192-93.

[44] Dallimore, *Heart Free,* 132-33.

[45] Richard Collier, *The General Next to God* (Glasgow, Scotland: William Collins Sons & Co., 1965), 91.

[46] Barlow, *Profiles,* 90.

[47] Ed Reese, *The Life and Ministry of David Livingstone (1813-1873)* (Glenwood, Ill.: Fundamental Publishers, 1975), 13.

[48] Tan, *7,700 Illustrations,* 1041.

[49] Dr. Jack Hyles, *The Blood, The Book And The Body* (Hammond, In.: Hyles-Anderson Publishers, 1992), 43.

Chapter XIII

[1] Ariel Durant and Will Durant, *The Story of Civilization,* vol. 7, *The Age of Reason Begins* (New York: Simon & Schuster, 1961), 141.

[2] Christopher Hibbert *et al., Tower of London* (New York: Newsweek, 1971), 86.

[3] J.R. Green, M.A., *A Short History of the English People* (New York: Harper & Bros. Publishers, 1884), 470.

[4] Gustavus S. Paine, *The Men Behind the King James Version* (Grand Rapids, Mich.: Baker Book House, 1959), 88.

[5] Hibbert *et al., Tower,* 87.

[6] Paine, *King James Version,* 89.

[7] *Ibid.*, 90.

[8] *Ibid.*, 47.

[9] Green, *English People,* 471.

[10] F.F. Bruce, *The Books and the Parchments,* 3d ed., rev. (Westwood, N. J.: Fleming H. Revell Co., 1963), 228.

[11] Will Durant, *The Story of Civilization,* vol. 6, *The Reformation* (New York:

Simon & Schuster, 1957), 418.

[12] Dave Hunt, *Global Peace and the Rise of Antichrist* (Eugene, Oreg.: Harvest House Publishers, 1990), 149.

[13] *Ibid.*, 105.

[14] Dr. Tim Dowley, ed., *Eerdmans' Handbook to the History of Christianity* (Grand Rapids, Mich.: Wm. B. Eerdmans Publishing Co., 1977), 323.

[15] John Foxe *et al.*, *Foxe's Christian Martyrs of the World* (Westwood, N. J.: Barbour & Company, 1985), 233.

[16] Dowley, *Handbook to Chritianity*, 639.

[17] *Ibid.*, 380.

[18] *Ibid.*, 639.

[19] John Fox, *Fox's Book of Martyrs*, ed. William Byron Forbush (Grand Rapids, Mich.: Zondervan Publishing House, 1967), 47.

[20] Durant, *Story of Civilization*, 6:397.

[21] Christopher Hibbert, *Rome, The Biography of a City* (New York: W.W. Norton & Company, 1985), 84.

[22] Edmond Paris, *Convert . . . or Die!*, trans. Lois Perkins (Chino, Calif.: Chick Publications, n.d.), 59.

[23] *Ibid.*, 130.

[24] Avro Manhattan, *The Vatican's Holocaust* (Springfield, Mo.: Ozark Books, 1986), 52.

[25] *Ibid.*, 49.

[26] Paris, *Convert*, 60.

[27] *Ibid.*, 135.

[28] Manhattan, *Holocaust*, 48.

[29] Paris, *Convert*, 106.

[30] *Ibid.*, 191.

[31] *Ibid.*, 106.

[32] Edmond Paris, *The Vatican Against Europe*, trans. A. Robson (London: Wickliffe Press, 1961), 209.

[33] Paris, *Convert*, 129.

[34] *Ibid.*, 189.

[35] Manhattan, *Holocaust*, 33.

[36] Alexander McClure, *Translators Revived*, with a Foreword and Update by R.E. Rhoades (Litchfield, Mich.: Maranatha Bible Society, 1858), 71-72.

[37] Edmond Paris, *The Secret History of the Jesuits*, trans. (Chino, Calif.: Chick Publications, 1975), 21.

[38] *Ibid.*, 26.

[39] *Ibid.*

[40] Clyde L. Manschreck, ed., *A History of Christianity*, 2d ed. (Englewood Cliffs, N. J.: Prentice-Hall, 1964), 134-35.

[41] Albert Henry Newman, D.D., LL.D., *A Manual of Church History*, vol. 2, *Modern Church History (A.D. 1517-1932)*, rev. (Valley Forge, Pa.: Judson Press, 1931), 374, 383.

[42] Durant, *Story of Civilization*, 6:915.

[43] Newman, *Church History*, 2:374.

[44] *Ibid.*, 383.

[45] Paris, *Secret History*, 30.

[46] Loraine Boettner, *Roman Catholicism* (Philadelphia, Pa.: Presbyterian & Reformed Publishing Co., 1962), 67.

[47] Paris, *Secret History*, 27.

[48] *Ibid.*, 191.

[49] *Ibid.*, 69.
[50] *Ibid.*, 75.
[51] Newman, *Church History*, 2:380.
[52] *Ibid.*, 374.
[53] *Ibid.*, 375.
[54] *Ibid.*, 383.
[55] *Ibid.*
[56] Manschreck, *History of Christianity*, 114.
[57] *Ibid.*, 144.
[58] Ariel Durant and Will Durant, *The Story of Civilization,* vol. 7, *The Age of Reason Begins* (New York: Simon & Schuster, 1961), 355.
[59] Durant, *Story of Civilization,* 6:413.
[60] Dowley, *Handbook to Christianity,* 377.
[61] Paul Lee Tan, *Encyclopedia of 7,700 Illustrations* (Rockville, Md.: Assurance Publishers, 1979), 204.
[62] Newman, *Church History*, 2:392-93.
[63] Paris, *Secret History,* 36.
[64] Newman, *Church History,* 2:410-11.
[65] Durant and Durant, *Story of Civilization,* 7:20.
[66] *Ibid.*
[67] Paris, *Secret History,* 43.
[68] Green, *English People,* 412.
[69] Durant and Durant, *Story of Civilization,* 7:21.
[70] Hibbert et. al., *Tower,* 89.
[71] Durant and Durant, *Story of Civilization,* 7:22.
[72] Hibbert et. al., *Tower,* 79.
[73] Durant and Durant, *Story of Civilization,* 7:35.
[74] Neil Munro, "Fleet's Threatening Approach," *Military History Magazine,* November 1990, 29.
[75] Durant and Durant, *Story of Civilization,* 7:35.
[76] Munro, *Fleet's Threatening,* 31.
[77] Durant and Durant, *Story of Civilization,* 7:36.
[78] *Ibid.*, 35
[79] Newman, *Church History,* 2:375.
[80] Henry Bettenson, ed., *Documents of the Christian Church,* 2d ed. (London: Oxford University Press, 1963), 375.
[81] Samuel C. Gipp, Th.D., *An Understandable History of the Bible* (Macedonia, Ohio: Bible Believer's Baptist Bookstore, 1987), 98-99.
[82] Elizabeth A. Livingstone, ed., *The Concise Oxford Dictionary of the Christian Church* (Oxford: Oxford University Press, 1977), 476.
[83] *Ibid.*, 314.
[84] *Ibid.*, 38.
[85] *Ibid.*, 468.
[86] *Ibid.*, 424.
[87] *Ibid.*, 117.
[88] *Ibid.*, 478-79.
[89] *Ibid.*, 161.
[90] *Ibid.*, 281.
[91] *Ibid.*, 556.
[92] *Ibid.*, 303.
[93] Gipp, *Understandable History,* 114.
[94] Arthur Fenton Hort, *Life and Letters of Fenton John Anthony Hort*

(London: Macmillan & Co., 1896), 2:186.

[95] Norman L. Geisler, Ph.D., *Decide for Yourself, How History Views the Bible* (Grand Rapids, Mich.: Zondervan Publishing Co., 1982), back jacket cover.

Chapter XIV

[1] Arthur Fenton Hort, *Life and Letters of Fenton John Anthony Hort* (London: Macmillan & Co., 1896), 1:279.

[2] Arthur Westcott, *Life and Letters of Brooke Foss Westcott* (London: Macmillan & Co., 1903), 1:ix.

[3] Hort, *Life and Letters of Hort,* 1:7-8.

[4] *Ibid.,* 191.

[5] Westcott, *Life and Letters of Westcott,* 1:290.

[6] Hort, *Life and Letters of Hort,* 2:165.

[7] Westcott, *Life and Letters of Westcott,* 1:13.

[8] *Ibid.,* 7.

[9] *Ibid.,* 19-20.

[10] *Ibid.,* 13.

[11] *Ibid.,* 52.

[12] *Ibid.,* 56-57.

[13] *Ibid.,* 52.

[14] *Ibid.,* 92.

[15] *Ibid.,* 94.

[16] *Ibid.,* 98.

[17] *Ibid.,* 111.

[18] *Ibid.,* 90.

[19] *Ibid.,* 254.

[20] *Ibid.,* 255.

[21] *Ibid.,* 119.

[22] *Ibid.,* 118.

[23] Hort, *Life and Letters of Hort,* 1:42.

[24] Samuel Gipp, Th.D., *An Understandable History of the Bible* (Macedonia, Ohio: Bible Believer's Baptist Bookstore, 1987), 121.

[25] *Ibid.,* 121-22.

[26] Sir Sidney Lee and Sir Leslie Stephen, eds., *Dictionary of National Biography* (London: Oxford University Press, 1960), 4:765-66.

[27] Elizabeth A. Livingstone, *The Concise Oxford Dictionary of the Christian Church* (Oxford: Oxford University Press, 1977), 286.

[28] Lee and Stephen, *National Biography,* 10:1180.

[29] Westcott, *Life and Letters of Westcott,* 1:79.

[30] Hort, *Life and Letters of Hort,* 2:455.

[31] *Ibid.,* 1:42.

[32] *Ibid.,* 202.

[33] Westcott, *Life and Letters of Westcott,* 1:175-76.

[34] Bob L. Ross, *A Pictorial Biography of C.H. Spurgeon* (Pasadena, Tex.: Pilgrim Publications, 1974), 109.

[35] Westcott, *Life and Letters of Westcott,* 332.

[36] *Ibid.,* 135.

[37] *Ibid.*

[38] *Ibid.,* 2:69.

[39] *Ibid.*, 1:53.

[40] *Ibid.*, 217.

[41] *Ibid.*, 163.

[42] *Ibid.*, 164.

[43] *Ibid.*, 223.

[44] *Ibid.*, 158.

[45] *Ibid.*, 2:309.

[46] Hort, *Life and Letters of Hort*, 1:231.

[47] *Ibid.*, 2:423.

[48] Westcott, *Life and Letters of Westcott*, 1:77.

[49] *Ibid.*, 95.

[50] *Ibid.*, 43.

[51] Hort, *Life and Letters of Hort*, 2:30.

[52] *Ibid.*, 68-69.

[53] *Ibid.*, 227.

[54] Avro Manhattan, *The Vatican in World Politics* (New York: Horizon Press, 1949), 67.

[55] Hort, *Life and Letters of Hort*, 2:393.

[56] Manhattan, *Vatican Politics*, 382-83.

[57] Avro Manhattan, *The Vatican Moscow Washington Alliance* (Chino, Calif.: Chick Publications, 1986), 338.

[58] *Ibid.*, 342-43.

[59] Westcott, *Life and Letters of Westcott*, 1:81.

[60] *Ibid.*, 183.

[61] *Ibid.*, 8.

[62] Hort, *Life and Letters of Hort*, 2:49-50.

[63] Westcott, *Life and Letters of Westcott*, 1:33.

[64] *Ibid.*, 321.

[65] *Ibid.*, 353.

[66] Hort, *Life and Letters of Hort*, 1:34.

[67] *Ibid.*, 43.

[68] *Ibid.*, 59-60.

[69] *Ibid.*, 77.

[70] *Ibid.*, 2:86.

[71] *Ibid.*, 51.

[72] Westcott, *Life and Letters of Westcott*, 1:160.

[73] Hort, *Life and Letters of Hort*, 1:76.

[74] *Ibid.*, 2:81.

[75] *Ibid.*, 224.

[76] *Ibid.*, 273.

[77] Westcott, *Life and Letters of Westcott*, 1:189.

[78] *Ibid.*, 292.

[79] *Ibid.*, 207.

[80] Hort, *Life and Letters of Hort*, 1:420.

[81] *Ibid.*, 421-22.

[82] *Ibid.*, 77.

[83] *Ibid.*, 2:329.

[84] *Ibid.*, 1:414.

[85] *Ibid.*, 416.

[86] *Ibid.*, 2:398.

[87] *Ibid.*, 1:473-74.

[88] Westcott, *Life and Letters of Westcott*, 2:49, 253, 394.

[89] *Ibid.*, 308.
[90] *Ibid.*, 268.
[91] Hort, *Life and Letters of Hort,* 1:136.
[92] *Ibid.*, 219.
[93] *Ibid.*, 428.
[94] *Ibid.*, 2:64.
[95] *Ibid.*, 335.
[96] *Ibid.*, 1:387.
[97] *Ibid.*, 121.
[98] *Ibid.*, 117.
[99] *Ibid.*, 120.
[100] *Ibid.*, 275.
[101] *Ibid.*, 2:336.
[102] Westcott, *Life and Letters of Westcott,* 2:349.
[103] *Ibid.*, 184.
[104] *Ibid.*, 37.
[105] Ed Reese, *The Life and Ministry of William Booth (1829-1912)* Christian Hall of Fame Series, no. 6 (Glenwood, Ill.: Fundamental Publishers, 1975), 5.
[106] Westcott, *Life and Letters of Westcott,* 1:348.
[107] Reese, *William Booth,* 9-10.
[108] *Ibid.*, 12.
[109] *Ibid.*
[110] Westcott, *Life and Letters of Westcott,* 2:14.
[111] Richard Collier, *The General Next to God* (Glasgow, Scotland: William Collins Sons & Co., 1965), 193.
[112] Susannah Spurgeon and Joseph Harrald, eds., *C.H. Spurgeon Autobiography,* vol. 1, *The Early Years,* rev. ed. (Carlisle, Pa.: Banner of Truth Trust, 1962), 193-94.
[113] Hort, *Life and Letters of Hort,* 1:358.
[114] *Ibid.*, 359.
[115] Spurgeon and Harrald, *Autobiography,* 1:533.
[116] Hort, *Life and Letters of Hort,* 1:388.
[117] *Ibid.*, 360.
[118] *Ibid.*, 2:207.
[119] *Ibid.*
[120] *Ibid.*, 1:280.
[121] *Ibid.*, 49.
[122] W.P. Strickland, ed., *Autobiography of Peter Cartwright, The Backwoods Preacher* (New York: Carlton & Porter Publishers, 1857), 444.
[123] Westcott, *Life and Letters of Westcott,* 1:302.
[124] *Ibid.*, 2:175.
[125] *Ibid.*, 1:317.
[126] John Pollock, *George Whitefield and the Great Awakening* (Bellville, Mich.: Lion Publishing Corporation, 1972), 263.
[127] Paul Lee Tan, *Encyclopedia of 7,700 Illustrations* (Rockville, Md.: Assurance Publishers, 1979), 1044.
[128] Westcott, *Life and Letters of Westcott,* 2:288-89.
[129] Fred Barlow, *Profiles in Evangelism* (Murfreesboro, Tenn.: Sword of the Lord Publishers, 1976), 169-70.
[130] Westcott, *Life and Letters of Westcott,* 2:17-18.
[131] Hort, *Life and Letters of Hort,* 1:138-41.
[132] Westcott, *Life and Letters of Westcott,* 1:309.

[133] *Ibid.*, 263-305.

[134] Robert L. Sumner, *Bible Translations* (n.p.: Biblical Evangelist, 1979), 6.

[135] Stewart Custer, *The Truth About the King James Version Controversy* (Greenville, S. C.: Bob Jones University Press, 1981), 26.

[136] Hort, *Life and Letters of Hort,* 1:240.

[137] *Ibid.*, 424.

[138] *Ibid.*

[139] Westcott, *Life and Letters of Westcott,* 2:69.

[140] *Ibid.*, 407.

Chapter XV

[1] Arthur Fenton Hort, *Life and Letters of Fenton John Anthony Hort* (London: Macmillan & Co., 1896), 1:139-41.

[2] *Ibid.*, 2:34.

[3] *Ibid.*, 1:459.

[4] Arthur Westcott, *Life and Letters of Brooke Foss Westcott* (London: Macmillan & Co., 1903), 2:23.

[5] Hort, *Life and Letters of Hort,* 1:264.

[6] *Ibid.*, 125.

[7] Westcott, *Life and Letters of Westcott,* 2:284.

[8] Hort, *Life and Letters of Hort,* 1:211.

[9] Westcott, *Life and Letters of Westcott,* 1:228-29.

[10] *Ibid.*, 2:85.

[11] Hort, *Life and Letters of Hort,* 1:400.

[12] *Ibid.*, 212-13.

[13] *Ibid.*, 2:133.

[14] *Ibid.*, 1:264.

[15] Westcott, *Life and Letters of Westcott,* 1:218.

[16] *Ibid.*, 256.

[17] *Ibid.*, 252.

[18] Hort, *Life and Letters of Hort,* 1:400.

[19] *Ibid.*, 445.

[20] *Ibid.*, 403.

[21] *Ibid.*, 2:283.

[22] *Ibid.*, 1:424.

[23] Westcott, *Life and Letters of Westcott,* 1:319-20.

[24] Hort, *Life and Letters of Hort,* 1:369.

[25] *Ibid.*, 2:246-47.

[26] Samuel C. Gipp, Th.D., *An Understandable History of the Bible* (Macedonia, Ohio: Bible Believer's Baptist Bookstore, 1987), 162.

[27] John William Burgon, B.D., *The Revision Revised* (Paradise, Pa.: Conservative Classics, 1883), 3.

[28] *Ibid.*, 6.

[29] Hort, *Life and Letters of Hort,* 2:136.

[30] Burgon, *Revision Revised,* 507.

[31] *Ibid.*

[32] Westcott, *Life and Letters of Westcott,* 1:394.

[33] *Ibid.*, 168.

[34] Hort, *Life and Letters of Hort,* 2:140.

[35] *Ibid.*

[36] *Ibid.*, 139.

[37] Burgon, *Revision Revised*, 515.

[38] *Ibid.*, xlii.

[39] *Ibid.*, 368-69.

[40] *Ibid.*, 368.

[41] *Ibid.*, 2-3.

[42] *Ibid.*, 3.

[43] Hort, *Life and Letters of Hort*, 2:237.

[44] David Otis Fuller, D.D., ed., *Which Bible?*, 5th ed., rev. (Grand Rapids, Mich.: Grand Rapids International Publications, 1975), 290.

[45] *Ibid.*

[46] Westcott, *Life and Letters of Westcott*, 1:390.

[47] *Ibid.*, 391.

[48] *Ibid.*, 392-93.

[49] *Ibid.*, 393.

[50] Fuller, *Which Bible?*, 282.

[51] Burgon, *Revision Revised*, 6.

[52] Fuller, *Which Bible?*, 291.

[53] Hort, *Life and Letters of Hort*, 2:248.

[54] Burgon, *Revision Revised*, 307.

[55] *Ibid.*, 307-8.

[56] *Ibid.*, 355.

[57] *Ibid.*, xxv.

[58] Fuller, *Which Bible?*, 293.

[59] *Ibid.*, 291.

[60] Hort, *Life and Letters of Hort*, 2:237-38.

[61] *Ibid.*, 236.

[62] *Ibid.*

[63] *Ibid.*, 1:10.

[64] Westcott, *Life and Letters of Westcott*, 1:5.

[65] *Ibid.*, 396.

[66] David Otis Fuller, D.D., ed., *True or False?* (Grand Rapids, Mich.: Grand Rapids International Publications, 1973), 93.

[67] Hort, *Life and Letters of Hort*, 2:236.

[68] Burgon, *Revision Revised*, 109.

[69] *Ibid.*, 229.

[70] Fuller, *Which Bible?*, 291.

[71] Burgon, *Revision Revised*, iv.

[72] Edward Miller, *A Guide to the Textual Criticism of the New Testament* (Collingswood, N. J.: Dean Burgon Society, 1979), 3.

[73] D.A. Waite, Ph.D., *The King James Bible's Fourfold Superiority* (Collingswood, N. J.: Bible for Today, 1992), 31.

[74] Norman L. Geisler and William E. Nix, *A General Introduction to the Bible* (Chicago, Ill.: Moody Press, 1968), 424.

[75] Burgon, *Revision Revised*, 130.

[76] *Ibid.*, 3.

[77] *Ibid.*, 211.

[78] *Ibid.*, 237.

[79] Geisler and Nix, *General Introduction*, 424.

[80] Miller, *Guide to Textual Criticism*, 3.

[81] Burgon, *Revision Revised*, 127.

[82] *Ibid.*, 138.
[83] *Ibid.*, 127.
[84] Hort, *Life and Letters of Hort*, 2:236.
[85] Burgon, *Revision Revised*, 226.
[86] *Ibid.*, 112.
[87] *Ibid.*, 225-26.
[88] *Ibid.*, 155-56.
[89] *Ibid.*, 164.
[90] *Ibid.*, 217-19.
[91] *Ibid.*, 171.
[92] *Ibid.*, 174.
[93] *Ibid.*, 203.
[94] *Ibid.*, 207.
[95] Westcott, *Life and Letters of Westcott*, 1:229.
[96] Hort, *Life and Letters of Hort*, 2:243-44.
[97] Burgon, *Revision Revised*, 105-6.
[98] Hort, *Life and Letters of Hort*, 2:289.
[99] *Ibid.*
[100] Westcott, *Life and Letters of Westcott*, 1:404.
[101] Hort, *Life and Letters of Hort*, 2:239.
[102] Burgon, *Revision Revised*, 376.
[103] *Ibid.*, 514-15.
[104] Hort, *Life and Letters of Hort*, 2:239-42.
[105] Westcott, *Life and Letters of Westcott*, 1:404.

Chapter XVI

[1] John William Burgon, B.D., *The Revision Revised* (Paradise, Pa.: Conservative Classics, 1883), 312.
[2] *Ibid.*, 345.
[3] *Ibid.*, 508.
[4] Arthur Fenton Hort, *Life and Letters of Fenton John Anthony Hort* (London: Macmillan & Co., 1896), 2:139.
[5] David Otis Fuller, D.D., *Which Bible?*, 5th ed., rev. (Grand Rapids, Mich.: Grand Rapids International Publications, 1975), 304.
[6] *Ibid.*, 289.
[7] *Ibid.*, 305-6.
[8] Philip Schaff, *History of the Christian Church,* vol. 7, *Modern Christianity, The German Reformation*, 2d ed., rev. (Grand Rapids, Mich.: Wm. B. Eerdmans Publishing Co., 1910), 18.
[9] *Ibid.*, 355.
[10] Philip Schaff, *History of the Christian Church,* vol. 3, *Nicene and Post-Nicene Christianity; From Constantine the Great to Gregory the Great, A.D. 311-600*, 5th ed., rev. (Grand Rapids, Mich.: Wm. B. Eerdmans Publishing Co., 1910), 1027.
[11] Fuller, *Which Bible?*, pp. 308-9.
[12] William R. Moody, *The Life of Dwight L. Moody* (Murfreesboro, Tenn.: Sword of the Lord Publishers, 1900), 416-17.
[13] *Ibid.*, 415-16.
[14] *Ibid.*, 573-74.

[15] Curtis Vaughn, Th.D., ed., *The New Testament from 26 Translations* (Grand Rapids, Mich.: Zondervan Publishing House, 1967), Acknowledgements.

[16] Barry Burton, *Let's Weigh the Evidence* (Chino, Calif.: Chick Publications, 1983), 13.

[17] Avro Manhattan, *The Vatican Moscow Washington Alliance*, 2d ed. (Chino, Calif.: Chick Publications, 1986), 64.

[18] *Ibid.*, 63.

[19] Avro Manhattan, *Murder in the Vatican* (Springfield, Mo.: Ozark Books, 1985), 6.

[20] Avro Manhattan, *The Dollar and the Vatican* (Springfield, Mo.: Ozark Books, 1988), 76-77.

[21] Avro Manhattan, *The Vatican Billions* (Chino, Calif.: Chick Publications, 1983), 188-89.

[22] *Ibid.*, 184.

[23] *Ibid.*, 207.

[24] Samuel C. Gipp, Th.D., *An Understandable History of the Bible* (Macedonia, Ohio: Bible Believer's Baptist Bookstore, 1987), 196.

[25] Lockman Foundation, *New American Standard Bible* (Glendale, Calif.: Gospel Light Publishers, 1960), vi-vii.

[26] "Zondervan, Blessed with Bible Contract, Lifts Profit Forecast," *Wall Street Journal*, 16 November 1978, 18.

[27] The Holy Bible, Revised Standard Version (Camden, N. J.: Thomas Nelson, New Testament, 1946, Old Testament, 1952), Preface.

[28] The Holy Bible, New King James Version (Nashville, Tenn.: Thomas Nelson, 1982), iii, vi.

[29] Annetta Miller, "He Reaps What He Sows," *Newsweek*, 26 October 1992, 57.

[30] Holy Bible, New International Version (East Brunswick, N. J.: International Bible Society, 1978), v.

[31] *Ibid.*, vi.

[32] *Ibid.*, v.

[33] *Ibid.*

[34] Jaspar James Ray, *God Wrote Only One Bible* (Eugene, Oreg.: Eye Opener Publishers, 1983), 33-34.

[35] "Advertisement," *Moody Monthly*, April 1991, 11.

[36] Leslie R. Keylock, "The Bible That Bears His Name," *Moody Monthly*, July/August 1985, 89.

[37] Jack P. Lewis, *The English Bible from KJV to NIV* (Grand Rapids, Mich.: Baker Book House, 1981), 5.

[38] Florencio Merasol, "Evaluating Versions of the New Testament" (unpublished notes, Fundamental Baptist Church, Pearl City, Hawaii, n.d.), 14-19.

[39] New International Version, iv.

[40] Gipp, Understandable History, 207-8.

[41] *Ibid.*, 212-13.

[42] *Ibid.*, 213-14.

[43] Bruce Lackey, *Why I Believe the Old King James Bible* (Chattanooga, Tenn.: By the author, 3020 Northway Lane, 1987), 62-63.

[44] Bernard Ramm, *Protestant Biblical Interpretation*, 3d rev. ed. (Grand Rapids, Mich.: Baker Book House, 1970), 8-9.

[45] *Ibid.*, 209.

[46] Stewart Custer, *The Truth About the King James Version Controversy*

(Greenville, S. C.: Bob Jones University Press, 1981), 6.

[47] *Ibid.*

[48] Nancy Gibbs and Richard N. Ostling, "God's Billy Pulpit," *Time*, 15 November, 1993, 74.

[49] Mrs. Sam P. (Laura) Jones and Walt Holcomb, *Life and Sayings of Sam P. Jones* 2d ed., rev. (Atlanta, Ga.: Franklin-Turner Co., Publishers, 1907), 89.

[50] Lewis, *English Bible*, 363-64.

[51] *Ibid.*

Chapter XVII

[1] The Holy Bible, New King James Version (Nashville, Tenn.: Thomas Nelson, 1982), 1233-34.

[2] *Ibid.*, 1234.

[3] "Advertisement," *Moody Monthly*, June 1982, back cover.

[4] "Advertisement," *Moody Monthly*, November 1982, 143.

[5] New King James Version, iii.

[6] *Ibid.*, iv.

[7] "Advertisement," *Moody Monthly*, June 1982, back cover.

[8] New King James Version, v.

[9] D.A. Waite, Th.D., Ph.D., *Defects in the New King James Version* (Collingswood, N. J.: Dean Burgon Society, 1987), 21.

[10] *Ibid.*, 12.

[11] New King James Version, 1235.

[12] "Advertisement," *Moody Monthly*, June 1982, back cover.

[13] New King James Version, v.

[14] Waite, *Defects in NKJV*, 7.

[15] New King James Version, iii.

[16] "Advertisement," *Moody Monthly*, May 1982, 4.

[17] C.I. Scofield, ed., Holy Bible, New Scofield Reference Edition (New York: Oxford University Press, 1967), Frontispiece.

[18] *Ibid.*, 334.

[19] *Ibid.*, v.

[20] *Ibid.*

[21] *Ibid.*

[22] *Ibid.*

[23] David O. Beale, *In Pursuit of Purity* (Greenville, S. C.: Unusual Publications, 1986), 46.

[24] *Ibid.*, 36-37.

[25] *Ibid.*, 38.

[26] Scofield, Scofield Reference Edition, 1174.

Chapter XVIII

[1] Edward F. Hills, *The King James Version Defended*, 4th ed. (Des Moines, Iowa: Christian Research Press, 1984), 9.

[2] Gustavus S. Paine, *The Men Behind the King James Version* (Grand Rapids, Mich.: Baker Book House, 1959), 23.

[3] *Ibid.*, 25.

[4] John Fox, *Fox's Book of Martyrs,* ed. William Byron Forbush (Grand Rapids, Mich.: Zondervan Publishing House, 1967), 184.

[5] *Ibid.*, 209.

[6] *Encyclopedia Americana,* 1991 ed., *s.v.* "Mayflower Compact."

[7] "Behold, rap Bible stories are born on radio," *USA Today,* 19 November 1992, 1(D).

[8] "Roman Catholics are Leading Denomination in Congress," *Chicago Tribune,* 18 December 1992, 8(B).

Bibliography

Manuscript Evidences

Beale, David. *A Pictorial History of Our English Bible*. Greenville, S.C.: Bob Jones University Press, 1982.

Bruce, F.F. *The Books and the Parchments*. 3d. ed., rev. Westwood, N. J.: Fleming H. Revell Co., 1950.

_____. *The Canon of Scripture*. Downers Grove, Ill.: InterVarsity Press, 1988.

_____. *The New Testament Documents*. 5th rev. ed. Leicester, England: InterVarsity Press, 1943.

Burgon, John William, B.D. *The Causes of the Corruption of the Traditional Text of the Holy Gospels*. Edited by Edward Miller. London: George Bell & Sons, Publishers, 1896.

_____. *The Revision Revised*. Paradise, Pa.: Conservative Classics, 1883.

_____. *The Traditional Text of the Holy Gospels Vindicated and Established*. Edited by Edward Miller. London: George Bell & Sons, Publishers, 1896.

Burton, Barry. *Let's Weigh the Evidence*. Chino, Calif.: Chick Publications, 1983.

Colwell, E.C. *The Origin of Text-types of New Testament Manuscripts. Early Christian Origins*. Edited by Allen Wikgren. Chicago: Quadrangle Books, 1961.

Custer, Stewart. *The Truth About the King James Controversy*. Greenville, S. C.: Bob Jones University Press, 1981.

Fuller, David Otis, D.D., ed. *True or False?* Grand Rapids, Mich.: Grand Rapids International Publications, 1973.

_____. *Which Bible?* 5th ed., rev. Grand Rapids, Mich.: Grand Rapids International Publications, 1975.

Garrison, Webb. *Strange Facts About the Bible*. Nashville, Tenn.:

Abingdon Press, 1968.

Geisler, Norman L. *Decide for Yourself: How History Views the Bible.* Grand Rapids, Mich.: Zondervan Publishing Co., 1982.

Geisler, Norman L., and William E. Nix. *A General Introduction to the Bible.* Chicago: Moody Press, 1968.

Gipp, Samuel C., Th.D. *The Answer Book.* Shelbyville, Tenn.: Bible & Literature Missionary Foundation, 1989.

_____. *An Understandable History of the Bible.* Macedonia, Ohio: Bible Believer's Baptist Bookstore, 1987.

Green, Jay P., ed. *Unholy Hands on the Bible.* Vol. 1, *An Understanding to Textual Criticism, Including the Complete Works of John W. Burgon, Dean of Chichester.* Lafayette, Ind.: Sovereign Grace Trust Fund, 1990.

Hefley, James C. *What's So Great About the Bible?* rev. Elgin, Ill.: David C. Cook Publishing Co., 1973.

Hills, Edward F. *Believing Bible Study.* 2d ed. Des Moines, Iowa: Christian Research Press, 1977.

_____. *The King James Version Defended.* 4th ed. Des Moines, Iowa: Christian Research Press, 1984.

Hoskier, Herman C. *Codex B and Its Allies.* Vol. 1, *A Study and an Indictment.* London: Bernard Quaritch, Publisher, 1914.

_____. *Codex B and Its Allies.* Vol. 2, *Chiefly Concerning ℵ, but covering three thousand differences between ℵ and B in the Four Gospels.* London: Bernard Quaritch, Publisher, 1914.

Kubo, Sakae and Walter Specht. *So Many Versions.* Grand Rapids, Mich.: Zondervan Corporation, 1975.

Lackey, Bruce. *Why I Believe the Old King James Bible.* Chattanooga, Tenn.: By the author, 3020 Northway Lane, 1987.

Lewis, Jack P. *The English Bible from KJV to NIV, A History and Evaluation.* Grand Rapids, Mich.: Baker Book House, 1981.

Lindsell, Harold. *The Battle for the Bible.* Grand Rapids, Mich.: Zondervan Publishing House, 1976.

Miller, Edward. *A Guide to the Textual Criticism of the New Testament.* Collingswood, N. J.: Dean Burgon Society, 1979.

Mirasol, Florencio. "Evaluating Versions of the New Testament." Unpublished notes. Fundamental Baptist Church, Pearl City, Hawaii: n.d.

Moorman, Jack, ed. *Forever Settled.* Collingswood, N. J.: Bible for Today, 1985.

Nolan, Frederick. *An Inquiry into the Integrity of the Greek Vulgate, or Received Text of the New Testament.* London: F.C. & J. Rivington, Publishers, 1815.

Pickering, Wilbur N. *The Identity of the New Testament Text.* rev. Nashville, Tenn.: Thomas Nelson Publishers, 1980.

Ray, Jasper James. *God Wrote Only One Bible.* Eugene, Oreg.: Eye Opener Publishers, 1983.

Report of the Committee on Versions to the Board of Managers of the American Bible Society. By Rev. James W. McLane, Chairman. New York: n.p., 1852.

Scrivener, Frederick H.A., M.A., D.C.L., LL.D. *A Plain Introduction to the Criticism of the New Testament for the Use of the Biblical Student.* Edited by Edward Miller. Vols. 1 and 2, 4th ed. London: George Bell & Sons, 1894.

_____. *The Authorized Edition of the Bible (1611), Its Subsequent Reprints and Modern Representatives.* London: Cambridge University Press, 1884.

Sumner, Robert L. *Bible Translations.* n.p.: Biblical Evangelist, 1979.

Waite, D.A., Th.D., Ph.D. *Defects in the New International Version.* Collingswood, N. J.: Dean Burgon Society, 1991.

_____. *Defects in the "New King James Version."* Collingswood, N. J.: Dean Burgon Society, 1988.

_____. *The King James Bible's Fourfold Superiority.* Collingswood, N. J.: Bible for Today, 1992.

Church Histories

Armitage, Thomas. *Bright Lights in Dark Times.* Oak Park, Ill.: Bible Truth Publishers, 1978.

Beale, David O. *In Pursuit of Purity.* Greenville, S. C.: Unusual Publications, 1986.

Bede, The Venerable. *The Ecclesiastical History of England.* Edited by Cecil Jane. Mobile, Ala.: R.E. Publications, 1473.

Bettenson, Henry, ed. *Documents of the Christian Church.* 2d. ed. London: Oxford University Press, 1963.

Cairns, Earle E. *Christianity Through the Centuries, A History of the Christian Church.* rev. Grand Rapids, Mich.: Zondervan Publishing House, 1954.

Chadwick, Owen, ed. *The Pelican History of the Church.* Vol. 3, *The Reformation.* rev. Middlesex, England: Penguin Books, 1972.

Davies, J.G. *The Early Christian Church, A History of Its First Five Centuries.* Grand Rapids, Mich.: Baker Book House, 1965.

Dowley, Dr. Tim, ed. *Eerdmans' Handbook to the History of Christianity.* Grand Rapids, Mich.: Wm. B. Eerdmans Publishing Co., 1977.

Edersheim, Alfred. *The Life and Times of Jesus the Messiah.* Grand Rapids, Mich.: Wm. B. Eerdmans Publishing Co., 1971.

Eusebius, Pamphilus. *The Ecclesiastical History of Eusebius Pamphilus.* Translated by Dr. Hanmer. Grand Rapids, Mich.: Baker Book House, 1989.

Fisher, George Park, D.O., LL.D. *History of The Christian Church.* New York: Charles Scribner's Sons, 1887.

Fox, John. *Fox's Book of Martyrs.* Edited by William Byron Forbush, D.D. Grand Rapids, Mich.: Zondervan Publishing House, 1967.

Foxe, John. *Foxe's Christian Martyrs of the World.* Westwood, N. J.: Barbour & Company, 1985.

Gordon, A.J., D.D. *The Holy Spirit in Missions.* New York: Fleming H. Revell Co., 1893.

Hardman, Keith J. *The Spiritual Awakeners.* Chicago: Moody Press, 1983.

Latourette, Kenneth Scott. *A History of Christianity.* New York: Harper & Bros. Publishers, 1953.

Luibheid, Colm. *The Essential Eusebius.* n.p.: Mentor Omega Book for New American Library, 1966.

Manschreck, Clyde L., ed. *A History of Christianity*. 2d. ed. Englewood Cliffs, N. J.: Prentice-Hall, 1964.

Menzies, Allan, D.D. *The Ante-Nicene Fathers*. Vol. 10, *Original Supplement to the American Edition*. 5th ed. Grand Rapids, Mich.: Wm. B. Eerdmans Publishing Co., 1990.

Musurillo, Herbert A. *Fathers of the Primitive Church*. New York: New American Library, 1966.

Newman, Albert Henry, D.D., LL.D. *A Manual of Church History*. Vol. 1, *Ancient and Medieval Church History (To A.D. 1517)*. rev. Valley Forge, Pa.: Judson Press, 1933.

_____. *A Manual of Church History*. Vol. 2, *Modern Church History (A.D. 1517-1932)*. rev. Valley Forge, Pa.: Judson Press, 1931.

Qualben, Lars P. *A History of the Christian Church*. rev. New York: Thomas Nelson & Sons, 1936.

Reese, Ed. "History of Evangelism and Evangelists." Unpublished lecture notes, Hyles-Anderson College, n.d.

Roberts, Alexander, D.D., and James Donaldson, LL.D., eds. *The Ante-Nicene Fathers*. Vol. 1, *The Apostolic Fathers with Justin Martyr and Irenaeus*. Grand Rapids, Mich.: Wm. B. Eerdmans Publishing Co., 1989.

_____. *The Ante-Nicene Fathers*. Vol. 2, *Fathers of the Second Century*. Grand Rapids, Mich.: Wm. B. Eerdmans Publishing Co., 1989.

_____. *The Ante-Nicene Fathers*. Vol. 3, *Latin Christianity: Its Founder, Tertullian*. Grand Rapids, Mich.: Wm. B. Eerdmans Publishing Co., 1989.

_____. *The Ante-Nicene Fathers*. Vol. 4, *Fathers of the Third Century*. Grand Rapids, Mich.: Wm. B. Eerdmans Publishing Co., 1989.

_____. *The Ante-Nicene Fathers*. Vol. 7, *Fathers of the Third and Fourth Centuries*. Grand Rapids, Mich.: Wm. B. Eerdmans Publishing Co., 1989.

Schaff, Philip. *History of the Christian Church*. Vol. 2, *Ante-Nicene Christianity, A.D. 100-325*. Grand Rapids, Mich.: Wm. B. Eerdmans Publishing Co., 1910.

_____. *History of the Christian Church*. Vol. 3, *Nicene and Post-Nicene Christianity; From Constantine the Great to Gregory the*

Great, A.D. 311-600. 5th ed., rev. Grand Rapids, Mich.: Wm. B. Eerdmans Publishing Co., 1910.

_____. *History of the Christian Church.* Vol. 4, *Medieval Christianity, From Gregory I to Gregory VII, A.D. 590-1073.* Grand Rapids, Mich.: Wm. B. Eerdmans Publishing Co., 1910.

Schaff, David, and Philip Schaff. *History of the Christian Church.* Vol. 6, *The Middle Ages, from Boniface VIII; 1294, to the Protestant Reformation, 1517.* Grand Rapids, Mich.: Wm. B. Eerdmans Publishing Co., 1910.

Schaff, Philip. *History of the Christian Church.* Vol. 7, *Modern Christianity, The German Reformation.* Grand Rapids, Mich.: Wm. B. Eerdmans Publishing Co., 1910.

Smith, George. *A Short History of Christian Missions.* London: T.T. Clark, Publishers, 1902.

Theron, Daniel. *Evidence of Tradition.* Grand Rapids, Mich.: Baker Book House, 1958.

Thompson, Charles L. D.D. *Times of Refreshing. A History of American Revivals from 1740 to 1877, with their Philosophy and Methods.* Chicago: M.W. Smith & Company, 1877.

Thynne, Charles J., ed. *Church Leaders in Primitive Times.* 2d ed. London: Wycliffe House, 1896.

Vedder, Henry C. *A Short History of the Baptists.* Valley Forge, Pa.: Judson Press, 1907.

Walker, Willison. *A History of the Christian Church.* 4th ed. New York: Charles Scribner's Sons, 1918.

Secular Histories

Durant, Ariel and Will Durant. *The Story of Civilization.* Vol. 7, *The Age of Reason Begins.* New York: Simon & Schuster, 1961.

Durant, Will. *The Story of Civilization.* Vol. 1, *Our Oriental Heritage.* New York: Simon & Schuster, 1963.

_____. *The Story of Civilization.* Vol. 2, *The Life of Greece.* New York: Simon & Schuster, 1966.

_____. *The Story of Civilization.* Vol. 3, *Caesar and Christ.* New

York: Simon & Schuster, 1972.

_____. *The Story of Civilization*. Vol. 4, *The Age of Faith*. New York: Simon & Schuster, 1950.

_____. *The Story of Civilization*. Vol. 5, *The Renaissance*. New York: Simon & Schuster, 1953.

_____. *The Story of Civilization*. Vol. 6, *The Reformation*. New York: Simon & Schuster, 1957.

Green, J.R., M.A. *A Short History of the English People*. New York: Harper & Brothers Publishers, 1884.

Hibbert, Christopher. *Rome, The Biography of a City*. New York: W.W. Norton & Co., 1985.

Hibbert, Christopher and the Editors of the Newsweek Book Division. *Tower of London*. New York: Newsweek, 1971.

Judd, Gerrit P. *A History of Civilization*. New York: Macmillan Co., 1966.

Reader's Digest Association. *Quest for the Past*. Pleasantville, N. Y.: Reader's Digest Association, 1984.

Sachse, William L., ed. *English History in the Making*. Vol. 1, *Reading from the Sources, to 1689*. Lexington, Mass.: Zerox College Publishing, 1967.

Starr, Chester G. *The Roman Empire, 27 B.C. - A.D. 476*. New York: Oxford University Press, 1982.

Strayer, Joseph R., and Hans W. Gatzke, eds. *The Mainstream of Civilization; to 1715*. 3d. ed. New York: Harcourt Brace Jovanovich Publishing Co., 1979.

Tuchman, Barbara W. *A Distant Mirror*. New York: Alfred A. Knopf, 1978.

Wells, H.G. *The Outline of History*. rev. Garden City, N. Y.: Garden City Books, 1961.

Theological Works

Chafer, Lewis Sperry. *Major Bible Themes*. 1st ed., rev. Grand Rapids, Mich.: Zondervan Publishing House for Academie Books, 1974.

Fisher, George Park, D.D., LL.D. *History of Christian Doctrine.* New York: Charles Scribner's Sons, 1896.

Gaussen, Louis, D.D. *Divine Inspiration of the Bible.* Translated from the French by David D. Scott. Grand Rapids, Mich.: Kregel Publications, 1841.

Ramm, Bernard. *Protestant Biblical Interpretation.* 3d rev. ed. Grand Rapids, Mich.: Baker Book House, 1970.

Thiessen, Henry Clarence. B.D., Ph.D., D.D. *Introductory Lectures in Systematic Theology.* Grand Rapids, Mich.: Wm. B. Eerdmans Publishing Co., 1949.

Unpublished Prepared Class Notes. Biblical Introduction Extension Class, "Inspiration." Philadelphia: Philadelphia College of the Bible, 1970.

Catholicism

Boettner, Loraine. *Roman Catholicism.* Philadelphia: Presbyterian & Reformed Publishing Co., 1962.

Hunt, Dave. *Global Peace and the Rise of Antichrist.* Eugene, Oreg.: Harvest House Publishers, 1990.

Manhattan, Avro. *The Vatican Billions.* Chino, Calif.: Chick Publications, 1983.

_____. *The Vatican Moscow Washington Alliance.* Chino, Calif.: Chick Publications, 1986.

_____. *The Vatican in World Politics.* New York: Horizon Press, 1949.

_____. *The Vatican's Holocaust.* Springfield, Mo.: Ozark Books, 1986.

Paris, Edmond. *Convert . . . or Die!* Translated by Lois Perkins. Chino, Calif.: Chick Publications, n.d.

_____. *The Secret History of the Jesuits.* Translated from the French. Chino, Calif.: Chick Publications, 1975.

_____. *The Vatican Against Europe.* Translated by A. Robson. 2d ed. London: Wickliffe Press, 1961.

Thompson, R.W. *Footprints of the Jesuits.* Cincinnati, Ohio: Cranston & Curtis Publishing Co., 1894.

Biographical

Anderson, Dwight and Nancy Scott Anderson. *The Generals, Ulysses S. Grant and Robert E. Lee.* New York: Alfred A. Knopf, 1987.

Barlow, Fred. *Profiles in Evangelism.* Murfreesboro, Tenn.: Sword of the Lord Publishers, 1976.

Collier, Richard. *The General Next to God.* Glasgow, Scotland: William Collins Sons & Co., 1965.

Dallimore, Arnold A. *A Heart Set Free.* Westchester, Ill.: Crossway Books, 1988.

_____. *George Whitefield, The Life and Times of the Great Evangelist of the Eighteenth-Century Revival.* Vol. 1, Edinburgh, Scotland: Banner of Truth Trust, 1970.

Entzminger, Louis. *The J. Frank Norris I Have Known for 34 Years.* St. John, Ind.: Christian Book Gallery, n.d.

Finney, Charles G. *Revival Lectures.* n.p. Fleming H. Revell Co., n.d.

Grubb, Norman. *C.T. Studd, Cricketer and Pioneer.* Fort Washington, Pa.: Christian Literature Crusade, 1982.

Hort, Arthur Fenton. *Life and Letters of Fenton John Anthony Hort.* Vols. 1 and 2. London: Macmillan & Co., 1896.

Jones, Mrs. Sam P. (Laura) and Walt Holcomb. *Life and Sayings of Sam P. Jones.* 2d ed., rev. Atlanta, Ga.: Franklin-Turner Co., Publishers, 1907.

Lawson, James Gilchrist. *Deeper Experiences of Famous Christians.* Anderson, Ind.: Warner Press, 1911.

Martin, Roger. *R.A. Torrey, Apostle of Certainty.* Murfreesboro, Tenn.: Sword of the Lord Publishers, 1976.

McClure, Alexander. *Translators Revived.* Foreword and Update by R.E. Rhoades. Litchfield, Mich.: Maranatha Bible Society, 1858.

Moody, William R. *The Life of Dwight L. Moody.* Murfreesboro, Tenn.: Sword of the Lord Publishers, 1900.

Paine, Gustavus S. *The Men Behind the King James Version.* Grand Rapids, Mich.: Baker Book House, 1959.

Pollock, John. *George Whitefield and The Great Awakening.* Tring, Herts, England: Lion Publishing, 1972.

Reese, Ed. *Christian Hall of Fame Series.* Vol. 1, *The Life and Ministry of Gipsy Smith, (1860-1947).* Glenwood Ill.: Fundamental Publishers, 1975.

_____. *Christian Hall of Fame Series.* Vol. 6, *The Life and Ministry of William Booth, (1829-1912).* Glenwood Ill.: Fundamental Publishers, 1975.

_____. *Christian Hall of Fame Series.* Vol. 8, *The Life and Ministry of Reuben Torrey, (1856-1928).* Glenwood Ill.: Fundamental Publishers, 1975.

_____. *Christian Hall of Fame Series.* Vol. 19, *The Life and Ministry of David Livingstone, (1813-1873).* Glenwood Ill.: Fundamental Publishers, 1975.

_____. *Christian Hall of Fame Series.* Vol. 23, *The Life and Ministry of George Mueller, (1805-1898).* Glenwood Ill.: Fundamental Publishers, 1975.

Ross, Bob L. *A Pictorial Biography of C.H. Spurgeon.* Pasadena, Tex.: Pilgrim Publications, 1974.

Spurgeon, Susannah, and Joseph Harrald, eds. *C.H. Spurgeon's Autobiography.* Vol. 1, *The Early Years.* rev. ed. Carlisle, Pa.: Banner of Truth Trust, 1962.

Strickland, W.P., ed. *Autobiography of Peter Cartwright, The Backwoods Preacher.* New York: Carlton & Porter Publishers, 1857.

Taylor, Dr. Howard and Mrs. Howard Taylor. *J. Judson Taylor, A Biography.* Chicago: Moody Press, 1965.

Towns, Elmer L. *The Christian Hall of Fame.* Grand Rapids, Mich.: Baker Book House, 1971.

Vineyard, Jim. *Great Preachers and their Preaching.* Vol. 1, *John Knox.* Hammond, Ind.: First Baptist Church of Hammond, 1975.

Watkinson, W.L. *The Life of John Wicklif.* Litchfield, Mich.: Maranatha Bible Society, n.d.

Westcott, Arthur. *Life and Letters of Brooke Foss Westcott.* Vols. 1 and 2. London: Macmillan & Co., 1903.

Whitefield, George. *George Whitefield's Journals*. Edinburgh, Scotland: The Banner of Truth Trust, 1960.

Reference Works

Dictionary of National Biography. 1960 ed. *S.v.* "James I."

Dictionary of National Biography. 1921-1922 ed. *S.v.* "William Tyndale."

Edwards, Jonathan. *Sinners in the Hands of an Angry God*. Murfreesboro, Tenn.: Sword of the Lord Publishers, n.d.

Encyclopedia Americana. 1991 ed. *S.v.* "Mayflower Compact."

Encyclopedia Brittanica. 1910 ed. *S.v.* "English Bible."

Holy Bible, The, New Scofield Reference Edition. New York: Oxford Press, 1967.

Kelly, J.N.D. *The Oxford Dictionary of Popes*. Oxford, England: Oxford University Press, 1986.

Lee, Sir Sidney, and Sir Leslie Stephen, eds. *Dictionary of National Biography*. Vol. 4. London: Oxford University Press, 1960.

Livingstone, Elizabeth A., ed. *The Concise Oxford Dictionary of the Christian Church*. Oxford, England: Oxford University Press, 1977.

Mack, Maynard, ed. *The Norton Anthology of World Masterpieces*. 5th ed. Vol. 1, *Literature of Western Culture Through the Renaissance*. New York: W.W. Norton & Co., 1985.

Miller, Madeleine S., and J. Lane Miller. *Harper's Encyclopedia of Bible Life*. 3d rev. ed. San Francisco: Harper & Row, Publishers, 1978.

New Standard Encyclopedia. 1990 ed. *S.v.* "Alexandria, Egypt."

New Standard Encyclopedia. 1990 ed. *S.v.* "James I."

Reid, Daniel G. *Dictionary of Christianity in America*. Downers Grove, Ill.: InterVarsity Press, 1990.

Tan, Paul Lee. *Encyclopedia of 7,700 Illustrations.* Rockville, Md.: Assurance Publishers, 1979.

Modern Translations

Holy Bible, New International Version. Grand Rapids, Mich.: Zondervan Corp., 1978.

Holy Bible, The, New King James Version. Nashville, Tenn.: Thomas Nelson, 1982.

Holy Bible, The, Revised Standard Version. Camden, N. J.: Thomas Nelson, New Testament, 1946; Old Testament, 1952.

Lockman Foundation, The. *New American Standard Bible.* Glendale, Calif.: Gospel Light Publications, 1960.

New World Translation. Brooklyn, N. Y.: Watchtower Bible & Tract Society, 1961.

Scofield, C.I., ed., *The Scofield Study Bible.* New York: Oxford University Press, 1945.

Vaughan, Curtis, Th.D., ed. *The New Testament from 26 Translations.* Grand Rapids, Mich.: Zondervan Publishing House, 1967.

Periodicals

"Advertisement." *Moody Monthly,* April 1991, 11.

"Advertisement." *Moody Monthly,* May 1982, 4.

"Advertisement." *Moody Monthly,* June 1982, back cover.

"Advertisement." *Moody Monthly,* November 1982, 143.

"Advertisement." *Saturday Evening Post,* March 1991, inside back cover.

"Behold, Rap Stories Are Born on Video." *USA Today,* 19 November 1992, 1(D).

Gibbs, Nancy and Richard N. Ostling. "God's Billy Pulpit." *Time,* 15 November 1993, 74.

Keylock, Leslie R. "The Bible That Bears His Name." *Moody Monthly,* July/August 1985, 89.

Kohlenberger, John R. III. "Which Bible Translation Is for Me?" *Moody Monthly,* May 1987, 17-19.

Miller, Annetta. "He Reaps What He Sows." *Newsweek,* 26 October 1992, 57.

Munro, Neil. "Fleet's Threatening Approach." *Military History Magazine Presents Great Battles*, November 1990, 26-33.

"Roman Catholics Are Leading Denomination in Congress." *Chicago Tribune.* 18 December 1992. 8(B).

Ryrie, Charles C. "Before the King James." *Moody Monthly*, May 1987, 21-24.

Sumner, Robert L. "Dear Abner!" Review of *Dear Abner, I Love You, Joab,* by Dr. Roy L. Branson. *The Biblical Evangelist,* 1 November 1992, 1-24.

Wojahn, Karen Ann. "The Real King James." *Moody Monthly,* July/August 1985, 87-88.

Yorks, Cindy Lafavre. "McChurch." *Daily Courier News, U.S.A. Weekend,* 13-15 April 1990, 4-7.

"Zondervan, Blessed with Bible Contract, Lifts Profit Forecast," *Wall Street Journal.* 16 November 1978, 18.

Index